.

European traders first appeared in India at the end of the fifteenth century and began exporting goods to Europe as well as to other parts of Asia. In a detailed analysis of the trading operations of European corporate enterprises such as the English and Dutch East India Companies, as well as those of private European traders, this volume considers how, over a span of three centuries, the Indian economy expanded and was integrated into the pre-modern world economy as a result of these interactions. The book also describes how the essentially market-determined commercial encounter between Europe and India changed in the latter half of the eighteenth century as the colonial relationship between Britain and the subcontinent was established. By bringing together and analysing the existing literature, the author provides a fascinating overview of the impact of European trade on the pre-colonial Indian economy which promises to be of great value to students of Indian, European and colonial history.

THE NEW CAMBRIDGE HISTORY
OF INDIA

European commercial enterprise in pre-colonial India

THE NEW CAMBRIDGE HISTORY OF INDIA

General editor GORDON JOHNSON
President of Wolfson College, and Director, Centre of South Asian Studies,
University of Cambridge

Associate editors C. A. BAYLY
Vere Harmsworth Professor of Imperial and Naval History, University of Cambridge,
and Fellow of St Catharine's College

and JOHN F. RICHARDS
Professor of History, Duke University

Although the original *Cambridge History of India*, published between 1922 and 1937, did much to formulate a chronology for Indian history and describe the administrative structures of government in India, it has inevitably been overtaken by the mass of new research over the past fifty years.

Designed to take full account of recent scholarship and changing conceptions of South Asia's historical development, *The New Cambridge History of India* will be published as a series of short, self-contained volumes, each dealing with a separate theme and written by a single person. Within an overall four-part structure, thirty-one complementary volumes in uniform format will be published. Each will conclude with a substantial bibliographical essay designed to lead non-specialists further into the literature

The four parts planned are as follows:

I The Mughals and their contemporaries

II Indian states and the transition to colonialism

III The Indian Empire and the beginnings of modern society

IV The evolution of contemporary South Asia

A list of individual titles in preparation will be found
at the end of the volume.

THE NEW CAMBRIDGE HISTORY OF INDIA

II · 5

*European commercial enterprise
in pre-colonial India*

OM PRAKASH

UNIVERSITY OF DELHI

CAMBRIDGE
UNIVERSITY PRESS

PUBLISHED BY THE PRESS SYNDICATE OF THE UNIVERSITY OF CAMBRIDGE
The Pitt Building, Trumpington Street, Cambridge CB2 1RP

CAMBRIDGE UNIVERSITY PRESS
The Edinburgh Building, Cambridge CB2 2RU, United Kingdom
40 West 20th Street, New York, NY 10011–4211, USA
10 Stamford Road, Oakleigh, Melbourne 3166, Australia

First published 1998

Printed in the United Kingdom at the University Press, Cambridge

Typeset in Garamond 10.5/13pt [CE]

A catalogue record for this book is available from the British Library

Library of Congress cataloguing in publication data
Om Prakash, 1940–
European commercial enterprise in pre-colonial India / Om Prakash.
p. cm. – (New Cambridge history of India : II.5)
Includes bibliographical references.
ISBN 0 521 25758 1
1. India – Commerce – Europe – History.
2. Europe – Commerce – India – History.
3. India – Economic conditions.
I. Title. II. Series.
DS436.N47 1987
[HF3788.E8]
954 s–dc21
[382′.094054] 97–25536 CIP

ISBN 0 521 25758 1 hardback

DEDICATED TO THE MEMORY OF MY PARENTS

CONTENTS

List of figures	*page*	x
List of maps		xi
List of tables		xii
General editor's preface		xiv
Preface		xvi
Introduction		1
1 India in the Indian Ocean trade, circa 1500		8
2 The Portuguese in India, 1500–1640		23
3 The European trading companies: exports from Europe and the generation of purchasing power in Asia		72
4 The companies in India: the politics and the economics of trade		111
5 Euro-Asian and intra-Asian trade: the phase of Dutch domination, 1600–1680		175
6 The VOC and the growing competition by the English and the French, 1680–1740		211
7 The supremacy of the English East India Company, 1740–1800		268
8 European trade and the Indian economy		315
9 Conclusion		337
Bibliographic essay		352
Index		366

FIGURES

2.1	Pepper imported by the Portuguese Crown, 1503–98	*page* 41
3.1	The export of precious metals by the VOC to Asia, 1602–1794	87
3.2	English East India Company exports to Asia, 1601–1760	107
4.1.1–4.1.6	Triennial totals and composition of the Dutch East India Company's imports into Europe, 1619–1780	
4.1.1	1619–21	116
4.1.2	1648–50	116
4.1.3	1668–70	116
4.1.4	1698–1700	117
4.1.5	1738–40	117
4.1.6	1778–80	117
4.2.1–4.2.4	Triennial totals and composition of the English East India Company's imports into Europe, 1660–1779	
4.2.1	1668–70	121
4.2.2	1698–1700	122
4.2.3	1738–40	122
4.2.4	1758–60	122
4.3	Regional distribution by origin of English Company imports into Europe, 1660–1779	123
5.1	Dutch East India Company's exports from Coromandel, 1608–90	181
5.2	Dutch East India Company's export of goods from Gujarat, 1621–1792	187
5.3	Dutch East India Company's exports from Bengal, 1645–1785	200
5.4	Regional distribution of the VOC's average annual exports from Bengal, 1660–1736	200
5.5	Share of Bengal goods in total Dutch exports to Europe, 1665–1736	203
6.1	Composition of Dutch exports from Bengal, 1675–1785	213
6.2	Dutch exports of textiles from Coromandel, 1691–1770	223
6.3	Dutch exports from Malabar, 1701–85	229
6.4	French East India Company's imports from Asia and India, 1725–71	255

MAPS

1 Important trading centres in Asia in the seventeenth and   *page* 10–11
  eighteenth centuries
2 Portuguese seaborne empire, c. 1580   24–5
3 The Indian Ocean in the seventeenth and eighteenth centuries   112–13
4 India: main textile-weaving areas, 1600–1750   176–7
5 South India: weaving areas, c. 1720   179
6 Gujarat: textile towns, c. 1700   183
7 Bengal: main textile towns   197

TABLES

2.1 Shipping movements between Portugal and Asia, 1497–1700   *page* 32

2.2 Composition of cargoes imported into Lisbon from Asia,   35
1505–18

2.3 Composition of cargoes imported into Lisbon from Asia,   36
1513–1610

2.4 Pepper imported by the Portuguese Crown, 1503–98   40

2.5 Major concession voyages and the rate of return c. 1580   58

3.1 The export of precious metals (coined and uncoined) by the   87
VOC to Asia, 1602–1794

3.2 The *assignaties* redeemed by the chambers of the Dutch East   89
India Company, 1640–1795

3.3 Value and the regional distribution of precious metals imported   98
by the VOC into India, 1640–1785

3.4 The Dutch East India Company's import of precious metals   102
from Holland and Japan into Batavia, 1621–99

3.5 Dutch East India Company shipping arriving at and leaving   104
Asia, 1602–1794

3.6 English East India Company exports to Asia, 1601–1760   106

3.7 French East India Company's exports to Asia, 1725–69   109

4.1 Triennial totals and composition of the Dutch East India   115
Company's imports into Europe, 1619–1780

4.2 Triennial totals and composition of the English East India   120
Company's imports into Europe, 1660–1779

4.3 Regional distribution by origin (percentagewise) of English   121
Company imports into Europe, 1660–1779

5.1 Dutch East India Company's exports from Coromandel,   180
1608–90

5.2 Dutch East India Company's exports from Gujarat,   185
1621–1792

5.3 Dutch East India Company's exports from Bengal, 1645–1785   196

5.4 Regional distribution of the Dutch East India Company's average   198
annual exports from Bengal, 1660–1736

5.5 Share of Bengal goods in total Dutch exports to Europe,   203
1665–1736

6.1 Composition of Dutch exports from Bengal (percent),   213
1675–1785

6.2 Value of the Dutch textile exports from Coromandel, 1691–1770   222

6.3 Value of the Dutch exports from Malabar, 1701–85   229

6.4 The French East India Company's imports from Asia and India,   254
     1725–71
7.1 Average annual value of the Danish Asiatic Company's imports   310
     from India, 1734–1807

GENERAL EDITOR'S PREFACE

The New Cambridge History of India covers the period from the beginning of the sixteenth century. In some respects it marks a radical change in the style of Cambridge Histories, but in others the editors feel that they are working firmly within an established academic tradition.

During the summer of 1896, F.W. Maitland and Lord Acton between them evolved the idea for a comprehensive modern history. By the end of the year the Syndics of the University Press had committed themselves to the *Cambridge Modern History*, and Lord Acton had been put in charge of it. It was hoped that publication would begin in 1899 and be completed by 1904, but the first volume in fact came out in 1902 and the last in 1910, with additional volumes of tables and maps in 1911 and 1912.

The *History* was a great success, and it was followed by a whole series of distinctive Cambridge Histories covering English Literature, the Ancient World, India, British Foreign Policy, Economic History, Medieval History, the British Empire, Africa, China and Latin America; and even now other new series are being prepared. Indeed, the various Histories have given the Press notable strength in the publication of general reference books in the arts and social sciences.

What has made the Cambridge Histories so distinctive is that they have never been simply dictionaries or encyclopaedias. The Histories have, in H.A.L. Fisher's words, always been 'written by an army of specialists concentrating the latest results of special study'. Yet as Acton agreed with the Syndics in 1896, they have not been mere compilations of existing material but original works. Undoubtedly many of the Histories are uneven in quality, some have become out of date very rapidly, but their virtue has been that they have consistently done more than simply record an existing state of knowledge: they have tended to focus interest on research and they have provided a massive stimulus to further work. This has made their publication doubly worthwhile and has distinguished them intellectually from other sorts of reference book. The editors of *The New Cambridge History of India* have acknowledged this in their work.

The original *Cambridge History of India* was published between 1922 and 1937. It was planned in six volumes, but of these, volume 2 dealing with the period between the first century AD and the Muslim invasion of India never appeared. Some of the material is still of value, but in many respects it is now out of date. The past fifty years have seen a great deal of new research on India, and a striking feature of recent work has been to cast doubt on the validity of the quite arbitrary chronological and categorical way in which Indian history has been conventionally divided.

The editors decided that it would not be academically desirable to prepare a new *History of India* using the traditional format. The selective nature of research on Indian history over the past half-century would doom such a project from the start and the whole of Indian history could not be covered in an even or comprehensive manner. They concluded that the best scheme would be to have a *History* divided into four overlapping chronological volumes, each containing about eight short books on individual themes or subjects. Although in extent the work will therefore be equivalent to a dozen massive tomes of the traditional sort, in form *The New Cambridge History of India* will appear as a shelf full of separate but complementary parts. Accordingly, the main divisions are between I. *The Mughals and their contemporaries*, II. *Indian states and the transition to colonialism*, III. *The Indian Empire and the beginnings of modern society*, and IV. *The evolution of contemporary South Asia.*

Just as the books within these volumes are complementary so too do they intersect with each other, both thematically and chronologically. As the books appear they are intended to give a view of the subject as it now stands and to act as a stimulus to further research. We do not expect the *New Cambridge History of India* to be the last word on the subject but an essential voice in the continuing discussion about it.

PREFACE

The rise of a pre-modern world economy, facilitated by the great discoveries of the closing years of the fifteenth century, held important implications for the Indian subcontinent. The availability of an all-water route between Europe and Asia via the Cape of Good Hope, and of a growing amount of American silver for export to Asia, involved a substantial expansion in the volume and the value of Euro-Asian trade. The Portuguese monopoly of the all-water route was challenged at the beginning of the seventeenth century by the English and the Dutch East India companies, who eventually came to dominate this trade. The only other body of any consequence engaged in this enterprise was the French East India Company. The so-called minor companies – the Danish, the Ostend, the Swedish and others – never really accounted for more than an insignificant proportion of the total trade between the two continents. At least one of the corporate enterprises, namely the Dutch East India Company, also carried on a substantial amount of trade within Asia. Employees of corporate enterprises also engaged in intra-Asian trade in their private capacity. By far the most important category of these employees was that in the service of the English East India Company.

India was at the centre of the Europeans' trading activities in respect of both Euro-Asian as well as intra-Asian trade. The Portuguese procured all their pepper for Europe in India: their intra-Asian trading network largely revolved around the Bay of Bengal. When textiles and raw silk dominated Euro-Asian trade from the last quarter of the seventeenth century onward, India also became central to the northern European trading companies' imports into Europe. India similarly dominated the Dutch East India Company's as well as the English private traders' intra-Asian trade.

In this volume, I have tried to analyse the trading operations of both the European corporate enterprises as well as the private traders in so far as these pertained to India within the overall Asian context. The time span covered is the three centuries between the beginning of the sixteenth century and the end of the eighteenth. The period

xvi

witnessed the transition in the latter half of the eighteenth century from an essentially market-determined commercial encounter between Europe and India to the beginnings of a colonial relationship between Britain and the subcontinent. One of my concerns in this volume has been an analysis of the implications of the European trade for the subcontinent's economy during the pre-colonial period. An investigation into the working of the English East India Company during the early colonial period has helped bring into sharp relief the altered state of affairs between the two phases.

It is inevitable that a synthetic work of this kind would draw upon the scholarship of fellow researchers. In my case this debt has been particularly large and my work made considerably easier by the availability of a large body of high-quality work. In particular, the availability of K. N. Chaudhuri's definitive study on the English East India Company, published less than two decades ago and still easily accessible, has rendered it unnecessary for me to go into the Company's trading operations in India in any great detail. It was only in respect of the period between 1760 and 1800 that a reference to a selected body of material in the India Office Records was found necessary. The absence of a counterpart to Chaudhuri's work for the Dutch East India Company obliged me to refer to the VOC's documentation for filling in some of the major gaps in the literature relating to the Company's trading activities in different parts of the subcontinent, particularly in the quantitative domain. The VOC archives also yielded an interesting body of correspondence between the English and the Dutch East India companies which considerably illuminated the working of the former during the early colonial period.

Over the past several years when this book was under preparation, a great deal of kindness and help came my way. I can hope to be able to acknowledge only a small part of it. In the early stages, when I was planning the format of the volume, discussions with Sanjay Subrahmanyam were extremely useful. S. Arasaratnam and Femme Gaastra were kind enough to read the first draft as it was being written. John Richards and Christopher Bayly commented extensively on another draft. The present version owes a great deal to the extremely useful and detailed suggestions made by the two of them. Others who have helped through discussions and advice include Leonard Blussé, Satish Chandra, Jurrien van Goor, Hugo s' Jacob, Ravinder Kumar, the late

Denys Lombard, Peter Marshall, Michael Pearson, Roderich Ptak, Hans van Santen and Niels Steensgaard. I am grateful to all of them.

As always, Henk Wesseling, Jan Heesterman and Dirk Kolff have provided support in ways far too numerous to be enumerated. I would also like to put on record the generous intellectual and other support received from Maurice Aymard, Dietmar Rothermund and Wim Stokhof.

This book would never have been written but for the constant and unfailing support of my wife and the continuing love and under-standing of my children.

INTRODUCTION

The history of commercial traffic in the Indian Ocean goes back to at least the early centuries of the Christian era. Networks of trade covering different segments of the Ocean have a history of remarkable resilience without being resistant to innovation. In other words, without disrupting the rhythm of the overall flow, variables such as the share in total trade of different communities of merchants engaged in a given network, the goods carried, and the relative volume of trade carried on at the ports called at, were fully reflective of evolving situations. Over the centuries, India has played a key role in the successful functioning of these trading networks. This undoubtedly was related in part to her location at midpoint geographically, but it also had a good deal to do with her capacity to put on the market large quantities of relatively inexpensive and highly competitive manufactured goods in addition to a whole range of other goods. In return, she provided an important outlet for the specialized agricultural, mineral and other products offered by her trading partners. Trade thus satisfied different kinds of needs for India as compared with her major trading partners, and this by itself provided an excellent basis for a significant and growing level of trade. The key role of India can thus be conceptualized essentially as one of contributing significantly to the expansion of the basis of trade in the Indian Ocean.

To the east of India, there were very long-standing and wide-ranging links between the Indian Ocean and the South China Sea. In addition to the Indonesian archipelago, a considerable amount of trade was traditionally carried on with China and Japan. Westward, however, the link with the Mediterranean through the Persian Gulf and the Red Sea channels involved the use of a certain amount of river-cum-land transportation, more so in the case of the Persian Gulf route than in that of the Red Sea route. In the western sector, the European merchants' involvement in the trade in Asian goods began only after the goods had reached the southern coast of the Mediterranean, to which these merchants regularly travelled to buy them.

I

This pattern of trade between Asia and Europe, which had been in operation for centuries, underwent a structural modification following the discovery by the Portuguese at the end of the fifteenth century of the all-water route to the East Indies via the Cape of Good Hope. Among the historic consequences of the discovery was the overcoming of the transport-technology barrier to the growth of trade between the two continents. The volume of this trade was no longer subject to the capacity constraint imposed by the availability of pack-animals and river boats in the Middle East. Both the old and the new routes were in use throughout the sixteenth century, but by the early years of the seventeenth, when the northern European companies had successfully challenged the Portuguese monopoly of the all-water route, the new route had almost completely taken over in the transportation of goods between the two continents. In addition to their transportation, the procurement of the Asian goods also was now organized by the Europeans themselves, who had arrived in the East in any number for the first time. The goods procured had to be paid for overwhelmingly in precious metals. This was an outcome essentially of the inability of Europe to supply goods which could be sold in Asia in reasonably large quantities at competitive terms. The new vistas of the growth of trade between the two continents opened up by the overcoming of the transport-technology barrier could have been frustrated by the shortage of silver for export to Asia that the declining, or at best stagnant, European output of this metal might have occasioned. But, fortunately, the discovery of the Cape route had coincided with that of the Americas. The working of the Spanish American silver mines had tremendously expanded the European silver stock, a part of which was available for diversion to Asia for investment in Asian goods. A continued expansion in the volume and the value of the Euro-Asian trade could now take place.

The Portuguese had been followed in the early years of the seventeenth century by the English and the Dutch, and on a much smaller scale by the Danes. The French East India Company was established in 1664, though it was not until the 1720s that the French presence in India became significant. The short-lived Ostend Company also functioned in India during this decade. In addition to these corporate groups, there were the private European merchants operating simultaneously. An overwhelming proportion of these persons had travelled to the East with one or the other of the corporate groups. Many of them engaged in private trade while still in the service of the relevant corporate group with or without permission. Others engaged in private trade on a full-time basis. The Euro-Asian trade was carried on overwhelmingly by the corporate groups, leaving the trade within Asia by and large to the individual traders, the largest group amongst whom eventually was that of the English private traders. The only major exception to this pattern was the large scale and systematic participation in intra-Asian trade by the Dutch East India Company (VOC) as an integral part of its overall trading strategy. In the sixteenth century, the Portuguese Crown had also participated in intra-Asian trade, but the scale and the duration of that operation had been relatively limited.

Throughout the sixteenth and the first half of the seventeenth century, the Euro-Asian trade carried on by the Portuguese was centred on India. But since the Dutch and the English procured their pepper and other spices mainly in Indonesia, the Asian loci of the Euro-Asian seaborne trade shifted at the beginning of the seventeenth century from India to the Indonesian archipelago. It was nearly three quarters of a century before the Asian loci shifted back to India. This was a consequence of the change in European fashions assigning an increasingly important role to textiles and raw silk in the Asian imports into Europe. It was only in the second half of the eighteenth century that the growing role of Chinese tea in these imports again deflected somewhat from the central position of India in Euro-Asian trade. India also played a key role in the Dutch intra-Asian trade. Indeed, it was the long-established pattern of the Indonesian spice growers asking for Indian textiles in exchange for their wares which had set the VOC on the path of intra-Asian trade in the first place. Later in the seventeenth century, Bengal raw silk and opium had played an extremely important role in the successful functioning of the Dutch network of intra-Asian trade. Among the private European traders engaged in this trade, the largest group, namely the English private traders, also operated overwhelmingly from India.

The organizational structure of procurement and trade that the trading companies as well as the European private traders encountered in India was both efficient and sophisticated. The production for the market was organized mainly on the basis of contracts between merchants and producers, specifying the quantity to the supplied, the price and the date of delivery. The contract system was a variant of the standard European putting-out system in so far as in the Indian system raw materials were provided by the merchants only rarely. A highly developed credit organization contributed to the efficient working of the system. Merchants could raise short-term loans at remarkably low rates of interest. The institution of the respondentia loans was also quite widespread. Funds could be transferred from one place to another relatively cheaply by using the *hundi*. The *sarrafs* who ran the credit and the banking structure were also indispensable to the working of the currency and the monetary system. The Mughal coinage system, with its uniform imperial standards of weights and measures, was imposed throughout the empire over dozens of local monetary systems. Centrally appointed functionaries of the imperial mints accepted bullion or coin from local *sarrafs* or other private individuals. The system of free minting ensured that the Mughal coins retained their high degree of fineness without any known debasement for nearly two centuries. Following the incorporation of Golconda into the Mughal empire in the closing decades of the seventeenth century, the only major region in the subcontinent where Mughal coinage did not circulate was the Malabar–Kanara coast.

The Europeans – both the companies as well as the individual traders – had no option but to operate within the given organizational structure of procurement and trade. An important group with which they had to deal all the time was that of the intermediary merchants of various kinds. It could be an easy relationship, but it could also be an exasperating one, with the merchants ordinarily calling the tune. The following description of the Bengal merchants by the Dutch Commissioner Hendrik Adriaan van Rheede is at one level indicative of who the Europeans were up against. Van Rheede wrote:

The merchants . . . are exceptionally quick and experienced. When they are still very young and in the laps of their parents and hardly able to walk, they already begin to be trained as merchants. They are made to pretend to engage in trade while playing, first buying *cauris*, followed by silver and gold. In this training as moneychangers, they acquire the capability of engaging in large-scale trade. They are always sober, modest, thrifty, and cunning in identifying the source of their profit, which they are always at pains to maximize. They have an exceptional capacity of discovering the humour of those who are in a position to help or hurt them. They flatter those they know they need to be in the good books of. In case of loss, they console themselves easily and can hide their sorrow wonderfully . . . In general, they are a people with whom one could get along well so long as one is on one's guard.[1]

An important problem that the Europeans faced on an almost perennial basis while procuring goods for export was that of bad debts. This happened in situations where, under the contract system, the value of the goods supplied to and accepted by a European company from a particular contract-merchant was less than the sum of money given to him in advance. The VOC tried to tackle this problem on the Coromandel coast by encouraging the merchants supplying textiles to it to form 'joint stock companies'. Under this arrangement, the merchants operated on the basis of funds contributed by themselves to a central pool and were jointly responsible for the contract given out to them. The innovation indeed worked for a while on the coast, but does not seem to have been found to be feasible elsewhere. On the whole, however, one could argue that the organizational framework within which the Europeans were obliged to work operated with a reasonable degree of efficiency and effectiveness. In the course of time, the Europeans not only mastered the intricacies of the system but indeed came to dominate many elements of it, forcing the indigenous merchants to adapt themselves to the new situation.

The Europeans' dependence upon and assimilation into existing networks comes out even more clearly when one looks at their participation in intra-Asian trade. Within two decades of their arrival in the East, the Portuguese had managed to carve out for themselves a trading network of goods and routes with Malacca as the centrepoint. But it is important to realize that this network grew basically along the lines defined by the pre-existing commercial system. The period of Portuguese apprenticeship was shortened considerably by the advice and assistance provided by the Tamil *keling* merchants of Malacca. In the seventeenth century, the Dutch East India Company's extensive participation in intra-Asian trade also grew along carefully chosen but pre-existing routes. It is another matter that by the middle of the century, the Company had emerged as the largest single participant in this trade with trading stations all over what one might call the great

---

[1] Instructions by Commissioner van Rheede to the Dutch factors at Hugli, 21.2.1687, *Algemeen Rijksarchief* (ARA), *Verenigde Oost-Indische Compagnie* (VOC) 1435, ff. 132v–133, 150v–152v.

arc of Asian trade stretching from the Persian Gulf in the northwest to Japan in the northeast. It was only in the latter half of the eighteenth century that, on the basis of their newly found political leverage and expanded resource base, the private English traders operating from India were able to make their way beyond the eastablished networks of trade and carve out new niches and routes for themselves.

The relationship between the Europeans and the Indian maritime merchants engaged in coastal and high-seas trade was, of course, not always one of cooperation but, at times, also one of conflict. An early example of the latter is the resistance offered by the *pardesi* and later the Mappila merchants of Malabar to the Portuguese pepper monopoly in the western Indian Ocean. But overall, the Indian maritime merchants adjusted remarkably well to the pressures generated by the Europeans' presence. If it was there at all, the negative effect on the volume and the value of the Indian merchants' maritime trade would seem to have been quite small.

As we noted earlier, the European companies were obliged to pay for the goods they procured in India predominantly in precious metals. The export surplus generated in the process, coupled with the reasonably high degree of market orientation and flexibility in the structure of output in the economy, involved, at a macroeconomic level, an increase in the level of income, output and employment in the subcontinent. There were, of course, variations in this regard across both space and time. Thus the Malabar coast, where the Portuguese, and later the Dutch, enjoyed, in principle, monopolistic privileges, was different from the other regions of the subcontinent. Across time, the availability in Bengal of special privileges to the English East India Company following its emergence as the formal ruler of the province in the second half of the eighteenth century basically altered the nature of the impact of the European trade on the economy of the region.

In analysing the trade of the Europeans, an attempt has been made to incorporate the trading operations of the various corporate groups as well as of individual traders functioning in India over the three centuries starting with the arrival of the Portuguese at the end of the fifteenth. In respect of the corporate groups other than the Portuguese, the story has been woven around the trading operations of the Dutch East India Company. The benchmarks used are those of the VOC and to facilitate comparison, the value of the trade carried on by the English and the French East India companies has often been expressed in terms of the Dutch florin. This reflects basically the fact that the VOC was the only major European trading body to engage in intra-Asian trade on a substantial scale with India playing a key role in the network, besides being the largest carrier of goods from India to Europe well into the eighteenth century.

CHAPTER 1

INDIA IN THE INDIAN OCEAN
TRADE, CIRCA 1500

An analysis of the structure and the mechanics of the early modern Indian Ocean trade, alternatively referred to as Asian trade, ought perhaps to start with a recognition of the simple fact that this trade transgressed the boundaries of both the Indian Ocean and Asia. While in the east it intruded prominently into the South China Sea, in the west it embraced maritime trade with East Africa. Traditionally, the great arc of Asian trade included the Persian Gulf and the Red Sea in the northwest and Japan in the northeast. The principal natural divisions of this huge area were the Arabian Sea, the Bay of Bengal and the South China Sea. Within each of these zones, there were important blocks of ports across which a large amount of trade had traditionally been carried on. The western or the Arabian Sea zone included ports in the Persian Gulf, the Red Sea, those on the East African coast and on the west coast of India. The Bay of Bengal network included ports in Sri Lanka, the Coromandel coast, Bengal, Burma, Thailand, Malaya and Acheh in Sumatra. Ports such as Canton and Zaiton in the South China Sea had extensive contacts both with the Indonesian ports as well as with ports in the straits of Malacca.

Within each of these zones, there were also clearly identifiable sub-zones. To take an example, in the west the ports of Aden, Ormuz, Cambay and Calicut formed one such sub-zone, while those of Kilwa, Mogadishu, Aden and Jeddah constituted another. Needless to emphasize, in terms of the ability of different constituents of a given zone to put important tradable goods on the market, for which there was adequate demand elsewhere in the zone, there was a very definitive basis for trade within each of the zones. Such a basis also existed to an important degree across zones, leading to the creation of significant long-distance trade flows in the Indian Ocean and beyond.

By far the longest distance was covered by the route that connected Aden to Canton traversing a very large part of the total area covered by the great arc of Asian trade. There is evidence to suggest that this route was in regular use at least from the seventh century. The principal group which had initiated trade on the route was the Persian merchants who had, however, been supplanted by and large by Arab merchants since about the ninth century. The principal stops on the way were either Cambay or Calicut on the Indian west coast and a port such as Palembang in Sumatra. It would seem that at some time during the twelfth century Chinese junks also began operating on this route. There is evidence that the Chinese merchants established commercial contacts with places such as Sri Lanka, Kollam on the Malabar coast and Ormuz in the Persian Gulf. The Chinese participation in trade on this route would appear to have reached important levels by the early years of the fifteenth century. Between 1404 and 1433, a series of seven commercial-cum-naval expeditions was dispatched from China under the command of Admiral Cheng Ho. The first of these expeditions is believed to have consisted of as many as 62 ships and 28,000 men. The fourth voyage is reported to have reached Ormuz and Aden, while those that followed claimed to have touched even the East African ports of Mogadishu and Malindi. But in 1433 the Chinese authorities abruptly withdrew from these ventures and, indeed, there is no record of these long-distance voyages having ever been resumed. The precise circumstances behind this development are not quite clear but it would seem that the depredation of pirates infesting the South China Sea and the criticism that the profit earned from these voyages was not sufficiently attractive contributed to the decision of the Chinese authorities. In the meantime, the Arabs had also gradually pulled out of this long-distance route.

Whatever the reasons behind the Chinese and the Arab withdrawal from long-distance trade, it signalled a basic alteration in the organizational structure of Asian trade. The new structure was based on the segmentation of the great arc of Asian trade into the three divisions mentioned earlier – the Arabian Sea, the Bay of Bengal and the South China Sea. The ports of Cambay or Calicut and Malacca (founded at the beginning of the fifteenth century), which had until then served essentially as victualling and stopping points on the long route between west Asia and China, now became terminal ports. The role of these ports in providing a reasonably assured market in the goods brought in, as well as in making available those sought after by the visiting ships, besides offering facilities such as anchorage, warehousing and banking, cannot be overemphasized. In the course of the fifteenth century, Malacca became a truly major centre of international exchange and a meeting point of traders from the East and the West.

Map 1 Important trading centres in Asia in the seventeenth
and eighteenth centuries

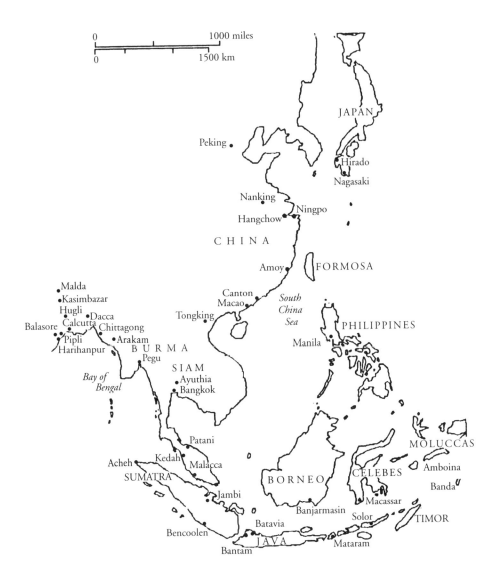

Allegedly, as many as eighty-four languages were spoken at this port. Also, each of the four major communities of merchants resident in and operating from Malacca – the Gujaratis, other 'western' merchants mainly from India and Burma, the merchants from southeast Asia up to and including the Philippines, and finally the East Asians including the Chinese, the Japanese and the Okinawans – were allowed to have *shahbandars* of their own who managed the affairs of their communities autonomously of the local authorities.

India played a central role in this structure of Asian trade. In part, this indeed was a function of the midway location of the subcontinent between west Asia on the one hand and southeast and east Asia on the other. But perhaps even more important was the subcontinent's capacity to put on the market a wide range of tradable goods at highly competitive prices. These included agricultural goods, both food items such as rice, sugar and oil as well as raw materials such as cotton and indigo. While the bulk of the trade in these goods was coastal, the high-seas trade component was by no means insignificant. The real strength of the subcontinent, however, lay in the provision of large quantities of manufactured goods, the most important amongst which was textiles of various kinds. While these included high value varieties such as the legendary Dhaka muslins and the Gujarat silk embroideries, the really important component for the Asian market was the coarse cotton varieties manufactured primarily on the Coromandel coast and in Gujarat. There was a large scale demand for these varieties both in the eastern markets of Indonesia, Malaya, Thailand and Burma as well as in the markets of the Red Sea, the Persian Gulf and East Africa. While it is impossible to determine precisely what proportion of total domestic demand for mass consumption textiles in these societies was met by imports from India, the available evidence would seem to point in the direction of this not being altogether insignificant. India's capacity to manufacture these textiles in large quantities and to put them on the market at highly competitive terms made it in some sense the 'industrial' hub of the region surrounded by west Asia on one side and southeast Asia on the other.

This circumstance also determined to a large extent the nature of India's demand for imports from the rest of Asia. This demand consisted essentially either of consumption goods which were not produced domestically for soil, climatic or other reasons, or of minerals and metals of various kinds whose domestic supply was either nil or substantially below the total demand. In the first category were items such as fine spices like cloves, nutmeg and mace from Indonesia, and horses and rosewater from west Asia. The second category included rubies and other precious stones from Burma, as well as metals – both precious and non-precious. By far the most important non-precious metal imported was tin from Malaya. Precious metals, mainly silver, were imported overwhelmingly from west Asia. It was for this reason that, from the sixteenth century onward, the port of Mocha was repeatedly referred to as the 'treasure-chest' of the Mughal empire. It is really immaterial for our purposes whether the imported precious metals are treated as a commodity import or as a means of settling the adverse balance of trade that the concerned trading partner of the subcontinent had with it. The important point to emphasize is that by virtue of her relatively more advanced structure of manufacturing production and her capacity to provide large quantities of a basic manufactured consumption good such as inexpensive cotton textiles at highly competitive terms, India significantly enhanced the basis of trade in the Asian continent. She not only provided the textiles and, on a more modest scale, the foodgrains and the provisions in great demand in the neighbouring societies but also provided an important outlet for their specialized agricultural, mineral and other products. Trade satisfied different kinds of consumption needs for India as compared with her numerous trading partners in the Indian Ocean region. This by itself provided an excellent basis for a significant and growing level of trade. It is really in this sense that the critically important role of India in the structure of early modern Asian trade needs to be assessed.

The key position of India in the structure of Asian trade was also reflected in the important role of the Gujarati and other Indian trading groups in the actual conduct of this trade. This role, if anything, was strengthened in the course of the fifteenth century which, as we have seen above, witnessed the fragmentation of Asian trade into well-defined segments. Increasingly, the participation of the Arab merchants became confined to the trade between west Asia and the west coast of India. This left the trade between the west and the east coasts of India on the one hand, and the eastern Indian Ocean region on the other, almost exclusively in the hands of Indians – the Gujaratis more than anyone else, but also the Chettis, the Chulias and other groups from the Coromandel coast, besides the Oriyas and the Bengalis. The participation of the Chinese merchants was now restricted by and large to controlling the trade between China and Malacca, while the Indonesian and the Malay merchants hardly seem to have ventured beyond the inter-island and the port-to-port trade in the Malay–Indonesian region. In sum, Indian merchants from different regions of the country constituted an important trading group operating in the Ocean.

From the vantage point of India, the two principal segments of maritime Asian trade were the western Indian Ocean and the Bay of Bengal. In the west, the link through the Red Sea and the Persian Gulf extended overland to the southern coast of the Mediterranean. The Bay of Bengal littoral extended through the straits of Malacca to the South China Sea going all the way to Japan. In the west, the area of operation of the Indian merchants stopped at the Red Sea and the Persian Gulf ports, while in the east it extended as far as Malacca. While there were clear-cut and by and large autonomous areas of operation and linkage in each of these two broad segments and there is a certain amount of merit in analysing each of these separately, it must be recognized that there was a considerable amount of interdependence and interaction across the two segments and that neither of the two should be regarded as a fully autonomous and self-contained system. One only needs to refer to the large volume of direct trade between Gujarat and Indonesia to realize the significance of this caution. This was equally true at the level of coastal trade as well, and one only has to remind oneself of the regular trade links in the fifteenth century between the ports of Bengal on the one hand and those of the west coast – in both Malabar and Gujarat – on the other.

In both the Arabian Sea and the Bay of Bengal, a considerable amount of trade was carried on both on the high-seas as well as on the coastal trade circuits. The coastal circuits were often dominated by trade in agricultural products such as foodgrains and other bulk goods, and were usually characterized by the use of relatively small craft which would ordinarily not be usable on the high-seas runs. Also, in comparison to the high-seas connections, the role of the monsoon winds was comparatively limited in determining the rhythm of trade on the coastal circuits.

THE WEST COAST

The west coast of India could conveniently be conceived of as consisting of four distinct segments divided roughly at the ports of

Chaul, Karwar and Cannanore. To the north of Chaul lay the Gujarat coast; from Chaul to Karwar was the Konkan coast; south of Karwar to Mount Eli immediately to the north of the port of Cannanore was the Kanara coast; and to its south the Malabar coast. During the fifteenth century, the ports of Cambay in Gujarat and Calicut in Malabar were the two major international ports on the west coast of India, and between them they handled a considerable amount of re-export trade. Gujarat was a major trading area in the subcontinent and the Gujaratis – mostly Muslims but also including Hindu traders – had traditionally been a dominant group amongst the Indian mercantile communities. Over the course of the fifteenth century, the trading activities of this group increased to a point where it emerged probably as the largest of all the groups engaged in trade in the Indian Ocean. This development would seem to be related to the cessation of the long-distance trade between west Asia and China, and the rise of segmented Asian trade. The most important of the new ports to emerge during the fifteenth century was Malacca, to which the Gujarati merchants shifted their trade from the Javanese and the Sumatran ports on which they had concentrated until then in their eastern trade. The growth of Malacca continued in the second half of the fifteenth century, and so did the Gujarati share in the trade of the port. According to Tomé Pires, writing at a somewhat later date, about a thousand Gujarati merchants travelled each year to Malacca together with between 4,000 and 5,000 sailors. It is true that the ships that left Cambay for Malacca each year included many owned and operated by Arab, Persian, Turkish and other merchants from west Asia, but all these groups together were overshadowed by the Gujaratis who controlled the bulk of the trade on the route. The goods that the Malacca-bound ships leaving Cambay carried were, in part, coloured woollen clothes and glassware from the Mediterranean, and items such as rosewater, opium, indigo and silver from west Asia. But a large part of the cargo would seem to have consisted of textiles manufactured in Gujarat – mainly of coarse cotton, though more expensive varieties including those manufactured from fine-quality cotton and silk also seem to have figured in the list. The cargo obtained in exchange at Malacca included Chinese goods such as silk and porcelain, Indonesian spices such as pepper, cloves, nutmeg and mace, besides woods and aromatics, and precious and non-precious metals such as Malayan tin. In addition to Malacca, the Gujarati ships from Cambay called at ports such as Acheh, Kedah, Tenasserim/ Mergui and Pegu. The goods carried to these ports were broadly similar to those carried to Malacca: the goods brought back were largely of local origin, rather than cosmopolitan as in the case of Malacca.

There was also a large amount of coastal trade carried on between Cambay and other smaller ports of Gujarat on the one hand, and ports on the Konkan, Kanara and the Malabar coasts to the south, and those in Bengal, on the other. The principal commodity procured in the Konkan ports of Chaul and Dabhol was textiles, while the main item procured in Kanara and Malabar was pepper. A certain amount of rice was also procured in Kanara. At Calicut, limited quantities of Chinese and Indonesian goods were also picked up. Bengal provided food-grains and provisions such as sugar, butter and oil in addition, of course, to textiles of different varieties.

A part of the large conglomerate of goods brought to Cambay was obviously destined for consumption in Gujarat, as well as the large north Indian hinterland supplied by it. But a good proportion would seem to have been re-exported mainly to west Asia, the most important ports in the region at this time being Aden and Jeddah. The other important constituent of the cargo to west Asia was textiles manufactured in Gujarat. These were predominantly those manufac-tured from coarse cotton and intended for mass consumption, though superior varieties manufactured from fine cotton and silk also figured in the list. The route from Cambay to Aden would seem to have been dominated by the Arab, Persian and other west Asian merchants, though the Gujarati merchants also operated on this route in an important way.

The Indonesian spices and other items imported from Cambay into Aden and other west Asian ports found their way in significant quantities, in addition to the markets of west Asia, to Europe via the Mediterranean. The two routes used for the purpose were those via the Red Sea and the Persian Gulf. While the Red Sea route terminated at the Egyptian port of Alexandria on the southern coast of the Mediterranean and involved only a small stretch of overland transpor-tation, the Persian Gulf route made use of the Tigris or the Euphrates rivers and a fair amount of caravan transportation across Iraq and the Syrian desert. Important among the Mediterranean destination ports on this route were Tripoli (of Syria) and Beirut. This traffic was handled exclusively by the west Asian merchants. At the Mediterranean ports, the goods were procured mainly by the merchants from Venice and Genoa. While both the Red Sea and the Persian Gulf routes had been in use since antiquity, the relative amount of traffic on either at any given point in time depended partly on political circumstances. While during the eighth and the ninth centuries the Persian Gulf route was the dominant one, the decline of the Abbasid caliphate and the rise of the Fatimids in Egypt tilted the balance from the eleventh century onward significantly in favour of the Red Sea route. This was also the period which witnessed a significant expansion in the volume of Euro-Asian trade. Evidence from the end of the fourteenth and the early years of the fifteenth century suggests that volume-wise the Alexandria trade was considerably larger than – nearly double on average – the one via Beirut. However, since the latter handled the expensive spices much more, the difference between the two ports was much smaller in terms of value.[1]

Another direction in which the cargo arriving at Aden – particularly the coarse cotton textiles from Gujarat – moved was southwards to the East African ports of Mogadishu, Malindi and Kilwa through the agency of the west Asian merchants. There was also a certain amount of direct trade between Cambay and the East African ports carried on by the Gujarati merchants, but the extent of this trade was perhaps quite small.

On the southwest coast, the main ports in Konkan were Chaul and Dabhol. The principal orientation of these ports was towards west Asia, though the merchants of Dabhol are also known to have gone on to Bengal to join the fleet to Malacca. The volume of the latter traffic would seem, however, to have been quite small. The ports on the Kanara coast included Mirjan, Honawar, Bhatkal, Barkur, Basrur, Mangalore and Kumbla. Bhatkal was the principal port, the others being relatively minor and catering only to the coastal trade. Bhatkal was oriented exclusively to the west with connections to the Persian Gulf and the Red Sea. The principal exports from the port were white rice, sugar, iron, textiles, ginger and pepper, while the imports included copper, gold and horses from Arabia and Persia. The non-Islamic components of the trading community operating from the

---

[1] C.H.H. Wake, 'The changing pattern of Europe's pepper and spice imports, ca. 1400–1700', *The Journal of European Economic History*, vol. 8 (2), 1979, pp. 364–9.

region consisted of Jains and the Saraswats, while the Muslims, who seem to have constituted the dominant group, included both the Navayat Muslims who claimed origins in Persia, as well as the so-called *pardesi* Muslim merchants, who were temporary residents in the area and came from the Arabian peninsula, Cairo, Turkey, Iraq and Persia.

The principal port on the Malabar coast was Calicut followed by smaller ports such as Cannanore, Cochin and Kollam. The principal orientation of the high-seas trade from the coast was westward with the Red Sea and the Persian Gulf, though a fair amount of trade was also carried on with the eastern littoral of the Bay of Bengal and with Malacca. The coastal connections stretched both northwards up to Gujarat as well as around the Cape with Sri Lanka, and via Coromandel as far north as Bengal. The principal exports from the coast were pepper, other spices such as ginger and cardamom, textiles, coconut and its ancillary products. The principal imports from west Asia were gold, silver and horses and, from the east, spices and aromatics. The *pardesi* merchants dominated the trade to the west, while the coastal trade and the high-seas trade to the east was controlled by the local Mappila merchants.

THE EAST COAST

The two principal trading regions on the east coast of India were the Coromandel coast and Bengal. The Coromandel coast is convention-ally defined as including the stretch between Point Godavari and the island of Manar, south of which lies the Fishery coast. To the north of Point Godavari is the Gingelly coast which is sometimes also included in the Coromandel coast. For our purposes, Bengal would be defined as including the Orissa ports of Pipli and Balasore. There was a fair amount of coastal trade between the ports of the two regions, dominated, it would seem, by the merchants of Bengal. At the beginning of the sixteenth century, the principal Coromandel port was Pulicat linked via Tirupati and Penukonda to the imperial city of Vijayanagar to the northwest. The port next in importance was that of Nagapattinam in south Coromandel, which also had two minor ports at Kunjimedu and Naguru. The northern Coromandel port of Masuli-patnam was of little consequence at this time. In Bengal, by far the most important port was Chittagong which was linked to the capital city of Gaur. Satgaon was next in importance until about 1580 when, due to the silting up of the waterway on which it was situated, it was succeeded by Hugli. Pipli and Balasore in Orissa were the other important ports in the region.

The high-seas trade from Pulicat was basically in two directions: to Mergui and the ports of the Irrawaddy delta in southern Burma on the one hand, and to Malacca and ports further east in the archipelago on the other. While the trade with Mergui was marginal, that with Pegu and lower Burma, in particular the ports of Martaban and Cosmin, was more substantial. The principal exports from Pulicat consisted of textiles produced all over the Coromandel coast and red yarn from the Krishna delta. The imports into Coromandel included items such as gold, rubies, timber, tin, ivory and copper. In 1516, Antonio Dinis, sometime Portuguese factor at Martaban, reported that on an average four or five ships were engaged each year in the trade between Cosmin and Coromandel. The link to Malacca was perhaps even more important. Until its capture by the Portuguese in 1511, the annual traffic to the port from Coromandel usually consisted of one large ship and as many as five smaller ships. The average annual value of the textiles cargo imported into Malacca from Pulicat in the early years of the sixteenth century has been put at 175,000 cruzados. There usually was also an annual ship to Pidie in northern Sumatra, as well as traffic from Pasai to Coromandel. The principal items imported into Pulicat included Indonesian spices, various kinds of woods, Chinese silk and other goods, gold and non-precious metals such as tin, copper, quicksilver and vermilion. A major trading group at Pulicat was that of Muslims, a few of Arab origin, but mainly members of the Muslim communities of coastal southeastern India, known as Chulias in parts of southeast Asia and Marakkayars on Coromandel. The trading community also included Telugu-speaking Chettis of the Balija and Komatti communities as well as Armenians. At the Malacca end, the mercantile community consisted largely of the so-called *keling* merchants of Tamil and Telugu origin led by people like Nina Chatu and Nina Suryadev. The sultan of Malacca himself is also known to have participated in this branch of commerce.

In addition to the high-seas trade carried on from Pulicat and other Coromandel ports, there was also a fair amount of coastal trade carried on with the Bengal ports in the north, the Sri Lankan and other ports in the south, and with ports on the Malabar coast. The precise position at the beginning of the sixteenth century remains somewhat obscure for the available data pertain mainly to the sixteenth and the early seventeenth centuries. The changes, if any, over the intervening period, however, do not appear to have been particularly marked, except in the matter of the growing role of Masulipatnam through the sixteenth century in the coastal, as in the high-seas, network. The available information suggests that there was regular trade between Bengal and Coromandel based on the import into ports such as Masulipatnam of rice, gram, wheat, long pepper, opium, clarified butter and Bihar saltpetre by an annual coastal fleet from Bengal. In the late sixteenth and early seventeenth centuries, the number of vessels in the fleet was between thirty and forty. While the ships from Bengal usually returned from north Coromandel itself, those from the Gingelly coast went further south to supply central Coromandel as far as Pulicat and São Tomé. The Coromandel cargo carried back to Bengal was raw cotton, tobacco, iron and crucible steel, and some textiles, but the profit seems to have been made largely on the outward journey. The pattern of coastal trade originating in southern Coromandel, however, was quite different. The ports of the Kaveri delta were all rice exporters, but this trade was directed southwards rather than towards the deficit pockets to the north. Nagapattinam supplied rice to the west coast of Sri Lanka, Jaffna and, on a more limited scale, to southern Malabar in addition to Acheh, on which route rice was used mainly as a ballast item. The principal items brought back from Sri Lanka were areca, cinnamon, timber and elephants. It is somewhat intriguing that the sources do not mention any coastal contacts between the Coromandel ports on the one hand and the Kanara, Konkan and Gujarat ports on the other.[2]

As far as Bengal was concerned, in addition to the coastal trade with southeastern India, the major commercial links extended to the eastern littoral of the Bay of Bengal and Malacca, to Sri Lanka, the Maldives and Malabar, and finally to the Gujarat, the Red Sea and the Persian Gulf complex. The eastward trade was dominated by the trade to Malacca. According to Meilink-Roelofsz., five or six ships sailed on average each year in the early part of the sixteenth century from Bengal to Malacca and ports such as Pasai and Pidie. Most of these

---

[2] Sanjay Subrahmanyam, *The Political Economy of Commerce, Southern India 1500–1650*, Cambridge, 1990, pp. 50–3, 93–8.

were rather small vessels but they did include one or two larger ones whose cargoes may have been worth as much as 80,000–90,000 cruzados. The exports from Bengal included textiles, rice, sugar and conserves, while the imports were a varied lot. These included Borneo camphor, Moluccan spices, pepper, sandalwood, Chinese porcelain and silk, precious metals – perhaps mainly silver – as well as base metals such as copper, tin, lead and mercury. The connection with Burma was mainly through the ports at Martaban, Dagon and Cosmin. According to the 1516 testimony of Dinis, four or five Bengal ships visited Cosmin each year carrying mainly textiles which were exchanged primarily against silver made into rings or small hoops.

The exports to Sri Lanka, the Maldives and the Malabar coast were again mainly textiles and foodstuffs, including large quantities of rice. Indeed, besides Kanara, Bengal was the principal rice surplus area in the entire region and areas such as the Maldives depended mainly on Bengal for their rice requirements. The principal items brought back by the Bengal vessels were cinnamon and areca from Sri Lanka, *cauris* (used extensively in Bengal both for ornamental purposes as well as in the form of low denomination currency) from the Maldives, and pepper, of which again Bengal was an important consumer, from Malabar. The trade to Gujarat was carried on primarily through Cambay, while the trips to Mocha in the Red Sea were often made after a stopover at the Maldives. The principal goods carried were textiles, sugar and long pepper, while the principal item brought back from Mocha was silver. The evidence regarding the Persian Gulf connection is, however, somewhat ambiguous.

The accounts of Tomé Pires and Barbosa also enable one to decipher the principal components of the mercantile community operating from Bengal. The indigenous merchants of Bengal are described as 'merchants with great fortunes' and were an important constituent of the trading community. But a large part of the trade would seem to have been controlled either by merchants based at the partner ports or by foreign merchant groups settled in the Bengal ports. Thus the trade with Malacca was dominated by the *keling* merchants settled there. The pepper trade with Pasai and Pidie was carried on by Persian merchants settled at the Port of Chittagong. This last-mentioned group would seem also to have dominated the trade to the middle and the western Indian Ocean ports, though the traders on these routes also included Turks, Arabs, Rumis, Abyssinians and merchants from Chaul, Dabhol and Goa.[3]

To sum up, around the time that the Europeans' participation in the maritime trade of India started, at the beginning of the sixteenth century, India occupied a position of key importance in the structure of Indian Ocean trade. Of the three principal segments of this trade, the Western Indian Ocean, the Bay of Bengal and the South China Sea, the first two were dominated by India. This domination was accounted for only in part by India's midway location. Perhaps more important was her capacity to put on the market a wide range of tradable goods – particularly manufactured goods, the most important amongst which was coarse cotton textiles – at highly competitive prices. In the process, she helped to expand the basis of trade in the region. This was a structure of trade in which the Europeans – of whom the Portuguese were the first – had no problem in finding a niche for themselves.

[3] Sanjay Subrahmanyam, 'Notes on the sixteenth century Bengal trade', *The Indian Economic and Social History Review*, vol. 24 (3), 1987, pp. 265–89.

CHAPTER 2

THE PORTUGUESE IN INDIA, 1500–1640

The arrival of three Portuguese ships under the charge of Vasco da Gama at Calicut on 20 May 1498 marked the inauguration of a new era in the history of Euro-Asian contacts in general, and of trade between the two continents in particular. Ever since the conquest in 1415 of the Moroccan city of Ceuta, the Portuguese had been increasingly involved in trading off the Saharan coast of Africa and importing gold and slaves from there. The legendary Prince Henry the Navigator participated in the profits from this trade, and in some sense personified the central role of the Portuguese Crown in encouraging further thrust into the Atlantic southwards. This phase culminated in the rounding of the Cape of Good Hope by Bartolomeu Dias in 1488 providing for the first time the potential of an all-water route connecting Europe to Asia. Apart from anything else, the Cape route implied the overcoming of the transport-technology barrier to the growth of Euro-Asian trade. The volume of this trade was no longer subject to the capacity constraint imposed by the availability of pack-animals and river boats in the Middle East.

EURO-ASIAN TRADE

Since it was the Portuguese who had discovered the Cape route, they promptly monopolized it and even asked the Pope to legitimize the arrangement. The result was that for a whole century, until this arrangement was successfully challenged by the Dutch and the English in the 1590s, the only merchant group engaged in trade between Europe and Asia along the all-water route was the Portuguese. Partly because of the absence of a strong mercantile tradition among the Portuguese comparable in any sense to that of the northwestern Europeans, and partly because the Crown had taken the lead in providing finance and the infrastructural support to the efforts which had culminated in the discovery of the Cape route, the overseas enterprise in Asia was dominated from the very beginning by the Portuguese Crown. The principal organizing unit at the Lisbon end

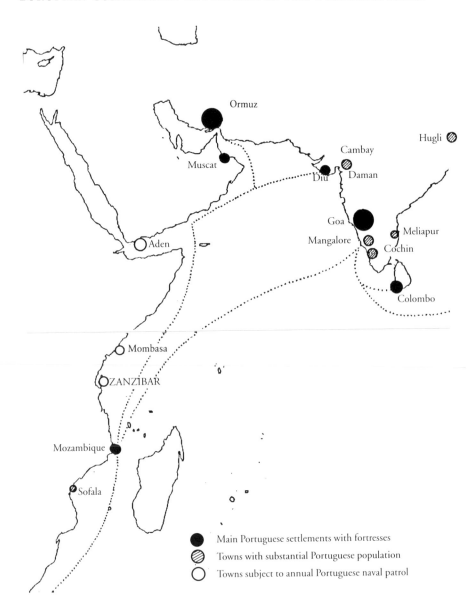

Map 2 Portuguese seaborne empire, c. 1580

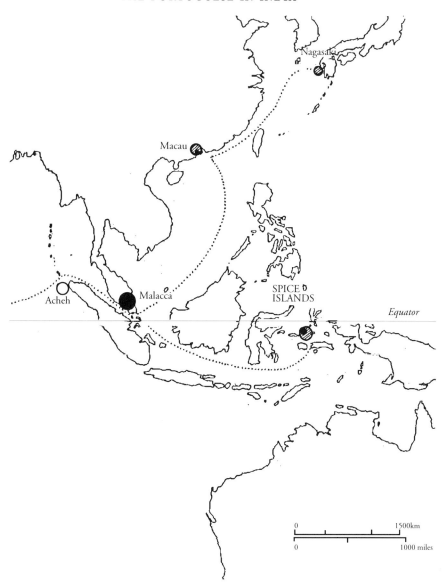

was the Casa da Índia, a royal trading firm entrusted with the overall charge of the trade with Asia. The Asian end of the enterprise was supervised by an administrative set-up described from the 1560s onwards as the Estado da Índia. This had its headquarters theoretically in Lisbon but for all practical purposes in Goa under the charge of the Viceroy nominated by the Crown. The Viceroy was assisted by, among others, informal councils which by 1563 had evolved and become more institutionalized as the Council of State. Its members, apart from the Viceroy as President, were the archbishop of Goa, the chief inquisitor, two or three of the older *fidalgos* resident in Goa, the head of the High Court, the Captain of the city of Goa and the Vedor de fazenda or chief financial official. The Viceroy had command over all Portuguese posts as well as military and naval forces from the Zambezi valley in Africa to Macao in China. The subordinate settlements followed the structure of control established in Goa. As a recent study puts it, in the first half of the sixteenth century, 'Portuguese India' did not designate 'a space that was geographically well defined but a complex of territories, establishments, goods, persons and administrative interests in Asia and East Africa, generated by or subordinate to the Portuguese Crown, all of which were linked together as a maritime network.'[1]

The Portuguese enterprise comprised a variety of interest groups which at times pulled in different directions. At the Lisbon end, in addition to the Crown, there were the syndicates of merchants, financiers and bankers of various European nationalities who were an essential constituent of the operation. Often, these syndicates also played an important role in the procurement and the transportation of the return cargo from Asia. Within Asia, also, the Portuguese presence had a multiplicity of facets. In its economic dimension, there was in the first place the official presence in the form of the Estado da Índia, which was supposed to take care of the commercial interests of the Crown. But the employees of the Estado from the Viceroy down simultaneously engaged extensively in trade on their private account under a variety of arrangements. And, finally, there were the private Portuguese traders who operated either under the protection of the

---

[1] Sanjay Subrahmanyam and Luís Filipe F. R. Thomaz, 'Evolution of empire: the Portuguese in the Indian Ocean during the sixteenth century', in James D. Tracy (ed.), *The Political Economy of Merchant Empires, State Power and World Trade 1350–1750*, Cambridge, 1991, p. 304.

Estado or outside of it. It is important to realize that over time through the sixteenth and the first half of the seventeenth century, there were important shifts in policy in respect of one or more of these constituents. The Portuguese enterprise can then be seen to have had an evolutionary character rather than a well-defined or unchanging profile.

In keeping with the traditional composition of the Asian imports into Europe, the principal item sought by the Portuguese Crown in Asia was spices – overwhelmingly pepper – though some other goods were also procured. On the basis of the better known cases of the Dutch and the English East India companies' trade in pepper and other spices, one ordinarily associates the spice trade primarily with the Indonesian archipelago (Sumatran pepper and Moluccan cloves, nutmeg and mace) and only marginally with Sri Lanka (cinnamon) and the southwest coast of India (pepper). This characterization, however, is totally inapplicable to the Portuguese case. Their early occupation of Malacca (1511) notwithstanding, the overwhelming bulk of their pepper procurement was done in the Malabar region (and later Kanara as well) on the southwest coast of India. This made India their principal theatre of operation throughout the century and a half of their trading history between Europe and Asia. It was only in the context of the intra-Asian trade that the Portuguese connection with other parts of Asia, including China and Japan, became quantitatively significant. The detailed documentary evidence available in respect of the Dutch and the English East India companies' trade is conspicuous by its absence in the case of the Portuguese. This makes it impossible to reconstruct in any detail the history of the Portuguese Euro-Asian trade. But the basic outlines of the story can be put together.

On the return of Vasco da Gama to Lisbon in 1499, the Portuguese government had formed a syndicate for trade with Asia, in which both the Crown and certain private interests participated. In the voyage of Pedro Alvarez Cabral which left Lisbon on 9 March 1500 with thirteen ships, for example, ten were on the account of the Crown, while the remaining three belonged to different syndicates of Portuguese noblemen and Italian financiers. But from 1506 onward, the trade in precious metals from Portugal to India, and that in pepper and other major spices in the reverse direction, was reserved as a royal monopoly. Private trade in monopoly items was, however, allowed to naval personnel, and to certain privileged institutions and individuals under royal license. More importantly, it would seem that the participation of private enterprise in the role of financiers continued. On occasions, this could be quite important. Thus the fleet of 1510 under the command of Diogo Mendes de Vasconcelos was largely staffed and financed by the Florentine commercial house of Sernigi and its associates. The procurement of pepper in India was organized by the Estado while the sales in Europe were through contract sales based until the middle of the century at Antwerp and thereafter at Lisbon.

The mounting liquidity problems of the Crown forced a major reorganization of the trade with Asia in 1564 when the first of a series of contracts giving over trade on the Cape route to private parties was concluded. The remaining part of the century witnessed a variety of experiments carried out in an attempt to identify the optimal strategy that would ensure the Crown maximum monopoly revenue without obliging it to be directly involved in the conduct of the trade with Asia. In 1570, the trade in pepper and other spices was opened to free competition, although the Crown also continued to participate in the trade itself and retained its monopoly on the export of precious metals to Asia.[2] The Asian contract system was introduced in 1575. The first beneficiary of the new arrangement was the Augsburg merchant Konrad Rott together with his associates who included the Milanese merchant, Giovanni Batista Rovalesca. Under this arrangement, Rott received intact the royal monopoly of the Cape route – the procurement of spices in Asia, their shipment to Europe, the provisioning of the carracks in Lisbon and Goa, and the distribution of pepper in Europe. Just before his death in 1580, dom Henrique renewed the Rott–Rovalesca contract for another five years. Under the terms of the contract, the contractors were supposed to purchase each year in India a total of 30,000 quintals of pepper – 15,000 on their own account and 15,000 on the king's account. The contractors were free to sell their half of the pepper as they chose; the king would also sell all of his 15,000 quintals (which cost him nothing) to the Rott–Rovalesca consortium at 32 cruzados per quintal. The consortium thus enjoyed exclusive European distribution of Portuguese pepper.[3] A sharp decline in the European price of pepper, however, forced Rott out of

---

[2] Subrahmanyam and Thomaz, 'Evolution of empire', pp. 310–11.
[3] James C. Boyajian, *Portuguese Trade in Asia under the Habsburgs 1580–1640*, Baltimore and London, 1993, p. 20.

business. In February 1586, a new Asian contract was concluded for a period of six years with Rovalesca in association with Giraldo Paris. They were authorized to take in other associates subject to the approval of the Crown. In April, the Augsburg firm of Welser joined in with a five-twelfths share. In 1587, the Fugger brothers also came in with a share of a quarter. This group was required to supply to the king 30,000 quintals of pepper per annum at a price of 16 cruzados per quintal.[4] The Casa da Índia sold the pepper to the European contractors at prices negotiated each year in Lisbon. The European distributors included, besides Welser and Fugger, several investors who were not party to the Asian contract. The consortium marketed pepper through a network of correspondents in Hamburg, Lubeck, Middelburg, Amsterdam, Leghorn and Venice. By not awarding the European distributorship to the group holding the Asian contract, the king gambled that he could bargain more effectively in Lisbon for a premium price for his pepper.[5] The contract system continued until 1598 when, following the English and Dutch intervention in the seaborne spice trade, private enterprise was no longer willing to take up the pepper contracts. In any event, the experiment with the contract system had not been particularly satisfactory for either side. The syndicates were consistently unable to import the quantities specified in the contracts and never managed to make adequate profits. The bankruptcy of Rott has already been noted: his Milanese counterpart Rovalesca was also forced to follow suit.

In the context of the continuing problem of liquidity, the formation of the English and the Dutch East India companies in 1600 and 1602 respectively would seem to have been instrumental in spurring the Portuguese (and Spanish) Crown to consider the establishment of a Portuguese India Company.[6] The Company was finally founded in 1628, but the experiment was not particularly successful, and as early as April 1633 it was decided to dissolve the Company. The last batch of cargo on the account of the Company left Goa in 1634. The Crown monopoly of pepper was partially relaxed in 1642 with the rights of

---

[4] Hermann Kellenbenz, 'Autour de 1600: le commerce du poivre des Fugger et le marché international du poivre', *Annales Economies-Sociétés-Civilisations*, vol. 11 (1), 1956, pp. 1–28.

[5] Boyajian, *Portuguese Trade in Asia*, p. 22.

[6] The details of the project can be followed in A.R. Disney, *Twilight of the Pepper Empire, Portuguese Trade in Southwest India in the Early Seventeenth Century*, Cambridge, Mass., 1978, Chapters V and VI.

the Casa da Índia being confined to purchasing the pepper on arrival in Lisbon at a pre-determined price. But the arrangement failed to stimulate the trade to any significant extent. The tonnage leaving Asia for Lisbon, which had stood at 13,710 tons during 1631–40, went up during 1641–50 only to 16,030 tons. In the second half of the seventeenth century, it was only during 1671–80 that this figure exceeded 10,000 tons (Table 2.1).[7]

The exports to Asia

The cargoes sent out from Portugal to Asia to facilitate the procurement of pepper and other return goods included precious metals (West African gold and, from 1570 onward, primarily rials coined from American silver), non-precious metals such as copper, lead, tin, quicksilver and mercury, and other goods such as coral and alum, wines and olive oil, and fine textiles such as scarlets, damasks, taffetas and silks. Valuewise, metals overwhelmingly dominated the exports, and copper was by far the most important of these for quite some time. Thus, of the average annual value of 103,295 cruzados sent out to Cochin between 1510 and 1518, copper accounted for 49,464 cruzados (47.88 per cent), silver and specie for 30,274 cruzados (29.31 per cent), while the remainder was accounted for by other non-precious metals and coral.[8] According to Magalhães-Godinho, the average annual value of the exports to Asia went up during the second quarter of the century to between 150,000 and 250,000 cruzados. But a spectacular increase both in the value of the average annual exports as well as in the share of silver rials in the total took place only over the last third of the century. He estimates the value of the precious metals alone sent out over this period at between one and one and a half million cruzados per annum.[9] This, however, would seem to be a gross overestimate. Elsewhere in his own work, Magalhães-Godinho

---

[7] In a recent paper, Glenn Joseph Ames has argued that 'as opposed to the dismal period from 1640–1663, when the *Carreira* was virtually moribund and contact between Lisbon and Goa was interrupted for years at a time, a regular seaborne trade between the metropolis and India was definitively re-established' from 1668 onward when Prince Regent Pedro assumed power in a palace coup. Ames' data cover the period between 1668 and 1682 and are broadly in agreement with the Duncan data. (Glen Joseph Ames, 'The Carreira da Índia, 1668–1682: maritime enterprise and the quest for stability in Portugal's Asian empire', *The Journal of European Economic History*, vol. 20 (1), 1991, pp. 7–27.)

[8] V. Magalhães-Godinho, *Os Descobrimentos e a Economia Mundial*, Lisbon, 1963–71, vol. III, p. 11.

[9] Magalhães-Godinho, *Os Descobrimentos e a Economia Mundial*, vol. III, p. 71.

has suggested for the 1580s a silver export figure of between 180,000 and 210,000 cruzados per annum.[10] Also considering the fact that the period would seem to have been marked by at least no increase in the average annual value of the cargoes imported from Asia, the enormously high figure of precious metal exported, as suggested by Magalhães-Godinho, would pose the problem of what eventually happened to all this additional purchasing power in Asia. Based on data from Luís de Figueiredo Falcão (c. 1610), Niels Steensgaard has suggested for the years between 1588 and 1592 an average annual export figure to Asia of 250,000 cruzados. The silver component of this figure at the end of the century was between 150,000 and 200,000 cruzados.[11]

Shipping movement between Asia and Europe

As far as the return cargoes from Asia are concerned, information regarding value is totally missing and one has to depend entirely on movements in shipping and tonnage and on some data on the volume of these cargoes. The number of ships that returned from Asia was obviously related to that sent out, though in any given year there could be a fair discrepancy between these two numbers because of shipwrecks on the way, the holding back of ships in Asia, or, conversely, the construction of new ships in the Asian shipyards. In a paper published in 1970, Steensgaard presented three series of ship departures from Portugal to India based respectively on the lists of Luís de Figueiredo Falcão (1491/2 to 1610/11), Pedro Barreto de Rezende (1491/2 to 1630/1) and Faria e Sousa (1491/2 to 1630/1).[12] According to Steensgaard, the Rezende series was the most reliable. The estimates given by Magalhães-Godinho also show that he has broadly followed the Rezende series.[13] More recently, based on a wide range of materials, T. Bentley Duncan has presented a new series of shipping movements between Portugal and Asia which largely supersedes earlier work not only because of its more comprehensive data base but also because it provides, in addition, the movements of

[10] Magalhães-Godinho, *Os Descobrimentos e a Economia Mundial*, vol. II, graph on p. 113.
[11] Niels Steensgaard, *The Asian Trade Revolution of the Seventeenth Century: The East India Companies and the Decline of Caravan Trade*, Chicago, 1974, p. 87.
[12] Niels Steensgaard, 'European shipping to Asia, 1497–1700', *The Scandinavian Economic History Review*, vol. 18 (1), 1970, Table 1, p. 5.
[13] Steensgaard, 'European shipping to Asia', pp. 5–6.

Table 2.1 *Shipping movements between Portugal and Asia, 1497–1700*

| Years | Europe–Asia | | | | Asia–Europe | | | |
| | Lisbon departures | | Asia arrivals | | Asia departures | | Lisbon arrivals | |
	Ships	Tonnage	Ships	Tonnage	Ships	Tonnage	Ships	Tonnage
1497–1500	17	2,665	10	1,640	3	290	2	170
1501–10	151	42,775	135	38,695	88	26,085	73	21,115
1511–20	96	38,690	87	35,830	60	26,060	59	25,760
1521–30	81	37,720	67	32,290	55	28,520	53	27,020
1531–40	80	44,660	76	42,610	61	39,110	57	36,410
1541–50	68	40,800	56	34,100	58	34,550	52	30,550
1551–60	58	39,600	46	32,500	47	33,650	35	25,750
1561–70	50	37,030	46	35,580	45	36,250	40	32,150
1571–80	50	42,900	48	40,800	42	38,250	39	35,150
1581–90	59	55,420	45	42,870	51	48,450	42	39,290
1591–1600	43	49,200	39	42,540	40	45,350	22	25,000
1601–10	71	77,190	45	49,540	36	43,390	28	32,290
1611–20	66	60,990	47	44,060	32	40,350	28	35,550
1621–30	60	48,000	39	31,410	28	24,150	19	15,050
1631–40	33	20,020	28	15,770	21	13,710	15	9,910
1641–50	42	22,840	28	14,280	32	16,030	24	12,030
1651–60	35	14,320	35	18,990	16	7,970	16	8,120
1661–70	21	8,635	14	5,635	14	6,070	13	4,820
1671–80	25	11,700	29	13,900	22	10,730	21	9,680
1681–90	19	11,650	19	11,650	16	9,300	15	8,600
1691–1700	24	14,900	21	13,700	14	8,950	13	7,550
1497–1700	1,149	721,705	960	598,390	781	537,215	666	441,965

Source: T. Bentley Duncan 'Navigation between Portugal and Asia in the sixteenth and seventeenth centuries', in E.J. van Kley and C.K. Pullapilly (eds.), *Asia and the West: Encounters and Exchanges from the Age of Explorations*, Notre Dame, 1986, p. 22.

shipping in the reverse direction as well as the extent of losses on the way.[14] Duncan's findings for the period 1497 to 1700 are presented in Table 2.1.

If one looks at movements in the number of ships departing from Asia (which would best capture the extent of the Portuguese trading operations in Asia), it is clear that there was a continuous and

[14] T. Bentley Duncan, 'Navigation between Portugal and Asia in the sixteenth and seventeenth centuries', in E.J. van Kley and C.K. Pullapilly (eds.), *Asia and the West: Encounters and Exchanges from the Age of Explorations*, Notre Dame, 1986, pp. 3–25.

significant downward trend in the number of ships operating. From a peak of eighty-eight ships in the first decade of the sixteenth century, the number comes down to forty-seven in the sixth decade and to forty in the last. The trend continues in the seventeenth century with only twenty-one departures listed during 1631–40. The downward trend is even more marked if one looks at the number of ships that left Lisbon for Asia over the same period. What conclusions can be drawn from this regarding the volume of Portuguese imports from Asia? It need hardly be emphasized that the movements in the number of ships alone cannot be a satisfactory index to movements in the volume of trade, particularly when it is known that the average ship size increased considerably over the period. Until 1540, Portuguese East Indiamen rarely exceeded 400 tons. But in the following decades, a number of ships of 1,000 tons or more were employed, taking the average up to perhaps 600 tons. By the 1570s, the average *nau* was a four-decked carrack of over 1,000 tons and 'monsters' of up to 2,000 tons were not unknown. What then is needed clearly is information on tonnage in addition to the number of ships operating on this route. Unfortunately, the records of the Carreira da Índia yield tonnage figures in respect of only 11 per cent of the total number of ships that left Lisbon for Asia between 1497 and 1590. But by carefully putting together the available information on the type of ships, the manner of their employment, the number of people aboard and the quantity of cargo carried, Duncan has produced a plausible tonnage series as a counterpart to his shipping movement series (Table 2.1). The important conclusion that his tonnage series brings out is that an increase in the average tonnage of the ships employed in the Portugal–India run over time more than neutralized the decline in the number of ships employed. Thus the decade 1581–90 witnessed more tonnage leaving Lisbon as well as Asia than any previous decade.[15] Duncan's work would thus cast serious doubt on the validity of the generally held notion of a decline in the volume of Portuguese India–Europe trade in the latter half of the sixteenth century.

The volume, value and composition of the return cargo

The information on the volume of the Portuguese return cargoes from India is quite limited and in part problematic. On the basis of

[15] Bentley Duncan, 'Navigation between Portugal and Asia', pp. 9–10.

information in the Sanudo diaries and the official summaries of the registers of cargo aboard the returning ships for the years 1501 to 1506 and 1513 to 1548, Magalhães-Godinho has suggested that the average annual volume of the return cargo for the first third of the sixteenth century was not less than 40,000 quintals and was possibly more than 50,000 quintals. Later in the century, according to him, this figure went up to between 60,000 and 75,000 quintals.[16] The substantially higher figures of Magalhães-Godinho in comparison with the earlier estimates of Frederic C. Lane were partly the result of an upward adjustment to correct for a suspected element of unregistered cargo not reflected in the books. The unregistered cargo arose because of the private trade carried on by the mariners and royal officials as perquisites of office. Magalhães-Godinho estimated this cargo at around 25 per cent of the total.[17] As for the composition of the imports, Magalhães-Godinho's data for the average annual exports from the Cochin factory from 1510 and 1518 show that, of the total value of 50,656 cruzados, pepper accounted for 84.64 per cent. The percentages for cloves, nutmeg, mace, cinnamon and lac were 3.64, 2.60, 2.76, 2.32 and 4.00, respectively.[18] The remainder of the information, unfortunately, provides the figures only in terms of weight and not of value. The data published by Geneviève Bouchon and relating to 1505 and 1518 respectively are summarized in Table 2.2. Based on Magalhães-Godinho's and C.H.H. Wake's data for 1513–48 and his own for 1587–1610, Niels Steensgaard has suggested the scenario summarized in Table 2.3.

What can be said on the basis of this information? The first point to be stressed is that in so far as the bulk of the information is in physical rather than value terms, its usefulness is somewhat limited. After all, the comparison of a quintal of pepper or indigo with the corresponding weight of a bale of raw silk or textiles can produce absurd results. At a general level, it could be argued that, given the nature of the commodities involved in the return cargoes from Asia, data in terms of weight would generally overstate the role of pepper and understate that of high-value spices such as cloves, nutmeg and mace.

[16] Niels Steensgaard, 'The return cargoes of the Carreira in the 16th and early 17th century', in Teotonio R. de Souza (ed.), *Indo-Portuguese History; Old Issues, New Questions*, New Delhi, 1985, pp. 13–14.

[17] Steensgaard, 'The return cargoes of the Carreira', pp. 13–14.

[18] Calculated from Magalhães-Godinho, *Os Descobrimentos e a Economia Mundial*, vol. III, p. 11.

Table 2.2 *Composition of cargoes imported into Lisbon from Asia,
1505–18 (percent by weight)*

	1505 (first estimate) Number of ships = 13 Cargo imported = 21,826 quintals	1505 (second estimate) Number of ships = 13 Cargo imported = 22,237 quintals	1518 Number of ships = 6 Cargo imported = 2,242,112 kg = 38,196 quintals (at 58.7 kg per quintal)
Pepper	95.73	94.84	94.95
Ginger	2.53	2.38	–
Cloves	0.63	0.78	0.24
Cinnamon	0.78	1.57	0.06
Indigo	0.11	–	–
Lac	0.03	0.26	2.96
Silk	–	–	0.11
Red sandalwood	–	–	1.24
Miscellaneous	0.15	0.14	0.40
TOTAL	99.96	99.97	99.96

Source: The estimates for 1505 are from Geneviève Bouchon, 'L'inventaire de la cargaison rapportée de l'Inde en 1505', in *Mare Luso Indicum*, vol. III, Paris, 1976. The estimate for 1518 is from Geneviève Bouchon, *Navires et cargaisons retour de l'Inde en 1518*, Paris, 1977.

Thus against 95 per cent in physical terms in 1505 and 1518, valuewise pepper accounted for less than 85 per cent between 1510 and 1518. The reverse was the case with the finer spices. As long as this particular inbuilt bias in the physical figures is kept in mind, a comparison in terms of such figures over time can generate a reasonably accurate picture. The other problem that is encountered in this is that of the coverage of the data. While Bouchon's figures would seem to take into account all the incoming ships (note that her numbers are 13 for 1505 and 6 for 1518 against an annual average of 7.3 between 1501 and 1510 and of 5.9 between 1511 and 1520), the coverage in the Steensgaard data is incomplete. In blocks of years such as 1608–10, when the coverage is particularly incomplete, perhaps it is not safe to derive any conclusions from these data. For the rest, a certain amount of care in their interpretation is called for. Thus against the figure of 95 per cent for pepper given by Bouchon, the Steensgaard data for 1513–19 suggest a figure of only 80 per cent, though the figure for 1523–31

Table 2.3 *Composition of cargoes imported into Lisbon from Asia, 1513–1610 (percent by weight)*

	1513–19 Number of ships = 24 Average cargo per ship = 6,223 quintals	1523–31 Number of ships = 17 Average cargo per ship = 4,345 quintals	1547–8 Number of ships = 10 Average cargo per ship = 6,789 quintals	1587–8 Number of ships = 8 Average cargo per ship = 6,638 quintals	1600–3 Number of ships = 12 Average cargo per ship = 7,891 quintals	1608–10 Number of ships = 3 Average cargo per ship = 6,110 quintals
Pepper	80.00	84.00	89.00	68.00	65.00	69.00
Moluccan spices	9.00	6.20	4.50	1.60	5.00	0.03
Ginger	7.30	6.10	4.20	3.70	2.50	1.60
Cinnamon	2.10	3.30	0.90	6.30	8.70	9.30
Indigo	0.00	0.00	0.00	8.40	4.40	7.70
Textiles	0.20	0.00	0.00	10.50	12.20	7.80
Miscellaneous	1.40	0.40	1.40	1.50	2.20	4.60
TOTAL	100.00	100.00	100.00	100.00	100.00	100.03

Source: Niels Steensgaard, 'The return cargoes of the Carreira in the 16th and early 17th century', in Tectonio R. de Souza (ed.), *Indo-Portuguese History: Old Issues, New Questions,* New Delhi, 1985, Tables 2.2 and 2.3, p. 22.

goes up to 84 per cent. These limitations notwithstanding, the totality of the data would strongly suggest the declining role of pepper in the second half of the sixteenth century to less than 70 per cent. The Moluccan spices and ginger also become proportionately less important over time. Sri Lankan cinnamon, on the other hand, becomes increasingly more important. Also, indigo emerges in the cargoes in the second half of the century in a reasonably important way: the same is even more true of textiles, though, as pointed out earlier, one has to be particularly careful while interpreting weight figures in relation to textiles.

James Boyajian has recently suggested a major reformulation of this broad scenario for the period 1580 to 1640. He has argued that during this period the volume and the value of the Portuguese Euro-Asian trade was in fact much larger than has traditionally been believed. At the heart of Boyajian's analysis is his almost revolutionary revision of current orthodoxy in the matter of the relative role of the private Portuguese traders in the Euro-Asian carreira trade. It has traditionally been conceded that the carreira ships operated on the account of the Estado da India did indeed transport on a regular basis a certain amount of private cargo under a variety of arrangements. The novelty of Boyajian's estimates consists in his view of the magnitude of the private cargoes carried aboard these ships overwhelmingly on the account of the New Christian merchants who were descendants of Iberian Jews forcibly converted to Christianity at the end of the fifteenth century. According to Boyajian, private cargoes accounted for an almost unbelievable 90 per cent of the total value imported over the period 1580–1640 from Asia. By far the most important constituent of this cargo was textiles, accounting for as much as 62 per cent of the total imports valuewise, followed by items such as precious stones (14 per cent), pepper (10 per cent), indigo (6 per cent) and spices other than pepper (5 per cent).[19] In all of these items, except for pepper, the private traders accounted for nearly the whole of the trade. What is the statistical basis of these estimates? As the 1755 Lisbon earthquake destroyed the Casa da India's records, Boyajian is obliged to use other evidence. According to him, Luís de Figueiredo Falcáo's data and a few manifests from 1586–98 indicate that total shipments of royal pepper and private goods of the carreira da Índia (excluding

[19] Boyajian, *Portuguese Trade in Asia*, p. 44.

privileged cargo not subject to duties) amounted to 67 million cruzados, giving an average of 5.1 million cruzados for each of thirteen years. Of this total, private cargo constituted almost 60 million cruzados, or just about 90 per cent, averaging 4.6 million cruzados annually. The inclusion of additional shipments of non-dutiable liberties and unregistered private cargo would raise the total value of the private cargo to well above 5 million cruzados per year.[20]

A close examination of the Boyajian estimates, however, suggests that the picture is indeed not quite as straightforward and unambiguous as he would have us believe. The data that form the basis of Boyajian's estimates are put together in Appendix A of the book, entitled 'Some manifests of carreira shipping, ca. 1580–1640'. For the period between 1586 and 1598, the information in respect of the years 1587 and 1588 has been taken from Steensgaard's *Asian Trade Revolution of the Seventeenth Century*, Table 10, p. 166, with chests of cloth being converted into bales at the rate of 1.5 bales per chest (1 bale = 2 quintals). This information lists the volume of imports separately in respect of each important commodity and is based on bills of lading of the relevant ships. For the remaining years over the period 1586–98, however, in the absence of similar detailed and original information, Boyajian imputes values in respect of the two principal commodity groups, namely cloth and miscellaneous drugs (the precise coverage of this category is not defined but would seem to consist of a number of items including spices other than pepper), on the basis of 'an average taken from total deliveries' of these commodity-groups during 1586–92 and 1593–8. But these total deliveries are again not based on direct evidence such as bills of lading or anything similar, but are assumed following the procedure explained in note 68 on pp. 271–2 of his book. Basically, Boyajian uses information relating to *obra pia* duties to fund charitable establishments in Lisbon assessed on private shipments of drugs and cloth at a rate of 200 reis per quintal to estimate the volume of private imports. For the period 1586–92, this gives him a figure of 37,879 bales and chests of drugs and cloth together. He next calculates the drug component of this as 25,739 bales by using information relating to the *colégio* duty to support the Jesuit College of Santo Antao in Lisbon collected at the rate of 100 reis per bale. This leaves the cloth component at 12,140 bales. A similar

---

[20] Boyajian, *Portuguese Trade in Asia*, pp. 41–4.

procedure for the period 1593–8 gives him a figure of 27,922 bales of drugs and 11,741 bales of cloth. The total for the period then is assumed to be 53,661 bales of drugs and 23,881 bales of cloth. These quantities are then distributed pro rata over years with the missing information according to the number of vessels known to have arrived in a given year. Clearly, the critical elements in this procedure are the reliability and the coverage of the information relating to both the *obra pia* and the *colégio* duties.

The considerable infirmity of the Boyajian estimates of the physical imports of cloth and drugs is compounded a great deal by the procedure he follows for converting these into value figures at an assumed uniform rate for the entire period. While talking of import and export figures, one ordinarily speaks in terms of invoice values so that the information one looks for relates to cost price. But, curiously, Boyajian instead calculates sale values by assuming a sale price of 2,000 cruzados per bale of cloth and 150 cruzados per bale of miscellaneous drugs. Given the extreme heterogeneity characterizing each of these two items with no clue with respect to the relative weights of different varieties in the case of cloth or different commodities in the case of the package of miscellaneous drugs, any figure assumed with respect to the average sale price will not command adequate respectability. Also, considering that the mark-up assumed in the case of both cloth and drugs is considerably greater than that in the case of pepper (where the sale price is assumed to be 45 cruzados per quintal except for 1686 when it is assumed to be 49 cruzados), calculating the relative shares of the Crown and the private trade in terms of sale values rather than invoice values would considerably vitiate the results in favour of the private traders and against the Crown. These problems with the Boyajian estimates, however, raise questions only about the precise extent of the private Portuguese merchants' inter-continental trade between Europe and Asia, not about their considerably more important role in this trade than has traditionally been believed. Boyajian's significant upward revision of this role is certainly in the right direction and must be duly taken note of.

The import of pepper

The data regarding the quantity of pepper imported by the Portuguese Crown into Lisbon over the sixteenth and the early part of the seventeenth century are limited and characterized by wide gaps.

Table 2.4 *Pepper imported by the Portuguese Crown, 1503[1]–98 (in quintals)[2]*

Year	Quantity	Year	Quantity
1503	26,000[3]	1548	23,827
1504	10,000	1587	10,378
1505	22,000	1588	22,963
1506	>17,300	1589	26,750
1513	20,020[4]	1590	23,682
1514	20,415	1592	9,939
1517	44,032	1593	4,994
1519	35,000	1594	6,516
1523	7,500	1595	17,611
1526	>20,000	1596	2,714
1530	15,438	1597	16,927
1531	18,870	1598	7,895
1547	36,412		

Note:

1. The years 1501 and 1502 have not been included because the figures for these years appear to be very incomplete.
2. Generally, the transactions in Europe were in terms of the lesser or lighter quintal of Lisbon, equivalent to 51.4 kg. That is the quintal used by Magalhães-Godinho throughout his work (for example, see vol. II, p. 196, where figures are given in both quintals and kilograms).
3. The figure given by Magalhães-Godinho is 18,000 quintals but following C.H.H. Wake, it has been revised up to 26,000 because the figure of 6,000 to 10,000 for cinnamon would in fact seem to pertain to pepper.
4. The figures for 1513 and the first figure for 1514 have been put together, because the 1514 figure relates to the two *naus* of 1513.

Source: V. Magalhães-Godinho, *Os Descobrimentos e a Economia Mundial*, Lisbon, 1963–71, vol. III, pp. 73–5.

The findings of Magalhães-Godinho for the sixteenth century are summarized in Table 2.4. An independent check on the reliability of Magalhães-Godinho's figures is not possible, but the two observations for 1505 and 1518 respectively available in Bouchon's work broadly corroborate his figures. Against Magalhães-Godinho's figure of 22,000 quintals for 1505, Bouchon's two estimates for the year are 20,895 and 21,090 heavy quintals. Converted into the light quintal of 51.4 kilograms used by Magalhães-Godinho, these would be 23,862 and 24,085 quintals respectively. As for 1518, against the Magalhães-Godinho

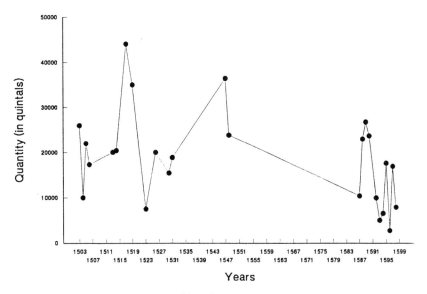

Fig. 2.1 Pepper imported by the Portuguese Crown, 1503–98

figure of 44,032 quintals for 1517, the Bouchon figure of 2,128,962 kilograms would amount to 41,419 light quintals.

If one looked at the Magalhães-Godinho evidence in specific blocks of years, it turns out that the average annual figure of pepper imported goes up from 18,825 quintals in 1503–6 to 29,866 quintals in 1513–19. After a trough of 15,452 quintals during 1523–31, the figure of 30,119 quintals is reached during 1547–8. But the last fourteen years of the century witness a sharp down-trend with the annual average imports standing at only 20,943 quintals during 1587–90 and at an incredibly low figure of 9,513 quintals during 1592–8. A part of the explanation of the particularly low figure in the 1590s is to be found in the extraordinarily high rate of losses at sea during the decade amounting in terms of both the number of ships as well as tonnage to as much as 45 per cent.[21] The shipwrecks, together with delayed departures forcing ships to return to Goa, created a situation where extraordina-

[21] Calculated from Bentley Duncan, 'Navigation between Portugal and Asia', Table 1, p. 22.

41

rily large gaps emerged between the amount of pepper loaded at Goa in a particular year and that eventually reaching Lisbon.[22]

Later researchers have sought to plug the gaps in the Magalhães-Godinho series by using the information on shipping and imputing pepper carrying capacity to these ships. C.H.H. Wake attempts such an exercise for the period between the 1530s and the 1580s where the gaps in the Magalhães-Godinho evidence are the most striking. He assumes a figure of 6,000 quintals of pepper per vessel for the 1540s, 5,872 quintals for the 1550s and the 1560s, and 5,000 to 5,353 quintals per vessel for the 1570s and the 1580s. On this basis, and after allowing for such things as spoilage and shipwrecks, he works out a net figure of 22,000 quintals of pepper per annum in the 1540s (and probably also in the 1530s), 17,100 quintals in the 1550s and the 1560s, and 19,500 to 20,800 quintals in the 1570s and the 1580s.[23] Wake's figures would thus change the Magalhães-Godinho scenario quite drastically, but, of course, the basis of the Wake calculations must remain a matter of debate.

Finally, for the seventeenth century, reasonably complete information is available for the period between 1612 and 1634. The average annual imports over the period were 10,054 light quintals: for the years between 1630 and 1634 alone when the Portuguese India Company carried on this trade, the figure was 8,840 light quintals.[24]

Pepper procurement in India

Throughout the sixteenth and the first half of the seventeenth century, an overwhelming proportion of the pepper imported into Lisbon was procured on the southwest coast of India. Thus, against the total of approximately 17,300 quintals imported into Lisbon in 1506, the average amount imported each year from Cochin alone during 1506 and 1507 was 13,214 quintals. Between 1510 and 1518, the latter figure went up slightly to 13,293 quintals. As against this, the total amount imported into Lisbon was 20,020 quintals in 1513 and 20,415 quintals in 1514.[25] In the early part of the seventeenth century, the significance

---

[22] Thus against 21,679 quintals loaded at Goa in 1594, only 6,516 quintals reached Lisbon. The corresponding figures for 1596 were 18,131 and 2,714 quintals, and for 1597, 21,299 and 16,927 quintals (Magalhães-Godinho, *Os Descobrimentos e a Economia Mundial*, vol. III, p. 75).

[23] C.H.H. Wake, 'The changing pattern of Europe's pepper and spice imports ca. 1400–1700', *The Journal of European Economic History*, vol. 8 (2), 1979, pp. 382–3.

[24] Disney, *Twilight of the Pepper Empire*, Appendix 2.2, p. 162.

[25] For the total amount imported, see Table 2.4. For the amounts imported from Cochin, see Magalhães-Godinho, *Os Descobrimentos e a Economia Mundial*, vol. III, pp. 10–11.

of Malabar/Kanara pepper increased even further. Thus between 1612 and 1634 pepper procured at Malacca, the only source other than the southwest coast of India, accounted for only 3.26 per cent of the total amount of pepper shipped to Lisbon.[26]

On the southwest coast of India, the procurement of pepper was begun at Calicut on the Malabar coast, where the Portuguese had first arrived. But relations with the *pardesi* merchants of the town as well as the Samudri raja deteriorated fast. The conflict with the merchants had its origin mainly in the Portuguese insistence on being provided with pepper before the Red Sea merchants had been served. The Portuguese attack on a *sambuk* was retaliated by their factory being looted which, in turn, led to an attack on the port and a bombardment of the town in 1501 that lasted for two days. The era of peaceful trading which, occasional instances of violence notwithstanding, had been the norm in the Asian waters for centuries, had finally been shattered by the Portuguese. At any rate, it was found more expedient to shift the centre of pepper procurement to Cochin where the more cooperative Mappila and the Syrian Christian merchants were used as brokers and intermediaries. With the aid of the dependent raja of Cochin, the Portuguese tried to establish a monopoly in pepper there. But since the raja had no real control over the areas where pepper was grown or over the routes used for its transportation, the monopoly never really worked in any effective sense. At his own level, of course, the raja provided all help by giving protection to the river boats bringing pepper to Cochin, by guaranteeing loans raised by the Portuguese from private sources, as well as by providing loans himself.[27] The friendly relationship between the Estado and the Mappila merchants at Cochin, however, did not last very long. By the end of the third decade of the century, the merchants had declared a holy war – *jihad* – against the Estado. This hostility continued in one form or another into the seventeenth century.

In the second half of the sixteenth century, in addition to Cochin, Kollam and marginally Cannanore on the Malabar coast, the Estado also began procuring pepper on the Kanara coast. Shipments from the mid-1560s onward generally included some Kanara pepper and, from the last decade of the century onward, Kanara definitely outstripped

---

[26] Calculated from Disney, *Twilight of the Pepper Empire*, Appendix 2.2. p. 162.
[27] Jan Kieniewicz, 'The Portuguese factory and trade in pepper in Malabar during the sixteenth century', *The Indian Economic and Social History Review*, vol. 6 (1), 1969, pp. 68–9.

Malabar as a source of pepper. Information available for the period 1612 to 1634 suggests that, roughly speaking, Kanara provided two-thirds of the total Indian supplies as against Malabar's one-third.[28]

The new route vs the old route

Until the English and the Dutch challenged it in the last decade of the sixteenth century, the Portuguese enjoyed a largely unqualified monopoly of the trade along the Cape route. Was their trade on this route a net addition to the Euro-Asian trade in spices and other goods or did it represent largely a diversion of the trade along the long-established water-cum-land route via the Levant? There is very little doubt that in the early years of the sixteenth century the Portuguese policies were indeed instrumental in spelling almost a total disaster for the trade along the old route. The attempt at monopolizing the spice trade was unambiguous. It called for a total exclusion of Asian shipping from the Persian Gulf and the Red Sea: the instructions to Pedro Alvares Cabral, in charge of the first major commercial voyage to India that left Lisbon in March 1500, included the initiation of steps designed at blockading the passage to the Red Sea. The rest of the Asian trade would be regulated to exclude trade in spices. The instrument used to implement this policy was the *cartaz*, a safe-conduct that all Asian ships were obliged to carry on pain of seizure in the event of non-compliance. The document obliged the Asian ship to call at a Portuguese-controlled port and, following the establishment of the Portuguese customs houses there, to pay customs duties before it proceeded on its voyage. Enemies of the Portuguese and banned goods such as spices were not to be carried. There is some evidence that an equivalent of the *cartaz* existed in the Asian seas before the arrival of the Portuguese, but there can be little doubt that the scale on which this restrictive measure was used by the Portuguese was unprecedented. The measure indeed represented an institutional constraint on the freedom of navigation on the high seas.

The policy of exclusion of the merchants from Calicut, Cambay and other ports on the west coast of India from the Red Sea and the

---

[28] Between 1612 and 1634, the share of Kanara pepper in the total amount procured on the southwest coast of India was 63.38 per cent as against 36.06 per cent from Malabar. If the small quantities procured at Malacca are also included, the share of the Kanara pepper works out at 61.31 per cent, that of the Malabar pepper at 34.88 per cent, and that procured at Malacca at 3.26 per cent. (Calculated from Disney, *Twilight of the Pepper Empire*, Appendix 2.2, p. 162.)

Persian Gulf was highly successful. Ormuz at the entrance to the Persian Gulf was captured in 1515: the failure to capture Aden was made up for by the dispatch each season from Goa of a fleet to lie off the entrance to the Red Sea, usually cruising between Aden and Bab-el-Mandeb and returning to Ormuz in April. Raids on departing fleets at Calicut were common and the result was practically a ruination of the spice trade with the Persian Gulf and the Red Sea. It was reported as early as 1504 that the Venetian galleys calling there found no spices at either Alexandria or Beirut. Two years prior to that, concerned at the loss of the substantial revenues that the spice trade used to bring him, the Mamluk of Egypt had sought the good offices of the Pope to try and dissuade the Portuguese from choking the flow of spices through the Red Sea!

The dislocation in the spice trade, however, proved only temporary. By the second decade of the sixteenth century cracks had already begun to appear in the Portuguese system. A series of circumstances combined to produce this result. A key element in the situation was the financial priorities and compulsions of the Estado da Índia. Given the rather precarious state of the finances of this body, it was imperative that no opportunity of taxing Asian shipping by making it call and pay duties at Portuguese controlled ports such as Malacca, Goa and Diu be missed. Ormuz, taken in 1515, was one such strategically located port. Pepper and other spices passing through the port and destined for consumption within west Asia posed no problem: the choice between tax revenue and the cost of the infringe-ment of the European monopoly arose only in respect of that part of the cargo which would eventually reach Venice or Genoa via Aleppo. The choice was made in favour of the tax revenue and, as Steensgaard has suggested, between 1524 and 1543 an average of 90,000 xerafins was earned as customs duties per annum at Ormuz. Steensgaard's characterization of the Portuguese enterprise as 'redistributive' in character has in part at its base such parasitical siphoning off of a part of the profits of Asian trade. Another circumstance that prompted the Portuguese to allow pepper shipments to pass Ormuz was the desire to earn the goodwill of Persia against an increasingly aggressive Ottoman empire. Whatever the motivation, the Portuguese decision involved a diversion of the spice trade from the Aden–Cairo–Alexandria axis to the Basra–Baghdad–Aleppo axis.

But that diversion was strictly temporary, and from the late 1530s onward the Red Sea spice trade began to revive. After an initial vigorous and successful phase, the Portuguese blockade of the Bab-el-Mandeb became increasingly ineffective for a variety of reasons. For one thing, considerations of strategy as well as of economics often obliged the Portuguese authorities to issue a limited number of *cartazes* for the Red Sea ports. Thus, as early as 1515 Albuquerque found it necessary to grant the Samudri raja a certain number of *cartazes* for the merchants based at his port, enabling them to resume trade with Aden and Jeddah. On other occasions, a similar concession was extended to other puppet rulers. Important business associates such as Khwaja Shams-ud-din Gilani as well as merchants providing credit to the Estado had to be similarly accommodated. In some cases, such as in that of Gilani, trade in pepper was explicitly permitted, while in most others the understanding was that pepper would continue to be treated as a prohibited article. But for all practical purposes, the distinction made little difference and nearly all ships going to the region carried pepper legitimately or clandestinely. And then, of course, there was the trade in pepper carried on by various categories of the Portuguese in contravention of the official policy. The network of this trade included the Red Sea and there was very little the Portuguese official machinery was able to do about it

It needs to be emphasized that the Estado simply lacked the resources in men and ships to sustain an effective blockade of the Red Sea year after year. The only area in which the Portuguese were reasonably successful was in preventing ships from Malabar from going to the Red Sea. But shipping from Kanara and the Bay of Bengal continued to carry Indian pepper to the Red Sea from the late 1530s and the early 1540s onward, mainly through the agency of the Gujarati merchants. It seems that considering the expense and the poor rate of success, the Portuguese abandoned the Red Sea expeditions around 1569, clearing the way for a full-fledged revival of the Red Sea traffic in pepper. C.R. Boxer, who has traced this revival, is of the opinion that the volume of Acheh pepper reaching Jeddah at the end of the sixteenth century was larger than what the Portuguese were taking to Lisbon by the Cape route.[29]

[29] C.R. Boxer, 'A note on Portuguese reactions to the revival of the Red Sea spice trade and the rise of Atjeh, 1540–1600', *Journal of Southeast Asian History*, vol. 10 (3), 1969, pp. 415–28.

Portuguese share of the European pepper market

That brings us to the question of the Portuguese share of the European pepper market during the sixteenth and the first half of the seventeenth century. In the late 1570s or the early 1580s, Konrad Rott estimated the size of the European pepper market at 28,000 light quintals.[30] In 1611, Hans Kampferbek, the Hanseatic Consul at Lisbon, put this figure at 30,000 light quintals.[31] Magalhães-Godinho's figure of 10,378 light quintals in 1587 would put the Portuguese share in the 1580s at 37 per cent: the figure would go up to 75 per cent if the annual average of the Portuguese imports between 1587 and 1590 was taken into account. As for 1611, the Portuguese import figure of 10,869 light quintals in 1612 would account for 36 per cent of the total European market: the figure is not changed perceptibly even if the average of the imports between 1612 and 1634 is taken into account.

The historiography on this question is quite extensive and wide-ranging. In two papers published in *The American Historical Review* in 1933 and 1940 respectively, Frederic C. Lane first talked of the revival of the Levantine trade to Europe and suggested that the economic importance of the Cape route in the sixteenth century may have been seriously exaggerated. According to him, Venice imported as much or more pepper from Alexandria in the 1560s as it had done in the late fifteenth century.[32] In his 1974 book, Steensgaard argued that in the 1570s and the 1580s the Portuguese average annual import

[30] The regional distribution of this figure was as follows:

Portugal (including Africa and Peru)	=	1,500 light quintals
Spain	=	3,000 " "
France	=	2,500 " "
England, Scotland and Ireland	=	3,000 " "
Italy	=	6,000 " "
Poland, Bohemia, Hungary, etc.	=	12,000 " "
TOTAL		28,000 " "

(Kellenbenz, 'Autour de 1600', pp. 1–28)

[31] The regional distribution of this figure was as follows:

Spain and Portugal	=	3,000 light quintals
Italy	=	2,000 " "
France	=	3,000 " "
Flanders	=	2,000 " "
Germany (and other northern provinces)	=	20,000 " "
TOTAL		30,000 " "

(Kellenbenz, 'Autour de 1600', pp. 1–28)

[32] Frederic C. Lane, 'Venetian shipping during the commercial revolution', *American*

of about 20,000 quintals would have accounted for only about 40 per cent of the total amount of pepper brought into Europe. In the decade of the 1590s marked by unprecedented shipping losses, this would have been halved to about 20 per cent.[33] In a paper published in 1979, C.H.H. Wake maintained that the Steensgaard scenario needed a drastic revision because he had both overestimated the size of the European market and underestimated the extent of the Portuguese imports. On the basis of his reinterpretation of the Magalhães-Godinho data on pepper imports, Wake argued that until 1550, and again in the 1570s and the 1580s, the Portuguese accounted for upward of 75 per cent of Europe's pepper imports. Regarding the role of the Levant trade, Wake emphasized the existence of an important spice market in west Asia itself and the consequent need to distinguish between the total Asian supplies entering the Red Sea and the Persian Gulf, and the part that eventually reached Europe. He then argued that the supplies bought by the Venetian and other European merchants in the Levant were regulated strictly in accordance with the quantities brought to Lisbon earlier in the year by the Cape route. As a result, 'the Levantine trade ebbed and flowed with the changing fortunes of the Portuguese enterprise'. In the 1560s, for example, when the Portuguese imports are known to have been limited, the Venetian imports from Alexandria are generally believed to have been very large. The Venetian revival was cut short by the Cyprus war of 1570–3 which, in the analysis of Wake, coincided with the recovery in the Portuguese trade. Finally, when Portugal's imports were marked by unprecedented maritime disasters in the 1590s, the Venetian trade again enjoyed a revival.[34]

As for the period from the early part of the seventeenth century onward, the area of disagreement is considerably less. It is generally agreed that the rise of the Dutch and the English East India companies spelt the near ruination of both the Levant routes as well as the Portuguese Euro-Asian trade. Pieter van Dam, the historian of the Dutch East India Company writing at the end of the seventeenth century, refers to an estimate dated 1622, according to which the

Historical Review, vol. 38, pp. 228–9; 'The Mediterranean spice trade, further evidence on its revival in the sixteenth century', *American Historical Review*, vol. 45, p. 586.

[33] Niels Steensgaard, *The Asian Trade Revolution*, pp. 163, 168.

[34] C.H.H. Wake, 'The changing pattern of Europe's pepper and spice imports', pp. 385–7.

Portuguese were supplying only 20 per cent of the total European demand of 7 million pounds of pepper, the remainder being divided between the Dutch and the English.[35]

INTRA-ASIAN TRADE

Throughout the sixteenth and the first half of the seventeenth century, trade between Portugal and Asia remained the *raison d'être* of the Portuguese enterprise in the East. But that should not lead us to lose sight of the fact that trade within Asia – or what the Portuguese termed 'trade from India to India' – was also a very important component of the Portuguese commercial presence in Asia. Indeed, beginning as early as the period of Afonso de Albuquerque (1509–15), the intra-Asian trade of the Portuguese was considerably larger in value and substantially more lucrative than the trade between Goa and Lisbon. It is another matter that, while a large part of the profit in the intercontinental trade went to the Portuguese Crown, the profit from the intra-Asian trade accrued overwhelmingly to private individuals. Precise quantitative data are hard to come by but the available evidence would seem to establish the broad orders of magnitude. A Dutch estimate pertaining to 1622 put the working capital invested annually by the Portuguese Crown and country traders in the intra-Asian trade at the enormously high figure of *f.*50 million. But in all likelihood, this particular estimate was grossly inflated on purpose in order to obtain larger amounts of capital from the Netherlands. That the value of the Portuguese intra-Asian trade around this time was nevertheless quite impressive is, however, borne out by the 1630 Bocarro estimate of the annual investment in this trade from Goa alone being 2.85 million xerafins (the equivalent of *f.*6.6 million) – about fifteen times the value of the Portuguese India Company merchandise exported to Lisbon that year.[36] The Portuguese participation in intra-Asian trade was substantial during the sixteenth century as well. Luís Filipe F.R. Thomaz has argued, for example, that even in respect of an item such as cloves, of the total amount bought by the Crown factors (which did

---

[35] Pieter van Dam, *Beschrijvinge van de Oost-Indische Compagnie* (ed. F.W. Stapel and others), The Hague, 1927–54, Book I, Part II, p. 167. Quoted in K. Glamann, *Dutch–Asiatic Trade 1620–1740*, Copenhagen/The Hague, 1958, p. 74.

[36] George B. Souza, *The Survival of Empire: Portuguese Trade and Society in China and the South China Sea, 1630–1754*, Cambridge, 1986, p. 169; Disney, *Twilight of the Pepper Empire*, p. 24.

not amount to more than 12.5 per cent of the estimated output in the Moluccas), less than a third (32 per cent) found its way to Lisbon, the rest being sold in places such as China, Burma, Indonesia, India and Persia. As for profitability, Thomaz has pointed out that against an annual average of 33,000 cruzados earned by the Captain-Major together with the captains of each of the *naus* of the returning fleet from Goa to Lisbon between 1570 and 1590, the average annual profit earned in the intra-Asian voyages around 1580 was five times as much.[37]

Some of the Portuguese intra-Asian trade fed the export of Moluccan spices to Lisbon: indeed these spices were procured overwhelmingly against Indian textiles. But the bulk of this trade was aimed simply at earning profit. Quite early in the sixteenth century, mainly with the help of Tamil *keling* merchants settled at Malacca, the Portuguese managed to make their way into a complex intra-Asian trading network of goods and routes with Malacca as the centre-point. The goods that figured in this network originated, apart from southeast Asia, in China, in India and, on a limited scale, in the Middle East. The southeast Asian goods included cloves from the Moluccas, nutmeg and mace from Banda, and pepper from Sumatra and Sunda, besides items such as sandalwood from Timor, camphor from Borneo, gold from Sumatra, tin from Malaya and precious stones from Burma. These goods were first collected at Malacca and then re-exported to China, Japan, and to various ports in the Indonesian archipelago as well as those around the Bay of Bengal. Some of the cargo was also sent on to the west coast of India, whence a part found its way to Persia and the Near East and another to Europe via the Cape route.

The principal item procured in China was porcelain, though silk, lacquer, jewellery and copper coins were also obtained there. Malacca served as the principal transit point for redistribution to the western India, Near East and Europe complex as well as to the archipelago and the Bay of Bengal complex. After the founding of Macao in 1557, however, the transit role of Malacca for the archipelago was increasingly eroded and direct connections were established. India, as noted earlier, mainly provided textiles which were used primarily to buy the

---

[37] Luís Filipe F.R. Thomaz, 'The Portuguese in the seas of the Archipelago during the 16th Century', pp. 81–5. Originally published as 'Les Portugais dans les mers de l'Archipel au XVIe siècle', *Archipel*, 18 (1979). Available in translation in *Trade and Shipping in the Southern Seas, Selected Readings from Archipel (18), 1979*, Paris 1984, pp. 75–91.

Indonesian spices and drugs. This practice was so established and so extensive that in many of the treaties concluded between the Portuguese and the suppliers of spices the prices of the latter were specified in terms of Indian textiles, rather than in any currency. As far as goods available in the Middle East were concerned, the Portuguese involvement was rather limited and confined to goods such as silk, carpets and worked leather, and base metals such as iron, copper, lead and mercury.

The voyages undertaken included both those on the high-seas circuits as well as those on the coastal ones. From Tomé Pires, we know the details of one of the coastal voyages from Malacca to the Moluccas. A direct route via Brunei, which the Portuguese initiated around 1525, would have taken only forty days. But the preferred route was a much longer one taking as many as eleven months to traverse. The principal commodity carried on the outward trip was Indian textiles and the first stop was in eastern Java at ports such as Gresik and Panarukan where the better quality textiles were exchanged against *caxas* and *sapecas*, Chinese copper coins of small value. The coins were employed to buy rice as well as low-quality cotton textiles at Bima which, in turn, together with the remainder of the Indian textiles loaded at Malacca, were used to buy mace, nutmeg and cloves in Banda and the Moluccas respectively. The hopping trip was extremely profitable and fully justified the much longer time taken.

Crown participation in intra-Asian trade

The extensive Portuguese network of intra-Asian trade grew basically along the lines defined by the pre-existing commercial system. As it happened, the period of the Portuguese apprenticeship was shortened considerably by the advice and assistance provided by the *keling* merchants of Malacca. In the wake of the Gujarati merchants' increasing withdrawal from the city following its conquest in 1511, the Tamil *keling* merchants had emerged as the single most important group of Indian merchants operating from Malacca. Amongst the Portuguese, the lead in the matter of getting into intra-Asian trade in a big way was taken by the Crown, though the period over which the Crown's involvement in this trade lasted was not very long.

An important branch of Asian trade that the Crown initially monopolized for itself was the spice trade with the Moluccas. However, from the very beginning, the monopoly was a rather loose one with crew members of the royal ships being allowed participation. In addition, rights were also granted to selected state officials to engage in a limited amount of trade in the 'forbidden goods'. On occasions, a shortage of resources also obliged the Crown to permit private participation: thus in 1523 a cargo of cloves was loaded in Ternate on private ships because the royal factory did not have the wherewithal to buy it. This was repeated two years later because the factory did not have a Crown ship with adequate capacity. There were also cases, as in 1524 and 1536, when private Portuguese traders managed to violate the royal monopoly by paying more for the cloves than the Crown factor was willing to pay. All these problems persuaded the Crown in 1539 formally to declare the trade in cloves and nutmeg free subject only to the condition that anybody dealing in these spices would be obliged to provide one third of the quantity bought to the Crown factors at cost price.[38]

The Crown also participated in several other branches of Asian trade – mostly those linking Malacca to the Bay of Bengal but marginally also in the western Indian Ocean – basically as a 'merchant among merchants'. In the decade 1511–20, the Fazenda Real (or royal treasury) carried out a number of exploratory commercial voyages and a whole series of crown routes (carreiras) was created. This was done in close cooperation with the *keling* merchant community of Malacca, whose doyen at the time was one Nina Chatu. The cooperation often took the form of ventures undertaken jointly by the Crown and Nina Chatu. One such venture was the voyage of the *São João* which left Malacca for Martaban in Burma in August 1512, returning in May 1513. The same ship was then sent to Pulicat, again in partnership with Nina Chatu and on similar terms. There was an equal division of the cargo space between the Crown and Nina Chatu, each party sending factors on board to administer its share of the cargo. All expenses during the voyage, whether on repairs, maintenance, food for the sailors, or loading and unloading charges, were divided equally between the two parties. On its trip to Pulicat, the vessel also carried individual Portuguese and other merchants on board together with their goods, evidently paying freight charges to the party in charge of the relevant shipping space. Persons not travelling aboard also participated in the venture by handing over money to those on board in

[38] Thomaz, 'The Portuguese in the seas of the Archipelago', pp. 75–91.

commenda. One Afonso Galego, for example, had handed over 200 cruzados to two *chatys* on board ship, on the understanding that they would give him 300 cruzados on their return, at 50 per cent on the principal sum.[39] According to Thomaz, this percentage usually was 35 to 50 on trips from Malacca to southeast Asia and 80 to 90, going up to as much as 200, on trips to India and China.[40]

By the late 1520s, the practice of sending a ship each to Pegu and Pulicat annually on the independent account of the Crown had become increasingly established. The Pegu run moved from an initial Malacca–Pegu–Malacca route to a Goa–Pulicat–Pegu–Goa pattern. The Coromandel voyage similarly moved from the Malacca–Pulicat–Malacca route to a Goa–Pulicat–Malacca–Goa route. The original practice of the *nakhuda* (or captain) of the vessel being an Asian was also given up, and all principal posts on board were now occupied by Portuguese officials. The posts of captain and factor were sometimes granted to the same individual and were remunerated by a share in the cargo space. This space could be used by the official himself or he could rent it out: in either case the goods carried in it were exempt from customs duties at Malacca.[41]

In 1518, a fleet of two vessels under the command of D. João da Silveira arrived in Chittagong on the newly created carreira de Bengala. Gradually, the Bengal voyage took on an annual character, and while most of the ships went to Chittagong, some called at Satgaon as well. Initially, these voyages originated in Goa and went to Bengal via Coromandel, but in the 1530s they are also known to have occasionally originated in Malacca. By the 1540s, there were two regular carreiras to Bengal, one each to Chittagong and Satgaon. Vessels operating on these routes were either owned or hired by the Crown and, as usual, the captain carried as perquisite a proportion of the cargo space and exemption from the payment of customs duties at Portuguese customs houses, whether at Malacca or Goa.[42]

As pointed out earlier, the period over which the involvement of the Portuguese Crown as an entrepreneur in intra-Asian trade lasted was comparatively brief. Indeed, already in the 1530s and the 1540s

[39] Sanjay Subrahmanyam, 'The Coromandel–Malacca trade in the 16th century: a study of its evolving structure', *Moyen Orient et Océan Indien*, vol. 3, 1986, pp. 55–80.

[40] Thomaz, 'The Portuguese in the seas of the Archipelago', p. 79.

[41] Sanjay Subrahmanyam, 'The Coromandel–Malacca trade', p. 60.

[42] Sanjay Subrahmanyam, 'Notes on the sixteenth century Bengal trade', *The Indian Economic and Social History Review*, vol. 24 (3), 1987, pp. 265–89.

changes in both the nature and the scale of Crown involvement in this trade were discernible. In the first place, Crown shipping was increasingly giving way to private shipping. Thus it was reported around the middle of the century that of the seven or eight ships that sailed each year from Malacca to Coromandel, only one belonged to the Crown.[43] Also, even on trips operated with Crown shipping, the investment of Crown capital in the cargo was on the decline and they were increasingly being converted into some kind of a freight service. Sanjay Subrahmanyam has discussed this development in relation to the carreira that operated on the route Goa–Pulicat–Malacca–Goa. A detailed account of the annual *nau* operating on this route is available for 1550 which shows that the Crown no longer invested capital of its own in the cargo on the Pulicat–Malacca run. The business was run purely as a freight service, the total charge on goods freighted being 12 per cent of value, half on account of freight charges and the other as customs duty in Malacca. The captain of the vessel received one-fourth of the freight space as a perquisite which he normally rented out, retaining the entire 12 per cent to himself. On the Malacca–Goa voyage, on the other hand, he was given only a sixth of the freight space, which again was free from duties at Goa.[44]

The 1540s and the 1550s witnessed a growing debate regarding the advisability of continued Crown participation in Asian trade in whatever capacity. The poor profitability of the venture in its incarnation as a freight service had a lot to do with this. It was repeatedly pointed out that the group that benefited most from this pattern of trading was that of the ships' captains. They almost always redistributed the cargo in such a way that the most profitable part of it (value for volume) fell to their share of the cargo space. The alternative of going back to the *status quo ante* of the Crown itself owning the cargo carried was scarcely practical given the state of the finances of the Portuguese state in India at this time. Available evidence points very strongly in the direction of a severe contraction in customs receipts – the principal component of state finance – in Portuguese Asia in the 1540s and the 1550s. Other circumstances also contributed to the gradual withdrawal of the Crown from participation in intra-Asian trade. One was what Magalhães-Godinho has termed the 'Atlantic

[43] Thomaz, 'The Portuguese in the seas of the Archipelago', p. 78.
[44] Subrahmanyam, 'The Coromandel–Malacca trade', pp. 64–5.

Turning' of Portuguese policy in consequence of the successful first stage of the colonization of Brazil. Another was the fact that the 'official perception of the Portuguese influence in the East became closer to the idea of empire, and put the emphasis on the sovereign role of the state to the neglect of its commercial activities'.[45] The result was a virtual completion of the process of Crown withdrawal from intra-Asian trade by about 1570. Only one carreira voyage – that from Goa to the Banda islands – is believed to have survived intact into the 1580s. But the Crown kept for itself the right to give benefices as rewards for service. Thus was born the so-called system of concession voyages, which came to constitute the backbone of the Portuguese private merchants' trade in Asia.

Portuguese private traders' participation in intra-Asian trade

The bulk of the Portuguese private traders engaged in intra-Asian trade were residents of the settlements which together constituted the Estado da India (as Portuguese Asia came to be termed from the mid-sixteenth century). These people operated under the jurisdiction and the patronage of the Estado. Those operating outside its jurisdiction were derisively called *chatins*. Within the Estado framework, the various categories of residents at a settlement such as Goa included government officials, soldiers, ecclesiastics, Jews and New Christians, and the *casados moradores* or married settlers. Members of each of these groups participated in trade to varying degrees. The government officials engaged in trade, for example, included persons at all levels beginning with the Viceroy himself. Thus, D. Miguel de Noronha, Fourth Count of Linhares and Viceroy between October 1629 and December 1635, is known to have been fairly active in intra-Asian trade, particularly that channelled through Goa. There is evidence that he extensively abused his official position in a variety of ways including trading in prohibited goods.[46]

But while each of the components of the Estado settlements community is known to have participated in Asian trade, by far the most important group would seem to have been that of the *casados*

---

[45] Thomaz, 'The Portuguese in the seas of the Archipelago', p. 77.

[46] Anthony Disney, 'The Viceroy as entrepreneur: the Count of Linhares at Goa in the 1630s', in Roderich Ptak and Dietmar Rothermund (ed.), *Emporia, Commodities and Entrepreneurs in Asian Maritime Trade, c. 1400–1750*, Stuttgart, 1991, pp. 427–44.

moradores. While a small segment of the *casado* community in Portuguese Asia did have a landed character, the bulk of the group made its money by engaging in maritime trade. Some of these traders are known to have amassed enormous fortunes. Thus four members of this group declared bankruptcy in 1633 in Japan to the amount of 1.25 million *taels'* worth of silver.[47] The group consisted of both white and black *casados* – the latter being native Christians. The whites themselves were subdivided between the *reinois* born of white parents in Portugal, the *casticos* born of white Portuguese parents in Asia, and the *mestizos,* born in Asia usually of a Portuguese father and an Asian or Eurasian mother. The exact number of the *casado* population in Portuguese Asia is not known for any point in time, but Bocarro does provide approximate numbers for 1635. These were 4,800 for white *casados* and 7,485 for black *casados*. The largest settlement was in Goa with 800 white and 2,200 black *casados*.[48] The *casado* traders had extensive dealings with other European and Asian trading groups as well as the Estado da India, in relation to which it also constituted some kind of a pressure group.[49] The privileges extracted from the Estado included occasional limited commodity monopolies and special rates of customs duties etc.

The *casado* traders were also a major, though by no means the only, beneficiary of the concession system introduced in the 1550s. A concession conferred on the grantee the right to make a voyage between two specified ports in the Indian Ocean and/or the China Sea. A concession route could either be to a so-called 'reserved' port in which case the concession holder, in principle, had the exclusive right to operate on the route. Or, alternatively, it could pertain to an 'open' route in which event the grantee was designated the captain-major of the fleet (including both Portuguese and non-Portuguese ships) operating on the route. The perquisites carried by this position included appointment as purveyor of the estates of the deceased in respect of all persons on the trading fleet, the right to buy and sell before anyone

---

[47] C.R. Boxer, *The Great Ship of Amacon, Annals of Macao and the Old Japan Trade, 1555–1640*, Lisbon, 1959, p. 131; Souza, *The Survival of Empire*, p. 30.

[48] Subrahmanyam and Thomaz, 'Evolution of empire', p. 322.

[49] It is known, for example, that Ferdinand Cron, an important *casado* trader, lent his own money or money raised using his personal credit and standing on numerous occasions to the Portuguese State in Goa. (Sanjay Subrahmanyam 'An Augsburger in Ásia Portuguesa: further light on the commercial world of Ferdinand Cron, 1587-1624', in Ptak and Rothermund (ed.), *Emporia, Commodities and Entrepreneurs*, p. 405.)

else, an occasional concession in the customs duty and so on. Important among the 'reserved' routes were those between Coromandel and Malacca and between Coromandel and Pegu. An example of an 'open' route was that between the ports of Orissa and Malacca. Some of the concession routes (viagem) were replacements for old Crown routes (carreira): others were newly created. Thus the voyage between Malacca and Pegu was a replacement: that to Pipli was a newly created one. In view of the privileges attached, all concession grants enjoyed a premium in varying degree and were fully transferable to another resident of the Estado settlements.[50]

While in its origin the grant was probably designed as a reward to members of the nobility or the army for services rendered, its character changed considerably over time. All residents of the Estado settlements, and even individuals/institutions not resident or functioning in Asia, eventually came to qualify for the grant. Thus in the second decade of the seventeenth century Queen Doña Margarita of Spain was allotted two Japan voyages. A few years earlier, on the intervention of the Queen, the Augustine monastery of Encarnacion had similarly been allotted two of the Japan voyages to facilitate the construction of its building near the royal palace in Madrid.[51] Such grants were almost always transferred at a premium. At times, concession grants were attached to particular offices as one of the perquisites. Thus in the 1580s the Captains of Malacca are known to have enjoyed the right to a number of concession voyages in the Bay of Bengal and the Indonesian archipelago. While ordinarily the Crown expected no *quid pro quo*, in times of grave financial stringency concession voyages are known to have been auctioned to the highest bidder.

The concession system began in the 1550s, and by the 1580s had become a major component of the Portuguese trading network in Asia. Thomaz has listed a total of thirty-four concession voyages in operation in the 1580s covering the China Sea, the Indonesian archipelago and the Bay of Bengal. The more important of these voyages are listed in Table 2.5.

In the Bay of Bengal, all the important concession voyages operating from Coromandel in the 1580s were, in principle, on reserved routes. These included two from São Tomé (one each to Malacca and

---

[50] Subrahmanyam, 'The Coromandel–Malacca trade', pp. 55–80.
[51] Subrahmanyam, 'An Augsburger in Ásia Portuguesa', pp. 407–8.

Table 2.5 *Major concession voyages and the rate of return c. 1580*

Route	Net average profit (in cruzados)	Selling price (in cruzados)
Goa–Macao–Nagasaki	35,000	20,000
Goa–Moluccas: captain	9,500	NA
Goa–Moluccas: factor	3,000	NA
Coromandel–Malacca	6,000	NA
Coromandel–Pegu	6,000	NA
Coromandel–Pipli	9,000	NA
Malacca–Macao	10,000	5,500
Malacca–Sunda	10,000	5,500
Malacca–Borneo	5,500	NA
Macao–Sunda	6,500	NA

Note: NA stands for not available.
Source: Thomaz, 'The Portuguese in the seas of the Archipelago', pp. 87–8; Subrahmanyam and Thomaz, 'Evolution of empire', p. 315.

Pegu) and four from Nagapattinam (one each to Martaban, Mergui, Ujang Salang (Phuket) and Kedah). Since the concession to Malacca provided for only one ship in a year, usually a large carrack was used laden, among other cargo, with the freight goods and persons of a hundred or more merchants. Given the Portuguese control over Malacca, the concession holder on this route could be reasonably certain of enjoying his monopoly status. But the same was not true of those operating between Coromandel and the Malayan ports, bringing down considerably the premium on the concession voyages to these ports.[52] The concession routes to Bengal were three in number. The ones to Chittagong and Satgaon (later to Hugli) were replacements of Crown routes, while the one to Pipli was a new route. None of these routes carried monopoly concessions.[53]

An analysis of the Goa–Malacca–Macao–Nagasaki concession voyage brings out certain interesting details. The voyage, started in the 1550s, resumed the practice of a single voyage connecting all the three geographical segments of Asian trade, namely the western Indian Ocean, the Bay of Bengal and the South China Sea – a tradition that had been lost ever since the cessation of the Cheng-Ho voyages in the 1430s. Until 1618, the annual voyage consisted of a single large carrack

[52] Subrahmanyam, 'The Coromandel–Malacca trade'.
[53] Subrahmanyam, 'Notes on the sixteenth century Bengal trade', pp. 265–89.

of between 1,200 and 1,600 tons, making it one of the largest ships engaged in intra-Asian trade. The voyage consisted of three segments – Goa–Malacca, Malacca–Macao and Macao–Hirado/Nagasaki. Different rates of return marked the three segments, often a characteristic feature of long-distance trade. On the Goa–Malacca segment, the outward voyage was not particularly profitable probably because of the competition faced. The Malacca–Macao segment presented other problems because the Captains of Malacca had the exclusive right to trade in pepper and other spices on this route. This often necessitated cooperative arrangements between the Captain of Malacca and the concession holder of the voyage. The real profit was made on the Macao–Nagasaki sector, and on the return trip from Nagasaki to Goa. The Macao–Nagasaki sector was, in principle, a monopoly sector, but other vessels are known to have plied this route, probably with the permission of the concession holder. The volume of trade carried on by the 'great ship' between Macao and Hirado/Nagasaki was quite substantial. As Boxer has noted, the chief of the Dutch factory at Hirado, Jacques Specx, reported in 1610 that

the ship coming from Macao usually has about 200 or more merchants on board who go ashore at once, each one of them taking a house wherein to lodge with his servants and slaves; they take no heed of what they spend and nothing is too costly for them; and sometimes they disburse in the seven or eight months that they stay in Nagasaki more than 250,000 or 300,000 taels, through which the populace profit greatly; and this is one of the reasons why they are still very friendly to them.[54]

There was a large demand for Chinese silk in Japan used mainly for the manufacture of ceremonial clothing for the ruling classes. In return for the silk, Japan provided large quantities of silver, the domestic output of which had been growing spectacularly throughout the sixteenth century as a result of the opening of new mines, better mining techniques and the application of the mercury amalgamation method to the refining of silver. These large quantities of silver were then exchanged against gold in Macao, where the gold/silver parity was much more favourable to silver. In addition to gold, copper and other Chinese goods were obtained in Macao and carried to India.

As Table 2.5 shows, the profitability of the Goa–Nagasaki voyage was estimated in the 1580s at 35,000 cruzados per annum. In the case

[54] Boxer, *The Great Ship of Amacon*, pp. 15–16.

of the concession holder deciding to alienate the privilege to another person, the selling price was reported to be around 20,000 cruzados, which suggests that ordinarily the share of the actual operator of the voyage in the total profit from the venture was somewhat smaller than that of the concession holder. Even after the entry of the Dutch (and marginally of the English) into the Japan trade in the early years of the seventeenth century, the Portuguese concession voyage to Nagasaki, which for security reasons was conducted after 1618 in groups of swift pinnaces or galliots, continued to be highly profitable. The profit figure mentioned for 1635 is as much as 172,000 xerafins (= 129,000 cruzados). Evidently the Dutch were not as yet in a position to interfere effectively: it would be highly risky to offend the many influential Japanese, including the Shogun, who invested in the cargoes carried by the Portuguese Japan ships. But circumstances favoured the Dutch when, in the late 1630s, the Japanese closed the country to all outsiders except the Chinese and the Dutch. The Portuguese of Macao even sent a deputation to plead with the Shogun's court for read-mission into Japan. On 4 August 1640, sixty-one members of the mission, including the ambassador, were beheaded for having dis-obeyed the orders not to return!

The trade outside the jurisdiction of the Estado was carried on by the so-called Portuguese *chatins*. These were mainly deserters from the Portuguese garrisons in quest of fortunes that they could never visualise making by continuing to work for the Estado. The principal region to which they spread out was the Bay of Bengal littoral. As early as the decade 1511–20, there is evidence of fair numbers of these people making contact with Bengal ports such as Satgaon and Chittagong, as well as with ports such as Pulicat on the Coromandel coast. At each of these ports, these Portuguese constituted one or more resident commu-nities with their own communal structure and leadership. As early as 1519, the number of these persons at Pulicat alone was reported to be between 200 and 300. In the early 1530s, there were some forty Portuguese households at Nagapattinam and a roughly equal number at São Tomé. In the decades that followed, their numbers went on increasing. The figure suggested for 1565 of these men settled in China as well as in the ports of the Bay of Bengal is 2,000.[55] On the ground

---

[55] Maria Augusta Lima Cruz, 'Exiles and renegades in early sixteenth century Portuguese India', *The Indian Economic and Social History Review*, vol. 23 (3), 1986, p. 259.

that 'one more merchant was one less soldier', the Estado generally adopted a hostile attitude towards these communities. As Luís Filipe Thomaz has pointed out, at Malacca, where the Hindus and the Muslims paid no more than 6 per cent as customs duty, these Portuguese private traders were obliged to pay as much as 10 per cent.[56] The Estado's hostility could take other forms as well, such as extending formal jurisdiction over such communities and subjecting them to taxes. Thus, the discovery in 1518 of a tomb, believed to be that of the Apostle St Thomas, in Mylapore, south of Pulicat, provided Goa with an excuse for extending its administrative network over Coromandel. A Portuguese Captain was appointed, probably in 1521, for the Coromandel and Fishery coasts. This man, with his head-quarters at Pulicat, had jurisdiction over all Portuguese residents on the Coast and was supposed to enforce the issuing of *cartazes* to shipping that operated in and around Coromandel.[57]

The decade of the 1630s witnessed catastrophic losses for the Portuguese country traders at the hands of the VOC. One Portuguese source estimated their losses between 1629 and 1636 at some 155 ships destroyed or captured, besides goods worth 7.5 million xerafins (= 5.62 million cruzados) lost.[58] This, however, does not imply, as is sometimes assumed in the literature, that the private Portuguese trade from India practically came to an end around this time. The 1640s were a peaceful decade for Dutch–Portuguese relations, which was a positive factor in the Portuguese merchants' trade from Nagapattinam. However, the Dutch pass policy forced a movement away from the Malay peninsular ports. But this turned out to be only temporary and, following a relaxation in the Dutch policy, trade with these ports was resumed in the 1670s. The loss of Nagapattinam to the Dutch in 1658 indeed constituted a setback to the Portuguese trade from Coromandel. But their response was to relocate themselves in large numbers at the port of Porto Novo to the north, which over the last quarter of the seventeenth century emerged as a major country trading port. An analysis on the basis of information available in the Dutch shipping lists of the ownership pattern of the ships, excluding Company ships and small coastal craft, that left this port between 1681–2 and 1685–6 for various Asian destinations shows that the

---

[56] Thomaz, 'The Portuguese in the seas of the Archipelago'.
[57] Subrahmanyam, 'The Coromandel–Malacca trade'.
[58] Souza, *The Survival of Empire*, p. 172.

Portuguese were a major group of merchants owning ships and operating from this port. The number of ships departing and owned by this group was seven out of a total of nineteen in 1681–2, six out of fourteen in 1682–3, six out of ten in 1683–4 and 1684–5, and seven out of fourteen in 1685–6. The single most important shipowner amongst the Portuguese was one Manuel Teixeira Pinto. By far the most important port of destination for the Portuguese shipping from Porto Novo was Acheh, followed by Pegu, Malacca, Goa and Manila.[59]

The Portuguese merchants' trade from Bengal too survived their expulsion from the port of Hugli in 1632. François Bernier noted the existence of a prosperous Portuguese mercantile community in Hugli in 1666. It included substantial traders and shippers such as João Gomes de Soto, who had the Bandel church at Hugli rebuilt, and who traded not merely on his own account, but also had close relations with the English Company. The Dutch shipping lists for the ports of Hugli and Balasore, pertaining to the last quarter of the seventeenth and the early years of the eighteenth century, do contain the names of several Portuguese merchants, ships on whose account arrived at and departed from the two ports over this period. The scale of this shipping would, however, seem to be somewhat smaller than that from southern Coromandel.[60]

The Portuguese merchants based at partner ports also carried on a certain amount of trade with ports on both the east and the west coasts of India. During the eighteenth century, by far the most important group of these merchants was the one based at Macao. The growing problems faced by this group in the early years of the century in the neighbouring markets of the South China Sea forced it to turn increasingly to markets in the Indian Ocean. An analysis of the Dutch shipping lists, as well as the information available in the English Company records for the period 1719 to 1754, shows that Portuguese ships called with varying frequency at the ports of Bengal, at Madras and Nagapattinam on the Coromandel coast, at Cochin, Tellicherry and Anjengo on the Malabar coast, and at Surat. Some of these ships,

---

[59] Sanjay Subrahmanyam, 'Staying on: the Portuguese of southern Coromandel in the late seventeenth century', *The Indian Economic and Social History Review*, vol. 22 (4), 1985, pp. 445–63.

[60] Om Prakash, 'The Dutch East India Company and the economy of Bengal 1650–1717', unpublished PhD dissertation, University of Delhi, 1967, pp. 479–82; Subrahmanyam, 'Staying on'.

particularly those calling at Surat, are known to have in fact been owned by Asian merchants flying the Portuguese flag for convenience. By far the most important ports of call for the genuine Portuguese shipping were Cochin, Tellicherry and Madras. Over the period 1719 to 1754, Portuguese shipping called at Cochin regularly between 1723 and 1742 except in 1733, with the number of ships each year varying between two and six. Between one and four of these ships were Macao based. From the early 1740s onward, the main Malabar port of call was Tellicherry, with the number of ships in a year often being as many as six and reaching the top figure of eight in 1749. This shipping was also dominated by that from Macao. The principal commodity carried to Malabar was Chinese sugar which was exchanged there mainly against pepper and sandalwood. In the case of Madras, the only years between 1719 and 1754 when Portuguese shipping did not call at the port were 1734, 1741, 1747 to 1749, and 1754. The numbers each year, however, were generally more modest than those at Cochin and later Tellicherry, varying between one and five. Most of these ships were also Macao based.[61] The emergence in the second half of the eighteenth century of English private traders as major competitors in the Indian Ocean and the South China Sea undoubtedly affected the trade of the Macao merchants adversely. But this did not prevent them from continuing to be an important segment of the trading community in the region.[62]

THE PORTUGUESE AND THE INDIAN MARITIME MERCHANT

As far as the Indian maritime merchant was concerned, the Portuguese intrusion into the western Indian Ocean at the end of the fifteenth century initially created a situation of utter chaos. We noted earlier that the Portuguese attempt at monopolizing the spice trade called for a total exclusion of Asian shipping from the Persian Gulf and the Red Sea. This involved frequent raids on ships departing from Calicut with pepper for the Red Sea. But this phase was a rather short-lived one

[61] Souza, *The Survival of Empire,* pp. 156–68.
[62] The Dutch shipping lists for the 1760s, for example, record the continuing arrival of Macao shipping at Nagapattinam. (See shipping list for 1764, *Algemeen Rijksarchief* (ARA) VOC 3077, ff. 1139–40 and for 1766, VOC 3164, ff. 607–8.)

and the financial compulsions of the Estado da Índia soon made it opt for taxing Asian shipping in the area rather than trying to smother it. This was done by requiring all Asian ships to ask for and to carry a *cartaz*. In the event of non-compliance, the vessel ran the risk of being seized by the Portuguese cruisers. The document authorized the vessel concerned to embark upon a specified trip and prohibited it from carrying goods monopolized by the Portuguese. The ports of call were specified and generally included a visit to a Portuguese-controlled port to pay duties on its cargo before proceeding to its destination. The fee charged for the grant of a *cartaz* was quite small: the principal pecuniary advantage derived by the Portuguese was the duties collected. The Portuguese were able to enforce such an arbitrary and high-handed requirement essentially because of the near absence of effective naval capability on the part of the Indian and most other Asian states at this time.

In order to ensure that the Indian vessels carrying the *cartazes* were not able to evade calling at the Portuguese-controlled ports and paying duties there, as well as to obviate the risk of Malabari pirate attacks on these vessels, the Portuguese introduced on the west coast of India the so-called *qafila* or caravan system in the second half of the sixteenth century. Under this system, Asian vessels operating between specified points were encouraged to sail in a group escorted by a Portuguese fleet. The practice was reasonably well established by the 1570s: in 1596, sailing in a *qafila* was made obligatory. Apart from the Cambay–Diu *qafila* and a more spasmodic one centred at Ormuz, all the *qafilas* came to Goa. The escorting vessels themselves also carried goods. For example, the private cargoes for the homeward-bound fleet were normally carried by such vessels. Two or three *qafilas* left Goa each year for Cambay via Chaul, Bassein, Daman and, in the seventeenth century, Surat as well. The Kanara *qafila* was also a regular one and made two to four voyages each year to Basrur, Mangalore and Honawar to fetch rice for the city of Goa. Yet another *qafila* travelled from Cape Comorin, via Cochin and Cannanore, to Goa. It included larger ships from Malacca, Siam, Bengal and Coromandel which were met by the guard fleet at Cape Comorin. In Cochin many smaller ships were picked up, and they all proceeded together to Goa.[63]

---

[63] M.N. Pearson, *Merchants and Rulers in Gujarat, The Response to the Portuguese in the Sixteenth Century*, Berkeley, 1976, pp. 39–47.

What implications did the Portuguese trade and policies have for the coastal and the high-seas trade carried on by the Indian merchants? Given the significant differences in this regard between one part of the subcontinent and another, an answer to this query is best attempted at a regional level.

The Western Indian Ocean

(a) Gujarat

To begin with Gujarat, one finds that, after an initial resistance, the response of the local merchants was one of acquiescence in the Portuguese system. By the middle of the sixteenth century, all Gujarati ships leaving the ports of the Gulf of Cambay were obliged to call at Portuguese-controlled Diu and pay duties there. This involved an additional fiscal burden of around 5 per cent of the value of the goods carried. The sixteenth century also witnessed a certain amount of reorientation of the Gujarati merchants' trade, with the share of the Red Sea sector in the total trade perhaps going up substantially. It is significant that the English and the Dutch documentation of the 1620s relating to Surat stresses the dependence in an important way of the merchants of the city upon the Red Sea trade. If this assessment is correct, Gujarat's trade with its other major trading partner, namely southeast Asia, would have suffered a possibly severe decline. What is likely to have been the role of the Portuguese in this process? Since a growth in the textile trade with the Red Sea would have brought them higher customs revenues at Diu, they would probably have welcomed this development and assisted it in whatever way they could. The picture is somewhat more complex in respect of the trade with southeast Asia. As Boxer has shown, the pepper shipments originating at Acheh and destined for the Red Sea operated in an important way through the half century starting around 1540. He has also pointed to the continuing important role of Gujarati shipping in this trade. If the Gujaratis increasingly withdrew from the spice trade from the closing years of the sixteenth century onward, this probably had more to do with the growing substitution of the old water-cum-land route to the Mediterranean by the Cape of Good Hope route after the appearance on the scene of the Dutch and the English East India companies, rather than to any specific Portuguese policies.[64]

---

[64] M.N. Pearson, *The Portuguese in India*, vol. 1.1 in *The New Cambridge History of*

(b) The Kanara coast

From about 1510 on, the Portuguese are known to have attacked the shipping from Bhatkal, particularly that bound for the Red Sea. But between 1518 and 1530, this port figured in the network of Portuguese Crown shipping, and annual voyages were organized to Ormuz with pepper and other goods such as iron, rice, sugar and ginger. In theory, the Indian merchants were not allowed to export pepper or import horses into Bhatkal which could be sold only at Goa, but the restrictions do not seem to have always been observed. The sailings to the Red Sea and South Arabia often seem to have been carried out even without a *cartaz*. From about 1530 onward, the amount of pepper exported from Bhatkal to the Red Sea went up considerably. Of the huge quantities of pepper reaching Jeddah in the 1560s, a large part would seem to have been from Kanara, the other part having originated in Acheh and the Sunda straits. But by about 1575, Bhatkal had suddenly disappeared from the Indian Ocean trading network. This would seem to be the combined outcome of the decline of the Vijayanagar empire and of Portuguese policies. Goods from west Asia designed for sale in the capital city of the empire no longer had a market, and the horse trade was adversely affected too. As for the Portuguese, the establishment of three fortresses – two to the south and one to the north of Bhatkal – in 1568–9 had involved a considerable tightening up of the vigil against the transportation of pepper to the Red Sea.

The Kanara port that took over the role of Bhatkal as the leading port of the coast from the late sixteenth century onward was Basrur. A Saraswat-dominated mercantile community referred to by the Portuguese as 'chatins de Barcelor' had traditionally carried on a fair amount of trade in rice, pepper and other goods from the port. By the early years of the seventeenth century, Basrur had become the leading rice-trading port of the Kanara coast. The rice was sent to Muscat, the Red Sea and the Persian Gulf, as well as to Goa and the Malabar ports. A Portuguese fort had been set up at Basrur in 1569 and a small settlement of white and black *casados* had come up there in the 1570s. The 'chatins de Barcelor' resisted the setting up of a customs house at the fort, which was eventually removed. There is evidence that the

India, Cambridge, 1987, pp. 52–5; Boxer, 'A note on the Portuguese reactions to the revival of the Red Sea spice trade'; Ashin Das Gupta, *Indian Merchants and the Decline of Surat c. 1700–1750*, Wiesbaden, 1979, pp. 4–5.

chatins' trade continued into the seventeenth century and, in addition to the rice trade, increasing amounts of pepper were now carried to Konkan and the Gujarat ports.[65]

(c) The Malabar coast

Given the Portuguese policy of monopolizing the trade in pepper, it is not surprising that a situation of conflict with the *pardesi* merchants developed very early in the history of Portuguese contact with the Malabar coast. The pepper fleets from Calicut, Kollam and Cannanore to the Red Sea were systematically attacked by the Portuguese squadrons both off the Malabar coast as well as at the entrance to the Red Sea. The relations with the Mappilas, however, were generally cordial at this time, and they were indeed used as intermediaries and brokers in the procurement of pepper. But the resistance and the successful evasion of the Portuguese control by the Mappilas of Cannanore under the leadership of their chief, Mamale, an ancestor of the Ali Rajas, must be recorded. They had resented, among other things, the forced diversion of the trade in horses and ginger from their port to Goa. By taking advantage of a palace revolution in Male, Mamale claimed sovereign rights in the Maldives and began collecting duties from ships calling there. The importance of this development lay in the fact that the Gujarati and other ships on their way from southeast Asia to the Red Sea carrying pepper and other goods could now call at the Maldives and evade the Portuguese on the Malabar coast. Malabarese pepper, Sri Lankan cinnamon and other goods were brought to these ships at the Maldives by the merchants of Bengal and Cannanore. The Portuguese attempts to disrupt this arrangement by operating from their fortresses at Pasai, Colombo, Male and Kollam were not particularly successful. With the cooperation of the Mappila traders from Calicut, who had put together an armed fleet under the command of the Kunjalis, spice shipments were also sent clandestinely to the Gujarat ports. This trade received a setback after the Portuguese gained control of the Gulf of Cambay. But a certain amount of spices continued to be smuggled, hidden in the bales of textiles.[66]

By about the middle of the sixteenth century, a change in the relative

[65] Sanjay Subrahmanyam, *The Political Economy of Commerce, Southern India 1500–1650*, Cambridge, 1990, pp. 124–35, 260–5.
[66] Geneviève Bouchon, 'Sixteenth century Malabar and the Indian Ocean', in Ashin Das Gupta and M.N. Pearson (ed.), *India and the Indian Ocean*, Calcutta, 1987, pp. 162–84.

stature of different Malabar ports had begun to be evident. Both Calicut and Cannanore were on the decline, while the rising port was that of Cochin which was now handling more and more of the trade both with Gujarat and the Persian Gulf as well as with southeast Asia. Needless to emphasize, the Portuguese were largely responsible for this. Indeed, from the very beginning of their contacts with the Malabar coast, they had consciously promoted Cochin at the expense of both Calicut and Cannanore. Before they had moved on to Goa in the second decade of the sixteenth century, the headquarters of the Portuguese administration was at Cochin and in course of time an important Portuguese settlement had arisen there. Quite early in the century, Cochin had also occasionally figured in the Crown shipping network.

In the second half of the sixteenth century, the trade from Cochin extended in both directions. There was, in the first place, the trade to the west coast north of Goa, mainly to Chaul, Surat and Diu. The goods exported were mainly pepper, ginger and other spices, as well as the goods brought in from Malacca and China. The imports were mainly opium, raw cotton and textiles, together with some grain. Since both pepper and opium were prohibited goods, it would seem that the trade was carried on with the connivance of the Estado. The other important trading link in the west was with Ormuz, while a relatively minor trade was also carried on with the Red Sea. Eastward, the principal links of Cochin were with the Coromandel coast, Malacca, Macao, Manila and, most important of all, Bengal. The trade to Coromandel was coastal and involved the export of timber, pepper, areca and other spices against the import of textiles and rice. The trade to Malacca and to Macao was essentially a re-export trade. Ships from Goa to Macao called at Cochin on both the outward and the return voyages to take in or to offload goods belonging to the *casado* merchants at Cochin. As for Bengal, António Bocarro estimated that, in its heyday, the total value of the trade on this branch was as much as 400,000 xerafins per annum, amounting perhaps to half of the total trade from Cochin. The exports to Bengal consisted above all of pepper, though some minor drugs and other spices also formed part of the cargo. The main items imported were opium, foodstuff, rice and textiles. The textiles included mainly *khasas* and *malmals* which often found their way into the liberty-chests of the carracks bound for Lisbon. The Cochin–Bengal link, however, nearly snapped after the Mughal expulsion of the Portuguese from Hugli in 1632, and this accounted in large measure for the decline of Cochin in the subsequent period.[67]

The Bay of Bengal

(a) Bengal

The Portuguese involvement in the trade of the Bay of Bengal began almost immediately after the capture of Malacca in 1511. As far as Bengal was concerned, the initial phase of Crown shipping was replaced from the 1560s onward by concession voyages. In addition, there were a certain number of private Portuguese individuals – traders and mercenaries – living in and operating from Bengal. Soon after the Mughal takeover of the province in 1576, the Portuguese settlement at Hugli was legitimized by a *farman* granted by Emperor Akbar in 1579. By the end of the sixteenth century, however, the Portuguese were expelled from Chittagong by Arakan's rulers. As noted above, the Mughals took similar action at Hugli in 1632.

Neither the carreira nor the concession routes to Bengal were monopoly routes and the Indian merchants' trade is known to have co-existed together with that of the Portuguese. There was, however, a certain amount of reorientation of the Bengal trade in the process. In the Bay of Bengal, the trade with Acheh increased substantially at the expense mainly of that with Malacca, which registered a progressive decline from the 1540s onward. The trade with the Coromandel coast, however, continued uninterrupted. As far as the trade with the ports west of Cape Comorin was concerned, one finds that by the middle of the sixteenth century, Indian merchants' trade with Gujarat and the Red Sea had ceased altogether. The only link with the region that survived at the end of the century was the *casado* merchants' trade between Hugli and Ormuz. It was only around the middle of the seventeenth century that the link between the Bengal ports and those in Gujarat and the Red Sea was revived.[68]

(b) The Coromandel coast

The situation was somewhat more complex on the Coromandel coast. *Casado* and other private Portuguese trading groups had already begun to settle down at Pulicat and the neighbouring port of São Tomé de Mylapore in the second decade of the sixteenth century. In

[67] Subrahmanyam, *The Political Economy of Commerce*, pp. 137–42.
[68] Subrahmanyam, 'Notes on the sixteenth century Bengal trade'.

the 1530s, another important Portuguese settlement had arisen at Nagapattinam. The monopolistic nature of some of the carreira routes to Coromandel notwithstanding, private Portuguese merchants' as well as Indian merchants' trade between Pulicat and Malacca is known to have continued on an important scale throughout the 1520s, 1530s and 1540s. But as Crown shipping gave way to the concession voyages to Coromandel on a reserved-route basis, the Indian merchants found themselves almost totally excluded from the Pulicat–Malacca run. They were now obliged to hire freight space aboard the concession holders' ships. An increase in the import duty at Malacca, combined with a rise in the freight charges, created further problems. This situation, together with the decline of the imperial city of Vijayanagar, led to an irreversible decline in the fortunes of the port of Pulicat. By the end of the sixteenth century, the port was only a shadow of its former self.

The port that succeeded Pulicat as the premier port of the Coromandel coast was that at Masulipatnam, which until the middle of the sixteenth century was a relatively minor port. The rise of Masulipatnam was in part related to the consolidation of the Sultanate of Golconda under Ibrahim Qutb Shah (1550–80). But it also had a good deal to do with the emergence of an alternative network of trade in the Bay of Bengal. This basically represented the Indian merchants' response to the Portuguese stranglehold over the Pulicat–Malacca sector. The other constituent ports of the newly emerging network were Acheh, Malay peninsular ports such as Perak and Kedah, and the Burmese ports of Pegu, Bassein, Tavoy and Martaban, all of which had taken on an anti-Portuguese character. In the 1590s, two or three ships regularly left Masulipatnam for Pegu laden with textiles and yarn. The links with Acheh were even stronger. In exchange for Coromandel textiles and rice, Acheh provided horses and elephants, southeast Asian pepper and spices, and the gold and copper of Minangkabau and the Far East. Acheh had turned out to be a worthy successor of Malacca as a major entrepôt port in the region. The other Coromandel port that traded with Acheh extensively was that of Nagapattinam.

The rise of the alternative network greatly alarmed the Estado which tried very hard to destroy it. Through official or unofficial *armadas*, attempts were made to disrupt trade both at Acheh and at Masulipatnam. The merchants of the latter port, who freely navigated without seeking the Portuguese *cartazes*, were sought to be countered by the grant of licences by the Estado to privateers to lie in wait outside Masulipatnam with ships with a view to capturing the local shipping. But these attempts were not particularly successful at any point: indeed, there were occasions when Portuguese captives from such attempts had to be ransomed from Masulipatnam by private Portuguese citizens. However, while the Portuguese authority could be ignored in the Bay of Bengal, it would have been dangerous to do so in the western Indian Ocean. Thus when a new link was established between Masulipatnam and the Red Sea in the 1580s in which Sultan Muhammad Quli Qutb Shah also participated, accommodation with the Portuguese became necessary. An agreement concluded between the Sultan and the Estado in 1590 provided for *cartazes* to be issued for the Mecca-bound shipping in exchange for 300 khandis of rice to be delivered to the Portuguese annually at Malacca or Sri Lanka. In 1598, it was decided to appoint a captain at Masulipatnam for the purpose of issuing *cartazes*. But while the Portuguese by and large kept their part of the agreement, the rice was never handed over to them. By the time the Dutch arrived at Masulipatnam in 1605, the Portuguese captain probably had been withdrawn from the port.[69]

To sum up, from the standpoint of the Indian maritime merchant, the Portuguese *cartaz* system, in so far as it entailed only a small additional fiscal burden, was indeed no more than a minor irritant. But to the extent that this device was used to keep the Indian merchants out of trade in specific commodities or on specific routes, the Portuguese were indeed at least partly instrumental in forcing certain changes in the structure of Indian maritime trade. One such change was an alteration in the relative stature of various Indian ports. Striking cases include the decline of Bhatkal in Kanara, that of Calicut and Cannanore in Malabar accompanied by the rise of Cochin, and the replacement of Pulicat by Masulipatnam as the principal port of the Coromandel coast. The Indian merchants, however, generally adjusted quite well to the evolving situations and did not allow the changes forced by the Portuguese to overwhelm them. Probably the best example of this resilience is the emergence of an alternative network of trade in the Bay of Bengal centred on Masulipatnam, Acheh and several Malay and Burmese ports which had assumed an anti-Portuguese character.

[69] Subrahmanyam, *The Political Economy of Commerce*, pp. 155–66.

CHAPTER 3

THE EUROPEAN TRADING COMPANIES: EXPORTS FROM EUROPE AND THE GENERATION OF PURCHASING POWER IN ASIA

The early years of the seventeenth century mark a sharp discontinuity in the volume and the value of the seaborne trade between Asia and Europe. This was the direct outcome of the successful challenge by the Dutch and the English of the Portuguese monopoly of this trade. The lead provided by these two countries was followed almost immediately by the Danes, though on a very modest scale, and, later in the century, by the French. The first half of the eighteenth century also witnessed the entry into the fray of motley groups of merchants from Ostend and other places trying to find ways and means of evading the great East India Companies' monopoly of this trade. On the whole, the two centuries witnessed not only a tremendous expansion in the volume and the value of the Euro-Asian trade, but also an enormous diversification in the composition as well as the origin of the cargo arriving from Asia into the ports of northwestern Europe. A related development was the near-wiping out early in the seventeenth century of the water-cum-land route between the two continents that had been in use for centuries.

THE DUTCH EAST INDIA COMPANY

The Dutch East India Company was founded in 1602 by a charter granted by the States-General, the national administrative body of the Dutch Republic. We have already noted that the Euro-Asian trade in pepper carried on by the Portuguese was running into serious problems in the last quarter of the sixteenth century. This, coupled with the loss, in 1585, of Antwerp's position as the staple market for Asian goods in northwestern Europe as a result of the blockade of the Scheldt, gave the merchants from the northern Netherlands a strong incentive to challenge the Portuguese monopoly of the Cape route and participate directly in the Euro-Asian spice trade. The substantial capital resource base of this group had recently been augmented by the arrival in Amsterdam of a number of wealthy merchants, who had folded up their business in Antwerp. Critically important inputs were provided by the technical/navigational expertise available in the person of the Flemish clergyman, Petrus Plancius, and the useful tips in the information provided on sailing instructions and other matters by Dutchman Jan Huyghen van Linschoten, who had served the Portuguese in the East for many years. In April 1595, the Amsterdam-based 'Company of Far Lands', which was the first among the so-called 'precompanies' and which had managed to raise a capital of ƒ.290,000, sent out four ships to the East Indies under the command of Cornelis de Houtman. One of the ships was lost but the remaining three came back in August 1597 with a cargo of pepper, nutmeg and mace. In the meantime, a number of new companies had been organized for trade with the East Indies. One of these was in Amsterdam, two in Zeeland, and another two in Rotterdam. The two Amsterdam companies were merged in 1598 and came to be known as the 'Old Company'. It was on the account of this company that eight vessels were sent out to the East in the spring of 1598. The profit on the voyage was estimated at around 400 per cent. By 1600, yet another four companies had been formed in the various provinces of the Netherlands. The inevitable result was an increase in the cost price of the pepper and other spices and a decline in their sale prices. To all those who realized the enormous potential of the East India trade, it was imperative that something be done to curb the cutthroat competition among the various companies.

The initiative was taken by the Old Company which, on the strength of being the pioneer in the East India trade and the most important participant in it, petitioned the States of Holland in 1601 for a monopoly of all trade east of the Cape of Good Hope for a period of twenty-five years. The request was turned down, but it was instrumental in setting in motion other moves to eliminate competition among the various companies. Mainly through the mediatory efforts of Johan van Oldenbarnevelt, the various units agreed to come together, and the Verenigde Oost-Indische Compagnie (VOC) was chartered on 20 March 1602. The Company was given the sole right for a period of twenty-one years to sail east of the Cape of Good Hope and west through the Strait of Magellan.

In view of the nature of its ancestry, the organizational structure of the Company was rather complicated. The precompanies which had been merged to form the VOC constituted the six *kamers* or chambers of the Company. These were Amsterdam, Zeeland, Rotterdam, Delft, Hoorn and Enkhuizen. The directors of these chambers nominated the all-powerful Board of Directors of the Company known as the Heren XVII. As the name indicates, the Board consisted of seventeen members and met consecutively for six years at Amsterdam and for the following two at Middelburg, which was the seat of the Zeeland chamber. Eight of the members were nominated by the Amsterdam chamber, four by that of Zeeland and one each by the four smaller chambers. The seventeenth member was nominated by one of the four smaller chambers by turn except during the two years in the eight-year cycle when the meetings were held at Middelburg and the right to nominate the seventeenth member was vested in the host chamber of Zeeland. The Amsterdam chamber accounted for half the overall business of the Company and Zeeland for a quarter. The remaining quarter of the business was shared equally by the two clusters of Rotterdam and Delft on the one hand and of Hoorn and Enkhuizen on the other. Although the charter provided that a stockholder might withdraw his stock at the close of each decade, this clause was withdrawn even before the first decade had closed. Shares could be sold but no longer withdrawn, so that a permanent joint stock was guaranteed. The initial share capital of the Company was $f.6.42$ million subscribed in holdings ranging in value from $f.20$ to $f.100,000$.[1] Over the following two centuries, the charter of the Company was renewed at regular intervals. Just before the charter of 1776 was due to expire in 1796, however, the Revolution of 1795 made the Heren XVII's position untenable. They were obliged to hand over control and were replaced by a 'Committee for the Affairs of the East India Trade and Possessions'. But simultaneously, the Company's charter was extended until the end of 1798, when it was decided to let it expire at the end of 1799.

All important decisions pertaining to the number of ships (all of which the Company owned) to be sent to the East each year, together with the volume and the value of the goods and the precious metals to be carried aboard them, the range and the volume of the goods to be ordered from the East, the procedure to be adopted with regard to the

---

[1] J.R. Bruijn, F.S. Gaastra and I. Schöffer, *Dutch–Asiatic Shipping in the 17th and 18th Centuries*, vol. I, The Hague, 1987, p. 9.

sale of the Asian goods in the Netherlands, and so on were taken at the meetings of the Heren XVII. The presiding chamber for the year determined in advance the agenda of the meetings and delegates from each of the other chambers came to them with specific briefs relating to each item on the agenda. Until 1751, these meetings were held thrice a year when their frequency was reduced to two per annum. The principal meeting of the year was held in the autumn and lasted as long as four to six weeks. The spring meeting where, among other things, the rate of dividend to be paid was usually determined, was held in February or March. The Heren XVII were assisted by a number of committees, which looked after matters such as the preparation of accounts, the organization of the auction sales and so on. A 'committee for secret affairs' determined the sailing routes for the fleets. A committee called 'Haags Besogne' met each spring for a period of four to eight weeks in The Hague to read and examine the voluminous correspondence received from Asia during the year.

The organization of the sale of the goods received from Asia was an elaborate affair. There were basically three devices the Company used to dispose of the Asian goods – contract sales, sales at a fixed price, and sales by public auction. Contract sales based on negotiations with major Dutch syndicates for the disposal of the entire lot of a particular commodity and often involving an undertaking by the Company not to sell any more of the commodity in question for a specified period of time giving the syndicate an absolute monopoly in the item, were the dominant device used during the first half of the seventeenth century, particularly in relation to pepper, by far the most important single item figuring in the list of goods imported by the Company. Some idea of the upper end of the size of a deal negotiated through this device can be formed by reference to the contract finalized by the Company on 19 October 1623 with a syndicate consisting of Gert Dircksz. Raedt, Cornelis van Campen and Hans Broer relating to the sale of the entire lot of pepper available in the Company's warehouses in addition to the lots that might arrive into the Netherlands before 1 May 1624. The *stilstand* – the period of no further sales by the Company agreed upon between the two parties – was twenty-four months. The value of the sale was a staggering four million florins.[2] The device of sales at a fixed price was followed in respect of spices such as cloves, nutmeg and mace

[2] Kristof Glamann, *Dutch–Asiatic Trade, 1620–1740*, Copenhagen/The Hague, 1958, p. 33.

following the attainment of an absolute monopoly in these items by the Company during the second half of the seventeenth century. The identification of an optimal monopoly price was, of course, not an easy task. The Company had to take into account the impact of a given price on sales as well as on the inducement it might offer for potential smuggling. Hard to believe as it is, it is nevertheless true that, for the entire period between 1677 and 1744, the Company sold cloves in Amsterdam at the fixed price of 75 stivers per Dutch pond.[3] The third device of sale by public auction was the dominant device used by the Company during the eighteenth century.

THE ENGLISH EAST INDIA COMPANY

The other major company engaged in the Euro-Asian trade was the English East India Company. The great success attendant upon the venture of the 'Old Company' of Amsterdam into the Euro-Asian trade with the successful return of its vessels in 1599 had caused great consternation among the English merchants engaged in the spice trade from the Levant. The fear of the Dutch domination of the spice market in northwestern Europe thus served as the catalyst that led a group of London merchants to apply to the Crown for a monopoly charter for the East India trade. The request was granted and on 31 December 1600 was born the 'Company of Merchants of London trading into the East Indies'. Between 1601 and 1612, the twelve voyages organized by the Company were on separate and terminable account. The capital subscribed for the first voyage in 1601 was £68,373 with the highest figure of £80,163 being reached in the sixth voyage sent out in 1609. The first joint stock lasted from 1613 to 1623, the second from 1617 to 1632 and the third from 1631 to 1642.[4]

In the meantime, in 1637, Charles I had granted a patent to the so-called Courteen's Association to trade to those parts of the East Indies where the English Company had not established a factory. But the Association turned out to be a dismal failure and constituted no real threat to the monopoly of the Company. The outbreak of the civil war in the 1640s caused a certain amount of dislocation for the Company's trade, but matters improved considerably after the charter of 1657

---

[3] Glamann, *Dutch–Asiatic Trade*, p. 92.
[4] K.N. Chaudhuri, *The English East India Company: The Study of an Early Joint-stock Company 1600–1640*, London, 1965, pp. 22, 28, 209.

which provided for a permanent joint stock. The monopoly privileges of the Company were threatened yet again in July 1698 when a rival body – usually described as the New English East India Company – received a charter from the Crown. This body was in effect a 'general society' of subscribers to a loan of £2 million to the State. But in April 1702, the two companies agreed to have a joint Board of Directors. The final amalgamation came in 1709 under an award by the Earl of Godolphin. From this point on there was no further challenge to the 'United' Company's monopoly until 1813, when the new charter legalized the entry of private traders into the East Indian trade. Twenty years later, the Company ceased to be a trading body and was entrusted solely with the running of the colonial administration of India, a process that had started in 1765 with the Company wresting from the Mughal emperor Shah Alam the *diwani* (revenue collection) rights in the province of Bengal. The Company was liquidated in 1858 following the assumption by the British Crown of direct responsibility for Indian affairs.

The general controlling body in the Company responsible for all entrepreneurial decisions – the counterpart of the Heren XVII in the case of the VOC – was the Court of Directors composed of twenty-four members. This larger committee was further subdivided into smaller working units, the most important of which in the early eighteenth century were the Committee of Correspondence, the Committee of Treasury, the Committee of Shipping, and a shadowy but extremely powerful body known as the Committee of Secrecy, composed of four members including the Chairman of the Company.[5]

In the early part of the seventeenth century, the Company built all its ships in one or other of its two shipyards on the Thames. But as the trade became well established and the possible demand for shipping required by the Company became known, the practice of direct construction was discontinued and the Court was able to charter its entire annual tonnage from shipowners who bore all the risks.[6]

As far as the organization of the sale of the goods imported from Asia was concerned, from the 1650s onward the Company adopted

---

[5] K.N. Chaudhuri, 'The English East India Company in the 17th and 18th centuries: a pre-modern multinational organization', in L. Blussé and F. Gaastra (eds.), *Companies and Trade*, The Hague, 1981, p. 38.

[6] K.N. Chaudhuri, *The Trading World of Asia and the English East India Company 1660–1760*, Cambridge, 1978, p. 133.

the practice of auctioning its goods in four quarterly sales held in London. The Company's main homeward fleet generally arrived back from the Indies during August and September, though a few ships could arrive earlier or later than during these two months. It was clearly inadvisable to try and sell the entire stock of goods brought home by the summer and autumn ships in one single auction. By spreading out the stocks over the whole year, the Company not only hoped to prevent a sudden slide in prices, but also provided the buyers with a means of predicting the market. In some cases, the Committee of Warehouses was prepared to go so far as to give a definite guarantee that once a certain quantity of a particular commodity was sold in an auction, no further stocks would be released on the market before a specified date. Such an assurance at once reduced the risk of market fluctuations arising from the Company's own action and it encouraged the buyers to offer higher prices at the public sales. Clearly the underlying assumption in the economic behaviour of the Company, as in the case of the VOC, was typically monopolistic. The crucial decision variable was the control over supplies, and demand was treated more or less as a given factor which varied according to a known random function. The quarterly sales were attended by dealers from Holland, Germany and eastern Europe. They knew intimately the actual conditions in these distant regional markets, the volume of stocks left in the hands of retailers, the price of substitute goods, the precise time for shipment through inland waterways before they froze up in winter, and changes in consumer taste.[7]

THE DANISH EAST INDIA COMPANY

The Dansk Ostindiske Kompagni chartered by King Christian IV on 17 March 1616 owed its origin to the initiative of two emigrants from the Netherlands. The influence of the Dutch East India Company was, therefore, quite evident in the Company's charter, valid in the first instance for twelve years. The capital resources available to the Company, however, were grossly inadequate from the very beginning and the enterprise could sustain itself even in the limited way it did only on the basis of continued state support. Indeed, from about 1630 on, Christian IV owned half the share capital of the Company. But

---

[7] Chaudhuri, *Trading World of Asia*, pp. 131–5.

that was not good enough, and the Company went into liquidation in 1650. A second East India Company chartered in 1670 lasted until 1729 and engaged partly in the smuggling trade in spices from Borneo and in the illicit trade with Manila. The Danish Asiatic Company, chartered in April 1732, did much better than its predecessors, but concentrated mainly on the China trade. The Asian trade, except that with China, was declared free in 1772 and private Danish enterprise also came to play a role, to a certain extent, in the trade between India and Denmark. But the Danish involvement in Indo-European trade was never particularly significant, except perhaps during the so-called golden age between about 1780 and 1807.

THE GENOESE COMPANY

The only other East India Company to be constituted in the first half of the seventeenth century was the Genoese Compagnia Genovese delle Indie Orientali founded in 1647. Dutch merchants Willem and Hendrik Meulman together with their associate Jakob van den Heuvel actively participated in the floating of this Company. But the venture really came to nothing and there is no evidence of any Genoese ships being sent to India.

THE FRENCH EAST INDIA COMPANY

The element of state support was particularly marked in the case of the French Compagnie des Indes Orientales founded by Jean-Baptiste Colbert on 1 September 1664, as well as in that of its successors. But in so far as state support involved state management to a degree not encountered in the case of any other East India Company, it constituted in the long run more of a liability than an asset and may perhaps legitimately be held largely responsible for the eventual failure of the French enterprise in Asia. The Company established in 1664 went into liquidation in 1684 and was succeeded the following year by a new Company subject to even greater control by the government. As many as 87 per cent of the shareholders of the defunct Company had now withdrawn from the enterprise.[8] The performance of the new

---

[8] Philippe Haudrère, *La Compagnie française des Indes au XVIIIe siècle (1719–1795)*, Paris, 1989, vol. I, p. 28.

unit turned out to be extremely unsatisfactory as well, and in May 1719 the Edict of Reunion merged the Compagnie des Indes Orientales with John Law's expanding enterprise. The new Compagnie des Indes had to be restructured only four years later into the Compagnie Perpetuelle des Indes, whose life-span lasted until 1769. From this point on, the East India trade was open to private individuals except between 1785 and 1790 when yet another East India Company had the monopoly of this trade.

THE OSTEND, THE SWEDISH AND OTHER MINOR COMPANIES

The eighteenth century witnessed the establishment of East India companies in several other European countries. By far the most interesting of these were the Ostend and the Swedish East India companies. Basically, these units were no more than 'covers' for groups of merchants of various European nationalities come together to get around the monopoly privileges of the great East India companies. The Ostend Company, which was a conglomerate of Dutch, Irish, Danish and Flemish interloping interests, was chartered by the Habsburg Emperor Charles VI at Vienna in 1722, though voyages to the East had been organized by this group from as early as 1713 when Austrian administration had been established in the Netherlands. Perceiving a threat to their respective monopoly privileges, both the Dutch and the English East India companies brought pressure on the emperor through their respective governments to have the enterprise withdrawn. Since the emperor needed the Anglo-Dutch support against Spain to secure for his daughter Maria Theresia the succession to all his dominions, the strategy worked. The Ostend Company was suspended in 1727 and abolished in 1731.

Several of the merchants involved in the Ostend venture transferred their capital to the Danish Asiatic Company of 1732. Others joined up with Scotsmen Hugh and Colin Campbell and the Goteborg merchant Henry Koenig and had a Swedish East India Company chartered in 1731. But as in the case of the Danish Asiatic Company, the principal preoccupation of the Swedish Company was with the China trade rather than with the trade to India. As the recent work of C. Koninckx shows, of the sixty-one voyages returning to Europe between 1733 and 1767 on the account of the Swedish Company, only three (those of 1735, 1740 and 1742) carried cotton and silk textiles and raw silk from Bengal. The other Indian port occasionally visited by the Swedish Company ships was Surat, from where again small quantities of cotton textiles were carried by the voyages of 1752, 1756 and 1762.[9]

Finally, mention might also be made of the Prussian 'Bengal' Company chartered in 1754 and based at Emden, an imperial company established at Trieste in the 1770s and the Philippine Company of the 1780s representing the Spanish attempt to enter the East India trade. The Prussian Company had been founded by the English country captains and company servants at Calcutta for remitting funds illicitly to Europe. The imperial East India Company of Trieste financed voyages from Ostend, Leghorn, Trieste and other European ports during the 1770s, but went into bankruptcy in 1782–3. Recognizing the impossibility of stopping such ventures, the English Company even supplied goods itself to the Philippine Company.[10] Quantitatively speaking, however, the trading activities of all these enterprises almost certainly added up to very little.

THE ASIAN TRADE REVOLUTION

While a whole host of East India companies participated in Euro-Asian trade, it was really the two giants, the Dutch and the English East India companies, who between themselves accounted for an overwhelming proportion of this trade through the seventeenth and the eighteenth centuries. The French East India Company was of importance only between about 1725 and 1770 and the Danish Asiatic Company over the last quarter of the eighteenth and the first few years of the nineteenth century. Niels Steensgaard has put forward the hypothesis that the Dutch and the English companies were instrumental in bringing about an institutional revolution in the organization and conduct of Euro-Asian trade as of the early years of the seventeenth century. He draws a sharp contrast between the seigneurial and redistributive nature of the Portuguese enterprise and the rational and productivity-maximizing policies of the companies. Thus, 'the Portuguese pepper monopoly was not a business but a

---

[9] C. Koninckx, *The First and Second Charters of the Swedish East India Company (1731–1766)*, Kortrijk, 1988, pp. 456–9.
[10] Holden Furber, *Rival Empires of Trade in the Orient 1600–1800*, Minneapolis and Oxford, 1976, p. 226.

custom house'.[11] On the other hand, the success of the companies was not based upon government monopolies or the use of violence but on their ability to compete in the market. For by adopting specific policies in relation to stocks, pricing and the mode of the disposal of their goods, the companies made impressive gains in the transparency and the predictability of the markets in which they operated.

While the core of Steensgaard's formulation is certainly valid, some of its components, when stretched to their logical outcome, present problems of one kind or the other. To begin with, in so far as the Dutch monopoly of finer spices (the details of which we will go into presently) involved a gross under-payment to the producers in the Spice Islands, the label of 'redistributive enterprise' would apply as much to this segment of the Dutch Company business as it would to the Portuguese pepper trade. Indeed, Steensgaard himself recognizes this when he says, 'the Dutch East India Company was not a "pure" type: it contained features in its constitution, in its structure and its policy, more reminiscent of a redistributive enterprise than of a business.'[12] Again, the absence of the 'use of violence' by the companies is a construct that poses certain problems at the margin. As we shall see later in detail, in its trade within Asia the Dutch East India Company took extensive steps to obtain exclusive rights in particular products and markets and to minimize competition by indigenous merchants, making a judicious use of violence in the process.[13] The Company also made an optimal use of the pass system, originally introduced by the Portuguese, to keep Asian competitors out of the trade in monopoly products such as spices and to regulate their trade in several others, such as Malayan tin.[14] If some violations of the prescribed policies and procedures, say by the Indian traders, was tolerated, it was only because the cost of unlimited conflict in the form

---

[11] Niels Steensgaard, *The Asian Trade Revolution of the Seventeenth Century: The East India Companies and the Decline of Caravan Trade*, Chicago, 1974, p. 100.

[12] Steensgaard, *The Asian Trade Revolution*, p. 141. A few pages earlier, Steensgaard writes, 'One may therefore raise the question as to whether the Dutch East India Company ought not to be considered a redistributive enterprise using organized violence with a view to the acquisition of income' (p. 133).

[13] As the Dutch historian Hans van Santen has put it, 'Violence was a necessary part of the market strategy of the VOC.' H.W. van Santen, *De Verenigde Oost-Indische Compagnie in Gujarat en Hindustan, 1620–1660*, Leiden, 1982, p. 208.

[14] Om Prakash, 'Asian trade and European impact: a study of the trade from Bengal 1630–1720', in Blair B. Kling and M.N. Pearson (ed.), *The Age of Partnership, Europeans in Asia Before Dominion*, Honolulu, 1979, pp. 43–70.

of possible disruptions to its trade in the Indian subcontinent would have been unacceptably high for the Company.[15]

If we go beyond Steensgaard and define the notion of 'ability to compete' to include both belief and confidence in competitive trade, the sustained opposition of the English and the Dutch companies to the entry of rival European companies into Euro-Asian trade creates problems. The Dutch Company, for example, was clearly hostile to the first Danish expeditions of the 1610s and the early 1620s to India.[16] The VOC's action in seizing two of the Genoese East India Company's vessels in the Sunda Straits in April 1649 was a clear example of the use of force to keep a potential competitor out, though ostensibly the step was taken because the vessels were carrying Dutch crews and merchants.[17] Also, as we shall note in some detail later, in the 1720s the Dutch and the English companies successfully formed a coalition both in Europe as well as in Bengal to keep the newly formed Ostend Company out of the lucrative Bengal trade. It was basically the pressure by the two companies that led to the suspension and later the abolition of the Ostend Company. There was, of course, nothing they could do about the same set of merchants regrouping themselves under different nomenclatures. It is, therefore, imperative that the question of the differences between the policies followed by the Portuguese on the one hand, and by the Dutch and the English on the other, which certainly were by no means inconsiderable, be kept in perspective.

EURO-ASIAN TRADE

Quite independently of whether or not there indeed was an institutional 'Asian trade revolution' at the beginning of the seventeenth century, it certainly is true that the process of the phenomenal expansion in the volume and value of Euro-Asian trade as well as of a diversification in the composition and the origin of the Asian cargo

---

[15] Om Prakash, 'Asian trade and European impact'; Sanjay Subrahmanyam has argued that the term 'age of contained conflict' captures the realities of the situation more appropriately than Holden Furber's 'age of partnership'. (Sanjay Subrahmanyam, *The Political Economy of Commerce, Southern India, 1500–1650*, Cambridge, 1990, ch. v.)

[16] Om Prakash (ed.), *The Dutch Factories in India, 1617–1623*, New Delhi, 1984, pp. 31–3, 35; Furber, *Rival Empires of Trade*, pp. 201–2; Subrahmanyam, *The Political Economy of Commerce*, p. 282.

[17] Subrahmanyam, *The Political Economy of Commerce*, p. 293.

entering this trade got under way around this time. Initially, both the Dutch and the English concentrated on the procurement of pepper and other spices which, as in the sixteenth century, continued to account for an overwhelming proportion of the total Asian imports into Europe. But unlike, and indeed mainly because of, the Portuguese, the Dutch and the English procured their pepper in Indonesia rather than on the southwest coast of India. The result was a marked shift in the Asian loci of the Euro-Asian seaborne trade from India to the Indonesian archipelago. This was the Asian counterpart of the shift of the European loci of this trade from Lisbon to Amsterdam and London. It was nearly three quarters of a century before the Asian loci shifted back to India in response to the change in European fashions assigning an increasingly important role to textiles and raw silk in the Asian imports into Europe. It was only in the second half of the eighteenth century that the growing role of Chinese tea again deflected somewhat from the central importance of India in Euro-Asian trade.

THE ROLE OF BULLION

The central characteristic feature of Euro-Asian trade, namely the necessity for the Europeans to pay for the Asian goods overwhelmingly in precious metals, however, remained unchanged throughout the entire period between the sixteenth and the eighteenth centuries. This particular phenomenon has sometimes been ascribed to the rigidity of consumer tastes in the East, which rendered the Asian markets for European goods extremely small and static. Alternatively, it has been suggested that the absorption of precious metals by India or China reflected the hoarding habits in these societies.[18] But perhaps a more convincing explanation of this phenomenon is the inability of Europe to supply western products with a potential market in Asia at prices that would generate a large enough demand for them to provide the necessary revenue for the purchase of the Asian goods. Europe at this time had an overall superiority over Asia in the field of scientific and technological knowledge but as yet did not have the cost advantage that came with the Industrial Revolution in the nineteenth century. This put the Asian, and particularly the Indian, producers,

---

[18] Rudolph C. Blitz, 'Mercantilist policies and the pattern of world trade, 1500–1750', *Journal of Economic History*, vol. 27, 1967, pp. 39–55.

with their considerably lower labour costs and a much longer history of sophisticated skills in handicrafts of various kinds, in a position of advantage over their European counterparts in the production of a variety of manufactured goods. The only major item Europe was in a position to provide to Asia was precious metals. The growth of the Euro-Asian trade, therefore, was critically dependent upon an increase in the availability of these metals. In this context, the working of the South American silver mines and the enormous import of American silver into Europe during the sixteenth and the early seventeenth centuries was a development of critical significance. Although the American silver initially arrived into Spain, a large part of it eventually found its way to Amsterdam, mainly via Hamburg. In fact, from the early years of the seventeenth century the Dutch were the undoubted masters of the European bullion trade and Amsterdam the leading world centre of the trade in precious metals.[19] It is an indication of the international standing of this city as a market for precious metals that the English East India Company also obtained a large part of its requirements of these metals in Amsterdam. An important implication of this 'bullion for goods' model of Euro-Asian trade was that as far as the Europeans were concerned, the profit from the trade was derived almost entirely from the sale of Asian goods in Europe rather than also from the sale of European goods in Asia.

DUTCH EXPORTS TO ASIA

An analysis of the Dutch and the English East India companies' exports to the East Indies over the seventeenth and the eighteenth centuries testifies to an unambiguous pattern where precious metals dominated the total exports throughout the period. In the case of the Dutch Company, the goods exported were woollen, silk and other textiles manufactured mainly at Leiden, and non-precious metals such as lead, iron, vermilion and mercury, besides sundry items such as wines and beer. Since the Company's accounts do not permit a clear-cut distinction between the cost of these goods and that of the equipment and consumption goods also sent along, a systematic analysis of the proportion that trade goods formed of the total exports

---

[19] J.G. van Dillen, 'Amsterdam als wereldmarkt der edele metalen in de 17de en 18de eeuw', *De Economist*, vol. 72, 1923, pp. 538–50, 583–98, 717–30.

is not feasible. But some information available for the eighteenth century in respect of the Amsterdam chamber alone suggests that this proportion was usually between 10 and 20 per cent.[20] The information base for the seventeenth century is much more fragmentary. But on the whole, it would seem to suggest a somewhat higher average figure for this century. According to the information available in the *Generale Missiven*, there were even some years in the second half of the seventeenth century when the value of trade goods exported matched that of the precious metals.[21]

Mercantilist prejudice against the export of precious metals notwithstanding, the Company never really had to face any particular restrictions on its export of these metals. The only restriction it had to contend with in the early stages of its trade was the prohibition on the export of precious metals in the form of bullion. In 1647, the States-General withdrew even this restriction, provided an amount equal to one third of that exported was surrendered to one of the state mints or the Amsterdam Exchange Bank. At any rate, practically throughout the period, the export of coins including Dutch coins specifically intended for export – the so-called *negotie-penningen* – was freely allowed.[22] The bulk of the Company's export of precious metals was in silver – mainly in Spanish rials, ducatons, *negotie-penningen* and bars. The limited amount of gold exported was in the form of dukaats and bars. As the proportion of the total precious metals absorbed in the Company's Indian trade increased considerably from the last quarter of the seventeenth century on, the fineness of the silver and the gold bars sent was sought to be regulated as far as possible by the fineness of the Bengal rupee and the Coromandel pagoda, respectively.[23]

The data on the Dutch Company exports of precious metals given below are actually the totals of the allotments made to individual chambers each year, but these corresponded closely to the actual amounts exported. The decadal totals are set out in Table 3.1.

---

[20] Bruijn, Gaastra and Schöffer, *Dutch–Asiatic Shipping*, vol. I, p. 183.
[21] This assumes that the term *koopmanschappen* (merchandise) has been used carefully to include only trade goods. (F.S. Gaastra, 'The exports of precious metals from Europe to Asia by the Dutch East India Company, 1602–1795', in J.F. Richards (ed.), *Precious Metals in the Later Medieval and Early Modern Worlds*, Durham, 1983, p. 461).
[22] van Dillen, 'Amsterdam als wereldmarkt', pp. 541–50.
[23] Gaastra, 'The exports of precious metals', p. 453; Bruijn, Gaastra and Schöffer, *Dutch–Asiatic Shipping*, vol. I, p. 225.

Table 3.1 *The export of precious metals (coined and uncoined) by the VOC to Asia, 1602–1794 (decadel totals in million florins rounded off to the nearest thousand)*

1602–10	5.207	1700–10	39.275
1610–20	10.186	1710–20	38.827
1620–30	12.360	1720–30	66.030
1630–40	8.500	1730–40	40.124
1640–50	9.200	1740–50	38.275
1650–60	8.400	1750–60	58.958
1660–70	12.100	1760–70	53.542
1670–80	11.295	1770–80	48.317
1680–90	19.720	1780–90	47.896
1690–1700	28.605	1790–94	16.972
		Total	573.789

Source: J.R. Bruijn, F.S. Gaastra and I. Schöffer, *Dutch–Asiatic Shipping in the 17th and 18th Centuries*, The Hague, 1987, vol. I, Table 39, p. 187.

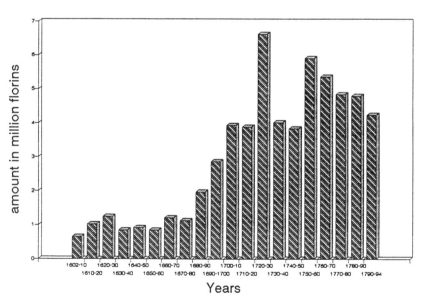

Fig. 3.1 The export of precious metals by the VOC to Asia, 1602–1794 (annual average)

It will be seen from the table that a relatively high figure of $f.12$ million had already been reached by the decade 1620–30. The big increase took place from about 1680 with an all-time peak of $f.66$ million being reached during 1720–30. A generally very high level was maintained throughout the second half of the eighteenth century. It should, of course, be realized that the decadal totals smooth out enormous annual fluctuations so characteristic of the entire period. To take an extreme example, the decade 1740–50 with an annual average of $f.3.82$ million included a year such as 1742–3 when the figure was no more than $f.1.6$ million, and the preceding one of 1741–2 when it was as high as $f.7$ million.[24]

THE BILLS OF EXCHANGE

The purchasing power made available to the factors in Asia did not consist only in the goods and precious metals sent aboard the outward bound ships. A second component of the 'assistance received from Holland' ('secours uit het lieve vaderland') was the funds raised locally by the factors in Asia (initially only at Batavia but later also by those at selected factories such as Bengal) by issuing bills of exchange (redeemable by the Heren XVII), which generally carried a 4 per cent interest. The bills were bought predominantly by the Company's servants on the look-out for a safe channel to remit their savings home. The Company realized very well that an overwhelming bulk of the savings was made by engaging in illicit private trade. But a refusal to accept these funds would simply have involved their diversion to rival companies. The other source used by the purchasers to buy the bills (called *assignaties*) was the private funds smuggled out from Holland to Asia to take advantage of the differential in the exchange rate. At the beginning of the eighteenth century, a silver ducaton could be bought in Holland at 63 stivers and converted into an *assignatie* at Batavia at 78 stivers, making a neat profit of nearly 24 per cent in addition to the 4 per cent interest. In 1734–5, a sum of as much as $f.4$ million is believed to have been smuggled out of Holland for the purpose.[25] In 1738, the Heren XVII issued instructions that the

[24] Bruijn, Gaastra and Schöffer, *Dutch–Asiatic Shipping*, vol. I, Table 46, p. 240.
[25] F.S. Gaastra, 'De Verenigde Oost-Indische Compagnie in de 17de en 18de eeuw: de groei van een bedrijf. Geld tegen goederen', *Bijdragen en Mededelingen betreffende de Geschiedenis der Nederlanden*, vol. 89 (2), 1976, pp. 244–72.

Table 3.2 *The assignaties redeemed by the chambers of the Dutch East India Company, 1640–1795 (decadel totals in million florins rounded off to the nearest thousand)*

1640–50	3.765	1700–10	6.387	1750–60	23.619
1650–60	4.506	1710–20	11.219	1760–70	37.900
1660–70	2.492	1720–30	7.956	1770–80	35.878
1670–80	4.304	1730–40	16.814	1780–90	40.015
1680–90	8.024	1740–50	13.982	1790–5	13.375
1690–1700	7.555				

Source: F.S. Gaastra, 'De Verenigde Oost-Indische Compagnie in de 17de en 18de eeuw: de groie van een bedrijf. Geld tegen goederen', *Bijdraden en Mededelingen betreffende de Geschiedenis der Nederlanden*, vol. 89 (2), 1976, pp. 244–72.

conversion rate at Batavia be reduced to 72 stivers and interest payment stopped. The transaction was still quite profitable and large sums of money continued to be smuggled out of Holland. The Company, on its side, considered the 13 per cent premium now involved reasonable in return for the use of the money for a fairly long period of time, and the fact that the risk involved in sending out equivalent sums of money to Asia was averted. In view of the liquidity crisis in Asia caused by the Fourth Anglo-Dutch War, the exchange rate of 78 stivers was restored in 1782. The amounts for which the *assignaties* were issued in Asia grew at a significant pace throughout the period. The valuewise decadal totals of the *assignaties* redeemed at the various chambers of the Company between 1640 and 1795 are tabulated in Table 3.2.

It will be seen from the table that from a relatively modest sum of f.3.76 million in 1640–50, the value of the *assignaties* redeemed had risen to f.11.22 million in 1710–20 and to an all-time peak of f.40 million in 1780–90. Read together with Table 3.1, this table brings out the important role of the *assignaties* in the total purchasing power made available by the Heren XVII particularly in the second half of the eighteenth century.

DUTCH INTRA-ASIAN TRADE

The 'assistance received from Holland' was supplemented considerably by the profits earned by the Company through participation in trade within Asia. Throughout the seventeenth century, not only were these profits considerable, but a large part of them was earned in precious metals. Indeed, the one characteristic feature that more than any other distinguished the Dutch Company from the other European enterprises operating in Asia was its large-scale official involvement in a highly profitable network of intra-Asian trade. Extensive participation in this trade was in fact an integral part of the overall trading strategy of the Company. In so far as the Crown had initiated and then sustained for a while the Portuguese involvement in intra-Asian trade in the sixteenth century, one could perhaps discern in the Portuguese case some kind of a precedent for the Dutch Company involvement in Asian trade. But after a brief phase of active participation, the Crown had withdrawn from the trade to become basically a dispenser of patronage through the concession system. More importantly, there was no specific commercial strategy involved in the way the Portuguese Crown had gone about participating in the intra-Asian trade. By and large, the Portuguese had simply become yet another group participating in an existing framework of trade, and initially at least operated with the assistance of and in collaboration with Indian and other Asian merchant groups. It is true that one of the branches of trade the Crown monopolized for itself was the trade in spices other than pepper designed to feed into the Euro-Asian trade. But, as we have seen, the control was rather lax throughout. The only important innovation that could be attributed to the Portuguese participation in Asian trade was the opening up of the long-distance trade between Goa and Nagasaki in the second half of the sixteenth century. But this was done not under the auspices of the Crown but under those of the private merchants operating under the concession system. The Dutch pattern of involvement in intra-Asian trade, on the other hand, had a definitive logic behind it besides involving the forging of important new commercial links across the Indian Ocean and the South China Sea.

The starting point of Dutch participation in the trade of the East Indies was, of course, the procurement of pepper and other spices for the European market. They realized from the very beginning that, if the spice trade was to continue to be highly profitable, they must strive to gain control of both the total amount reaching Europe and the cost price in the Indies. The 1602 merger of the precompanies into the United Company was only the first step in this direction. The ultimate aim was to eliminate the rivals in this trade – the Portuguese, the English and the Asian merchants. Between 1605 and 1609, the Company managed to wrest from the authorities in Amboyna and Ternate agreements obliging the producers to supply their cloves exclusively to the Dutch. A similar agreement was concluded in 1605 with the Banda group of islands regarding the procurement of nutmeg and mace. The latter agreement was renewed after the conquest of the islands by the Company in 1621.

By the early 1620s, then, the Dutch had acquired effective monopsony rights in nutmeg and mace. The case of cloves was somewhat more complex. There was a large-scale smuggling trade carried on between the producing areas and Makassar, enabling the English, among others, to obtain large quantities of this spice. Though from 1643 onward the Company had managed to reduce such smuggling, it was only after the conquest of Makassar in 1669 that the Dutch fully controlled the trade in cloves. As for pepper – which was a substantially more important item for investment in the Indies than all the other spices put together – in spite of the availability of formal monopsony rights in a number of states in the region, the Company never acquired effective monopsony rights in the spice.

The control exercised by the Company on the Spice Islands enabled it to procure spices other than pepper at incredibly low prices. This ensured a very high rate of gross profit on these spices, often exceeding 1,000 per cent. Before the arrival of the Dutch, the spice growers had been used to exchanging their wares for Indian cloth, rice and other necessities brought to them by Indian and other Asian merchants as well as by the Portuguese. The Company could have obtained the Indian textiles – by far the most important medium of exchange in the Spice Islands – at Acheh and other places in Indonesia, but its acute business instinct drove it to their source, the Coromandel coast, where four factories were established between 1606 and 1610 covering both the northern and the southern stretches of the coast. Gujarat, on the west coast of India, the other major Indian region supplying textiles to the Indonesian archipelago, was reached in 1618 with the establishment of a factory at Surat. Within a few years, subordinate factories had been opened at Cambay and Broach, and at Agra in northern India. Thus began the Company's participation in intra-Asian trade, which in course of time assumed important proportions and became an object of as much concern as the Euro-Asian trade itself.

It is important to realize that the idea of extensive participation in intra-Asian trade had originated not with the Heren XVII but with the officials at the Company's eastern headquarters established at Bantam in 1609 and shifted in 1618 to Jacatra, renamed Batavia in 1621. As early as 1612, Hendrik Brouwer, a future governor-general of the East Indies, had described the Coromandel coast as the 'left arm of the Moluccas and the surrounding islands because without textiles that come from there, the trade in the Moluccas will be dead'.[26] The driving force behind the project was a remarkable man, Jan Pietersz. Coen, who was named Governor-General of the East Indies in April 1618 at the young age of thirty-one years. The way Coen went about the whole thing displayed a remarkable grasp of the realities of Asian trade. He devised a carefully worked out strategy and followed it up with great tenacity. In 1619, he sent to the Directors a blueprint of the Company's intra-Asian trade: cloth from Gujarat (obtained against spices, other goods and Spanish rials) to be exchanged against pepper and gold in Sumatra; cloth from Coromandel (obtained against spices, Chinese goods and gold, and rials) to be exchanged against pepper at Bantam; sandalwood, pepper and rials to be exchanged against Chinese gold and goods, the latter also being used to obtain silver from Japan. Finally, rials of eight could be obtained in Arabia against spices and other sundry items. Since the Company already had spices available to it, all that was needed to turn this blueprint into reality was an adequate number of ships and enough capital for some time to establish the intra-Asian trading network – 'a little water to prime the pump'. The Company already had a permanently circulating capital of between $f.2.5$ million and $f.3.5$ million in the East Indies at this time, but Coen wanted more.

The Directors, however, found it very difficult to meet Coen's demands. Though there were no serious objections to the export of precious metals from Holland, there was a limit to the amount of capital that the Directors were in a position to send to the East Indies. Whereas the total share capital of the Company was less than $f.6.5$ million, its total debts in 1623 stood at $f.8$ million. Although merchants of good standing could obtain credit in Amsterdam at between 3 and 4.5 per cent, the Dutch East India Company in its early years

---

[26] J.E. Heeres (ed.), *Corpus-Diplomaticum Neerlando-Indicum*, The Hague, 1907, vol. 1, p. 154.

had to pay as much as 6.25 per cent. Resources for the development of intra-Asian trade, therefore, had to be found largely within Asia.

In addition to pepper and other spices, the key commodity in Coen's blueprint was Indian textiles, which had to be paid for in Coromandel mainly in gold, and in Gujarat mainly in silver. It was, therefore, imperative to establish trade relations with Asian sources of precious metals – whether they were themselves producers of these metals or were obtaining them through trade. By far the most important Asian producer of precious metals at this time was Japan. The discovery and working of new silver mines in the sixteenth century had turned Japan into the second largest producer of silver in the world next only to the Spanish American mines in the New World. In addition to its own output, Asia also received considerable quantities of the New World silver through trade. In addition to the lots brought in by the Portuguese and the European companies via the Cape of Good Hope, large quantities of this silver also reached the Red Sea and the Persian Gulf region via the Levant. Another route through which American silver reached Asia was the galleon trade between Acapulco and Manila. Since the Manila trade, controlled by the Spanish, was out of the reach of the Dutch, the two principal areas of interest to them were Japan and the Middle East.

A factory was established at Hirado in southwestern Japan in 1609. Although items such as fine-quality cotton textiles, spices, sugar, lead, quicksilver and musk could be sold in Japan, the principal items in demand there during the early period of Dutch trade were Chinese silk, silk textiles and other Chinese goods. The Dutch initially tried to obtain Chinese goods in the Indonesian archipelago and the Malay peninsula. Indeed, the establishment of trade relations with places such as Patani and Siam, and later with Cambodia, Annam and Tonkin, was partly in the quest for Chinese goods. But success was limited, and attempts were made almost from the very beginning of trading relations with Japan to establish a trading post, by force if necessary, on the coast of China or in its immediate vicinity. The efforts to blockade Chinese trade with Manila were followed by an attack on Macao in 1622 and the subsequent occupation of the Pescadores. But soon thereafter, in 1624, the Dutch were persuaded to move to Taiwan in return for an informal agreement that Chinese merchants would be allowed to go there to trade with them. The principal commodities procured by the Company in Taiwan were Chinese silk and silk textiles for the Japanese market. A part of the silver obtained from Japan in exchange for the Chinese goods was then invested in getting not only the next round of silk in Taiwan but also gold needed chiefly for the crucial Coromandel trade. Gold was procured in Taiwan rather than directly in Japan until the former was lost to the forces of Coxinga in 1662. This was done chiefly to take advantage of the very different gold/silver parity in the two places until 1637 favouring the procurement of gold in Taiwan. From 1641 in any case the export of gold from Japan was banned. This was a sequel to the 1636 closure of the country to all foreigners except the Chinese and the Dutch, the latter being required in May 1641 to move to the islet of Deshima off the Nagasaki harbour.

In the meantime, efforts had been going on to widen further the supply base of the raw silk and the silk textiles required for the Japan trade. From the early 1640s on, Bengal emerged as a major supplier of raw silk for Japan. Ever since 1615, the factors at Coromandel had been trying to find a foothold in Bengal, which at that time was looked upon basically as a potential source for textiles, sugar and saltpetre. But in so far as the Bengal goods could be procured at Coromandel itself, where they were regularly imported by the Indian merchants, the efforts to establish a factory in Bengal lacked intensity and seriousness of purpose. It was only after the factors at Agra drew Batavia's attention in 1630 to the import by Indian merchants of a large quantity of relatively inexpensive raw silk from Bengal into Agra each year and enclosed a sample of the product with their report that the requisite urgency was imparted to the Bengal project. The Mughal expulsion of the Portuguese from Hugli in 1632 helped. A factory was established at Hariharpur in Orissa in 1633, and another at Hugli in 1635. Bengal raw silk was included in the Dutch cargo for Japan for the first time in 1640 and soon became a major constituent item of this cargo.

The last of the major Indian regions figuring in the Company's intra-Asian trade was the southwest coast of India, comprising the Malabar and the Kanara coasts. After several abortive visits to the region by the Dutch factors, a treaty was signed between the Company and the Samudri raja of Calicut in January 1626. The treaty stipulated that all pepper and ginger grown in the region would be supplied to the Dutch at a fixed price, and that no export or import duties would be charged from the Company. But since no ships or capital could be spared for Calicut over the following several years, the treaty remained a dead letter. In 1633 and 1634, the fleets sent from Batavia to Surat were asked to call at the Malabar ports and trade there, without, however, setting up factories. Between 1636 and 1643, the Dutch fleet sent each year to blockade Goa also put in at Malabar and carried on a limited amount of trade there. In order to facilitate the blockade and generally to serve as a watchtower (*uitkijkpost*) over Goa, the Company established a small factory in 1637 at Vengurla in the kingdom of Bijapur on the Kanara coast under the direct jurisdiction of Batavia. In Malabar, a factory was eventually set up in Kayakulam in 1647. But the resumption of hostilities with the Portuguese after the end of the Ten Years' Truce in 1652 forced a withdrawal of the factory. It was only in 1663 when the Dutch, collaborating with the Raja of Cochin, managed to throw the Portuguese out that the Dutch trade at Malabar began on a regular and substantive basis. The strategic role of the Vengurla factory now came to an end. It was placed under the charge of the chief factory at Surat in 1673 and for all practical purposes abandoned in 1685, though formal orders for its closure were not issued until 1692.

Efforts to reach the other major Asian source of precious metals, namely the Red Sea and the Persian Gulf region at the other extremity of the great arc of Asian trade, had also been initiated quite early, using the Company's establishment at Surat as the base. As early as 1616, attempts were made to establish trade relations with Mocha. But in 1624, following problems arising out of the seizure of two ships belonging to the port of Dabhol, the Company had no option but to abandon the factory for good. As far as Persia was concerned, a factory was established at Gombroon in 1623. Initially, Persia was in fact a net absorber of precious metals rather than a net supplier. The principal item procured there at this time was raw silk in exchange for goods such as pepper and other spices, Japanese copper and Indian textiles, and precious metals. Between 1622 and 1634, several of the ships from Holland were sent directly to Surat and Persia with fair amounts of capital. In 1624–5, for example, three of these ships carried ƒ.600,000 to these factories, constituting nearly one third of the total precious metals sent to Asia that year.[27] But this pattern lasted only for a brief while, and from 1643 Persia emerged as

[27] Gaastra, 'De Verenigde Oost-Indische Compagnie in de 17de en de 18de eeuw', p. 261.

a net supplier of silver *abassies* and gold *ducats*, which were smuggled out on a regular basis, often by concealing them in cavities made into the bales of raw silk.[28] The resultant loss in the value of silk was evidently an acceptable price to pay for getting hold of the silver and gold coins. From a comparatively modest sum of $f.235,000$ in 1642–3, the value of these coins came to exceed a million florins in 1649–50. The average annual value of the coins smuggled out over the following decade was $f.660,712$.[29] But over the rest of the seventeenth century, the sums involved were extremely modest, if they were at all positive, and it was only around 1700 that, for a few years, Persia again became a major – in fact the most important – provider of precious metals in Asia.[30]

What the above analysis establishes quite definitively is that by about the middle of the seventeenth century the Dutch East India Company had become a major participant in intra-Asian trade with trading links all along the great arc of Asian trade. The crucial role played by this trade in the overall commercial strategy of the Company was summed up neatly by the Heren XVII in 1648 as follows: 'The intra-Asian trade and the profit from it are the soul of the Company which must be looked after carefully because if the soul decays, the entire body would be destroyed.'[31] Three years later, the Directors even expressed the hope that at some point it would be possible for Batavia not only to finance the exports to Europe (which in 1650–1 amounted to $f.2.49$ million) wholly out of the profits from intra-Asian trade, but also to send to them in addition some Asian precious metals. Although such extravagant hopes were never realized, the fact remains that, throughout the seventeenth century, participation in intra-Asian trade was of great advantage to the Company. Note that between 1640 and 1688 the invoice value of the return cargo from Asia amounted to approximately $f.150$ million as against $f.120$ million-worth of precious metals and goods exported to Asia over the same period. Thus about 20 per cent of the return cargo represented the profits from intra-Asian trade. Considering that the total proceeds from the sale of the return cargo amounted to $f.420$ million, the sales

[28] Glamann, *Dutch–Asiatic Trade*, p. 120.
[29] Gaastra, 'The exports of precious metals from Europe to Asia', Appendix 4, Table 1.
[30] The average annual sum exported between 1700–1 and 1703–4 was $f.873,560$ (calculated from Gaastra, 'The exports of precious metals from Europe to Asia', Appendix 4, Table 2, p. 475).
[31] *Algemeen Rijksarchief* (ARA), Heren XVII to Batavia, 22.9.1648, VOC 317, f.120v.

value of 20 per cent of the cargo would amount to ƒ.84 million. This amount was more than sufficient to cover the sum of ƒ.67 million paid out as dividend by the Company over the period.[32]

The expansion of trade into vitally important areas was critically dependent on the growing availability of precious metals, a large chunk of which was found throughout the greater part of the century within Asia. Evidence available in the Company's archives, including the 'General journals kept by the Bookkeeper-General at Batavia for the period 1700–1 to 1789–90', enables us partially to reconstruct the resource flows to the Indian factories over the two centuries of the Company's trade in the region. The findings are summarized in Table 3.3. It need hardly be emphasized that there are significant gaps in the information available. The non-availability of the regional distribution on a systematic basis of the origin of the precious metals brought by the Company into Gujarat and Bengal during the seventeenth century is only one of these. Even when such a distribution is available for the eighteenth century, and in the case of Coromandel also for the seventeenth, the degree of precision that can be achieved is limited. This is because the precious metals exported from Batavia included lots received from Holland as well as from sources within Asia. The figures in the column numbered 5 of the table, therefore, constitute only the floor of the amounts originating within Asia. But even if only the figures in this column are taken into account, the overwhelming role of Asia in the precious metals brought into Coromandel right through to 1680 is established conclusively. For Bengal, the occasional and non-systematic information available also underscores the important role of Asia, particularly Japan, in the mix of precious metals sent to the region in the seventeenth century. Finally, as far as Gujarat is concerned, the available information suggests a pattern where the precious metals imported until the 1630s originated mainly in Holland, and thereafter increasingly in Japan and the Middle East. The domination of Japan was particularly marked between 1638–9 and 1644–5, as was that of Persia over the following fifteen years or so.[33]

The table also provides strong confirmation of the dominant role of precious metals in the total imports of the Company into India. The

[32] F.S. Gaastra, *Bewind en Beleid bij de VOC. De Financiele and Commerciële Politiek van de Bewindhebbers 1672–1702*, Zutphen, 1989, p. 205.
[33] van Santen, *De Verenigde Oost-Indische Compagnie in Gujarat en Hindustan*, Table 2, p. 37.

Table 3.3 Value and the regional distribution of precious metals imported by the VOC into India, 1640–1785

Year[1]	Coromandel					Gujarat					Bengal					Malabar				
	1[2]	2	3	4	5	1	2	3	4	5	1	2	3	4	5	1	2	3	4	5
1640–50	1,846,411 (8 yrs)	NA	zero	36.8	63.2	700,500 (6 yrs)	87.6	NA	NA	NA	NA					NA				
1650–60	1,775,449 (5 yrs)	NA	zero	24.4	75.6	438,000 (3 yrs)	61.8	NA	NA	NA	NA					NA				
1660–70	1,482,339 (4 yrs)	NA	zero	36.3	63.7	66,872 (10 yrs)	15.2	NA	NA	NA	1,225,741 (7 yrs)	87.7	NA	NA	NA	NA				
1670–80	1,882,547 (1 yr)	NA	zero	24.0	76.0	zero (10 yrs)	zero	zero	zero	zero	1,090,386 (6 yrs)	77.8	NA	NA	NA	NA				
1680–90	NA					17,935 (10 yrs)	3.1	NA	NA	NA	1,167,650 (10 yrs)	74.6	NA	NA	NA	NA				
1690–1700	NA					zero (10 yrs)	zero	zero	zero	zero	2,120,169 (10 yrs)	85.1	NA	NA	NA	NA				
1701–2	905,929	73.7	zero	84.2	17.8	zero	zero				2,046,197	82.9	zero	62.0	38.0	81,198	50.2	zero	100.0	zero
1711–12	1,012,326	75.4	zero	100.0	zero	zero	zero				2,979,992	87.1	zero	100.0	zero	12,923	7.1	zero	100.0	zero
1722–3	1,180,714	75.4	zero	100.0	zero	1,502,875	85.1	zero	100.0	zero	3,884,482	95.5	zero	100.0	zero	zero	zero			
1731–2	561,689	58.8	zero	77.8	22.2[3]	zero	zero				1,781,999	84.9	zero	100.0	zero	zero	zero			
1741–2	zero	zero	zero			200,582	53.0	zero	100.0	zero	4,735,089	90.7	zero	68.3	31.7 (Coromandel)	870,167	69.3	zero	71.0	29.0 (Coromandel)
1751–2	1,005,067	42.2	zero	73.0	27.0	99,094	19.8	zero	zero	100.0 (Persia)	4,729,994	86.6	7.6	88.4	3.9	422,362	54.4	zero	5.3	94.7 (Surat)
1761–2	1,370,763	78.1	zero	100.0	zero	zero	zero				2,634,282	86.3	11.5	88.5	zero	150,000	23.0	zero	zero	100.0 (Surat)
1770–1	1,330,185	71.6	39.1	39.0	21.9	zero	zero				397,183	55.9	83.3	16.7	zero	179,535	83.6	zero	100.0	zero
1784–5[4]	zero	zero	zero			zero	zero				zero	zero				zero	zero			

Note:

[1] Until 1700, the figures are on an average annual basis.

[2] Explanation of column heading numbers:

1. Value of treasure imported in florins. The figures in parenthesis in this column for the period 1640–1700 refer to the number of years in a decade for which information is available.

2. Proportion of treasure to total value imported.

3. Proportion of treasure directly imported from Europe.

4. Proportion of treasure imported from Batavia.

5. Proportion of treasure imported from the rest of Asia.

[3] This is the amount of bills of exchange (*wissels*) issued at Coromandel and honoured by Sri Lanka.

[4] The funds invested in Bengal during this year were raised by issuing bills of exchange locally which were payable in Europe.

NA stands for not available.

Source: For the seventeenth century, the figures for Coromandel are based on information available in T. Raychaudhuri, *Jan Company in Coromandel, 1605–1690*, The Hague, 1962; for Gujarat in V.B. Gupta, 'The Dutch East India Company in Gujarat trade, 1660–1700: a study of selected aspects', unpublished PhD Thesis, University of Delhi, 1991; and for Bengal in Om Prakash, *The Dutch East India Company and the Economy of Bengal, 1630–1720*, Princeton, 1985. The eighteenth-century evidence is from the 'General Journals kept by the Bookkeeper-General at Batavia for the period 1700–1 to 1789–90', ARA, *Boekhouder-Generaal Batavia (BGB)*, 1075 I–801.

case of Gujarat, however, provides an interesting deviation from the norm of the 'bullion for goods' model for the subcontinent. While until 1660 or so precious metals constituted the bulk of the total imports into the region, the picture changed dramatically in the following decades. From a net importer of precious metals, Surat now became a net exporter of Mughal silver rupees, mainly to Bengal but also to places such as Coromandel coast and Malabar, as well as to Sri Lanka. The amounts involved, as we shall see later, were fairly large and formed an important segment of the total Dutch exports from the region. This transition from a 'bullion for goods' to a 'goods for goods and bullion' situation was made possible because of the unusually important role of Surat as a market for spices brought in by the Dutch. The other major commodity that contributed to this result was Japanese bar copper, in which again the Dutch had a monopoly. This situation lasted until the 1720s when it was again found necessary to bring precious metals into Surat. A small quantity of these metals was also imported in the 1740s. In the second half of the eighteenth century, Surat had once again turned into a net exporter of precious metals, now mainly to Cochin on the Malabar coast.

The two key factors that enabled the Dutch to achieve an enviable position in intra-Asian trade during the seventeenth century were the spice monopoly and the exclusive right to trade with Japan. The spice monopoly provided the Company with a staple item of trade in demand all over Asia and entailing an extraordinarily high rate of return. As was pointed out above, the special situation in Surat was the product largely of the Company's spice monopoly.

The Japan trade brought in large quantities of precious metals, mainly silver until 1668 and gold thereafter. It was pointed out earlier that in May 1641 the Dutch had been obliged to move to the islet of Deshima off the Nagasaki harbour. At the same time, their trade had been subjected to a variety of restrictions. For example, days were prescribed on which alone they could offer their goods for sale, until which time they had to be kept in sealed warehouses. Also, the *pancado* system was extended to the entire lot of Chinese raw silk the Company imported into Japan. This system required the Company to sell the silk at a price determined by a guild monopsony consisting of a group of merchants from the five imperial cities of Edo (Tokyo), Osaka, Kyoto, Sakai and Nagasaki. Commercially injurious as these restrictions were, the Dutch meekly accepted them. The Heren XVII, in fact, went so far as to instruct Batavia to maintain the trade, if necessary, 'even from the ships'. In a report submitted to the Directors in September 1652, Pieter Sterthemius, the chief of the Nagasaki factory during 1650–1, wrote,

But I seem to hear a whisper in my ear, that some vexations can surely be endured for the sake of Japan's sweet gains, since Japan is the strongest sinew of the Company's inland trade and of the Indies profits; and this (in so far as our self-respect allows us to endure it) is true.[34]

The 'sweet gains', of course, were the precious metals the trade provided. The relative positions of Holland and Japan in the matter of the supply of precious metals is set out in Table 3.4.

What this table suggests quite unambiguously is a clear an substantial lead for Japan between the late 1630s and the end of the 1670s. There were two further advantages associated with the procurement of precious metals in Japan as compared to Holland. In the first place, the Japanese supplies were obtained in exchange for commodities that were themselves sold at a good profit. Second, the cost per unit of silver procured seems to have been lower in Japan. If one assumes that the value that the factors in Batavia assigned to a tael of Japanese *schuit* silver in their books correctly represented its cost price, the cost of the Japanese silver works out to be 24.75 per cent lower than in Holland until 1636 and 35.58 per cent thereafter.[35] It might also be added that, in addition to the precious metals, Japan also provided large quantities of bar copper which sold at a good profit in both Asia and Europe.

In the course of the last quarter of the seventeenth century, however, things became increasingly difficult for the VOC in Japan. As Table 3.4 shows, there was a steep decline in the Dutch import of precious metals from Japan from about 1680. This was the cumulative outcome of the ban on the export of silver in 1668, the introduction of the appraised trade system in 1672 and of the limited trade system in 1685, and finally the debasement of the gold *koban* in 1696 with its gold content being reduced from 85.69 to 56.41 per cent without any reduction in its silver price of 6.8 taels.[36] In the absence of a major alternative Asian source of gold, the Company did continue to procure small quantities of gold *koban* occasionally

[34] Om Prakash, *The Dutch East India Company and the Economy of Bengal, 1630–1720*, Princeton, 1985, p. 121.

[35] Prakash, *The Dutch East India Company and the Economy of Bengal*, p. 21.

[36] Prakash, *The Dutch East India Company and the Economy of Bengal*, ch. 5.

Table 3.4 *The Dutch East India Company's import of precious metals from Holland and Japan into Batavia, 1621–99 (annual average in florins)*

Period	Holland	Japan
1621–4	1,215,000	157,924
1628–32	1,240,000	–
1633–6	1,075,000	921,044
1637	1,000,000	3,029,550
1640–9	940,000	1,518,871
1650–9	840,000	1,315,121
1660–9	1,200,000	1,454,913
1670–9	979,500	1,154,148
1680–9	1,972,000	298,383
1690–9	2,691,000	228,952

Source: The years included in the table are those for which information regarding Japan is available. Until 1637, the figures for Japan are based on Oscar Nachod, *Die Beziehungen der Niederländischen Ostindischen Kompagnie zu Japan im Siebzehnten Jahrhundert*, Leipzig, 1897, Appendix, Table E, pp. ccvii–ccviii. The figures for 1621–4 are given in Nachod directly in florins but those after 1624 are in taels. The rate of conversion used here is the same as that used by the Company: 61.5 stuivers to a tael until 1636 and 57 stuivers to a tael for 1637. The figures for 1640–99 are based on Glamann, *Dutch–Asiatic Trade*, Table III, p.51, who bases these on Nachod and other sources. Until 1662 the imports from Japan were entirely in silver, and from 1668 entirely in gold. For the period 1660–9, the component of gold in the average annual figure of ƒ.1,454,913 was ƒ.406,902 (or 28 per cent). The figures for Holland have been calculated from Bruijn, Gaastra and Schöffer, *Dutch–Asiatic Shipping*, vol. I. Appendix 4, Table 46 with a one-year lag.

until the middle of the eighteenth century, but the critical role of Japan in promoting the Company's intra-Asian trade had come to an end in 1696.

The declining volume as well as profitability of intra-Asian trade in precious metals was perhaps an important element in the changing fortunes of the Company in the matter of the profitability of the intra-Asian trade in general as between the seventeenth and the eighteenth centuries. It has been estimated that while in the seventeenth century as much as 90 per cent of the total income earned by the Company in Asia was derived from trade, the proportion came down over the eighteenth century to around 60 per cent, the remainder of the income being contributed by items such as taxes and tolls.[37] Of course, as the work of de Korte on the Company's finances shows, the eighteenth century also was not a homogeneous unit in this respect. Indeed, in the course of the century, the Company's Asian income from trade (*generale winsten*) fluctuated a great deal with a significant and irreversible decline being registered only from 1768–9 onward. The average annual income earned by the Company from Asian trade, calculated on a decadal basis, was over *f*.4 million during the first four decades of the century, over *f*.6 million during the 1740s and the 1750s, *f*.4 million during the 1760s, and a little over *f*.2.5 million during the 1770s and the 1780s.[38]

Another index that suggests a relatively declining participation by the VOC in Asian trade is the lower absorption rate into intra-Asian trade of shipping coming in from Holland in the eighteenth century. The relevant information is summarized in Table 3.5. Before we draw our conclusions from the table, however, it might be useful to note the limitations of this data base. For one thing, the absorption rate in the Asian trade worked out on the basis of the difference between the number of ships (and the volume of tonnage) arriving into and leaving Asia would overstate the real absorption rate for several reasons. In the first place, by virtue of its age or for other reasons, a ship might simply be pulled out of service after arrival in Asia. It would then not be included in the shipping returning to Europe, but at the same time would not have been available for use in intra-Asian trade. Also, of the shipping pressed into service in Asia, a certain amount was not used for purposes of trade but for patrolling, armed combat and so on. Besides, in the eighteenth century, the apparently high absorption rate of the 1780s is likely to have been related to the problems in sending

---

[37] F.S. Gaastra, *De Geschiedenis van de VOC*, Zutphen, 1991, p. 133.

[38] J.P. de Korte, *De Jaarlykse Financiele Verantwoording in de Verenigde Oost Indische Compagnie*, Leiden, 1984, Appendix 10. The precise average annual figures on a decadal basis were as follows:

1700/1–1709/10	*f*.4,192,286
1710/11–1719/20	*f*.4,487,979
1720/1–1729/30	*f*.4,287,878
1730/1–1739/40	*f*.4,514,343
1740/1–1749/50	*f*.6,081,362
1750/1–1759/60	*f*.6,267,012
1760/1–1769/70	*f*.4,086,227
1770/1–1779/80	*f*.2,537,701
1780/1–1789/90	*f*.2,768,002

Table 3.5 *Dutch East India Company shipping arriving at and leaving Asia, 1602–1794*

Years	No. of ships arriving in Asia	Tonnage arriving in Asia	No. of ships leaving Asia	Tonnage leaving Asia	Proportion of arriving ships absorbed in Asia	Proportion of arriving tonnage absorbed in Asia
1602–10	69	33,370	47	20,100	31.9	39.8
1610–20	114	55,410	46	26,590	59.6	52.0
1620–30	130	50,960	68	35,280	47.7	30.8
1630–40	154	62,640	72	38,890	53.2	37.9
1640–50	165	100,950	92	73,740	44.2	27.0
1650–60	196	118,341	102	84,200	48.0	28.8
1660–70	228	125,186	115	79,313	49.6	36.6
1670–80	218	142,289	129	91,975	40.8	35.5
1680–90	196	126,619	133	98,165	32.1	22.5
1690–1700	223	138,827	145	100,697	35.0	27.5
1700–10	271	180,620	188	133,437	30.6	26.1
1710–20	297	220,074	240	182,164	19.2	17.2
1720–30	353	272,103	308	243,314	13.7	10.6
1730–40	363	270,095	290	221,205	20.1	18.1
1740–50	307	246,565	215	170,155	30.0	31.0
1750–60	287	276,295	234	227,650	18.5	17.6
1760–70	288	287,845	223	222,450	22.6	26.7
1770–80	287	287,190	231	230,670	19.5	19.7
1780–90	288	233,850	197	144,093	31.6	38.4
1790–94	106	84,943	85	66,370	19.8	21.9

Source: Calculated from Bruijn, Gaastra and Schöffer, *Dutch–Asiatic Shipping*, vol. I, Tables 35 and 36, pp. 174–6.

ships back to Europe because of the Fourth Anglo-Dutch War. An acute shortage of sailors would have produced a similar result in the 1790s. On the other hand, in so far as the Company occasionally bought vessels in Asia which were used exclusively in intra-Asian trade, the absorption rate suggested by the table would understate the real absorption rate of shipping in Asian trade. In the absence of the relevant information, the bias in neither direction can be corrected, though perhaps it was not particularly pronounced in either and was in part at least self-cancelling. The other problem with the data pertains to the fact that the ships permanently absorbed in intra-Asian trade might very well have had very different working lifespans depending partly upon the stage of their life at which they had been kept back in Asia. This would necessarily leave a certain margin of error in the conclusions drawn from the table.

Subject to these limitations, the main conclusions suggested by the table are as follows. In terms of the absolute number of ships absorbed in Asian trade there was a decline from 744 in the seventeenth century (98 years) to 640 in the eighteenth (94 years). In terms of tonnage, however, the volume had gone up over the same period from 305,642 tons to 518,072 tons. But in relative terms, the decline between the seventeenth and the eighteenth century is unambiguous and fairly significant in terms both of the number of ships as well as the volume of tonnage. Thus the proportion of ships absorbed in Asian trade came down from an average of 44 per cent in the seventeenth century to 23.5 per cent during the eighteenth. The corresponding values for the volume of tonnage were 32.1 per cent and 22 per cent, respectively.

THE TRADING STRATEGY OF THE ENGLISH EAST INDIA COMPANY

The evolution of the English East India Company's trading strategy in Asia was along very different lines. Nevertheless, the pattern of its exports to the East was quite similar to that of the VOC. The commodities exported included broadcloth, draperies and lead, but the dominant item throughout was precious metals, mainly silver. As Table 3.6 shows, treasure accounted approximately for between 65 and 90 per cent of the total English exports to Asia. In the second half of the eighteenth century, an overwhelming proportion of the total purchasing power in the East was generated by issuing bills of exchange on London and other places in favour not only of the Company's own servants, but of a large range of other private European traders as well. The other major source used by the Dutch to supplement the resources received from home, namely the precious metals earned within Asia, was, however, never available to the English.

Like other Europeans, the principal interest of the English in the East, initially at least, was the procurement of pepper and other spices for the European market. The first two voyages were directed at Bantam in Java where a factory was established in 1602. From 1613,

Table 3.6 *English East India Company exports to Asia, 1601–1760*
(average annual value in £sterling (£1 = f.12)

Years	Total exports	Treasure (%)
1601–10	17,096	69.7
1611–20	76,009	64.5
1621–30	44,152	91.3
1631–40	47,670	79.1
1661–70	133,463	67.0
1671–80	342,891	74.2
1681–90	402,566	84.0
1691–1700	299,352	71.3
1701–10	407,662	87.4
1711–20	513,871	80.6
1721–30	650,008	83.5
1731–40	648,518	76.0
1741–50	819,287	73.6
1751–60	988,588	65.6

Source: The figures for the period 1601–40 have been calculated from Chaudhuri, *The English East India Company*, Table II, p. 115. It has been assumed that in the years not listed in the table the exports were zero.

The figures for the period 1661–1760 have been calculated from Chaudhuri, *The Trading World of Asia and the English East India Company, 1660–1760*, Appendix 5, Tables C1 and C4, pp. 507, 512.

Sumatra became the chief supplier of pepper to the Company. Factories were established at Acheh, Tiku and Priaman, but the factory at Bantam remained the headquarters of the Company's trading organization in the region. The crucial importance of the Coromandel textiles in facilitating this trade and making it more profitable had also been brought home to the Company quite early. In 1610, therefore, it accepted the offer of two Dutchmen, Peter Floris and Lucas Atheunis, to set up a factory on the coast of Coromandel and supply textiles for the southeast Asian markets. Floris and Atheunis established a factory at Masulipatnam in 1611, though the first Company voyage to the coast was organized only in 1614. In the meantime, given the Dutch monopolistic designs in the archipelago, a situation of armed conflict with the VOC was becoming inevitable. The hostilities erupted in 1618, and the English emerged distinctly the

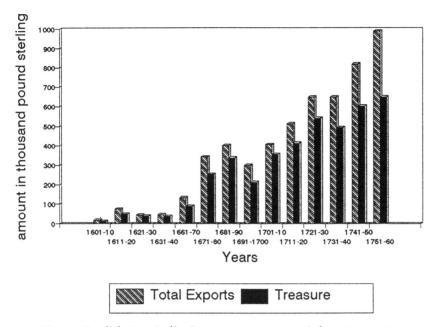

Fig.3.2 English East India Company exports to Asia, 1601–1760
(annual average)

worst of the two. The London agreement of 1619 provided for an English share of one third in the trade of the Spice Islands, and of one half in the pepper trade of Java subject to the English contributing one third of the cost of maintaining the Dutch garrisons in the area. The English headquarters in the area were moved to Batavia in 1620 and the two companies shared garrisons in the Bandas, Moluccas and Amboyna. But due both to Dutch hostility as well as to the shortage of resources of the English, the arrangement did not quite work. The 1623 incident at Amboyna led to a recall of the English factors from the shared centres in the archipelago to Batavia and hastened the process of the English withdrawal from the Spice Islands. By 1624, the factories at Patani, Ayutthaya and Japan had also been abandoned. From this point on, pepper was procured mainly at Bantam to which the English had moved back from Batavia, and cloves at Makassar, where a factory had been established in 1613. As D.K. Bassett has demonstrated, the English were among the major buyers of the cloves smuggled in large quantities into this port until 1643 both by the merchants from Makassar as well as by those operating from several of the Malayan ports. An important medium of exchange used in both Bantam and Makassar was the textiles from the Coromandel coast. In the mid-1620s, the English established another factory on the Coromandel coast at Armagon. The Anglo-Portuguese truce made possible the establishment of an English factory in 1640 at Madras as well, which in September 1641 was designated as the chief factory of Coromandel. In 1682, the Dutch forced the English out of Bantam, and from 1685 the only English establishment in the Indonesian archipelago was at Benkulen in Sumatra.

While the English had come to Coromandel in quest of textiles for the southeast Asian markets, their attempts to penetrate the Gujarat trade were linked directly to their Euro-Asian trade. Because of the possibility of a military engagement with the Portuguese and/or the Dutch, each of the English voyages to the East consisted of a certain minimum number of ships. But on the return voyage, a cargo consisting of pepper and other spices alone would fill perhaps only one of these ships. Hence the urgent need to diversify the return cargo by including in it items such as Indian textiles and indigo. Gujarat textiles could, of course, also be used for the southeast Asian trade to the extent necessary. The third voyage sent out in 1608, therefore, carried instructions to explore the commercial possibilities of the western coast of India. William Hawkins reached Surat in 1608 and went on to Agra the following year, but was unable to obtain trading rights. Henry Middleton, the commander of the sixth voyage, was also refused permission to trade at Surat. It was only in September 1612 that Thomas Best finally managed to obtain formal trading rights. A factory was established at Surat in 1613 and regular trade started there and at Ahmedabad, Burhanpur and Agra. A ship was sent back home directly from Surat for the first time in 1615. Between 1616 and 1617, while only four small ships were dispatched directly to Bantam from London, nine ships of large tonnage were sent to Surat. The President at Surat was also placed in charge of the Company's trade in Persia. The Crown leased Bombay to the Company in 1668: in 1687 it superseded Surat as the headquarters of the Company in western India. In the meantime, the Company's trade had extended into Bengal in the early 1650s with the establishment of a factory at Hugli.

Table 3.7 *French East India Company's exports to Asia, 1725–69*
(figures in livres tournois ($1 LT = f.o.5$)

(1) Years	(2) Average annual value of total exports (LT)	(3) Average annual value of treasure exported (LT)	(4) Proportion of treasure to total exports (%)	(5) Average annual value of treasure earmarked for India (LT)	(6) Treasure earmarked for India as proportion of total treasure (%)
1725/6 to 1734/5	6,976,174	6,014,325	86.2	3,891,666	74.2
1735/6 to 1744/5	11,428,789	9,419,610	82.4	7,293,689	77.5
1745/6 to 1754/5	13,095,305	9,857,508	75.2	9,095,913	92.2
1755/6 to 1764/5	4,300,516	2,971,994	69.1	NA	
1765/6 to 1768/9	10,113,855	5,596,522	55.3	NA	

Note: NA stands for not available.
Source: Calculated from Philippe Haudrère, *La Compagnie française des Indes au XVIIIe siècle 1719–1795*, Paris 1989, vol. IV, Tables II E and F, pp. 1196–98.

Information regarding India is available over the first decade for only three years, 1727/8 to 1729/30. The figure for this decade in column 5 is, therefore, a three-year average. In working out the proportion in column 6 also, information pertaining to only these three years has been taken into account for both India as well as the total. For the decade 1735/6 to 1744/5, the only year for which information for India is not available is 1735/6. This year has, therefore, been left out of account in working out the figure in column 6 as well. Information for the decade 1745/6 to 1754/5 is available for all years.

FRENCH EXPORTS TO ASIA

The last of the major European trading companies to engage in Euro-Asian trade was the French East India Company. Quantitative information available in respect of the Compagnie Perpetuelle des Indes suggests that the pattern of French exports to Asia in the eighteenth century was the usual one of the domination of the export bill by precious metals. The information is set out in Table 3.7. Over the period 1725 to 1755, for which a destination-wise regional breakdown of the precious metals exported is also available, the domination of India, accounting for between 74 and 92 per cent of the total treasure exported, is unmistakable. The involvement of the Company in the China trade, the other major theatre of French Company activity in Asia, was on a much smaller scale at this time.

The French started out in India in Surat where François Martin arrived in October 1668. Martin was also responsible for setting up the Company's establishment on the Coromandel coast at Pondicherry in 1674 after the dust raised by the fiasco of the capture and subsequent loss of São Tomé by Commander de la Haye had settled down. Pondicherry, which became the headquarters of the French in India, was seized by the Dutch in 1693 but restored to them in the peace of 1697. The French actually reoccupied Pondicherry only in 1699. The extension of French trade into Bengal had begun in 1686 when an agent had been sent there by Martin to found a factory. Trading posts were established at Balasore, Kasimbazar and Patna, but the real beginning of French trade in the region should perhaps be dated to the acquisition of Chandernagore by Martin's son-in-law Deslandes in 1690, the same year as Calcutta was founded by Job Charnock.

CHAPTER 4

THE COMPANIES IN INDIA: THE POLITICS AND THE ECONOMICS OF TRADE

The history of the European companies' trading operations in India over the seventeenth and eighteenth centuries in the context of their overall trade in Asia can be broadly divided into three fairly distinct phases with the cut-off points lying approximately around 1680 and 1740. In the case of the Dutch East India Company, the phase until about 1680 was basically one where the importance of the Indian trade was derived chiefly from its role in the Company's intra-Asian trade. Textiles from Coromandel and Gujarat were indispensable for the procurement of pepper and other spices, while raw silk from Bengal had become the mainstay of the bullion-supplying Japan trade. In the period after about 1680, the drastically altered composition of the imports into Europe, with a dominant role for Indian textiles and raw silk, ensured a continuing critical role for India, though it was now basically in the Company's Euro-Asian trade. This phase lasted until about 1740, when the dominant role of India was challenged to a certain extent by Chinese tea, which now accounted for around one third of the total imports from Asia, though later this figure came down to about a quarter.

Basically the same time division is applicable in the case of the English East India Company. Also, the English Company's emergence as a political power in the subcontinent in the latter half of the eighteenth century puts this period into a category by itself. The newly acquired power of the English had a variety of consequences. For the rival European trading companies, including the Dutch, this meant that they could no longer operate on a basis of equality, but were essentially on sufferance and subject to all kinds of arbitrary regulations and restrictions imposed on them by the English. The implications of European trade for the Indian economy were also altered significantly. In a region such as Bengal, the relationship between the English East India Company on the one hand, and the local producers and merchants on the other, was no longer determined

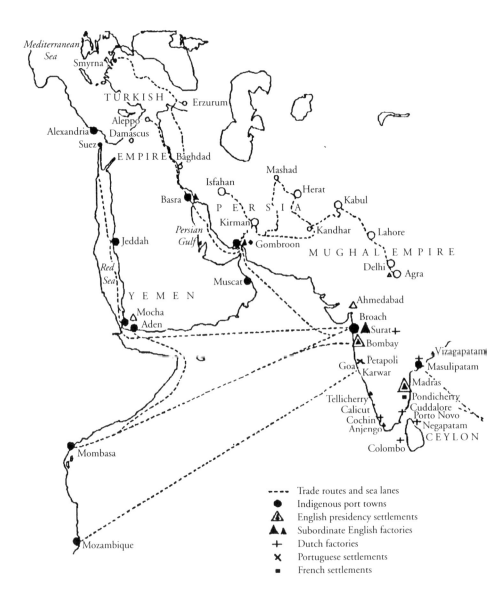

Map 3 The Indian Ocean in the seventeenth and eighteenth
centuries, showing the settlements of the English East India
Company and of other European nations

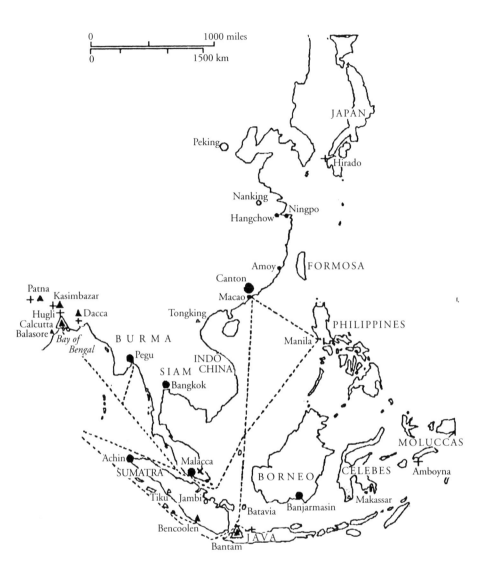

by the market but became one of domination by the Company over these groups, depriving them of the full extent of their legitimate share in the value of the output produced.

THE DUTCH COMPANY IMPORTS INTO EUROPE

The available evidence permits the construction of a fairly detailed quantitative profile of the trading operations of both the Dutch and the English East India companies. As far as the VOC is concerned, a broad idea of the growing value as well as the changing composition of the Company's imports from Asia into Europe through the seventeenth and the eighteenth centuries can be formed from the work of Kristof Glamann, recently extended by Bruijn, Gaastra and Schöffer. The information is set out in Table 4.1. As far as the value of the imports is concerned, there was a significant upward trend all the way. Thus from a modest figure of under $f.3$ million over the three-year period 1619–21, the imports had crossed the $f.10$ million mark by 1668–70 and stood at $f.15$ million during 1698–1700. Given the large base at the beginning of the eighteenth century, the rate of growth over that century was naturally much lower, but the absolute value of imports was nevertheless in excess of $f.19$ million during 1738–40 and nearly $f.21$ million during 1778–80. Equally important was the changing composition of the imports. Pepper and spices together came down from an imposing 74 per cent of the total imports in 1619–21 and 68 per cent during 1648–50 to 23 per cent during 1698–1700 and to a mere 12 per cent during 1778–80.[1] On the other hand, textiles and raw silk went up from 16 per cent in 1619–21 to an incredible 55 per cent at the end of the seventeenth century. There was a decline thereafter, but in 1778–80 this group again accounted for half of the total imports. Equally important was the rise in the share of tea and coffee in the eighteenth century. From a mere 4 per cent in 1698–1700, the figure went up to an impressive 27 per cent in 1778–80, with a peak of 32 per cent in between during 1738–40. The table also highlights the critical value of the Company's spice monopoly. Here was a group where the

---

[1] This, however, should not obscure the fact that, in absolute terms, the trend over the same period had been of a very different kind. The invoice value of this group had gone up from $f.2.15$ million in 1619–21 to $f.4.2$ million in 1648–50, down to $f.3.45$ million in 1698–1700 and finally to $f.2.5$ million in 1778–80. Note that the terminal value was actually higher than the initial one.

Table 4.1 *Triennial totals and composition of the Dutch East India Company's imports into Europe, 1619–1780*

Goods	1619–21		1648–50			1668–70²			1698–1700			1738–40			1778–80		
	1¹	2	1	2	3	1	2	3	1	2	3	1	2	3	1	2	3
Pepper	1,638,500	56.45	3,168,900	50.43	32.89	3,294,000	30.53	28.99	1,680,000	11.23	13.31	1,561,000	8.1	11.43	1,868,100	9.0	11.03
Other spices	510,400	17.55	1,127,700	17.85	26.36	1,306,800	12.05	28.43	1,755,000	11.70	24.78	1,182,600	6.1	23.63	642,900	3.1	24.43
Textiles and raw silk	466,900	16.06	894,600	14.16	17.54	3,942,000	36.46	23.77	8,205,000	54.73	43.45	7,918,600	41.1	28.27	10,283,200	49.5	32.66
Tea and coffee	—	—	—	—	—	—	—	—	630,000	4.24	4.10	6,202,100	32.2	24.22	5,652,300	27.2	22.92
Drugs, perfumes and dye-stuffs	284,200	9.84	535,500	8.52	7.35	626,400	5.84	5.86	1,245,000	8.29	6.57	532,000	2.8	2.70	380,700	1.8	2.29
Sugar	—	—	403,200	6.39	8.80	453,600	4.24	2.02	45,000	0.24	0.20	710,000	3.7	3.00	133,000	0.6	0.61
Saltpetre	—	—	132,200	2.07	4.30	550,800	5.08	7.63	585,000	3.92	4.00	504,400	2.6	3.54	909,700	4.4	2.79
Metals	2,900	0.10	31,500	0.50	0.70	615,600	5.74	2.99	795,000	5.26	2.94	202,100	1.1	0.58	569,000	2.7	1.37
Sundries	—	—	12,600	0.17	2.06	10,800	0.06	0.28	60,000	0.39	0.65	433,900	2.3	1.93	357,600	1.7	1.90
TOTAL	2,902,900		6,306,200			10,800,000			15,000,000			19,246,700			20,796,500		

Note: ¹ Explanation of column headings:

Column 1 = Total value of imports over the triennium (in florins)

Column 2 = Percentage of total invoice value

Column 3 = Percentage of total sales proceeds at Amsterdam.

² Only two out of nine ships from Sri Lanka included.

Source: J.R. Bruijn, F.S. Gaastra and I. Schöffer, *Dutch–Asiatic Shipping in the 17th and 18th Centuries*, The Hague, 1987, vol. I, Table 41, p. 192.

Figs. 4.1.1–4.1.6 Triennial totals and composition of the Dutch East India Company's imports into Europe, 1619–1780

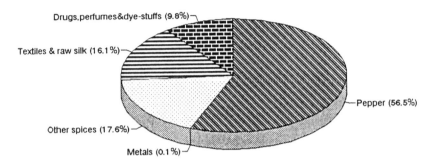

Fig. 4.1.1 1619–21

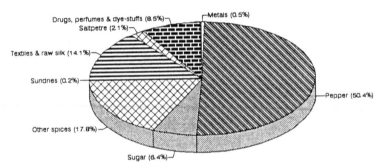

Fig. 4.1.2 1648–50

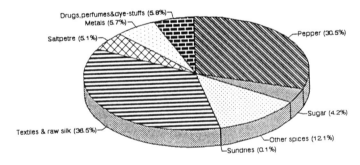

Fig. 4.1.3 1668–70

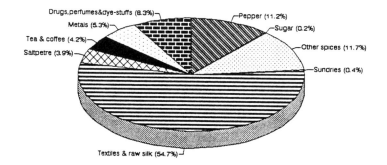

Fig. 4.1.4 1698–1700

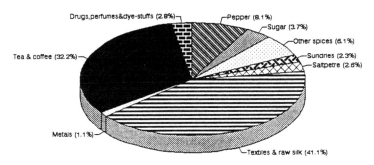

Fig. 4.1.5 1738–40

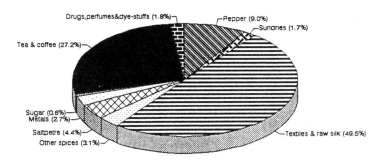

Fig. 4.1.6 1778–80

share in the sales proceeds was consistently higher than the share in the invoice value. Over time, this differential in fact increased fairly substantially till in 1778–80, against a share of a mere 3 per cent in the invoice value, the share in the sales proceeds was as much as 24 per cent. In the case of pepper, except in the years 1648–50 when the share in the sales proceeds was considerably lower, the two values were generally similar. Finally, in the case of both the textiles and raw silk and the tea and coffee groups, the share in the sales proceeds was generally lower – sometimes substantially lower – than the share in the invoice value. This was a necessary corollary of the differential in the case of spices being significantly in the other direction.

India figured prominently in the Company's trade within Asia as well as that between Asia and Europe. Items such as saltpetre and indigo, used extensively in the Europe trade, as well as opium, which figured prominently in the intra-Asian trade, were procured almost exclusively in India. The principal importance of the India trade, however, lay in the supply of textiles and raw silk for both the Asian and the European markets.

THE ENGLISH COMPANY IMPORTS
INTO EUROPE

The available data set in respect of the English East India Company covers the period from about 1660 to 1780. In order to facilitate a comparison with the VOC to the extent possible, this information has been put together in Tables 4.2 and 4.3 for the trienniums 1668–70, 1698–1700, 1738–40, 1758–60 and 1777–9. It will be noted that until 1670, the English Company was way behind the Dutch, accounting for only $f.4.32$ million worth of imports during 1668–70 against the Dutch figure of $f.10.78$ million. This gap had nearly been bridged by 1698–1700 when the English imports had reached $f.13.79$ million against the Dutch figure of $f.15$ million. This process continued in the eighteenth century, and by 1738–40 the English had actually forged ahead of the Dutch, accounting for $f.23$ million against the VOC figure of $f.19.24$ million. Note, however, that this comparison pertains only to the Euro-Asian trade carried on by the two companies. For the still substantial intra-Asian trade of the Dutch there was no English counterpart. Thus with regard to the total value of trade carried on in Asia, the Dutch, in all likelihood, were still considerably ahead of the English. But by the time the close of the 1770s is reached, there is no room for any ambiguity whatsoever. With a figure of $f.69$ million against the Dutch figure of under $f.21$ million, the English were so much ahead that an inclusion of the Dutch intra-Asian trade figure in the value of their total trade in Asia would make hardly any difference to the relative ranking of the two companies.

As far as the composition of the English imports is concerned, the absence of spices from the list is a reflection of the Dutch monopoly of this item. The changes over time included a decline in the share of pepper from 25 to under 5 per cent, and in the case of saltpetre from 8 per cent to 3 per cent. A minor item, indigo, disappeared from the list altogether in the eighteenth century. As in the case of the Dutch Company, the share of goods such as textiles, raw silk and tea, on the other hand, registered a major increase. Thus between 1668–70 and 1738–40 the share of textiles went up from 57 per cent to 70 per cent, though by 1758–60 it had come down to 54 per cent. By this time, raw silk had also become an important item of trade, accounting for 12 per cent of the total imports. The other spectacular increase was in the case of tea from nil in 1668–70 to 10 per cent in 1738–40 and as much as 25 per cent in 1758–60.

The changing composition of the imports was also reflected in the relative shares of India, southeast Asia and China in the total value imported (Table 4.3). The decline in pepper accounts for the eventual disappearance of southeast Asia from the list. The rise in the share of China was linked almost entirely to tea. India was central to the English Company trade throughout, accounting for 95 per cent and 84 per cent of total imports during 1698–1700 and 1738–40, respectively, when the textile trade was at its peak. During 1758–60, India and China accounted for two thirds and one third of the total imports, respectively. By 1777–9, the share of India had once again gone up to 78 per cent. Within India, by virtue of its status as the principal supplier of textiles and raw silk, Bengal completely dwarfed during the eighteenth century the other two Indian regions, namely Bombay and Madras.

THE FUNCTIONING OF THE COMPANIES IN INDIA: THE ABSENCE OF COERCION

The Dutch East India Company was the first northern European corporate enterprise to establish factories in India. Since the principal

Table 4.2 Triennial totals and composition of the English East India Company's imports into Europe, 1660–1779

Goods	1668–70		1698–1700		1738–40		1758–60		1777–9	
	1[1]	2	1	2	1	2	1	2	1	2
Pepper	90,996	25.25	80,719	7.02	64,701	3.37	91,585	4.37		
Textiles	203,976	56.61	850,559	73.98	1,333,094	69.58	1,119,540	53.51		
Raw silk	2,181	0.60	81,494	7.09	208,706	10.89	256,611	12.27		
Tea	120	0.03	13,082	1.13	195,951	10.22	527,901	25.23		
Coffee	1,603	0.44	22,164	1.93	50,853	2.65	–	–		
Indigo	15,325	4.25	32,532	2.82	–		–	–		
Saltpetre	27,671	7.67	17,460	1.51	35,480	1.85	62,287	2.97		
Miscellaneous		5.15		4.52		1.44		1.65		
Total value	£360,310 (=ƒ.4,323,720)		£1,149,599 (=ƒ.13,795,188)		£1,917,202 (=ƒ.23,006,424)		£2,092,040 (=ƒ.25,104,480)		£5,778,201 (=ƒ.69,338,412)	

Note: [1] Explanation of column headings:

Column 1 – Total value of imports over the triennium (in £sterling)

Column 2 – Proportion of invoice value.

Source: The figures for the years until 1760 have been calculated from K.N. Chaudhuri, *The Trading World of Asia and the English East India Company 1660–1760*, Cambridge, 1978, Appendix 5, Tables C.2, C.8, C.9, C.10, C.14, C.15, C.19 and C.24, pp. 507–48. The rate of conversion used is £1 = ƒ.12.

The figures for the years 1777–9 have been calculated from Appendix 22C, 'An account of the total prime cost of all cargoes purchased in India and China, to be shipped for Europe, for the different seasons from 1763 to 1778 inclusive, distinguishing each year', to Report from the Select Committee appointed to examine the Reports of the Directors of the East India Company dated 22 June 1784 (Parliamentary Board Collection 19, L/Parl/2/19, India Office Library). The rate of conversion used is £1 = ƒ.12. The cargoes that left Asia in 1776, 1777 and 1778 reached Europe with a time lag of a year. The commodity composition of these cargoes is not available. But the total value figure for these years is fully corroborated by information available for Bengal alone. We note in Table 4.3 that during these years, Bengal accounted for 54.28 per cent of the total English Company imports from Asia. That gives a figure of £3,136,407. Based on information available in Appendix 6 to the Ninth Report of the Select Committee, Chaudhuri puts the Bengal figure for these years at £3,136,980 (K.N. Chaudhuri, 'Foreign Trade and Balance of Payments 1757–1947' in Dharma Kumar (ed.), *The Cambridge Economic History of India*, Vol. II, Table 10.2C, p. 8 9, Cambridge, 1983).

Table 4.3 *Regional distribution by origin (percentagewise) of English Company imports into Europe, 1660–1779*

Region	1668–70	1698–1700	1738–40	1758–60	1777–9
Bombay	36.07	34.40	6.06	5.89	?
Madras	27.81	19.39	12.31	6.86	?
Bengal	12.33	41.64	65.92	52.85	54.28
Total for India	76.21	95.43	84.29	65.60	77.96
Southeast Asia	23.29	0.56	0.75	0.69	0.00
China	0.03	2.06	12.28	33.68	22.03

Source: The figures for the period until 1758–60 have been calculated from Chaudhuri, *The Trading World of Asia*, Appendix 5, Table C.2, pp. 508–10.

The figures for 1777–9 have been calculated from Appendix 22C, 'An account of the total prime cost of all cargoes purchased in India and China, to be shipped for Europe, for the different seasons from 1763 to 1778 inclusive, distinguishing each year'; and Appendix 22B, 'An account of the prime cost of investments imported from China from the year 1765 to the year 1779 inclusive, with an average for one year', to Report from the Select Committee appointed to examine the Reports of the Directors of the East India Company dated 22 June 1784 (Parliamentary Board collection 19, L/Parl/2/ India Office Library); and Appendix 6, 'Invoice amount of Investments from Bengal 1766–1780', to Ninth Report from the Select Committee appointed to take into consideration the state of the administration of justice in the provinces of Bengal, Bihar and Orissa dated 25 June 1783, L/Parl/2/15 India Office Library. The figures available are for total exports from India and China, those from China and those from Bengal. The percentage figure for India has been derived by deducting that from China from the total for India and China. To the extent that there might have been some imports from southeast Asia, the Indian figure would go down correspondingly.

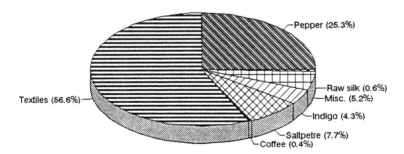

Fig. 4.2.1 1668–70

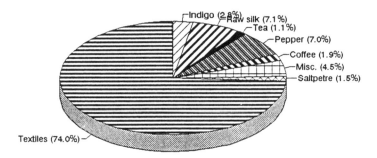

Fig. 4.2.2 1698–1700

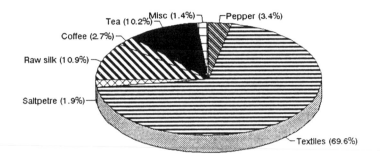

Fig. 4.2.3 1738–40

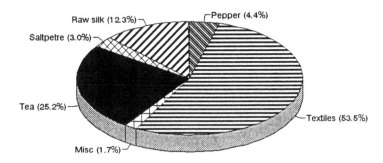

Fig 4.2.4 1758–60

Figs 4.2.1–4.2.4 Triennial totals and composition of the English
East India Company's imports into Europe, 1660–1779

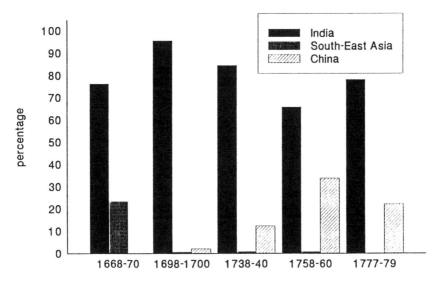

Fig. 4.3 Regional distribution by origin of English Company
imports into Europe, 1660–1779

attraction that India held for the Company at this early stage was the
possibility of procuring textiles for the Indonesian archipelago, it is
not surprising that the first establishments were set up on the
Coromandel coast, the principal source of these textiles. The other
major coastal centres of trade in the subcontinent were reached over
the following few decades. The English East India Company also
arrived on the subcontinent almost simultaneously. As we noted
earlier, there was a long tradition of foreign merchants being allowed
to operate at Asian ports under a variety of administrative arrangements. By virtue of being the leading centre of international exchange
and the meeting point of the Asian traders from the East and the West,
by far the most liberal in this regard was the port city of Malacca in
the fifteenth century. Asian merchants resident in and operating from
this port could be broadly divided into four groups: (a) the Gujaratis;
(b) other Indian merchant groups and merchants from Burma; (c) the
merchants from southeast Asia upto and including the Philippines;
and finally (d) the merchants from East Asia including the Chinese,
the Japanese and the Okinawans. Each of these four groups was
allowed to have a *shahbandar* of its own who managed the affairs of

that particular merchant-group autonomously of the local authorities. While such total autonomy was not the norm in most Asian ports and merchants visiting from other parts of the continent were subject to the discipline and the control of the local authorities, they were by and large treated well and left alone to manage their affairs themselves. This included the arrangements they might make with their local counterparts, their business dealings in the market and so on, without the administration making any undue interference in their decision-making processes. This generally positive attitude towards these merchants was in a large part conditioned by the revenue generated by these merchants for the authorities in the form of, for example, customs duties. On the arrival of the Europeans in Asia, a certain amount of deviation from this tradition was occasioned in the case of the Portuguese chiefly because of their belligerent behaviour and the use of armed strength in the initial stages of their operations in Asia. The troubles that the Portuguese had in 1501 with the samudri raja at Calicut is a case in point. The centre of pepper procurement was subsequently shifted to Cochin where the local raja was coerced into granting the Portuguese monopoly rights in pepper. It is another matter that, given the raja's lack of real control over the areas where pepper was grown or the overland routes used for its transportation across the western ghats, the monopoly never really worked in any effective sense. It is instructive to note that in 1663, when the raja of Cochin, in collaboration with the Dutch East India Company, eventually managed to throw the Portuguese out of his kingdom, he was obliged to grant identical monopoly privileges to the new European collaborator. Earlier in the century, the VOC had also managed to coerce authorities in various spice-producing islands in the Indonesian archipelago into granting to the Company monopoly rights in spices such as cloves, nutmeg and mace. The story was repeated later in the century in Sri Lanka with reference to cinnamon, areca-nuts and other goods.

From the vantage point of the Indian subcontinent, the case of the Portuguese and of the Malabar coast in general must be looked upon as exceptional. In the rest of the subcontinent, until at least the middle of the eighteenth century, the relationship between the ruling authority and the different European groups operating there was by and large an amicable one based essentially on perceived mutual advantage. The authorities basically looked upon the European companies' trade in their area as a net addition with the attendant benefits that such growth of trade entailed for the economy. More immediately, the resultant increase in the customs revenue, which in the case of the Mughal empire accrued directly to the central treasury and probably constituted a head of revenue in importance next only to land revenue, was an important consideration. An equally important consideration would seem to be the 'bullion for goods' character of the Europeans' trade. The fact that the companies paid for the goods obtained in the subcontinent overwhelmingly in terms of precious metals made them probably the single most important conduit for the import of these metals into the country. In the context of the domestic output of these metals being practically nil, their importation in reasonably large quantities was critically important for, among other things, the successful conduct of the subcontinent's monetary system. The result was that the Europeans' requests for permission to trade and the establishment of factories were granted almost as a matter of course by the imperial authorities in the case of Mughal India, and by the regional authorities in the case of the Coromandel coast. The rate of customs duty that the company concerned was obliged to pay was ordinarily the same as that payable by the Indian and other Asian merchants operating from the region. Indeed, the imperial administration often went a step further and exempted the companies from the payment of the transit (*rahdari*) duties, putting them in a position of differential advantage vis-à-vis their own nationals. It is another matter that the local and the provincial authorities, whose income streams would have been adversely affected by such an exemption, usually managed to ignore the imperial orders and continue charging the *rahdari* duties. Under this dispensation, the companies operated in the market basically as yet another group of merchants with no special privileges whatever being available to them in their dealings with the Indian merchants or artisans. By the same token, they were at liberty to function in the system like any other merchant group, indigenous or foreign, with no restrictions whatsoever on their using the various infrastructural facilities that the system had to offer. Their factors and representatives were allowed to travel anywhere in the empire, to buy and sell where they found it most profitable to do so, and to deal with their Indian counterparts on terms strictly determined by the market.

The critical significance for the Europeans of the market-determined nature of this relationship and the absence of coercion on either side is perhaps best illustrated by a brief reference to their experience in Japan both before and during the 'closed-country' era. Briefly stated, in their business dealings in this bullion-providing country the Europeans found themselves at the receiving end of an intensely coercive relationship. Under an arrangement introduced in 1604 and termed the *pancado*, the Portuguese were obliged to sell their principal import into Japan, namely Chinese raw silk, at a price determined by a guild monopsony consisting of a group of merchants from the five imperial cities of Edo (Tokyo), Osaka, Kyoto, Sakai and Nagasaki. This arrangement was part of a larger strategy adopted by the Japanese authorities to give them a measure of control over the merchants buying the imported raw silk. In 1631, when they protested against the arrangement, the Portuguese were told that they were free to leave the country. In 1633, they actually had to sell at prices lower than even the *pancado* price.[2] The same year the *pancado* arrangement was extended to cover a part of the Chinese raw silk brought in by the Dutch East India Company as well. Following the promulgation in June 1636 of the *kaikin* edict and the expulsion of the Portuguese in 1639 consequent upon the suspected involvement of the Catholic missionaries in the Shimabara rebellion in 1637, the Dutch became the only European merchant-group to be allowed to operate in Japan. In May 1641, they were ordered to move to the islet of Deshima off the Nagasaki harbour to which they were henceforth confined, cutting them off from the mainstream of Japanese life. The number of Japanese allowed access to the Dutch quarters at Deshima was kept to a minimum and the purpose of their visit limited to matters of trade. The Japanese were prohibited from learning Dutch and the Hollanders from learning Japanese; communication was permitted only through interpreters in Portuguese. The commercial restrictions imposed on the Company included a ban on the export of gold; the prescription of days on which it could offer its goods for sale, until which time they had to be kept in sealed warehouses; and the extension of the *pancado* system to the entire lot of Chinese raw silk the Company imported into Japan. The 1672 introduction of the system of *shih shobai*, which the Dutch translated as *taxatie-handel* (appraised trade), effectively extended the *pancado* system to all imports. On the basis of the

---

[2] George Bryan Souza, *The Survival of Empire: Portuguese Trade and Society in China and the South China Sea, 1630–1754*, Cambridge, 1986, p. 60.

samples collected from the Dutch factors, the different commodities imported were evaluated unilaterally by selected members of the Nagasaki Chamber of Commerce. This arrangement had an immediate and substantial adverse effect on the profitability of the trade, and in 1675 the Batavia Council wrote to the governor of Nagasaki that although the Company traded with 'all corners of the globe', it had 'never yet found a single other place where the purchaser fixed the price'.[3] The appeal that the 'appraised trade' system be rescinded, however, fell on deaf ears and the Dutch chief at Nagasaki, Martinus Ceaser, could do little but express his frustration as follows: 'But it seems that the Japanese have finally laid aside all sense of honour and decency whilst we perforce must dance to their piping in everything.'[4] It is indeed true that in spite of all this, exclusive access to the Japan trade was one of the principal differential advantages the Dutch had over their European rivals. Nevertheless, in their commercial operations in Mughal India and the Coromandel coast, they had good reason to be glad that if they did not have the monopoly privileges there that they had in the Indonesian archipelago and Sri Lanka, they were not subject there to the restrictive and coercive situation that they had to face in Japan either.

THE ESTABLISHMENT OF FACTORIES: PRIVILEGES, PERSONNEL AND SOCIAL LIFE

Coromandel

We noted above that the Dutch East India Company was the first northern European corporate enterprise to establish factories in India. The process was started on the Coromandel coast with the establishment of a factory at Petapuli on the northern segment of the coast in 1606. Another factory was established the same year in the neighbouring major port of Masulipatnam. The southern stretch of the coast was reached with the establishment of a factory at Tirupapaliyur in 1608. Finally, a factory was established in 1610 at the central Coromandel port of Pulicat which also became the headquarters of the Dutch directorate of Coromandel. The Fort Geldria was constructed

---

[3] Pieter van Dam, *Beschrijvinge van de Oost-Indische Compagnie* (ed. F.W. Stapel *et al.*), Book II, Part I, p. 454.

[4] C.R. Boxer, 'Jan Compagnie in Japan 1672–1674 or Anglo- Dutch rivalry in Japan and Formosa', *Transactions of the Asiatic Society of Japan*, second series, vol. 7, 1930, p. 170.

at Pulicat in 1613 and the Coromandel complex of factories was elevated in 1616 to the status of a 'government' with its seat at Fort Geldria. As a countermeasure against the local *havaldar*'s demands, the factory at Petapuli was closed in June 1616. Further, in view of the uncertain conditions created by the civil war that engulfed southern Coromandel following the death of king Venkata II of Vijayanagar, the Tirupapaliyur factory was also abandoned in 1618. While the overall head of the Coromandel factories was designated 'governor', the chief of the factory at Masulipatnam was to be the second-in-command and was designated 'president' in 1621. In 1690, the seat of the Coromandel 'government' was moved from Pulicat to Nagapattinam in southern Coromandel. A *farman* granted by the king of Golconda in August 1606 stipulated the payment by the Dutch of a 4 per cent customs duty on their exports and imports. The Company was exempted from the stamp duty on cloth amounting to about 12 per cent. In 1612, the 4 per cent duty at Masulipatnam was commuted to a fixed payment of 3,000 pagodas per annum.

In the year 1680, the personnel of the Dutch establishments on the Coromandel coast was reported to have totalled 441 of which 233 were Indians holding diverse jobs such as clerks with a knowledge of Persian, blacksmiths, carpenters, domestic servants, palanquin-bearers, stableboys, torch-bearers etc. Of the 208 European functionaries, as many as 128 were soldiers including a lieutenant, 5 sergeants and 7 corporals. The bulk of these constituted the garrison at Fort Geldria. Eleven of the European employees performed miscelleneous jobs and included a clergyman, five medical men and two trumpeters. The remaining sixty-nine functionaries directly looked after the Company's trade and included the governor, two chief factors, six factors, thirteen under-factors, four book-keepers and forty-three assistants.[5] The European employees essentially constituted self-contained communities who lived under communal discipline maintaining their own cultural traditions. The walled factory compounds served both as living quarters and as secure storage for valuable goods. Partly in order to impress the local inhabitants and the royal court with the wealth and the power of the Company, the senior members of the staff often lived in ostentatious style. For example, when Thevenot visited Golconda in 1666, he found that the Dutch chief factor at Masuli-

---

[5] van Dam, *Beschrijvinge*, Book III, p. 234.

patnam was escorted by standard-bearers and trumpeters whenever he went out. Baldeus, who was the minister on the coast during the 1660s, has left a detailed account of the daily habits and manner of living of the Dutch in Coromandel. They had adopted many of the local habits, like washing the mouth after every meal and chewing betel leaves. Their diet was on the whole the same as in Holland and a large proportion of the meat and bacon required was supplied from Holland as hopes of procuring victuals cheaply on the coast had proved to be false. Coromandel, in the opinion of a Dutch governor, 'was more a prey to Bacchus and Venus than any other place in India', and many of the coast factors believed that 'men must follow the ways of the land'. Their zeal in this respect often involved the Dutch in serious difficulties with the local people and the other European companies. It was decided, in 1633, to pay the Coromandel factors only the amount considered necessary for keeping house, the balance of their salary being paid when they returned to Batavia, so that they should have no surplus money in their hands during their stay on the coast. The measure was directed against both illegal private trade and habitual drunkenness and debauchery.[6]

As far as the English East India Company was concerned, a factory was established at Masulipatnam in 1611, though the first Company voyage to the coast was organized only in 1614. Initially, the Dutch factors at Pulicat had instructions to try and keep the English out of the Pulicat trade. But the 1619 Treaty of Defence that terminated the hostilities between the two companies in the Indonesian archipelago contained a clause entitling the English Company to a share in the trade at Pulicat provided they also shared half of the cost of the maintenance of the Dutch fort and the garrison there. An agreement signed at Batavia on 13 April 1621 provided that in the case where the two companies wished to buy identical varieties of textiles at Pulicat, these would be bought jointly. The Dutch also undertook to provide accommodation to the English factors inside the fort itself against the payment of rent at least till such time as alternative arrangements were made for them. The *Globe* arrived at Pulicat on 19 June 1621 and the cooperation between the two companies formally started.

But the accord ran into problems almost from the very beginning. The English complained that the Dutch did not offer them half of the

[6] T. Raychaudhuri, *Jan Company in Coromandel 1605–90*, The Hague, 1962, pp. 201–6.

total textiles procured but insisted on dividing the lot in proportion to the capital invested by the two companies respectively. They also complained about the inadequacy of the accommodation provided for them as well as about the procedure adopted to work out their share of the cost of the maintenance of the garrison. The Dutch retorted that the joint procurement of textiles ensured for the English the same price and quality that the Hollanders got for themselves on the basis of the experience acquired by them over a number of years. The English were not convinced and the result was a growing bitterness between the two companies. Governor-General Coen, who was in any case strongly opposed to any kind of accommodation with the English, wrote the following to the Directors in January 1622:

It was impossible to deal with the English. They would do as much damage to the Dutch interests as they could, and then claim that it was they who were the aggrieved party. The jealousy, the distrust and the envy that these people had was unlikely to be neutralized by any regulations, agreements or orders. The more apart the two stayed from each other, the greater were the chances of continued friendliness between the two.[7]

In May of the same year, he wrote to the factors at Masulipatnam:

Regarding the costs at the Moluccas, Amboina, Banda, and Pulicat, the English had nothing but complaints to make. Their ambition and greed could never be appeased. In all matters, big and small, they found themselves cheated, sunk, affronted and despised so much so that it appeared that the entire means at the disposal of the Company would not be enough to meet their claims.[8]

The Dutch factors at Coromandel, however, did not take such an extreme view of the situation at any stage and indeed consciously tried to accommodate the English whenever possible. The latter, however, found the burden of their share of the maintenance costs of the fort and the garrison at Pulicat crippling. In any case, all hopes of any continued cooperation between the two nations were dashed to the ground following the notorious 'massacre' of Amboyna in February 1623. The formal termination at Pulicat came with the English withdrawal from that place on 1 July 1623. Soon thereafter, a factory was established at Armagon. The Anglo-Portuguese truce also made the

[7] General letter from Coen at Batavia to the Directors at Amsterdam, 21 January 1622, *Algemeen Rijksarchief* (henceforth ARA), *Verenigde Oost-Indische Compagnie* (henceforth VOC), 1075, ff. 2–10v.
[8] Coen at Batavia to Andries Soury and Van Uffelen at Masulipatnam, 8 May 1622, ARA, VOC 849, ff. 82–5.

establishment of a factory possible at Madras in 1640. The Fort St George was constructed there and, in September 1641, Madras was designated the chief factory of Coromandel. Factories were also established at Cuddalore and Vizagapatnam on the coast.

Gujarat

The quest for textiles for the Indonesian archipelago next took the VOC to Gujarat where a factory was established at Surat in 1618 on the strength of a document granted by the *subadar*, Prince Khurram. Soon thereafter subordinate factories were established at Broach, Baroda, Cambay, Ahmedabad, Burhanpur and Agra. The establishments at Cambay and Burhanpur were, however, not found particularly useful and were soon withdrawn. The English East India Company had earlier established a factory at Surat in 1613 and had extended its trade to Ahmedabad, Burhanpur and Agra. Since it was not feasible to have garrisons in the Mughal territories, the Gujarat establishment of the VOC was relatively small. In 1619, a total of eighteen Dutch employees was recorded: by 1628, this number had gone up to thirty-five, of whom twenty-two were employed at Surat and the remaining at Ahmedabad, Agra, Broach and Baroda. After a decline in the famine-hit 1630s, the number in 1651 was reported to be fifty-one. The increase in the volume of trade in the second half of the century necessitated a further increase in the number to seventy-eight in 1687–8. The number of Indian functionaries at work in the Gujarat-Agra establishments at this time was reported to be 150. By the middle of the eighteenth century, this number had gone up to 300, though soon after a big drop was recorded.[9]

The VOC factors at Surat formed part of a Christian community which included the resident Portuguese, the Armenians and the English. Considerable differences in the domain of religion, politics and economics across these constituent units notwithstanding, they appeared from the outside to be a socially coherent group. Thus on the last journey of the wife of the VOC Director Paulus Croock in 1642 to the Dutch cemetery in the city (where her tombstone still stands), all resident Europeans were in attendance. The procession was headed by two trumpeters – a Dutchman and an Englishman – while

---

[9] H.W. van Santen, *De Verenigde Oost-Indische Compagnie in Gujarat en Hindustan, 1620–1660*, Leiden, 1982, p. 9.

the coffin was carried by four Dutch and four English Company servants. Then followed a carriage with the female slaves of the departed woman and two flag-carriers bearing the Dutch and the English colours. Next, clad in black, were the Dutch director, the English director, and, in hierarchical order, the factors and the assistants of the two companies. The rear was made up by the other resident Christians of the city totalling in all approximately sixty persons. Like their counterparts in Coromandel and elsewhere, the Dutch factors in Mughal India also liked to live in style. For example, whenever the Director left the factory, he was preceded by trumpeters, drummers and the Dutch flag. The Governor-General at Batavia could do little about this except to express his strong displeasure when rumours reached him regarding the 'splendour . . . with which the factors lived there, going about draped in gold'.[10]

Bengal

The extension of Dutch trade to Bengal in the 1630s was also in response to the imperatives of the Company's intra-Asian trade, though the commodity this time was not cotton textiles for the Indonesian archipelago, but raw silk and silk textiles for the critically important bullion-providing Japan trade. A factory was established at Hariharpur in Orissa in 1633, and another at Hugli in 1635. But the Hugli factory was abandoned in 1636 in favour of another at Pipli in Orissa. Soon after, the Hariharpur factory was also abandoned and a new one opened at Balasore, also in Orissa. The Hugli factory was re-established sometime between 1645 and 1647, but the chief factory of the Bengal region continued to be at Pipli. Sometime between 1645 and 1651, the Patna factory, originally founded in 1638 but abandoned the same year, was also re-established and a new factory opened at Kasimbazar, the principal silk emporium of the region. The Bengal factories came of age in 1655 when they were organized into a directorate independent of the 'government' at Pulicat. The following year, the factory at Hugli (in the village of Chinsura) was recognized as the chief factory of the region and continued to be the seat of the Dutch directorate of Bengal for nearly a century and a half. The Company leased the villages of Chinsura, Baranagar and Bazar

---

[10] van Santen, *De Verenigde Oost-Indische Compagnie in Gujarat en Hindustan*, pp. 10–11.

Mirzapur for an annual ground rent of Rs.1,574. In 1676, a factory was opened at Malda in north Bengal primarily for the procurement of textiles. But it was closed in 1687 in pursuance of Commissioner Van Rheede's directive to make do with as few establishments as possible.[11]

By three *farmans* granted between 1636 and 1638, Emperor Shahjahan had allowed the Company to trade freely in Bengal, though the rate of customs duty payable by it was left vague. By virtue of various documents granted to it, the Company was also exempted from the payment of transit (*rahdari*) duties in the province. The Van Adrichem embassy, sent to Delhi in 1662 to try and obtain from the new emperor Aurangzeb concessions that his late father Shahjahan had accorded the Company, did indeed manage to obtain a *farman* exempting the Company from transit and similar duties in the provinces of Bengal, Bihar and Orissa. As for the customs duties, the *farman* instructed the relevant officials to go on charging the Company at the 'formerly established' rate (which was 4 per cent at Hugli and 3 per cent at Pipli and Balasore). The rate of customs duty payable at Hugli was reduced to 3.5 per cent in 1679 or later. This might have been done to ensure uniformity with the rate at Surat, where it was 2.5 per cent prior to 1679, but was later increased to 3.5 per cent to include 1 per cent in lieu of the *jazia*. By a *farman* granted by Emperor Bahadur Shah in January 1709, the rate of customs duty payable at Surat and Hugli was reduced from 3.5 to 2.5 per cent. The 1709 rates were confirmed in August 1712 by a *farman* by Bahadur Shah's successor, Jahandar Shah. By a separate *farman* granted at the same time, the new emperor also confirmed the Company's exemption from transit and similar duties throughout the Mughal empire.[12]

The personnel of the Company's establishments in Bengal was reported in 1680 to be 64 European and 341 Indian employees. As in the case of Gujarat, the European employees did not include any soldiers. Apart from seven medical men and an equal number of those attending to miscellaneous jobs, all the European functionaries were basically assigned commercial duties. The main job of the law enforcement officer (the *fiscaal*) was to prevent illicit participation in private trade by the Company's factors. A career survey of 115 European

---

[11] Om Prakash, *The Dutch East India Company and the Economy of Bengal, 1630–1720*, Princeton, 1985, pp. 34–41.

[12] Prakash, *The Dutch East India Company and the Economy of Bengal*, pp. 37–43.

employees of the directorate of Bengal during the eighteenth century showed that only 34 of them (30 per cent) returned to Holland after an average Company service of 21 years. The other 81 employees died in Asia at the age of 45 plus after an average of $22\frac{1}{2}$ years of Company service.[13]

The English East India Company reached Bengal about the same time as the Dutch, and by 1651 had established a factory at Hugli. Soon thereafter, factories were established at Balasore, Kasimbazar, Patna, Dhaka and Malda. Following the outbreak of hostilities between the English Company and the Mughal authorities in 1686, the English moved to Sutanati which later became the nucleus of the city of Calcutta. The English had started out in Bengal with a distinct advantage over all their European rivals: the exemption from customs and transit duties that they had been able to obtain from the Mughal authorities subject to an annual tribute of a mere Rs.3,000. The concession had initially been obtained through fraudulent means. The 1651 *nishan* by *subadar* Prince Shah Shuja conferring this concession had been obtained by misrepresentation of facts pertaining to the *farman* granted by Emperor Shahjahan in 1650. From 1656 onward, however, the factors were obliged to pay to the port authorities at Hugli an annual tribute of Rs.3,000 as the price for continued exemption from the customs duty. A *hasb-ul-hukm* issued in February 1691 under the seal of Wazir Asad Khan formalized the duty-exempt status of the Company subject to an annual tribute of Rs.3,000. This privilege received royal sanction in the form of Farrukhsiyar's well-known *farman* of 1717. An idea of the magnitude of the distinct differential advantage that this concession would have conferred on the English would probably be conveyed by reference to the fact that, in the decade of 1711–20, the average annual liability of the Dutch East India Company on account of the customs duties payable by it in Bengal would have worked out at approximately Rs.120,000.[14]

Malabar

The last of the major Indian regions the northern European trading companies reached was the southwest coast of India, comprising the Malabar and the Kanara coasts. In 1637, the VOC had established a

[13] F. Lequin, *Het Personnel van de Verenigde Oost-Indische Compagnie in Azie in de Achttiende eeuw, meer in het byzonder in de vestiging Bengalen*, Leiden, 1982, pp. 206–11.
[14] Prakash, *The Dutch East India Company and the Economy of Bengal*, pp. 75–81.

small factory at Vengurla in the kingdom of Bijapur on the Kanara coast under the direct jurisdiction of Batavia. In Malabar, a factory was set up in Kayakulam in 1647. But the resumption of hostilities with the Portuguese after the end of the Ten Years' Truce in 1652 forced a withdrawal of the factory. It was only in 1663, when the Dutch, collaborating with the raja of Cochin, managed to throw the Portuguese out that the Dutch trade at Malabar began on a regular and substantive basis. The strategic role of the Vengurla factory now came to an end. It was placed under the charge of the chief factory at Surat in 1673 and for all practical purposes abondoned in 1685, though formal orders for its closure were not issued until 1692. The special nature of the Company's trade at Malabar, which in theory was run on the basis of monopoly privileges granted by the raja of Cochin in pepper – the principal item provided by the region – would be clear by reference to the division of the personnel of the Company's establishments in the region in the year 1680. In addition to 162 Indian employees, there were as many as 561 European employees at work in these establishments at this time. The significant thing to note is that of the 561 European functionaries, military officers and soldiers accounted for no fewer than 423.[15] Whatever of its theoretical monopoly rights the Company managed actually to enjoy in Malabar would have owed a great deal to this impressive military presence. The English East India Company also maintained factories at Tellicherry, Cochin and Anjengo on the Malabar coast but, given the absence of any special privileges, the nature of its presence was very different from that of the Dutch East India Company.

THE ADMINISTRATIVE FUNCTIONING OF THE FACTORIES: THE ROLE OF BATAVIA

In a given region, be it the Coromandel coast or Bengal or any other, the chief factory together with the subordinate factories constituted an administrative complex with clearly defined decision-making processes and procedures. In the case of the Dutch East India Company, the principal executive body at the chief factory level was the council headed by the Governor or the Director as the case might be. In Bengal, the Hugli Council consisted, besides the Director, of a senior

---

[15] van Dam, *Beschrijvinge*, Book III, pp. 240–1.

factor in charge of the Company's trade books, the *fiscaal*, the factor in charge of the warehouses, the factor in charge of the loading and the unloading of the ships and six junior factors, one of whom acted as secretary to the council. Each of the subordinate factories also had a council. The chief of the Kasimbazar factory, who held the rank of senior factor, was treated as second-in-command in the directorate and in the event of the death or incapacitation of the director took over the latter's functions pending the appointment of a regular incumbent to the position. As pointed out earlier, in Coromandel the position of the second-in-command was held by the President at Masulipatnam. A centralizing factor in the administrative structure of the Coromandel factories was the office of the *hoofd-administrateur*, i.e. chief administrator, who supervised the accounts for the entire coast before these were sent to Batavia. Besides these, there was the Council of Justice for the coast which had powers to judge and punish the employees in Coromandel.

The administrative structure was not very different in the case of the English East India Company with the principal decision-making powers lying with the chiefs of the factories at Madras, Surat (later Bombay) and Calcutta. In 1653, Madras was made a presidency and five years later all English settlements on the Coromandel coast and in Bengal were subordinated to it. In 1661, the centre of the Company's northern trade was still firmly located in Surat. The chief of the Surat factory carried the title of President and the area of his authority extended well beyond the subordinate factories of Broach and Ahmedabad in Gujarat. He was also in charge of the factories at Tatta in Sind, Karwal, Kayal and Rajapur further south down the coast and even Gombroon and Isfahan in Persia, Basra in the Persian Gulf and Mocha in the Yemen.[16] Following the construction of Fort William there in 1700, Calcutta also became an autonomous entity. Once this was the case, the respective chiefs of the three Presidency settlements at Madras, Bombay and Calcutta dealt directly with the Court of Directors in London.

A feature peculiar to the Dutch East India Company with far-reaching implications in a variety of directions, and which indeed has already been noted earlier, must be commented upon at this stage.

---

[16] K.N. Chaudhuri, *The Trading World of Asia and the English East India Company 1660–1760*, Cambridge, 1978, p. 47.

This was the office of the Governor-General and Council at Batavia with a large establishment acting essentially as an intermediate agency between the Board of Directors – the Heren XVII – and the Company establishments all over Asia. The decision to create this office, whose first occupant was Pieter Both, had been taken in September 1609. The office was initially located at Bantam but was shifted to the Batavia Castle after the founding of the town in 1619 (actually christened Batavia only in 1621). To begin with, the members of the Council, presided over by the Governor-General, numbered five but this was increased to nine in 1617. From 1650 onward, the Council consisted of six ordinary and two extraordinary members with the position of the Governor-General further strengthened in the set-up. The Batavia Castle functioned as the eastern headquarters of the Company and the Governor-General and the High Council were the supreme authority in Asia. The structure of command was for the Heren XVII to deal almost exclusively with the Governor-General and Council who, in turn, dealt with the chief factories in the individual Asian regions. Thus the Directors sent the consolidated orders-list for the year, listing the orders region by region, to Batavia, which arranged for the transmission of the relevant part of the list to each of the regions. By the same token, the chief factory of each individual region reported to Batavia which, in turn, communicated from this advice whatever it considered necessary to the Heren XVII in the form of one or more general letters each year. Whenever necessary, of course, there could indeed be direct communication between a chief factory and the Heren XVII, but this was ordinarily kept to the minimum. Individual chief factories dispatched cargoes to Batavia where they were centrally collected and then put on the homeward-bound ships, which would have earlier in the season travelled directly to Batavia from Holland. Of course, there were exceptions here too and direct shipments from Sri Lanka, Surat and Bengal, etc., to the Netherlands did indeed take place, though never on a large scale.

The availability of an intermediate high-ranking agency in Asia conditioned to a significant extent the functioning of the Dutch East India Company as well as the precise trading strategy it was able to evolve over the years. One could, for example, argue with a reasonable amount of certainty that extensive participation in intra-Asian trade, which in time became the single most important feature distinguishing the Company from its fellow European corporate enterprises functioning in Asia and which indeed contributed a great deal to its dominant position in Euro-Asian trade through at least the seventeenth century, would have been unthinkable without Batavia. The whole enterprise was the brainchild of Coen and his successors at Batavia which played the critical coordinating agency's role throughout the seventeenth and the eighteenth centuries. But at the same time, it must be recognized that there were other dimensions of Batavia's intermediate role, all of which were not necessarily to the Company's advantage in the long run. Take, for example, the procurement by the Company of Indian textiles for the European market following the fashion revolution of the last quarter of the seventeenth century when trade in these textiles became the most important single component of the Company's Euro-Asian trade. Bengal had emerged as the single largest provider of these textiles accounting at the turn of the eighteenth century for an incredible 55 per cent, by value, of the total of Asian textiles the Company imported into Europe. The Bengal–Europe trade in textiles was essentially a luxury trade in which exclusiveness and novelty in designs and patterns mattered a great deal. In 1681, for example, the English Court of Directors had written to their factors in Bengal,

> Now this for a constant and generall Rule, that in all flowered silks you change ye fashion and flower as much as you can every yeare, for English Ladies and they say ye French and other Europeans will give twice as much for a new thing not seen in Europe before, though worse, than they will give for a better silk for [of] the same fashion worn ye former yeare.

Later the same year, they had written, 'Of all silk wares, take it for a certain rule that whatever is new, gaudy or unusual will always find a good price at our candle.'[17] This exclusiveness, coupled with the intense competition among the Europeans for limited supplies, put a large premium on quick decisions by the local European factors. Such a decision might pertain to the purchase of a textile with a new pattern or a textile whose quality or size specification was substantially different from that stated in the relevant orders list. In this kind of situation, the English were able to score over the Dutch. Given the distance between England and India, the English Directors really had no option but to allow a considerable amount of discretion in such matters to factors in Calcutta and elsewhere on the subcontinent. The

---

[17] V. Slomann, *Bizarre Designs in Silks*, Copenhagen, 1953, p. 114.

result was a constant flow of new varieties, colour combinations and patterns in the textiles that Calcutta sent to London, though in the process the prices paid for these textiles continuously went up. The Dutch factors, on the other hand, were continuously denied such discretionary powers. The reason was the belief that considering that Batavia was only a few weeks away from Hugli and for that matter any other Asian chief factory, such discretion was best left only to the Governor-General and Council. The Directors' general perception that the factors in India, particularly those in Hugli, which was by far the most important centre from which clandestine private trade was organized, ordinarily worked to their personal advantage rather than to that of the Company contributed to this decision. But the fact of the matter was that Batavia was never really able to help the Bengal factors effectively in deciding what to buy. The net result was that the Bengal factors at no time were able to snatch the initiative from their English counterparts, with attendant negative consequences for profitability and growth.

THE SUPERIOR NAVAL POWER OF THE EUROPEANS: CONFLICT RESOLUTION

We had noted earlier the absence of coercion in the relationship between the Indian political authorities and the northern European trading companies. This was by and large true for all Indian regions other than the Malabar coast until the rise to power of the English East India Company in Bengal in the second half of the eighteenth century. Such absence of coercion, of course, did not by any means preclude the occasional emergence of areas of conflict between the two sides. But in such an event, both sides were concerned that the conflict should not be allowed to escalate beyond a certain point. At work was indeed a rather finely tuned balance between the Europeans' unquestioned superiority on the sea as against their almost total vulnerability on land for a long time. Scholars such as Frederic C. Lane and, more recently, Niels Steensgaard have gone to the extent of arguing that 'the principal export of pre-industrial Europe to the rest of the world was violence'. In the case of India, and more generally Asia, the capacity to inflict violence followed essentially from the immense armed superiority of European ships over their indigenous counterparts. A glaring example of this disparity was provided in April 1612 when six English ships congregated off the Arabian coast and hijacked, in succession, fifteen passing Mughal ships from India, culminating in the capture of the great 1,000–ton vessel *Rahimi*, which belonged to the mother of the Mughal emperor. The prizes were taken to a nearby anchorage and plundered at will. It is true that the *Rahimi* was armed with some fifteen pieces of artillery and that the soldiers aboard her carried muskets, but these were merely anti-personnel weapons. Indian vessels, which often relied on rope and treenails to hold their planks in place, lacked the strength either to suffer heavy artillery bombardment from without, or to absorb the recoil of large ordnance firing from within.[18] The fact that the English could do this with impunity reflected not only the vulnerability of the Indian mercantile vessels but also the absence of a Mughal Indian navy capable of retaliating against such high-handed action. The flotilla at Dhaka and the fleet maintained by the Sidis at Janjira near Bombay were clearly inadequate to support an offensive against the European ships. It was indeed not without reason that in 1662, on being approached on behalf of the king of the Maldive Islands to use his good offices to persuade Emperor Aurangzeb to impose a ban on English and Dutch shipping to the islands, the *faujdar* of Balasore pointed out that even if the emperor could be persuaded to oblige the king, he was in no position to do so since he was 'master only of land and not of the sea'.[19]

An early institutionalized consequence of the European naval superiority was the requirement that the Portuguese, almost immediately on their arrival in the western Indian Ocean, imposed on Asian shipping to obtain from them before each voyage a licence in the form of a *cartaz*. The document obliged the Asian ship to call at a Portuguese-controlled port and to pay customs duties before it proceeded on its voyage to ports enumerated in the document. While it is true that the distorting effects of this innovation in reorienting the direction of Indian merchants' trade were relatively limited, it was nevertheless instrumental in bringing about a quiet revolution in the organizational structure of Asian trade. For the first time in the history of this trade, the unfettered and absolute freedom of navigation on the high seas stood compromised.

In the seventeenth century, the Dutch, English and French compa-

---

[18] Geoffrey Parker, *The Military Revolution, Military Innovation and the Rise of the West, 1500–1800*, Cambridge, 1988, pp. 107–8.

[19] Prakash, *The Dutch East India Company and the Economy of Bengal*, p. 48, note 84.

nies also took over the *cartaz* system from the Portuguese, though in a modified format and under the nomenclature of the 'pass' or the 'passport' system. It was, however, only the Dutch East India Company which, given its high stakes in intra-Asian trade, took the system with a certain amount of seriousness. Even there, whenever the Company chose to enforce the restrictions it might prescribe for Indian shipping rigorously, it came into conflict with both the Indian merchants as well as the ruling authorities with consequences which were not altogether pleasant for either side. A case in point is the troubles the Company faced at Surat in 1648–9. Following the conquest of Malacca in 1641 and the subsequent conclusion of monopsony agreements with the principal tin-producing regions in the Malay peninsula, the Company had sought to restrict direct access for Indian vessels to the 'tin ports' north of Malacca, and to get them to carry out all their trade at Malacca itself. This strategy, however, proved largely ineffective as long as these vessels had continuing free access to the Bay of Bengal port of Acheh on the northern tip of Sumatra. The extensive trade carried on by the Acheh merchants with Sumatran and Malayan ports made Acheh a large market for Indian textiles, as well as a major procurement point for items such as pepper and tin. Indeed, on the basis of the passes issued by the queen of Acheh it was even possible for the Indian merchants to sail to the east Sumatran and west Malayan ports and carry on trade there. Particularly useful in this regard was the link to Perak which was then a vassal state of Acheh and was abundantly provided with tin. The implications of this for the VOC were quite severe. In 1646, no tin could be bought in the Malay peninsula and no pepper could be sold at Malacca. A full-scale response was evidently called for and on 3 July 1647, Batavia resolved that 'the Moors of Surat, Coromandel, Bengal, Pegu etc. be prohibited from the trade both in Achin [Acheh] and in the tin quarters [of peninsular Malaya] on pain of seizure [of their vessels] as legitimate prize if they come there in the future'. It was decided to intensify the cruising of the approaches to Acheh as well as to ports such as Kedah, Perak and Johor. The factors in India were instructed not to issue passes for Acheh or any of the other ports declared out of bounds.[20]

[20] S. Arasaratnam, 'Some notes on the Dutch in Malacca and the Indo-Malayan trade 1641–1670', *Journal of Southeast Asian History*, vol. 10 (3), 1969, pp. 480–90.

The reaction to this severely restrictionist policy was sharp at least at Surat. When passes for Acheh were refused, the Mughal authorities banned the loading of the Dutch ships at the port. That was not all: in April 1648, the local Dutch factory was stormed by a force of 150 men. One Dutchman was killed, two others wounded and goods worth f.27,000 plundered. The attackers were never identified, but it was a clear message signalling the gross displeasure of both the Mughal authorities as well as the local merchants. Johan Tack, the Company's man at Agra, made representation to the Court asking for the restitution of the plundered goods. With the help of one of the *amirs* at the Court, Haqiqat Khan, who was generally favourably inclined towards the Company, an audience with Emperor Shahjahan was obtained. The emperor promised to grant a *farman* directing the *mutasaddi* of Surat to compensate the Company for the plundered goods. But before the *farman* could be issued, a delegation of the Surat merchants arrived at the Court. They could not prevent the grant of the *farman*, but ensured that it was a very different kind of document. All that the *farman* did was to say that the local authorities at Surat would do their best to trace the plundered goods. The factors saw no point in even bringing the document to the attention of the *mutasaddi*. The Company then decided to retaliate on the sea. A fleet sent from Batavia for the purpose arrived too late in 1648 to attack the Indian shipping returning from Mocha. But the following year, two Gujarati ships on their way back from Mocha and carrying a cargo worth more than one and a half million guilders were seized just outside Surat. Following negotiations between the Company, the local authorities and some of the leading merchants of the city, the Company's twofold demand for compensation for the plundered goods and a promise to stop the Surat ships' attempted voyages to Acheh, Perak, Kedah and Phuket, etc. was accepted. In return, the Company released the seized ships and the cargo to the lawful owners.[21]

The implications of the Company's pass policy during these years were somewhat less severe on the Coromandel coast. The problems there revolved mainly around the issue of the refusal of passes for the ships of the all-powerful noble, Mir Jumla. Following the seizure in 1647 of tin worth 2,000 rials off Perak from a ship of the Mir because it

---

[21] van Santen, *De Verenigde Oost-Indische Compagnie in Gujarat en Hindustan,* pp. 21–4.

did not carry a Dutch pass, the governor of Masulipatnam, a subordinate of Mir Jumla, asked for restitution. Peace was bought temporarily by a promise to do the needful and by agreeing to sell the entire stock of cloves in the Company's warehouses in Coromandel together with a certain amount of copper to the Mir. But the tin had not been returned by 1651 leading to obstructions being placed on the Company's textile trade in the region. It was only after Commissioner Dirck Steur went to see Mir Jumla that an agreement emerged. The Company reiterated its promise to return the tin besides undertaking to buy its requirements of textiles at specified places only from the representatives of the Mir. But problems surfaced again following the seizure of one of Mir Jumla's ships, the *Nazareth*, off Malacca for flying the Portuguese flag after the Dutch–Portuguese truce had ended. Matters came to a head in 1653 when Mir Jumla threatened to attack Fort Geldria unless the *Nazareth* and its cargo were released immediately and passes granted for the Portuguese-controlled ports in Sri Lanka. It was then decided to meet a part of the Mir's claims in respect of the goods carried by the *Nazareth*. Besides, passes were to be issued to all subjects of Golconda for ports under the jurisdiction of the king of Kandi and for Acheh. The only stipulation made regarding the latter was that in the event of the blockade of the port by the Dutch, the ships sailing for Acheh would agree to proceed to another destination approved by the Company. It was, however, only at the end of 1655 that the compensation in respect of the *Nazareth* was paid. The Company also conceded the Mir's right to trade with Makassar, Bantam and Kedah as well as to send goods to Malacca aboard the Company's ships. In return, Mir Jumla agreed not to send ships to Jaffanapatnam in view of the ongoing Dutch–Portuguese struggle there.[22]

The naval superiority of the Europeans often had other dimensions as well. Naval assistance might be sought by the Indian provincial or other administrations for purposes such as organizing campaigns against neighbouring states and containing the depradations of the European pirates against Indian shipping. The general policy the companies followed in this regard was to avoid becoming involved as far as possible. When there was no alternative, the obligations were sought to be fulfilled with as little investment in men and materials as possible.

[22] Raychaudhuri, *Jan Company in Coromandel*, pp. 48–51.

The first such major involvement of the Dutch East India Company was in the Mughal campaign against Chittagong in 1665–6. The attempt to conquer Chittagong and, if possible, Arakan was intended to contain the Magh pirates who had rendered impossible any profitable trade along the river Meghna, which was one of the two estuaries serving Bengal. These pirates had joined hands with the Portuguese *chatins* and operated from Chittagong with the active connivance of the king of Arakan, who shared in the spoils. Between 1656 and 1664, campaigns were planned twice but not executed for various reasons. Matters came to a head in 1664, when 60 to 70 pirate vessels were reported to have captured as many as 160 boats of the imperial flotilla. Later the same year, the pirates were reported to have captured in one raid 2,700 to 2,800 Bengalis from Bhusna to be sold as slaves. The provincial authorities were ordered to reorganize the flotilla and execute the campaign. *Subadar* Shaista Khan asked the Portuguese, the English and the Dutch for assistance in the form of armed vessels. The Dutch were requested to provide ten to twenty vessels against the promise of a reimbursement of the costs incurred, the grant of one fourth of the territory that might be conquered (with the Company having the option to demand a cash payment in lieu thereof), and an exemption in perpetuity from the payment of customs duties throughout the Mughal empire. Even if it is assumed that not all the promises would have been kept, the very fact that such extravagant terms were offered only serves to underscore the pathetic state of naval capability in Mughal India. The Batavia Council agreed to provide two small ships, the *Landsmeer* and the *Purmerland*, for the campaign. But the vessels arrived at Chittagong only on 11 October 1666, long after the forts at both Chittagong and Rambu – midway between Chittagong and Arakan – had been captured by the Mughal forces under the command of Buzurg Ummed Khan, the son of *Subadar* Shaista Khan. Due to the shortage of supplies and other factors, the campaign had been suspended at this stage. Commander Van Leenen, therefore, proceeded with the vessels to Dhaka, where they were placed at the disposal of the local factors for commercial use. The planned campaign against Arakan did not materialize, and the Mughal forces returned to Dhaka.[23]

Another important area of potential conflict between the Europeans

[23] Prakash, *The Dutch East India Company and the Economy of Bengal*, pp. 49–50.

and the Mughal authorities was the demand made on the former to provide protection to Indian shipping against the depradations of European pirates operating from their bases in Madagascar. The 1692 plunder of four Surat vessels, two of which were owned by Mulla Abdul Ghafur, brought forth a demand on the Dutch, the English and the French companies to equip a warship each for the purpose of apprehending the pirate ships. The failure to comply with this demand led to a ban in February 1693 on the Europeans' trade throughout the Mughal empire. It was only through bribes to officials at the local and the provincial levels that the trade could be continued on a clandestine basis. The ban was formally withdrawn only in February 1694.

The plunder of the *Ganj-i-Sawai* in 1695 was instrumental in the introduction of the system of Dutch and English convoys to the Red Sea. A large ship of 1,000 khandies was paid a fee of Rs.20,000 for a round trip while a smaller vessel qualified for Rs.15,000. Half the sum was found by the *mutasaddi* of Surat from the customs duties, while the rest was jointly subscribed by the merchants whose ships were to make the trip. The Company was allowed to carry its own cargo or freight goods on the escort vessels it made available. This arrangement worked well until 1698, when Surat merchant Hasan Hamadani lost a richly laden ship. The ship had not formed part of the convoy, but each of the three companies was nevertheless obliged in February 1699 to give a bond (*muchalka*) accepting responsibility for any losses that vessels from Surat might in future sustain at the hands of the pirates. The English were made responsible for the vessels going to the southwest coast of India, the Malay peninsula and the Indonesian archipelago, the French for those going to the Persian Gulf, and the Dutch for vessels going to the Red Sea. Abdul Ghafur and other merchants interpreted the *muchalkas* as implying the companies' responsibility for losses whether or not a particular ship that might be captured formed part of the convoy, an interpretation that the Europeans contested.

An occasion for testing the enforceability of the *muchalkas* arose in September 1701, when news reached Surat that one of Abdul Ghafur's ships from the Red Sea, the *Husaini*, had been plundered. The Dutch refused to pay compensation, claiming that this was one of the ships that had broken convoy. Ghafur organized his fellow merchants, who decided that until the Dutch paid the compensation, no one would fit out a ship. They also demanded suspension of the Company's trade until a settlement was reached. The imperial court decreed in favour of the merchants, and ordered the Dutch to pay the compensation claimed. Pending this, their trade was banned throughout the Mughal empire. As was usual in such situations, however, the ban was only partially enforced. The demand for compensation was met but it was only in November 1702 that the ban on trade was withdrawn.

In August 1703, yet another of Abdul Ghafur's ships was attacked and captured while it was anchored at the Surat bar. The Dutch refused to pay compensation, as the piracy had not occurred on the high seas. A strong Dutch naval force made its appearance off Surat in September 1703 and again a year later. At the suggestion of the new governor of Surat, Najabat Khan, the emperor agreed to relieve the Dutch of the 1699 *muchalka*, thereby restoring the *status quo ante* of 1696 stipulating only the provision of convoy to the Surat ships. This was in January 1705, but the Dutch blockade of Surat was lifted only in 1707.[24]

THE RISE OF COASTAL CITIES

The rise of a number of port cities on both the east and the west coasts of India can be directly attributed to the commercial operations of the European trading companies. The most important among these cities, Madras, Bombay and Calcutta, eventually became the headquarters of the three presidencies. These new port cities essentially represented a shift away from regional political and economic systems that were based on a link between an inland centre and a port which complemented each other, to another system where the port combined the political, administrative and overseas trading roles. Since they functioned in an essentially alien and potentially hostile setting, they were duly fortified, rendering them capable of defending themselves. It is indeed not surprising that all three fortified port cities were founded by the English East India Company. They did not have the equivalent of Batavia together with the strong territorial base of the VOC in Java and the Spice Islands and felt vulnerable without fortified settlements in the Indian subcontinent.

We noted above that on the Coromandel coast the Dutch controlled

[24] Prakash, *The Dutch East India Company and the Economy of Bengal*, pp. 50–2. Further details can be followed in Ashin Das Gupta, *Indian Merchants and the Decline of Surat, c.1700–1750*, Wiesbaden, 1979, ch. II.

146

the port of Pulicat and protected it with the guns of Fort Geldria. Forty kilometres to the south, the English built a port in the 1630s on the open roadstead at Madras protected by Fort St George. Still further south, the French occupied Pondicherry. Finally, in 1690, the Dutch moved their Coromandel chief factory from Pulicat to Naga-pattinam in the far south where a considerable fortification was raised. By the time of François Martin's death in 1706, Pondicherry was no longer a mere trading station, but a flourishing commercial city of 60,000 defended by an impressive fortress and garrison. A dependable tax system supported a French administrative, judicial and religious establishment which ruled the city and its environs. In 1704, the Mughal *faujdar* of the Hyderabad Karnatak, Daud Khan Panni, an *amir* who was a confidant of Zulfiqar Khan, objected to the erection of fortifications in the city on the ground that Pondicherry was an integral part of the Mughal empire. As evidence of Mughal sover-eignty, Daud Khan demanded immediate payment of Rs.100,000 as tribute. Early in 1706, the French governor made a personal present of Rs.10,000 to Daud Khan when the latter marched to threaten the city. By this juncture – just prior to Aurangzeb's long-expected death – Daud Khan was unable to undertake a costly and difficult assault on Pondicherry and he let the matter rest.[25]

Madras

Madras was founded on the strength of a small grant of three square miles of beachfront land to the English Company by the Hindu *nayak* of Kalahasti in 1633. By 1640, walls had been constructed to enclose the factory and Fort St George came into existence. The meagre British garrison was supplemented by Eurasian and Indian soldiers, and, by the end of the year, an estimated 300 to 400 families of weavers had migrated to the settlement. Following the Mughal conquest of Golconda in 1687, Madras was threatened with Mughal attack in 1689–90, but the campaign against the Marathas at Jinji diverted the attention of the Mughal commanders. In fact, Madras supplied munitions, foodgrains and even gunners to the Mughal army besieging the Maratha fortress. The next threat to the city came in

---

[25] John F. Richards, 'European city states on the Coromandel coast', in P.M. Joshi and M.A. Nayeem (ed.), *Studies in the Foreign Relationships of India (from the Earliest Times to 1947)*, Prof. H.K. Sherwani Felicitation Volume, Hyderabad, 1975.

1702 when Daud Khan Panni, in the context of Aurangzeb's ban on the Europeans' trade in connection with the piracies against the Indian merchants, demanded payment of large arrears of presumed revenue from the English. He also announced that his officers would survey the Company lands in and around the city and send troops to occupy the unfortified Indian quarter of Madras. The British resisted and a seige ensued. Negotiations and desultory military action progressed simultaneously for three months until the two sides eventually came to terms. Daud Khan found it easier to compromise rather than make a serious assault on the defences of Madras. Thereafter, the issue of Mughal control over the city was settled by default. Saadutullah Khan, who by 1710 had become the independent nawab of the Karnatak, merely accepted the *status quo*.[26]

In the meantime, during the second half of the seventeenth century, Madras had been attracting a large number of artisans, mainly weavers, as well as brokers and merchants. This was related mainly to the security offered by the city in the midst of devastating warfare in the region. Also, many traders and artisans with the stigma of low caste attached to their ritualistic status found in English neutrality a welcome economic and social freedom, though even within the walls of Madras the inhabitants of the black town were not entirely free from bloody caste conflicts.[27] At the turn of the century, the population of Madras is reported to have gone up to about 100,000. Thomas Pitt, governor of Madras between 1698 and 1709, noted at the end of his term that the revenues of Madras amounted each year to between 700,000 and 800,000 pagodas of which about 10,000 pagodas came from the mint.[28]

During the eighteenth century, the Company extended its territory to include fifteen villages around Madras and their dependent hamlets, increasing the size of the settlement to more than 40 square miles. Around mid-century, the competition with the French at Pondicherry and wars with Mysore over political hegemony in the south transformed the character and functions of the trading outpost. The Karnatak wars increased the European military population of the city

---

[26] Richards, 'European city states'; John F. Richards, *The Mughal Empire, New Cambridge History of India*, Vol. I.5, Cambridge, 1993, pp. 240–1.
[27] Chaudhuri, *The Trading World of Asia*, p. 51.
[28] Richards, 'European city states'.

from about a dozen officers in 1750 to over 800 by the late 1780s and from a few hundred rank-and-file soldiers to several thousands. Its non-military European population saw a corresponding growth – from only slightly more than a hundred Company officials, private merchants and seamen, excluding their families, to an estimated 1,200 persons by 1800. The total population of the city at this time was estimated at around 300,000. The last three decades of the century also witnessed a decline in the easy symbiosis between Europeans and Indians in the city. Increasingly an exclusively European executive dominated both Indian and European commercial communities. The government intervened to regulate prices charged by Indian merchants and artisans and in 1787 a Board of Regulation was set up. Alongside the attempts to build an untrammelled European executive went various forms of social control initiated by European residents. In 1793, official policy barred people of mixed race from government service and emphasized the growing racial separateness of European residents.

Racial separateness, of course, was nothing new and had indeed characterized the growth of the city from the very beginning. The original settlement had been divided into Fort St George, with its surrounding white town for the European inhabitants, and the black town and its suburbs for the Indian residents. The white town developed on the north side of the Fort to house the European, the Eurasian and the Indian Christian populations of the settlement. Its streets formed a uniform grid pattern and had both British and Indian names. The black town was originally founded as an Indian town and had been laid out in a neat grid pattern of streets just beyond the walls of the Fort. It was provided with a centrally located temple and market; and the various resident castes were allocated separate streets. Economic and social influence and political authority in the black town were largely held by the Company's favoured merchants and *dubashes*, who were granted substantial powers over revenue, judicial and commercial matters. This original Indian town was demolished in the mid-eighteenth century in order to expand the buffer zone around the Fort. The Indian community now had to congregate within the suburban quarters of Muthialpet and Peddanaickenpet, just north of the old town. This new black town initially had less spatial and social cohesion than its predecessor. Rather than possessing a central temple and marketplace to provide a focus for its activities, the town was divided into several caste-defined neighbourhoods, each with its separate temple and bazaar.[29]

Bombay

Throughout the seventeenth century, both the Dutch and the English East India companies carried out their trade in northern and western India from their respective factories in the premier Mughal port of Surat. From early in the century, however, the English had their eye on the natural harbour of Bombay further south on the coast which was then under the control of the Portuguese. Indeed, as early as the 1620s, the English factors had urged the Directors to acquire the harbour city where a secure base for their operations could be put in place. In 1661, the island was ceded to England under the terms of the marriage treaty between the English king Charles II and Catherine of Braganza, sister of the king of Portugal. It was, however, not until 1664 that formal possession was taken in the name of the British crown which soon after ceded it to the English East India Company. The 1670s and 1680s witnessed a fairly sharp deterioration in the relations between the Company and the Mughal authorities. Thomas Pappillon and Josia Child, both wealthy merchants and government contractors, headed two opposing factions in East India House. Child's faction strongly supported and indeed initiated the changeover to the policy of armed trading, and he was instrumental in formulating a commercial and political strategy which would put an end to the English interlopers in the eastern waters. It was in this context that it was decided to engage in a short and effective naval war against the Mughal empire. The main aim of the war would be to make territorial conquests in the coastal areas of India and to fortify the new settlements. Formal permission to wage war on the Mughal empire was obtained from James II and the conflict finally broke out in 1686, affecting the Company's settlements both in western India as well as in Bengal. In an attempt to put pressure on the Mughal authorities to stop the English interlopers' trade at Surat, John Child, the governor of Bombay, ordered the capture of eighty Indian vessels sailing to Surat. In retaliation, Aurangzeb ordered the stoppage of all English trade and directed the Abyssinian sealord, the Siddi, who was tribu-

---

[29] Susan M. Nield, 'Colonial urbanism: the development of Madras City in the eighteenth and nineteenth centuries', *Modern Asian Studies*, 13 (2) 1979, pp. 217–46.

tary to the Mughal emperor, to attack Bombay. The Siddi's troops succeeded in occupying most of the island, but did not capture the city and its citadel. Frantic negotiations and offers to pay reparation by the English ended the affair. A few years later, Bombay was again in trouble. The European pirates' attacks on Surat shipping, and the unauthorized minting of rupees at Bombay which adhered to the Mughal standards for fineness and weight but bore the insignia of the English monarch, persuaded Aurangzeb to order Siddi Yakut Khan to attack Bombay again. But the Bombay fortifications held and the attack was repulsed.[30]

In the course of the eighteenth century, Bombay's defences became more formidable and its trade grew. Gradually, Bombay began to supplant Surat as the leading port of trade for western India, but it was a long time before the process was completed. In the meantime, migration into the city was growing and a population figure of 80,000 for 1780 and of as much as 200,000 for 1825 has been suggested. The pattern of settlement in the city was caste based, though highly influenced by Portuguese patterns of town planning and ethnic jurisdiction.[31]

Calcutta

The English East India Company's war with the Mughal empire was also intimately related to the rise of Calcutta. After being driven out of Hugli at the start of the hostilities in October 1686, the English moved down the river to a place called Sutanati. From their base there, they tried to inflict damage on the Mughals in a variety of ways, including an attempt to overrun Chittagong and offering their services to the king of Arakan in his offensive against the Mughals. But nothing helped and the English were eventually forced to sue for peace. They returned to Sutanati in 1690 and were granted a *hasb-ul-hukm* in 1691 under the seal of *Wazir* Asad Khan. Between the middle of 1695 and the close of 1697, the province was in a state of utter disorder because of the revolt of Zamindar Sobha Singh of Chatwa-Barda in Midnapore

---

[30] Richards, *The Mughal Empire*, pp. 239–42; Chaudhuri, *The Trading World of Asia*, pp. 116–17; K.N. Chaudhuri and Jonathan I. Israel, 'The English and Dutch East India Companies and the Glorious Revolution of 1688–9', in Jonathan I. Israel (ed.), *The Anglo-Dutch Moment, Essays on the Glorious Revolution and its World Impact*, Cambridge, 1991, pp. 407–38.
[31] C.A. Bayly, *Indian Society and the Making of the British Empire*, Cambridge, 1988, pp. 68–9.

district. Being unable to control the situation on the basis of his own resources, *Subadar* Ibrahim Khan appealed to the European companies for armed assistance in crushing the revolt. He also permitted them to strengthen their own defences and even to fortify their factories. In August 1696, the rebels succeeded in capturing the Mughal fort at Hugli, exposing the local Dutch factory to grave danger. The Dutch at this point decided to deploy a contingent of European soldiers to surround the fort, and the *Berkenstein* was stationed in the Hugli river at a point from which its guns could cover the fort. The known superiority of European weaponry persuaded the rebels not to put up a fight. The fort was promptly vacated and the Dutch restored Mirza Hasan Ali's control over it. The VOC, however, chose not to take advantage of the *subadar*'s permission to fortify their factory and, once the revolt had been crushed, even undid the temporary measures taken to strengthen the defences of the Hugli factory. It was only in 1743 that the factory of Hugli (Chinsura) was fortified and given the name of Fort Gustavus.[32] The English, on the other hand, immediately had a fortification raised, which a few years later was christened Fort William and declared the seat of the new Presidency independent of Madras. Earlier, in November 1698, the Company had bought the *zamindari* rights over the villages of Sutanati, Govindpur and Dihi-Kalkatta against a consideration of Rs.1,300 paid to the existing *zamindars* of the villages. By a *muchalka*, the Company undertook to deposit the *jama* of Rs.1,195 annually into the imperial treasury.[33] The city of Calcutta was born.

The eighteenth century witnessed an impressive growth in the size and population of Calcutta as well as in its role in the history of the subcontinent. As in the case of Madras, two distinct towns – the 'white town' and the 'black town' – which were only functionally related to each other emerged fairly rapidly. The white town came to consist of the East India Company's fort, its commercial buildings and offices, churches and private houses. Outside the white town and immediately to the north of it was the black town with the houses of Indians, including substantial ones for the richer members of the community, shops and bazaars. Within the black town, the population was fragmented by ethnic origin, caste and occupation. Arabs, Parsis, Gujaratis,

[32] Prakash, *The Dutch East India Company and the Economy of Bengal*, p. 50.
[33] Farhat Hasan, 'Indigenous cooperation and the birth of a colonial city: Calcutta c. 1698–1750', *Modern Asian Studies*, 26 (1), 1992, pp. 65–82.

Greeks and Armenians were the early non-Bengali groups to establish their distinct abodes. A few khatris and Marwaris from northern India also arrived early. Outside the defined black town, the hutments on the fringes of the settlement seem to have preserved distinct identities as communities of cultivators, fishermen and weavers.[34]

Calcutta's fortunes changed spectacularly in mid-century. In 1756, the nawab's troops captured it, sacking the white town. The following year the British retook Calcutta and, when the nawab had been overthrown after the battle of Plassey, its political importance changed out of all recognition. The Company was granted *diwani* rights in the province in 1765 and the administrative machinery for the government of Bengal was moved to Calcutta in 1772. In 1773, it was recognized by Act of Parliament as the seat of government for the supreme authority over British India.[35]

There were strong elements of continuity between the new capital and the old trading town. Growth took place within the old framework of white town, black town and outer villages. The white town was completely rebuilt with a new Fort William costing over £1,000,000. A new Town Hall, the famous Writers' Building and new churches, Anglican and 'Mission', followed. There was also some ambitious new building in the old established black town. Successful Indian families began to commission houses in a style which has been called 'comprador syncretism' reflecting Hindu, Muslim and British influences. As for the population of the city, a figure of 120,000 has been suggested for mid-century, while the Police Census of 1837 put it at 230,000.[36]

For most of the eighteenth century, very little was provided for Calcutta's inhabitants by those set over them. There was no 'native' hospital until 1793 and even then the funds made available were only sufficient for fifty in-patients. The connections between the black town and the white town were strictly functional. A few of the ambitious Indians such as Nabakrishna appeared on the fringes of European social life, but the majority appear to have kept themselves entirely aloof from Europeans outside business.[37]

[34] P.J. Marshall, 'Eighteenth century Calcutta' in Robert Ross and G.J. Telkamp (ed.), *Colonial Cities, Essays on Urbanism in a Colonial Context*, Leiden, 1985, pp. 87–104.
[35] Marshall, 'Eighteenth century Calcutta'.
[36] Marshall, 'Eighteenth century Calcutta'.
[37] Marshall, 'Eighteenth century Calcutta'.

THE ECONOMIC INFRASTRUCTURE

We noted earlier the pivotal position of India in the Indian Ocean trading network on the eve of the Europeans' arrival. It was pointed out that while this undoubtedly was related in part to India's location at midpoint geographically, it also had a good deal to do with her capacity to put on the market large quantities of relatively inexpensive and highly competitive manufactured goods in addition to a whole range of other goods. This made India in some senses the 'industrial hub' of the region surrounded by west Asia on one side and southeast Asia on the other. At the root of this 'industrial' capability was the availability in the subcontinent of a sophisticated infrastructure of institutions and services which rendered the system of production and exchange highly efficient, dynamic and fully market responsive. This sophisticated infrastructure was available in full measure to be made use of by the Europeans. The principal constituent elements of this infrastructure were things such as a high degree of labour mobility and the existence of a labour market, merchant groups capable of collective defence and good organization, development of accountancy skills, highly developed and price-responsive marketing systems and a sophisticated monetary and credit structure.

A highly developed exchange and trading network – both internal and external – served as a vital link between the agrarian and the non-agrarian sectors of the economy. Land revenue had traditionally accounted for an overwhelming proportion of state finance in Mughal India and adjustments in the procedures for assessing and collecting this revenue were a routine feature in all administrations. But under Akbar, these adjustments were rather extensive and, among other things, involved a continuing shift away from the collection of land revenue in kind to that in cash. Both at a qualitative as well as at a quantitative level, this innovation served to promote in an important way the growth of a money economy. Quite clearly, the land revenue assessees would have been marketing a certain proportion of their gross output in any case. But under the new dispensation of compulsorily having to generate a rather large cash flow to meet the revenue demand which could be up to 50 per cent of gross output, the volume of monetized transactions entered into by this group would have gone up significantly. This would have necessitated a continuously rising supply of money and perhaps an increase in its velocity of circulation.

The Mughal Indian coinage consisted of the gold muhr, the silver rupee, and the copper dam or paisa. Given the almost total absence of domestic production of precious metals, the supply of gold and silver available for coinage depended almost exclusively on the volume of their import into the country. This was also true of copper, though to a smaller extent. A continuing import of these metals, overwhelmingly from the Middle East in the pre-European trade phase and, thereafter, increasingly also from Europe and Japan, had thus assumed the role of almost a precondition to the successful functioning of the monetary system and the exchange networks. It was essentially on the basis of the continuing inflow of the *khalisa* revenue – the share of the imperial government in the total land revenue – in cash that the elite in the heartland of the empire around Agra/Delhi could afford to constitute an important market for the industrial and other products of the outlying regions of the empire. By the same token, these regions, such as Gujarat and Bengal, would have found it impossible to generate the revenue to be sent to Agra/Delhi without the heartland providing a substantial and continuing demand for their products enabling them to buy back, as it were, the cash flowing to the north as 'tribute'.

External trade by land

The maritime trading links of India which served to provide the empire with the necessary supply of precious metals and other goods have already been noted in Chapter 1. There were also significant, though not quite as extensive, overland trading links with Persia and Central Asia via the northwest. The route to Persia stretched from Agra to Lahore to Qandahar on to Isfahan – the central market of Persia. The volume and value of the trade on this route seems to have been reasonably large with 20,000–25,000 camel loads travelling each year from Lahore to Isfahan in the early part of the seventeenth century with all kinds of relatively high-value goods manufactured or grown in the north Indian plains. Ordinarily, overland transportation, particularly when it also involves a certain amount of protection cost payable to the tribes through whose jurisdictions the caravans would have to pass, is more expensive than transportation by sea. But in the case of the Indo-Persian trade, the Dutch East India Company factors at Agra maintained that the land route between Agra and Isfahan via Lahore and Qandahar cost less per unit of goods transported than the land-cum-sea route which would involve the transportation of the goods from Agra to Surat by land, on to Bandar Abbas by sea and finally from Bandar Abbas to Isfahan by land.[38]

The route connecting the Mughal heartland with central Asia also started at Agra and continued on to Lahore and Peshawar reaching Kabul via the Khyber Pass. It then continued on to a chain of Indian trading settlements which stretched far up into central Asia to Astrakhan and Lake Balkh. This was a significant trade which took Indian spices, textiles and other goods up to Bokhara and beyond in search of gold and silver, horses, silks and Chinese porcelain. The scale of this traffic may be judged by the effect of a single accidental fire in Peshawar fort in 1586. The disaster destroyed 1,000 camel-loads of goods belonging to the merchants who had sheltered there when the route was temporarily obstructed.[39] As long as the chiefs of the Afghan and other tribes were given their usual cut, the caravan trade on this route ordinarily moved quite smoothly.

Internal trade

A large volume of internal trade in items such as foodgrains, other agricultural produce such as cotton, other raw materials and finished manufactured goods across the length and breadth of the subcontinent contributed a good deal to the growth of productivity in both the agrarian and the non-agrarian sectors. The achievement of an extra-ordinarily high degree of market dependence is suggested by bits of evidence like the poor peasants of the rice-growing riverine systems of southeastern India consuming not the expensive paddy crops which they produced, but millets and dry grains from the interior.[40] Food-grains, raw materials and finished products travelled long distances for eventual consumption in production centres and markets providing the highest return. Bengal was known to be the 'granary' of the subcontinent and provided large quantities of items such as rice, sugar and oil to many parts of the country besides neighbouring countries such as Sri Lanka and the Maldive Islands. The cotton textile industry of the Coromandel coast depended for a large part of its raw material on Maharashtra and Berar. In Bengal, while the finest Dhaka muslins

---

[38] H.W. van Santen, 'Trade between Mughal India and the Middle East, and Mughal Monetary Policy, c. 1600–1660', in Karl Reinhold Haellquist (ed.), *Asian Trade Routes, Continental and Maritime*, London, 1991, pp. 87–95.

[39] Richards, *The Mughal Empire*, p. 50.

[40] D.A. Washbrook, 'Progress and problems: South Asian economic and social history c. 1720–1860', *Modern Asian Studies*, 22 (1),1988, pp. 57–96.

were woven from high-grade cotton grown in the vicinity of Dhaka itself, the bulk of the cotton used in the extensive cotton textile industry in the province was imported from areas such as Gujarat. The important silk textile industry in Gujarat, in return, obtained the bulk of its supply of high-grade raw silk from Bengal. The large volume of trade between the east and the west coasts was done via the heartland of the Mughal empire. Luxury silks and muslins were a staple item in the cargo sent from Bengal to Agra for use by the Mughal aristocracy. Some of these goods were re-exported from Delhi and Agra to the west coast along with indigo from Bayana and clothes produced in Hindustan. They were exchanged, among other goods, for Gujarati silk textiles and luxury items from the Middle East. The trading communities in north India included Punjabi Khatris and the Rajasthanis, but perhaps the most dominant group was that of the Gujarati merchants who controlled the great cross-country trade route from Surat to Murshidabad. Indeed, on the basis of their excellent market information and large capital resources, many of these Gujarati merchants had settled down in various parts of the country including Bengal, several branches of whose trade, both by land and water, they eventually came to dominate.[41]

The monetary and credit system

We noted earlier that the Mughal coinage consisted of coins of three metals – the gold muhr, the silver rupee and the copper dam or paisa. The basic coin constituting the principal unit of account was the silver rupee. The gold muhr was used mainly either for ceremonial purposes or for hoarding. The copper dam or paisa constituted a major medium of handling small-value transactions and was used extensively. A distinguishing feature of Mughal coinage was the extraordinarily high content of the relevant metal of a very high degree of purity in the coin. Thus the gold muhr, which weighed 169 grains troy, was practically of unalloyed metal of high purity. The alloy content in the silver rupee, which weighed 178 grains until Aurangzeb raised the weight to 180 grains, was also never more than about 4 per cent. The

---

[41] For example, a perusal of the Dutch shipping lists for Bengal suggests that the coastal and overseas trade of the port of Balasore was dominated by the immigrant Gujarati Shahs. (Om Prakash, 'The Dutch East India Company and the economy of Bengal, 1650–1717', unpublished PhD dissertation, University of Delhi, 1967, p. 35).

copper dam weighed 323 grains till 1663–4 when its weight was reduced to about two thirds of this figure. The coins were manufactured in imperial mints spread all over the empire. The procedure followed was that of 'free' mintage under which anyone could bring bullion, old coins or foreign coins to a mint and obtain after a lapse of time new coins in exchange. The number of coins delivered against a given quantity of metal depended upon the purity level of the metal surrendered. This was determined at the mint. A charge was made at the mint to cover the seigniorage, the loss of metal in the process of coining, and the cost of coining, which consisted partly of the cost of the necessary ingredients and partly that of the labour involved. As far as the question of the relative valuation of the coin of one metal in terms of each of the other two was concerned, this was left entirely to the market, and depended upon the relative market supply and demand of each of the three metals.[42]

In the case of the silver rupee, the new coin delivered by the mint was known as the *sikka* rupee. The value of this coin corresponded broadly to the value of the metal contained in it, plus the minting charges including seigniorage. The problem of wear and tear of a coin through use was tackled ingeniously by a complex system of equivalence based on a varying degree of premium being enjoyed by a new coin over older issues. The *sikka* rupee, defined as a coin minted during the current or the previous year, enjoyed such a premium over all older issues which routinely carried the year of issue on them. The rate of this premium was controlled for all practical purposes by a class of highly experienced and influential money dealers known as *sarrafs*. Once the premium enjoyed by a new over an earlier issue exceeded a threshold level, the old coin would simply be brought to the mint for recoinage. This would be encouraged by the government in so far as its income from seigniorage would go up. Since the coins were intrinsic and not token coins, the problem of debasement of coins did not plague Mughal coinage. It also seems that forgery of coins was generally not a major problem.

The Mughal coinage system involved monetary management by the state only in a limited way. The accretions to the supply of money

---

[42] Om Prakash, 'On coinage in Mughal India', *The Indian Economic and Social History Review*, 25 (4), 1988, pp. 475–91.

were determined by the public itself subject to the availability of metals in the system and the capacity of the imperial mints. In this regard, the government was formally no different from any other member of the public except that its resource base was naturally larger than that of any private individual and the minting of its bullion would get priority. Further, the government could, and did, occasionally exercise its authority in directing the use of a particular metal for coinage. Thus in 1657 when an increase in the demand for copper coins in Surat took the rupee:paisa ratio to 1:40, while in 1642 it had stood at only 1:56, the *mutasaddi* of Surat ruled that all copper imported into the city should be taken directly to the mint. In order to facilitate this, he banned the movement of the metal bought by the indigenous merchants from the Dutch East India Company (which was by far the single largest importer of this metal into the Mughal empire, mainly from Japan) to places outside the city. This ban remained in force over the two succeeding years. Mughal imperial mints were scattered all over the empire, though clearly some were more important than others, in terms of both the number of coins manufactured as well as the geographical area within the empire over which the issues of a mint ordinarily circulated. It is also important to realize that while the business of all the imperial mints was the crafting of refined metal into coins, this could be done under different entrepreneurial and technical arrangements. The available information suggests the existence of at least two distinct models along which the structure of a Mughal imperial mint was organized. The dominant model would seem to have been the one where Mughal state officials organized the work of production themselves. The alternative organizational arrangement involved the entrepreneurial function being delegated to the *sarrafs*. What was common to the two patterns was the strict control exercised by the government on the quality of the coins manufactured.[43]

The coinage system in south India was quite different. Until the Mughal conquest of Golconda in 1687, the monetary system of the region remained firmly based on gold. The standard coin was the pagoda or hun (53 grains) stamped with the image of Vishnu. The pagoda's subsidiary coins, the half-pagoda and the fanam (5 grains)

---

[43] Prakash, 'On coinage in Mughal India'.

were also gold. The latter, heavily alloyed, was one of the smallest gold coins known and was extensively used for ordinary commercial transactions. A copper coin weighing between 25 and 30 grains was called 'cash'. Since 1636, the Qutb Shahs had also been minting a limited number of Mughal silver rupees to symbolize their status as tributary chiefs. After 1687, of course, the Mughals issued gold muhrs, silver rupees and copper coins of the usual Mughal types from the Hyderabad mint. But the production of the older indigenous gold and copper coins as well as their extensive use in the region continued for quite some time. This flexibility was possible because a centrally controlled minting structure of the north Indian variety was conspicuous by its absence in the south. In the latter region, including Golconda and the Hindu territories further south, minting was decentralized subject to licence and a fairly large number of mints operated in the area, bringing out coins which were not always comparable in weight and fineness across mints. This applied with particular force to fanams, where the alloy content of the coins brought out by different mints could be very different.

The European trading companies were among the major beneficiaries of the decentralized system of minting on the Coromandel coast. Since the companies were allowed to convert their bullion and foreign coins into local coins in their own mints, they were spared the continuous tussle on a variety of issues that went on between themselves and the masters of the Mughal imperial mints in north India. Following the establishment of a factory at Armagon, the English East India Company had been granted the right to coin pagodas and fanams by the local *nayak* in 1626. A similar concession was made available in the grant under which the English transferred their factory to Madras. After the Mughal conquest of Golconda, the English mint at Madras coined large quantities of silver rupees which were not only used locally but also sent in large numbers to areas such as Bengal. The Dutch East India Company also operated a mint in Fort Geldria at Pulicat. Of the 0.75 per cent seigniorage on minting due to the government, the Company was allowed a concession of 50 per cent on the metal minted on its own account, and 33 per cent on that minted on the account of the local merchants and others. In 1658, the Company was also allowed to coin pagodas at Nagapattinam at 50 per cent of the usual duty. The Company minted both pagodas and fanams at these mints. These coins circulated freely throughout the region. Indeed, the Dutch pagodas minted at Pulicat were in great demand.[44]

Coined money constituted an important, perhaps an overwhelming, segment of the total money supply in the economy, but it by no means accounted for the whole of it. Small-value transactions were often carried out through an extensive use of uncoined non-standardized money. Important varieties of this kind of money were the small seashells known as *cauris*, bitter almonds known as *badams*, pieces of lead and tin, and so on.

Finally, there were the credit instruments constituting near-money which were used to settle mutual claims. The *sarrafs* constituted the core group around which the money and credit markets were organized. Perhaps the most highly developed of these markets in Mughal India was the one at Surat. This was partly because this port was the principal point of entry of foreign treasure into the Mughal empire. This treasure was minted locally before it found its way to other parts of the empire. Available evidence suggests that large sums of money could be raised in this market on loan for varying periods of time with relative ease. Thus the records of the Dutch East India Company's factory at Surat reveal that the Company regularly raised large sums of money locally on interest. The average rate of interest in a money market such as Surat was lower – at times substantially lower- than in a somewhat less developed market such as Hugli in Bengal.

We noted earlier that the revenue in respect of the *khalisa* lands belonged to the imperial exchequer and enormous sums of money needed to be transferred regularly from the provinces to the heartland of the empire in Delhi/Agra. The reverse flow consisted of funds needed to run the provincial administrations, for organizing military campaigns of various kinds, and for purposes of acquiring goods in the provinces either for trade or for consumption in the heartland. The large-scale business of remitting funds from one part of the empire to the other, and indeed to areas outside the empire but within the subcontinent, was also carried on by the *sarrafs*. There was an extensive network of branches, agents and correspondents that these *sarrafs* had, and the basic document used to effect the transfer of funds was the bill of exchange or the *hundi*. This document, which was

---

[44] Om Prakash, 'Foreign merchants and Indian mints in the seventeenth and the early eighteenth century', in John F. Richards (ed.), *The Imperial Monetary System of Mughal India*, New Delhi, 1987, pp. 171–92.

essentially a binding written promise to pay a named person or its presenter a certain sum of money at some future but proximate date usually in another town, was in extensive use to effect money transfers on a large scale. The standing of the *sarrafs* engaged in the *hundi* business ranged from relatively small dealers to very large houses with agents or correspondents all over. In the seventeenth century, one such major house was that of Virji Vohra with its headquarters in Surat. During the first half of the eighteenth century, by far the most important *sarraf* establishment in the empire was that of the Jagat Seth family operating from its headquarters in Murshidabad in Bengal. In addition to its other extensive activities, this house handled the remittance of the central revenues from Bengal to Delhi amounting to over ten million rupees per annum.[45]

The *hundi* was used both as an instrument for remitting funds from one place to another as well as for raising short-term credit which would be repaid on maturity at another place. In the case of the former, the amount to be transferred was handed over to the *sarraf* together with the cost of the transaction, which would depend upon the current rate of discount on *hundis* between the two cities. The *sarraf* would then issue the *hundi* to the party, who would arrange to send it on to its representative in the city to which the funds were to be transferred. This representative would present the document to the local agent or correspondent of the *sarraf* who had issued the *hundi* and collect payment at the expiry of the stipulated period. As far as the party remitting the funds was concerned, the arrangement did indeed involve a certain amount of risk arising from the possibility of the *sarraf* going bankrupt before the *hundi* had been encashed. The extensive interlinking of financial enterprises across firms of *sarrafs* made even a chain of bankruptcies a distinct possibility. It is true that such bankruptcies did not happen frequently or on any scale, but the possibility was always there. This risk could be avoided by using the alternative method of raising the resources locally. This was done by the local representative going to a *sarraf* and 'drawing' a *hundi* on his principal. In the case of the VOC, for example, this would mean that the Company's factor at Agra, rather than being provided with a *hundi* bought by the Company at Surat, would instead be asked to go

---

[45] Om Prakash, 'Sarrafs, financial intermediation and credit network in Mughal India', in E. Van Cauwenberghe (ed.), *Money, Coins and Commerce: Essays in the Monetary History of Asia and Europe (From Antiquity to Modern Times)*, Leuven, 1991, pp. 473–90.

to the local agent/correspondent of the Surat *sarraf* and ask for accommodation for a specified sum of money. The agent/correspondent would then provide the accommodation asked for less the commission/discount to be charged. The document exchanged between the agent and the factor would be sent by the latter to the chief of the Surat factory, who would arrange for the money to be paid to the local *sarraf* after the lapse of the stipulated period. Under this arrangement, the *hundi* really became an instrument for raising short-term credit. In addition to obviating the risk arising out of the bankruptcies, this method of drawing a *hundi* also implied that the Company had the use of the funds for the duration of the journey between Agra and Surat, and for the maturity period thereafter. The discount or commission charged at the time of drawing a *hundi*, therefore, was always greater than if a *hundi* had been bought for remitting the same sum of money.[46]

The organization of manufacturing production

The organizational structure of manufacturing production can perhaps best be analysed with respect to the textile sector which constituted by far the most important segment of the manufacturing industry in the subcontinent, turning it into perhaps the world's greatest producer of cotton textiles. The production of textiles for export was concentrated mainly on the Coromandel coast, in Gujarat and in Bengal, though these were also produced in limited quantities in other areas. The specialization of Coromandel consisted in the manufacturing of relatively inexpensive cotton textiles which were either plain or patterned on the loom. They were often dyed in bright colours with plant dyes. The printing or painting was done in floral and a variety of other motifs. While the northern Coromandel – the area between the rivers Krishna and Godavari – specialized in the production of plain textiles, the specialization of the south – the coastal stretch between Pulicat and Nagapattinam – consisted in the production of the famous painted textiles – the *pintadoes*. A census carried out by the Dutch East India Company in northern Coromandel in the 1680s provides useful details regarding the organization of textile manufacturing in the region. The weavers were not concentrated in towns but rather dispersed in industrial villages scattered throughout the coastal

[46] Prakash, 'Sarrafs, financial intermediation and credit network in Mughal India'.

districts. In the weaving villages of the Krishna delta, a good part of the production was of the finer grades of fancy cloth while weavers in the Godavari delta concentrated on the production of plain calicoes. The inland centres produced mainly fine calicoes. The census contains evidence regarding eighteen producing centres in the area around the Dutch factory at Draksharama in the east Godavari delta. These ranged from villages with 40 weaver households to others with as many as 900. The average number of weaver households per centre enumerated was 331, and the number of looms 418. The production in the area of high-quality red chay-roots used for dyeing was a great advantage. More specifically, in the east Godavari villages of Gole-pallem and Gondawaran, the existence of groundwater with specific chemical properties enabled the local painters and dyers to achieve distinctive results. The Krishna delta contained fewer weavers and smaller centres of weaving. The inland producing region had dispersed weaver settlements and its individual nodes were apparently less sizeable than in the east Godavari region.[47]

In western and northern India, the weavers producing for the export markets were usually either urban based or situated close to the main cities. Surat, for example, was the metropolitan market of three small weaving towns within a distance radius of 20 miles – Bardoli, Nausari and Gandevi. The other major textile centres of Gujarat, such as Ankleshwar, Broach, Baroda, Nediad, Dholka and Ahmedabad, were all urban and located close to the main caravan route to Delhi and Agra. While both inferior- and superior-grade cotton textiles were manufactured in large quantities in Gujarat, the region also provided high-grade silk and mixed textiles using mainly Bengal raw silk as raw material. Towns such as Ahmedabad and Sironj provided fine embroidered quilts, satins, chintz and the famous transparent muslin known as *ab-i-rawan* or flowing water. Tavernier ascribed the superiority of Sironj *chintz*, its lively colours and their fastness, to the river that passed through the town, the water of which 'possesses the property of giving the brightness to the colours'.[48]

The relative decentralization of the textile industry in Bengal owed

[47] Sanjay Subrahmanyam, 'Rural industry and commercial agriculture in late seventeenth century south eastern India', *Past and Present*, Number 126, February 1990, pp. 76–114; Joseph J. Brennig, 'Textile producers and production in late seventeenth century Coromandel', *The Indian Economic and Social History Review*, vol. 23, 1986, pp. 333–56.
[48] Chaudhuri, *The Trading World of Asia*, pp. 242–9.

a great deal to the extensive and comparatively inexpensive river transport network in the province. The comparative advantage of Bengal in relation to other textile-producing regions of India consisted in the manufacture of fine cotton and silk textiles. Based on special geographical features and the cumulative effect created by a hereditary concentration of craft skills, a number of specialized centres of production had emerged in the province. The best quality muslins were produced in the district of Dhaka in eastern Bengal, where a particularly well-known centre of production was Sonargaon, situated at a distance of about 15 miles east of the city of Dhaka. The exquisite quality of the Dhaka muslins owed a great deal to a particularly high-grade cotton grown in a small and narrow belt in the district which happened to possess the right soil. The other important manufacturing centres were the Malda district and Santipur in Nadia district. Comparatively less fine varieties of muslins were also produced in Patna in Bihar and Balasore in Orissa. The staple varieties of muslins procured by the Europeans were *khasa* and *malmal*. Usually, both these were plain muslins but they could also be brocaded in gold, silver or silk threads, usually in floral patterns. Less frequently, they were instead embroidered in coloured silks in chain-stitch, in gold and silver threads or in cotton itself, which is what probably later came to be known as 'chikan' embroidery. Many of the pieces also had their borders woven in gold threads. In the case of calicoes, the principal centres of production of the finer varieties were the Malda district and the area around Kasimbazar in Murshidabad district; the comparatively coarser varieties were manufactured in Birbhum district, in Patna, and in Pipli and Balasore in Orissa.[49]

Besides cotton textiles, the Europeans procured substantial quantities of mixed and silk piece-goods in Bengal, which was by far the most important producer of these textiles in India. Mixed piece-goods were woven by the simultaneous use of cotton and silk yarns, the latter having been derived either from the usual mulberry silk worm or from the silk worm *anthereap aphia*, which produced the wild *tussur* silk. The silk textiles procured by the Europeans were almost exclusively of mulberry silk. The principal areas of production were Malda and Kasimbazar, though limited amounts of particular varieties

---

[49] Prakash, *The Dutch East India Company and the Economy of Bengal*, ch. 3.

were also produced in Radhanagar and other centres in Midnapore district.[50]

Working on the basis of the cotton yarn procured from the spinner, the basic unit of production in the manufacturing of textiles was the weaver operating as an independent artisan. To a certain extent, the production of standardized varieties of textiles for traditional markets was carried on on the basis of the weavers' own resources and at their own risk. There is evidence, for example, that several varieties of comparatively coarse cloth were produced on this basis in the district of Malda in north Bengal for eventual sale to merchants engaged in trade with Pegu, north India (Hindustan) and Persia, which had traditionally been important markets for these varieties. The bulk of the marketed output, however, was produced on the basis of agreement between merchants – many of whom were intermediary merchants known in Bengal as *paikars* – and weavers specifying details such as the quantity to be produced, the price and the date of delivery. A part – often a substantial part – of the final value of the contract was given in advance to enable the weaver to buy the necessary raw materials as well as to sustain himself and his family during the period of production. Clearly, the three key elements in this system were the weavers' need of finance, their relatively limited access to the market, and a desire on their part to avoid risks arising out of their inability to forecast correctly the behaviour of the demand for a given variety of textiles. This structure, which could be described as the contract system, was essentially a variant of the standard European putting-out system. Unlike in the European case, the Indian weaver bought his own raw material and exercised formal control over his output until it changed hands. Of course, the merchant who had given the advance had first claim on the output, and debt obligations often rendered the artisans subject to coercive control by the merchants.

Though grossly inadequate and perhaps not entirely representative, the available evidence on the weavers' costs and the merchants' mark-up enables us to form some idea of the magnitudes involved. A 1670 report on Malda in north Bengal suggested that standardized textiles worth Rs.800,000 to Rs.1 million were sold in the district annually for export to places such as Pegu, Agra, Surat and Persia. If these were bought against cash directly from the producers who brought them

---

[50] Prakash, *The Dutch East India Company and the Economy of Bengal*, ch. 3.

into Malda rather than from the intermediary merchants, the saving in cost would be between 12 and 15 per cent. The mark-up by the merchant would, of course, be substantially greater under the contract system to compensate him for the additional risks borne. These risks were not inconsiderable. For example, a sudden rise in the cost of living in the wake of a famine, or the appointment of a particularly tyrannical official in a given area, might lead to a mass migration of the poor weavers to a more convenient location, to the great discomfiture and loss of the merchants who had entered into contracts with them and given them advances. Some data relating to 1686–7 in respect of *khasas*, a staple variety of muslin procured by the Dutch East India Company in fairly large quantities in Bengal, suggests that about two thirds of the price obtained by the weaver covered the costs of the raw material, the remainder being the reward for his labour. The mark-up by the intermediary merchant (calculated on the basis of the price agreed upon at the time of the contract between the Company and the merchant) was 35 per cent in the case of grade I, 55 per cent in that of grade II, and as much as 142 per cent in that of grade III.[51]

The structure of textile production in the areas catering to the export demand was reasonably flexible in responding to changes in demand for its output. Thus the phenomenal increase in the European companies' demand for Bengal textiles in the last quarter of the seventeenth and the first half of the eighteenth centuries was accompanied by a substantial rise in the output of the varieties demanded, though there were obviously frustrating time lags and shortages of particular varieties. Also, the sizes of the textiles as well as their texture, patterns, designs and colour combinations were constantly adjusted to meet changes in demand. Initial resistance to the adoption of such innovations was usually overcome by the offer of higher prices and an assured purchase of the entire output produced according to the new specifications. The VOC even started a unit within the precincts of its factory at Hugli where experiments in new designs, patterns and colour schemes were carried out.

The mode of procurement

In the case of both manufactured goods such as textiles, as well as processed agricultural goods such as opium and indigo, the Europeans

---

[51] Prakash, *The Dutch East India Company and the Economy of Bengal*, ch. 4.

made use of the existing procurement organization, though in course of time they did indeed introduce modifications and innovations with varying degrees of success in a variety of directions aimed at solving specific problems that they encountered. An important functionary made use of by the Europeans was the *dalal* (broker), an Indian employee with an intimate knowledge of both the local market and the intermediary merchants. He was ordinarily a salaried employee, and his duties included collecting information about the market price of various goods as well as identifying merchants with a good reputation for honouring contractual obligations. These merchants were brought by the *dalal* to the relevant company and agreements concluded between the company and each of the merchants willing to supply at mutually agreed terms. In the case of textiles, the agreement specified the quantity to be supplied, the period of delivery, and the price per piece of each of the different varieties contracted for. The merchants had the goods manufactured mainly on the basis of the contract system which, as we have seen, obliged them to give a part of the value of the contract to the producers in advance. The merchants, therefore, insisted that the company similarly give them an advance, which in the case of Bengal was ordinarily between 50 and 65 per cent. The intermediary merchants who did business with the Europeans were an extremely heterogenous group. In the case of the VOC in Bengal, at one end it included merchants such as Khem Chand Shah, who engaged in large-scale domestic and overseas trade and who owned several ships. At the other end, there were marginal merchants who genuinely could not have operated except on the basis of the advances received from the Company. Once the goods were delivered into the Company's warehouses, the deviation from the samples was worked out and the price finally paid to the merchants was adjusted accordingly.

There were occasional deviations from this broad structure of procurement. At places such as Dhaka and Pipli, for example, the VOC is known to have used the services of commission agents (also called *dalals*) to procure export goods. The agent was given a certain amount of money, which he invested among the weavers on behalf of the Company and at the Company's risk. After the goods had been delivered, the agent was entitled to a 2 per cent commission (*arhat*) on the total value of the transaction. Another interesting functionary whom we come across is the head weaver (*hoofd wever*). His precise status is not clear, but he acted as an intermediary between the weavers and the buyers of their produce. He appears to have exercised some authority over the members of his community, ensuring a certain amount of regularity in the supplies. His services were often utilized by the intermediary merchants, who would enter into a contract with him and give him an advance. On the limited occasions on which it was able to do so, the Company dealt directly with the head weavers and saved on the margin of the intermediary merchants. Thus, in 1670, a head weaver of Hugli agreed to supply *fotas* – an ordinary calico – at Rs.70 per twenty pieces, whereas the merchants were asking for a price of Rs.90. The corresponding figures in the case of sailcloth were Rs.36 and Rs.43 respectively. Such deals, however, had to be made very discreetly because the intermediary merchants were always on the lookout to sabotage them.[52]

The organization of procurement was broadly similar in respect of processed agricultural goods such as opium and indigo. However, in respect of indigo grown and traded in and around Bayana near Agra in the 1630s and 1640s, there were enough interesting deviations from the norm to merit a somewhat closer look. The commodity was a highly volatile one in so far as the fluctuations in both output and price could be fairly marked. It was perhaps because of this peculiarity that the normal procedure of procurement adopted in relation to other commodities was not followed in the procurement of Bayana indigo. Neither party wanted to commit itself to honouring a predetermined price. As a result, the norm developed in relation to this commodity was that contacts between the buyer and the producer were made only after the harvest was in and deals concluded at the ruling market price. This, however, did not prevent certain classes of buyers from nevertheless entering into prior contracts with the producers and giving them fairly large sums of money in advance. Ordinarily, the producers of indigo, including the fairly substantial ones, were in constant need of finance and welcomed any advances coming their way. But the conditions that accompanied such a contract were very different from those in the case of, say, opium or textiles. In the first place, the funds advanced to the producer of indigo were not interest free and ordinarily carried an interest rate of 1.5 per cent per month. Secondly, no mutually binding price was worked out at the time of the contract. Once the harvest was in, price negotiations would be held between the producer

[52] Prakash, *The Dutch East India Company and the Economy of Bengal*, ch. 4.

and the person who had given the advance. If a mutually acceptable price emerged, the deal would go through and the advance together with the interest on it would be adjusted in the final payment. Should the price negotiations, however, fail, the producer would be free to sell to anyone else and his obligation to the person giving the advance would be limited to returning the advance together with the interest on it. The only firm right that the person giving the advance had was the right to be offered the output first. In other words, he had the first right of refusal, but nothing else. Note that this was a radically different situation from that obtaining in respect of other commodities where the contract obliged the producer to supply under all situations at the mutually agreed predetermined price. Why did anybody then give out advances? It would seem that different categories of persons giving out advances had a different set of objectives. In the first place, there were the speculative dealers in the commodity. This group emerged essentially in the 1630s when the international demand for the product was rapidly on the increase. The basic idea was that by using the right of first purchase at the current market price soon after the processed output was in, they would be able to cash in on the continuously rising market price. The other important category engaged in the business of giving advances to indigo producers was that of the employees of the Dutch East India Company, who did it clandestinely and without the approval of their employers. The considerations that led these employees to do this were quite different from those of the speculative buyers. Often, the funds given out as advances belonged to the Company but were not officially entered in the books as advances. The implication was that whether or not the deal with the producer went through, the proceeds of interest at 1.5 per cent per month between the time of the giving of the advance and that of the coming of the output onto the market would be available to the employees to be pocketed. In situations where Company funds were not available for such advances, the employees borrowed the money in the Agra money market in the name of the Company at 1 per cent per month. In that case, the difference of $\frac{1}{2}$ per cent per month would still be available to them.

From the point of view of both the speculative buyers as well as the VOC servants, the giving of advances to the producers of indigo carried with it certain inherent risks. In the event of a poor crop, it might not always be possible to recover the full extent of the money advanced together with the interest earned on it in the form of either indigo or cash. This is precisely what happened in 1637 to both the speculators as well as the Dutch Company servants. Several of the speculators went bankrupt as a result. After 1645 or so when the international demand for Bayana indigo registered a steep decline, the remaining speculative buyers also had really no option but to go out of business. The 1637 crop failure also hit the Company servants hard and when the matter accidentally came to the attention of the higher authorities a major scandal was created. Eventually, in 1642, the Company was obliged to write off the bad debts still outstanding in the names of the indigo producers.[53]

The problem of bad debts, however, was not peculiar to the special case of Bayana indigo but indeed plagued all commodities that the Europeans procured in India. In the case of textiles, the intermediary merchants almost always supplied less than they had undertaken to, either because the producers had not fully honoured their obligations toward them or because they themselves had chosen to divert a part of the goods procured to a third party at better terms. Second, of the goods received by the companies, a part was usually found unacceptable as being of too poor a quality. Finally, even in respect of goods accepted, for reasons of quality deviation, the final price paid to the merchants was ordinarily lower than that originally agreed upon. The result was that quite often the value of the goods accepted by a company from a particular intermediary merchant was less than the sum of money given to him in advance. The balance constituted a bad debt. Preventive measures taken by the VOC in Bengal included a closer investigation into the credentials of the intermediary merchants before contracts were given out to them, and a denial of fresh contracts to those of them who owed money to it. But since the Company did not want to lose the bulk of its suppliers to its rivals, the latter measure was invoked only in the case of habitual offenders. The others were simply required to clear at least a part of their earlier obligations simultaneously with the new ones.

An interesting innovation the VOC tried out on the Coromandel coast with a view to solving or at least minimizing the problem of bad debts was the institution of the so-called 'joint stock companies' in the region. The innovation in this arrangement consisted essentially in the

[53] van Santen, *De Verenigde Oost-Indische Compagnie in Gujarat en Hindustan*, pp. 153–8.

fact that the funds needed for investment in textiles were raised jointly by the intermediary merchants themselves rather than being provided by the Company in the form of advances to the customary extent of 50 to 70 per cent of the value of the contract. Each merchant was supposed to subscribe to the pool of funds in accordance with his share in the total value of the contract given out by the Company. These merchants were also encouraged to operate in different seg-ments of the production areas so as to minimize competition amongst themselves leading to a rise in the cost price of the textiles procured. This was a highly welcome development from the point of view of the Company. But over time, the distinct characteristic feature of the institution – namely, the investment by the participating merchants of their own funds in procuring the textiles obviating the need for the Company to give them advances and run the risk of bad debts arising – tended to disintegrate and the joint stock system increasingly followed the norms of the ordinary cash-advance contracts. Thus, in the 1760s at Jagannathpuram in northern Coromandel, the Company dealt with two joint stock companies. One of these consisted of the Masulipatnam merchants (or their descendants) who had moved with the Company to Jagannathpuram in 1750, while the other was constituted by the local merchants.[54] In southern Coromandel, the arrangement was much looser. An ordinary partnership between two merchants, or even a single merchant unit, qualified to be designated as a joint stock company there. Thus in the 1760s, the VOC procured textiles both at Nagapattinam and at Porto Novo through six joint stock companies each. At each of the two places, two of the companies consisted of two merchants each, while the remaining four contained only one merchant each.[55] Each of the units received an advance from the Company and was expected to settle its accounts at the end of the year. Bad debts nevertheless arose on a regular basis and the best that

[54] ARA, Memoir of the outgoing Governor of Coromandel, Pieter Haksteen, for his successor, Reynier van Vlissingen, dated 20 September 1771, *Hooge Regering Batavia* (HRB) 344, ff. 53–5.

[55] At Nagapattinam, one of the partnership companies consisted of Palikonda Kistna Chettiar and Venkatasala Mudaliar, while the other had Kondapilly Venkata Kistna Rama Chetty and Kondapilly Venkatasalam Chetty as members. The four individual merchants constituting a company each were Tirumani Chetty, Ramalinga Pillay, Muthu Venkatalinga Mudaliar and Godawarti Sadasiva Chetty. In Porto Novo, Tambu Naikar and Rangasay Chetty constituted one of the two partnership companies, while the other consisted of Papa Chetty and Ramalinga Chetty. The four single merchant companies there consisted of Masulimani Mudaliar, Shiva Chidambaram Mudaliar, Vedenada Muthu Chetty and Rama Sama Chetty (ARA, Haksteen memoir, HRB 344, ff. 206, 146).

the Company could do was to oblige each unit to clear each year, in addition to meeting its obligation for that year, a part of its outstanding obligations from earlier years. It was again the desire to minimize bad debts that prompted the Company to allow a deceased merchant's heir(s) almost automatically to succeed him. The relatively less well-off among the merchants were also obliged to produce a guarantor acceptable to the Company.[56] To counter the problem of the poor quality of the *chintz* supplied, the Nagapattinam factors also decided in 1767 to depute a 'supervisor' to oversee the work of the artisans engaged by the joint stock units to produce this variety. The innovation was reported to have produced positive results and was extended to other varieties such as *muris*.[57]

The emergence of bad debts was not the only problem the companies faced. Another serious problem was the receipt of goods from the intermediary merchants much later than the date mutually agreed upon. Part of the explanation lay in nonadherence to the schedule by the artisans, but in some cases at least the delay was deliberate. The delivery of goods only a few days prior to the scheduled departure of the ships left very little time for the factors to examine the goods received carefully, thereby increasing the chances not only that substandard items would be accepted but also that they would be evaluated at the same price as the others. Also, the fact that the quality of the goods received was usually poorer than that of the samples given to the intermediary merchants had important ramifications other than contributing to the emergence of bad debts. Given the structure of demand in most of the markets supplied with Indian goods by the companies, the loss in total revenue consequent upon a deterioration in the quality offered was usually much greater than the saving in total cost. The commodity for which the problem of poor quality occurred in its most intense form was raw silk. Various qualities of unreeled silk were mixed together before they were reeled. In addition, the reeling itself was often very defective, with threads running into each other.

---

[56] This requirement at times created rather peculiar situations. For example, when they succeeded their father, the late Godawarti Sadasiva Chetty, his two sons pleaded with the Nagapattinam factors not to enforce the requirement of a guarantor in their case, for this would adversely affect their standing and credit in their community. The Company agreed on the condition that they would ensure that no bad debts ever arose on their account (Haksteen memoir, ARA, HRB 344, ff. 206–8).

[57] ARA, Haksteen memoir, HRB 344. ff. 208–10.

Various measures were taken at different points in time by the companies to solve these problems to the extent possible. But given that, on the whole, the rate of growth of the Europeans' demand for Indian goods far exceeded the rate of growth of their supply turning the market increasingly into a sellers' market, the companies were not really in a position to impose punitive measures on the suppliers with any degree of success. An interesting innovation that had a certain measure of success that might briefly be noted is the silk-reeling unit that the Dutch East India Company installed within the precincts of its factory at Kasimbazar in Bengal in 1653. This was a measure designed to solve the twin problems of the use of inferior grades of unreeled silk and the poor quality of the reeling of raw silk supplied by the merchants. The unit had an extraordinarily chequered life, at times reeling nearly all of the raw silk exported by the Company, and at others practically none. When operating at full capacity, it could reel about 1,500 bales (227,625 ponds) of raw silk per annum, and employed over 3,000 men. Initially, the unit was organized on the basis of a contract with a so-called 'master reeler'. This individual was provided with the equipment necessary for reeling raw silk, working space for the reelers, and the necessary raw materials. Against a certain amount of unreeled silk supplied to him, he was supposed to provide the Company with a specified amount of properly reeled silk by a certain date. He was paid in advance a sum calculated at the rate of Rs.5 per maund of reeled silk he had undertaken to supply. The organizational structure of the unit was changed in 1674 with the Company itself assuming all risks and the master reeler being demoted from the position of contractor to that of a manager at a salary of Rs.200 per annum. In 1715, additional working space was constructed so as to make it possible to accommodate as many as 4,000 reelers. Production on this scale under one roof was almost certainly unprecedented in Mughal India. Also, the imperial and other workshops (*karkhanas*) were not fully comparable to the Dutch unit for two reasons. First, the goods manufactured in *karkhanas* were intended almost exclusively for use by royalty, the nobility, rich merchants and others, and for the army, rather than for sale in the market. Second, at least some of the big *karkhanas* appear to have been operated on the basis of underpaid drafted labour rather than with free market labour.[58]

[58] Prakash, *The Dutch East India Company and the Economy of Bengal*, ch. 4.

CHAPTER 5

EURO-ASIAN AND INTRA-ASIAN TRADE: THE PHASE OF DUTCH DOMINATION, 1600–1680

THE DUTCH COMPANY TRADE

The Coromandel coast

We noted earlier that the first Indian region to be reached by the Dutch East India Company was the Coromandel coast where a factory was established as early as 1606. While the region had the potential of providing items such as indigo, saltpetre and diamonds for the European market, its principal attraction consisted in the availability of large quantities of textiles initially primarily for southeast Asia, but eventually also for the European market. The staple varieties included the 'long cloth', dyed in bright colours and with stripes and checks, and re-exported extensively by the Dutch from Europe to the West Indies under the title of 'Guinea linen'. A variant, bleached white or dyed blue, was also extensively used in the southeast Asian trade under the designation of 'negro-cloth'. Other staple varieties exported to Europe included *bethilles, salampuris, muris* and *parcallas*. The range of the varieties exported to the Asian markets was much larger. The principal consuming markets served by the Dutch were in southeast Asia and included the Spice Islands (the Moluccas, Banda and Celebes), Java, Sumatra, the Malay peninsula, Siam and Burma. In the Far East, limited quantities of Coromandel textiles figured in the exports to Taiwan and Japan. Other Asian markets supplied with these textiles were Sri Lanka and Persia. In Indonesia, these textiles were used primarily to procure pepper and other spices, but were often also used as a medium of payment to the soldiers in the service of the Company. Throughout the archipelago, these textiles were used primarily as wearing apparel by all sections of the community. While the bulk of the demand seems to have been for the relatively coarser and inexpensive types, there was also a fairly large market for the more expensive and ornamental varieties. In Java, for example, the principal varieties sold were *tapis* (including *tapi sarassas* and *tapi*

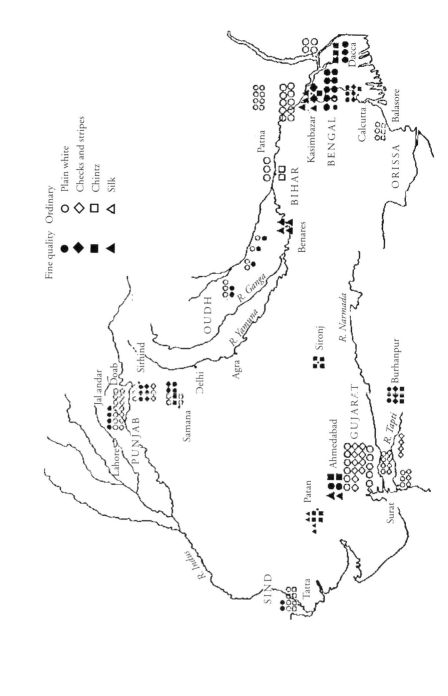

Fine quality Ordinary

● ○ Plain white
◆ ◇ Checks and stripes
■ ☐ Chintz
◀ ◁ Silk

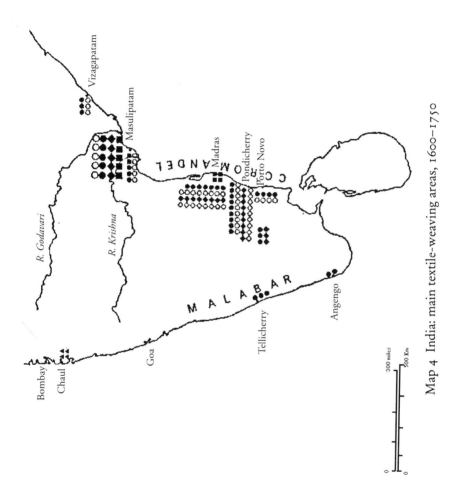

Map 4 India: main textile-weaving areas, 1600–1750

chindaes) and *goulongs*. While the coarser varieties of *tapis* were partly for 'the peasants in the hills',[1] the *goulongs*, which were patterned on the loom and often incorporated gold thread, were obviously for the better-off sections. In a letter to Masulipatnam in 1617, Coen emphasized that 'it was essential that only the best quality *goulongs* and *tapi-sarassas* were procured for Java since these people were very particular about the quality and, given their good buying power on the basis of the high price of pepper, would pay a very good price for the right kind of textiles'.[2] It would, therefore, be quite inaccurate to classify these markets as absorbers merely of coarse cottons. Also, each of the consuming markets, with several sub-segments, was a distinct unit with its own specific tastes and preferences with regard to the colours of the dyes, as well as the patterns and designs created through printing and painting. The orders lists sent by Batavia to Coromandel, therefore, were elaborate affairs, often running into several folios, indicating in great detail the market-wise requirements in terms of variables such as the size of the piece, the colours preferred, the size of the stripe, the pattern of the border, the exact floral design that was to be duplicated, and so on. Thus the eighty packets of *tapi-sarassas* asked for in 1623 were to have 'bright red borders and small flower work in lively colours'.[3]

The Company's trade on the Coromandel coast registered a significant increase over the seventeenth century. The growth in the average annual value of the Company's total exports from the region is set out in Table 5.1. It will be seen from the table that while between 1620 and 1640 the annual exports averaged only *f*.0.5 million, the subsequent period witnessed an impressive growth. The *f*.2 million mark was crossed in the early 1650s with a value of *f*.2.67 million being reached during 1661–5. After that, there was a slight decline, but the period 1686–90 was again marked by the highest ever figure of *f*.3.78 million.[4] The available data do not

---

[1] *Algemeen Rijksarchief* (ARA), Coen at Batavia to Masulipatnam, 8 May 1622, VOC 849, ff. 82v–85v.

[2] ARA, Coen at Jacatra to Masulipatnam, 30 November 1617, VOC 1067, ff. 31v–35v.

[3] 'An estimate of Coromandel clothes that could be sold in a year in the Moluccas, Amboina, Banda, Java, Jambi, Patani and other southern quarters.' Prepared at Batavia, 27 April 1623, ARA, VOC 1080, ff. 89v–90v.

[4] Note, however, that in this quinquennium, as in some others, the average annual figure is based on information available only for one year. During 1686–90, that year was 1686.

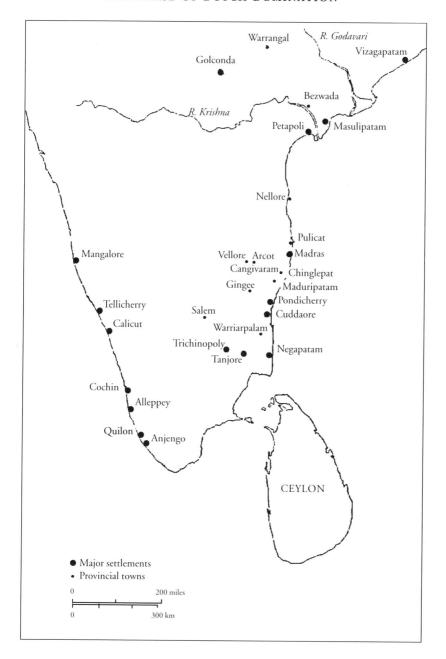

Map 5 South India: weaving areas, c. 1720

Table 5.1 *Dutch East India Company's exports from Coromandel, 1608–90 (annual average value in florins)*

Years[1]	Value (f.)
1608	110,143
1614	279,975
1621–5	567,366
1626–30	657,207
1631–5	419,839
1636–40	652,270
1641–5	1,017,559
1646–50	1,725,692
1651–5	2,011,313
1661–5	2,673,815
1666–70	2,564,026
1671–5	2,300,000
1676–80	2,008,536
1686–90	3,781,568

Source: The figures until 1645 are based on Subrahmanyam, *The Political Economy of Commerce*, p. 170. The figures for the remaining period are based on Raychaudhuri, *Jan Company in Coromandel*.
Note: [1] Note that in most quinquennial periods, information for all five years is not available, and the annual average is based on whatever number ot years information was available for within the quinquennium. Over the quinquennium 1686–90, for example, information was available in respect of only one year, namely 1686.

permit a disaggregation of the value of the total annual exports between Europe and Asia. This is mainly because the exports for Europe and southeast Asia were sent to Batavia and were listed together under that factory. It is only for the brief period between 1616 and 1626 when shipments were also sent directly from Coromandel to Holland that the value of the exports to Europe alone can be worked out. As a proportion of total exports, the exports to Europe during this period usually fluctuated between 20 and 25 per cent, though there were years such as 1624 when this proportion was only 15.5 per cent and 1619 when it was as high as 42.3 per cent. Note, however, that in so far as during this period the export of Coromandel goods to Holland also took place via Batavia, the proportions above

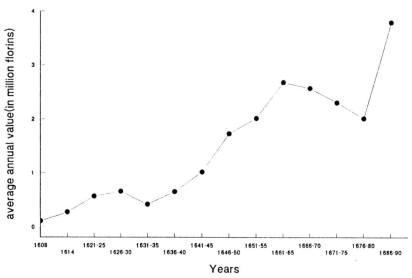

Fig. 5.1 Dutch East India Company's exports from Coromandel,
1608–90

capture only the lower bound of the exports to Europe, not their
average value.[5]

The southeast Asian markets accounted for an overwhelming
proportion of the total Asian market for Coromandel textiles. This is
borne out clearly by the annual order lists sent from Batavia to
Masulipatnam which, incidentally, are our only source for a partial
reconstruction of the quantitative profile of the Dutch intra-Asian
trade in Coromandel textiles over the greater part of the seventeenth
century. Instructions from Batavia repeatedly required Coromandel to
attach priority to the textile orders from different parts of Asia over
those from Europe. The extent to which the orders were under-
fulfilled (which was mostly the case) depended mainly on the availability of capital with the factors at any given point in time. The value
of the textile orders for southeast Asia at 1640–1 prices registered a
rapid rise from around *f*.300,000 in 1617 to *f*.455,000 in 1626 and to

[5] Information on the value of exports by direct shipments from Coromandel is available
in J.R. Bruijn, F.S. Gaastra and I. Schöffer, *Dutch–Asiatic Shipping in the 17th and 18th
Centuries*, The Hague, 1987, vol. III. The figures above are from Sanjay Subrahmanyam, *The
Political Economy of Commerce, Southern India 1500–1650*, Cambridge, 1990, pp. 170–3.

f.824,000 in 1640. Thereafter the rise was even more rapid, and the value increased to *f*.1.3 million in 1644, and *f*.1.55 million in 1650.[6]

The Company had a nearly captive market in the Spice Islands and exploited this advantage in full by charging prices which were considerably higher than those that other traders used to charge earlier. In fact, in 1618 these prices were reported to be so high as to be almost counterproductive in so far as they adversely affected the delivery of cloves in the Moluccas.[7] With a brisk procurement by the Chinese, Malay and other traders, the sales in the Java market picked up considerably from the 1630s. The average rate of profit around this time was reported to be between 60 and 100 per cent.[8] The 1641 conquest of Malacca helped, and the subsequent decades witnessed a considerable increase in the trade in Coromandel textiles in southeast Asia. Indeed, until the 1680s this market continued to be supplied overwhelmingly by Coromandel. Thus of the total of *f*.1.26 million-worth of textiles the Batavia Council ordered for this market for 1696 from Coromandel, Bengal and Gujarat together, the respective share of the three sources was 93 per cent, 4 per cent and 3 per cent.[9] It was only from about this time onward that the Company was confronted by the problem of growing competition in Java by the locally produced cheaper supplies of painted textiles.[10]

The composition of the Coromandel goods exported to Europe was more diverse. Commodities such as indigo, cotton yarn and saltpetre figured in the export invoices more or less regularly throughout the first half of the seventeenth century, and in some cases until later, though as time passed the relative importance of goods other than textiles declined. As far as Coromandel textiles were concerned, the domination of the group by Guinea linen was unchallenged throughout. In 1642, the Directors' orders for cotton textiles from Asia amounted to *f*.246,250 worth constituting 7.7 per cent of the total orders for the year. The five Coromandel varieties, namely Guinea linen, *bethilles*, *salampuris*, *muris* and *parcallas*, accounted for

[6] Subrahmanyam, *The Political Economy of Commerce*, p. 174.

[7] General letter from Governor-General Laurens Reael to the Directors at Amsterdam, 20 August 1618, VOC 1068, ff. 218–29.

[8] In 1633, the profit on white cloth was reported to be as much as 125 per cent (T. Raychaudhuri, *Jan Company in Coromandel*, The Hague, 1962, p. 159).

[9] Calculated from Pieter van Dam, *Beschrijvinge van de Oost-Indische Compagnie*, II.II, pp. 79–80 and 220–1; II.III, pp. 104–5. This is the only comprehensive list of orders available.

[10] Raychaudhuri, *Jan Company in Coromandel*, p. 162.

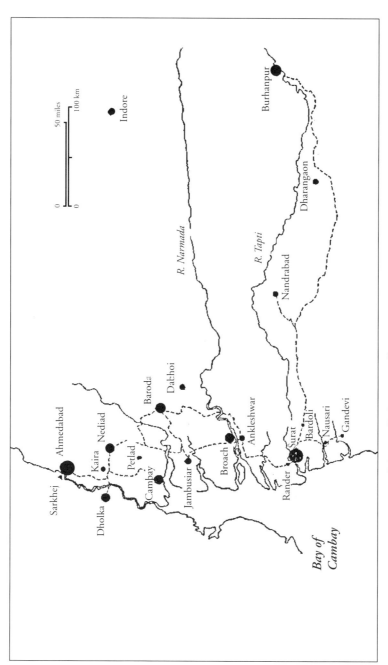

Map 6 Gujarat: textile towns, c. 1700

$f.157,500$ which, in turn, amounted to 63.9 per cent of the total Asian orders for cotton textiles.[11] By 1652, the orders for these five varieties had gone up to $f.397,000$ (an increase of more than 150 per cent) in a total Coromandel textile order of $f.500,000$ for Europe. The orders for Europe accounted for 30 per cent of the total Dutch orders from Coromandel.[12] By the mid-seventeenth century, then, Europe had become an important trading partner of Coromandel. The 1670s witnessed further substantial increases in the European orders for Coromandel textiles. The gross profit fetched by these textiles around this time was reported to be between 65 and 160 per cent.[13]

Gujarat

The Company's trade with the other major Indian region supplying textiles to southeast Asia, namely Gujarat, was taken up in earnest from about 1620 onward. The growth in the value of the Company's exports from the region is set out in Table 5.2. Until the early 1640s, this growth was a continuous one, and the annual exports had by then crossed the $f.1$ million mark. There was, however, a decline from that point on and the $f.1$ million mark was not reached again until the early 1670s, around which level the exports stayed until the early 1680s. A major development of the period was the emergence of Gujarat from about 1660 onward as a net exporter of precious metals in the form of Mughal silver rupees. As we noted earlier, Gujarat now conformed to a 'goods for goods and bullion' pattern rather than the usual 'bullion for goods' pattern. By the late 1670s, the average annual export of silver rupees had reached an all-time peak of $f.700,000$ worth and accounted for as much as two thirds of the total Dutch exports from the region. In the following period, however, there was a steep decline in the number of rupees sent out. Among the principal beneficiaries of the Surat silver rupees were the Dutch establishments at Bengal, Sri Lanka, the Malabar coast and Coromandel.

The fact that the Surat factors were able to finance the procurement of the export cargo for Europe and Asia, meet the establishment and other costs of the factories in the region, and still spare funds for export in the form of rupees to Batavia or directly to another Indian/Asian region, without receiving any monetary assistance from Batavia

---

[11] K. Glamann, *Dutch–Asiatic Trade 1620–1740*, Copenhagen/The Hague, 1958, p. 136.
[12] Subrahmanyam, *The Political Economy of Commerce*, pp. 171–2.
[13] Raychaudhuri, *Jan Company in Coromandel*, p. 161.

Table 5.2 *Dutch East India Company's exports from Gujarat, 1621–1792 (annual average value in florins)*

Years	Goods for Europe (f.)	Goods for Asia (f.)	Total of goods (f.)	Cash for Asia (f.)	Grand total (f.)
1621/2–1625/6			358,833	–	358,833
1626/7–1630/1			385,667	–	385,667
1631/2–1635/6			731,350	–	731,350
1636/7–1640/1			997,880	–	997,880
1641/2–1645/6			1,017,200	–	1,017,200
1646/7–1650/1			731,750	–	731,750
1651/2–1655/6			744,000	–	744,000
1656/7–1660/1			579,523	240,300	819,823
1661/2–1665/6			754,831	173,069	927,900
1666/7–1670/1	263,744	255,202	518,949	249,044	767,993
1671/2–1675/6	232,471	236,770	469,241	574,629	1,043,870
1676/7–1680/1	143,378	228,866	372,244	699,268	1,071,512
1681/2–1685/6	293,540	274,869	568,409	497,243	1,065,652
1686/7–1690/1	352,281	227,593	579,874	218,933	798,807
1691/2–1695/6	383,499	300,357	683,856	188,007	871,863
1696/7–1700/1	603,737	480,654	1,084,391	152,571	1,236,962
1701/2–1705/6	671,117	159,361	830,478	NA	
1706/7–1710/11	240,452	199,683	440,135	NA	
1711/12–1715/16	169,225	246,053	415,278	NA	
1716/17–1720/1	225,571	137,526	363,097	NA	
1721/2–1725/6	178,789	177,423	356,212	NA	
1726/7–1730/1	130,295	209,359	339,654	NA	
1731/2–1735/6	152,699	217,275	369,974	NA	
1736/7–1740/1	175,103	186,937	362,040	NA	
1741/2–1745/6	188,518	238,644	427,162	NA	
1746/7–1750/1	268,006	695,547	963,553	300,000	1,263,553
1751/2–1755/6	265,227	657,846	923,073	354,564	1,277,637
1756/7–1760/1	169,845	602,496	772,341	508,200	1,280, 541
1761/2–1765/6	212,548	276,657	489,205	360,000	849,205
1766/7–1770/1	353,486	222,510	575,996	400,500	976,496
1784/5–1788/9	175,862	176,439	352,301	NA	
1789/90–1791/2	251,579	158, 689	410,268	NA	

Note: NA stands for not available.
Source:
1. The figures for the years 1621/2 to 1655/6 have been calculated from van Santen, *De Verenigde Oost-Indische Compagnie in Gujarat*, Table 1, pp. 32–3. The regional breakdown of the goods exported is not available for this period.

Table 5.2 (*contd*)

2. The figures for the period 1656/7 to 1665/6 have been calculated from V.B. Gupta, 'The Dutch East India Company in Gujarat trade 1660–1700: a study of selected aspects', unpublished PhD thesis, University of Delhi, 1991.

3. The figures for the period 1666/7 to 1749/50 are from two sources. The figures for goods exported, including the regional breakdown, have been calculated from Appendix 1, entitled, 'Aanwysing van het bedragen der versondene retourneren in 80 jaren sedert anno 1665/66 tot 1749/50 inclusief als', to 'Memorie wegens den toestand der Souratsen Directie opgemaakt en te gelyk met het bestier aangegeven door den ondergetekenden afgaanden directeur Jan Schreuder aan synen vervanger den heer geeligeert directeur Johannes Pecock in 't Nederlands comptoir te Souratta den 30 September anno 1750', ARA, *Hooge Regering Batavia* (HRB) 838, ff. 1–139, appendices independent pagination 1–261. Appendix 1, ff. 249–52.

   The figures for cash exported between 1666/7 to 1699/1700 have been calculated from Gupta, 'The Dutch East India Company in Gujarat trade'. Information regarding cash exported between 1700/1 and 1749/50 is not available. The figure for cash shown against the quinquennium 1746/7 to 1750/1 is based on information available only for 1750/1.

4. The figures for the period 1750–1 to 1767–8 have been calculated from Appendix 14 to the memorandum left by the outgoing director C.L. Senff for his successor M.J. Bosman dated 31 December 1768, ARA, HRB 848.

5. The figures for the period 1784–5 to 1791–2 have been calculated from appendix B to the memorandum left by the outgoing director A.J. Sluisken for his successor Pieter Sluisken dated 31 December 1792, ARA, HRB 854. Information regarding cash exported during this period, if any, is not available.

or elsewhere, was, of course, the outcome of the factors' ability to generate enormous sums of money locally by the sale of Asian goods. Because of its command over the large north Indian market as its hinterland, Surat easily constituted by far the largest single market the Company had anywhere in Asia. The most important of the Asian goods sold there were Indonesian spices and Japanese bar copper, in both of which the Company enjoyed monopoly status. In order to tide over short-term problems of liquidity, the proceeds from the sale of goods were often supplemented by funds borrowed in the local money market, in which sphere again the city of Surat had attained a level of development and maturity not found anywhere else in the subcontinent.

As early as 1623, Pieter van den Broecke, the VOC director at Surat, had visualized a situation where the proceeds from the sale of spices would be adequate to finance the procurement of export cargo

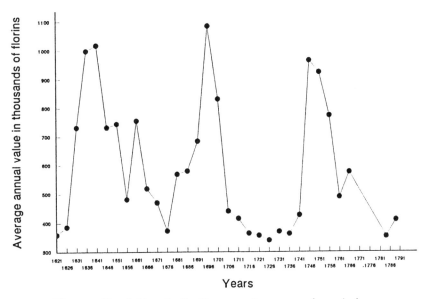

Fig. 5.2 Dutch East India Company's export of goods from
Gujarat, 1621–1792

for Europe as well as the rest of Asia.[14] The principal spices sold by
the Company were cloves, nutmeg and mace. The Company's factory
at Agra, which was under the administrative control of Surat, with its
concentration of the Mughal Court and the aristocracy, was a major
outlet for the spices. Being a luxury consumption good, one would
ordinarily expect the price elasticity of demand in respect of spices to
have been reasonably high. But in fact the demand for spices in India
was inelastic over a very broad price range. The reason evidently was
that while the rich Muslim aristocracy with its fondness for spiced
food, as well as other well-off sections, were willing to pay extremely
high prices for the coveted spices, most other sections of the community found them beyond their reach even if there was to be a sharp
decline in the price. Initially, this was something the Directors found
hard to believe. Given the extraordinarily cheap procurement price of
spices, the profit margin was very good and the Directors were not at

---

[14] ARA, Surat to De Carpentier at Batavia, 25 December 1623, VOC 1083, ff. 138–45.

all averse to a reduction in price in the interests of promoting sales and generating a larger purchasing power. In course of time, however, the Directors accepted the special nature of the demand for spices in India. There were other complicating circumstances as well. The Company was concerned that the Asian prices of the spices should not be allowed to fall to a level that would make it worth their while for the English and others to buy spices in India or elsewhere in Asia and take them to Europe, thus compromising the crucial European monopoly of the Company. This was by no means an imaginary fear and there were cases of this actually happening.[15] Taking all these factors into account in conjunction with the monopoly position of the Company, the natural thing for the Company to do would be to keep the sale prices in India pegged at a high level and maximize the monopoly revenue. But the identification of the optimal price for each of the major spices was not an easy matter at all. The suspicious conduct of the factors of the Company at the Surat factory did not help matters either.

Since the first Indian establishments of the Company were on the Coromandel coast, the sale of spices began there. The Surat market was at this time supplied from Masulipatnam, but already in 1618, even before a regular factory was established there, Coen was contemplating concentrating the Indian spice sales at Surat.[16] In 1619, the price of cloves and nutmeg in Surat was reported to be higher even than in Amsterdam.[17] The Company also began sending spices to Agra around this time. The position was quite satisfactory on the Coromandel coast as well. The lot of spices worth ƒ.40,000 sent there in 1622 had afforded a net profit of ƒ.180,000.[18] This was notwithstanding the fact that the price in Coromandel was usually substantially lower than in north India. Early in 1627, Francisco Pelsaert wrote that the Coromandel price of cloves was only ƒ.1.80 per pond against the price of ƒ.3.84 at Agra. This encouraged a large-scale

---

[15] In 1680, for example, several English captains had bought spices sold by the Dutch at Surat. They were reported to have sold them in England at a profit of more than 100 per cent. The English Directors advised their factors at Hugli to follow a similar course of action (India Office Library, English Court of Directors to factors in Hugli, 30.12.1681, Letter Book 6, f. 437). Also see Glamann, *Dutch–Asiatic Trade*, pp. 104–8.

[16] Coen at Bantam to Masulipatnam, 19 September 1618, VOC 1068, ff. 76–82.

[17] General letter from Coen at Jacatra to the Directors at Amsterdam, 22 January 1620, VOC 1070, ff. 162–77.

[18] Coen aboard the *Mauritius* at St Helena to the Directors at Amsterdam, 20 June 1623, VOC 1077, ff. 3–40.

overland trade between the two regions which, in turn, threatened to spoil the Agra market. In 1628, at the suggestion of the Agra factors, Batavia agreed to increase the share of Surat/Agra in the spice shipments to India at the cost of that of the Coromandel coast. In view of Shahjahan's campaign against Ahmadnagar, the routes from the Deccan had also become rather unsafe at this time. The result was a spectacular rise in the Agra price of cloves from ƒ.3.00 in 1627 to ƒ.6.60 per pond in 1630.[19]

The 1630s witnessed a significant increase in the volume of cloves procured at Makassar by the English and the Danes as well as by the Asian merchants. The result was a pressure on spice prices both in Europe as well as in Asia. The Surat price of cloves, for example, came down from ƒ.4.76 in 1630 to ƒ.3.07 in 1633 and further to ƒ.2.35 per pond in 1635.[20] The Coromandel price around this time was only ƒ.1.50 per pond.[21] The response of the Company was to try and compete the rivals out of the market by a further marked reduction in price, usually referred to as the strategy of dumping. As a result, the Surat price was brought down in 1636 to an unprecedentedly low level of ƒ.1.22 per pond. The following year, of the total of 269,000 ponds of cloves sent to the various Asian factories, Batavia sent as much as 167,000 ponds or 62 per cent to India.[22] The Company's strategy might very well have worked but for the collusion between the Company's servants in Surat and a few leading merchants of the city. Evidently in return for a consideration, the factors confined the sale of the cheap cloves to a very small number of merchants, at whose request the price was not publicly disclosed. In the few cases where information regarding both the wholesale price paid by these merchants as well as the price at which they retailed the cloves is available, the margin of profit earned by them is uniformly high and probably considerably in excess of the normal level.[23]

It was only in the second half of the seventeenth century, and particularly from the 1660s onward when the Company had finally managed to control the problem of smuggling, that the price of cloves

---

[19] H.W. van Santen, *De Verenigde Oost-Indische Compagnie in Gujarat en Hindustan, 1620–1660*, Leiden, 1982, pp. 44, 217.

[20] van Santen, *De Verenigde Oost-Indische Compagnie in Gujarat*, p. 217.

[21] Raychaudhuri, *Jan Company in Coromandel*, p. 194.

[22] W. P. Coolhaas (ed.), *Generale Missiven van Gouverneurs-Generaal en Raden aan Heren XVII der Verenigde Oost-Indische Compagnie*, The Hague, 1960, vol. I, p. 613.

[23] van Santen, *De Verenigde Oost-Indische Compagnie in Gujarat*, p. 45.

recovered both at Surat and on the Coromandel coast.[24] The increasingly strong position of the Company in the spice market, as also the desire to ensure that the European monopoly was not compromised by unusually low sale prices in Asia, were both reflected in the announcement by the Directors in 1653 of minimum sale prices for each of the major spices for Asia. These were $f.2.40$ per pond for cloves, $f.1.65$ for the whole kernels of nutmeg called 'noten' and $f.1.20$ for the broken variety called 'rompen', and $f.3.50$ per pond for mace.[25] The actual sale price in any given Asian factory could, of course, exceed these figures. From 1654 on, the Surat price of cloves was only marginally in excess of the prescribed minimum, except in particularly good years such as 1658 when it touched $f.3.65$ per pond. In the early 1660s, the Amsterdam price was $f.4.85$ per pond and the Directors believed that if they could fetch anywhere between $f.3.50$ and $f.4.00$ per pond in India, it would be relatively more profitable to sell in India. The Surat market did better than that and the price was reported to have gone up to $f.4.18$ per pond in 1663.[26]

The sale of cloves at Surat picked up considerably in the 1670s and the 1680s. Thus, against an annual average of 46,000 ponds during the 1660s, the figure went up to 75,000 ponds in the 1670s, and further to 85,000 ponds in the 1680s.[27] The Directors believed that an increase in the minimum Asian price would not have an adverse effect on the total amount sold. In 1687, therefore, these prices were revised upward to $f.4.35$ per pond for cloves, $f.2.50$ for the 'rompen' variety of nutmeg, and $f.4.75$ per pond for mace. These prices were only marginally lower than the prices in Europe. At Surat, things proceeded relatively smoothly until 1692, when the average annual sale of cloves was reported to have fallen to an unprecedentedly low level of 12,687 ponds. On enquiry, it was established that this was not because the

---

[24] Coolhaas (ed.), *Generale Missiven*, vol. III, p. 459; van Santen, *De Verenigde Oost-Indische Compagnie in Gujarat*, pp. 217–18; Raychaudhuri, *Jan Company in Coromandel*, p. 194.

[25] van Dam, *Beschrijvinge*, II.III, pp. 118–25.

[26] van Santen, *De Verenigde Oost-Indische Compagnie in Gujarat*, pp. 217–19; van Dam, *Beschrijvinge*, II.III, p. 118; Coolhaas (ed.), *Generale Missiven*, vol. III, p. 459.

[27] van Dam, *Beschrijvinge*, II.III, Appendix IIc, 'Nagelen, in 28 jaren in Suratte ter quantiteyt en pryse als volght verkoft', p. 131; van Santen, *De Verenigde Oost-Indische Compagnie in Gujarat*, pp. 47, 217–19. Between 1 September 1670 and 31 August 1680, a total of 1.67 million ponds of cloves, 2.13 million ponds of nutmeg and 0.2 million ponds of mace was sold in Asia. The corresponding figures of export to the Netherlands over the same period were 3.52 million ponds, 2.54 million ponds and 0.9 million ponds, respectively. (F.S. Gaastra, *Bewind en Beleid by de VOC 1672–1702*, Zutphen, 1989, p. 103).

effect of the minimum prices had now begun to be felt, but because Pieter van Helsdingen – one of the two acting directors of the Dutch factory at Surat – had rejected offers of prices higher than the minimum. It was pointed out that the factory could have sold 96,500 ponds of cloves at $f.4.50$ per pond and made a profit of $f.420,000$. Van Helsdingen was dismissed from the service of the Company, and the Surat factors were instructed to sell at $f.4.35$ per pond. A new set of minimum prices was announced by Batavia in 1696. The price of cloves was maintained at the 1687 level, but those of the other spices were increased. In the meantime, Van Helsdingen had succeeded in convincing the Directors that the 1687 prices were far too low, and that the sales would not suffer if the minimum prices for Asia were further revised upward. Yet another set of minimum prices for Asia was, therefore, announced by the Directors in 1697. The new price of cloves was $f.5.00$ per pond, which was about 6.7 per cent higher than the European price. It also happened to be considerably higher than the current market price in a number of Asian factories, with the result that the total sales dropped for a while.

By their secret letter of 12 August 1698, the Batavia Council authorized the factors at Surat to sell cloves, if necessary, at a price lower than the 1697 minimum but no lower than the 1687 minimum of $f.4.35$ per pond. In March 1701, Director Van Zwaardecroon wrote to Batavia that they had not been able to sell more than 40,000 ponds at about $f.4.70$ per pond. Doubts were also expressed in Holland regarding the wisdom of fixing the Asian minimum prices. A commission was, therefore, appointed late in 1702 to go into the question. Pieter van Dam, the celebrated historian of the Company, who served on the commission, advocated a reduction in the Asian prices.[28] The principal advocate of keeping the prices at a high level was Pieter de Witt who justified the policy on considerations of preventing illegal private trade in spices in Asia as well as safeguarding the Company's monopoly in Europe. The latter view prevailed and the commission recommended no reduction in prices.[29]

A statement available in the Company's archives pertaining to the years 1688–9 and 1689–90 and other information enables us to document the relative importance of Gujarat (and north India) as a

---

[28] van Dam, *Beschrijvinge*, II.III, pp. 120–5.
[29] ARA, Hugli to Batavia, 19.9.1697, VOC 1596, f. 94; Glamann, *Dutch–Asiatic Trade*, pp. 104–8.

market for spices. Of the total profit of *f*.1.89 million made by the Company on the sale of cloves, nutmeg and mace in Asia during 1688–9 and 1689–90 together, sales in Persia accounted for 12.83 per cent. The remaining 87.17 per cent of the profit was made on sales in India: Gujarat – 50.23 per cent, Coromandel – 28.06 per cent, Bengal – 7.01 per cent and Malabar – 1.87 per cent.[30]

The sale of goods was, of course, only a means towards an end, which was the procurement of textiles and other goods for the Asian and the European markets. Information regarding the relative share of Europe and the rest of Asia in the goods exported by the Company from Surat is available on a systematic basis only from the mid-1660s onward. Between that time and the mid-1680s, the value of goods intended for Europe was broadly the same as that for the rest of Asia (not taking into account the export of silver rupees from Surat which were intended exclusively for other Indian/Asian factories), except during the late 1670s when the relative share of Europe was distinctly smaller (Table 5.2). As a proportion of the total Dutch exports to Holland during this period, goods procured in Gujarat for Europe usually accounted for 6 to 7 per cent, though in an unusual year such as 1670–1 it could be as large as 14 per cent.[31] For the period until the mid-1650s, the commodity composition of the export cargo suggests that the share of Europe would have been distinctly larger until about 1641, and somewhat lower than that of the rest of Asia thereafter. This was the result essentially of the dramatically altered role of indigo, destined almost exclusively for Europe, in the total exports from Surat. While until 1641 indigo generally accounted for anywhere between 35 and 60 per cent of the total exports, its share during the 1640s and the early 1650s was generally under a quarter.[32] Indigo was procured by the Company at both Bayana (near Agra) and Sarkhej (near Ahmedabad).

Indigo's domination of the export cargo during the early years of the Company's trading operations in Gujarat and Agra is somewhat difficult to rationalize. In letter after letter, Batavia was asking Surat to go slow on the procurement of indigo and to invest the bulk of the

---

[30] This statement is available in ARA, VOC 1504, ff. 271–4.

[31] Calculated from Table 5.2 in conjunction with information on total Dutch imports into Holland available in Bruijn, Gaastra and Schöffer, *Dutch–Asiatic Shipping*, vol. III.

[32] van Santen, *De Verenigde Oost-Indische Compagnie in Gujarat*, Table 1, pp. 32–3.

limited funds available in textiles for the southeast Asian markets, because 'without these textiles, it was difficult to carry on trade in the southern quarters'.[33] When, in 1622, the *Weesp* arrived at Batavia with no Gujarat textiles for Indonesia, Coen wrote to Surat to register his strong displeasure, even adding that Van den Broecke 'dreamt of nothing but indigo'.[34] But for some inexplicable reason, the emphasis on indigo in the total procurement continued. It was only in the 1640s when competition by the better-quality and cheaper supplies from the West Indies brought about a slump in the market for Indian indigo in Europe that the procurement of this item was reduced. There was a revival in the demand for Indian indigo from the mid-1650s, but the amount exported between 1660 and 1680 was rarely above 100,000 ponds against the figure of over half a million ponds reached between 1638 and 1641.[35]

As for textiles, the varieties exported to Europe were initially mainly finer varieties of *baftas*, *dariabadis* and *cangans*. No Gujarat silk piece-goods were exported to Europe at this time, and the number of cotton and silk mixed piece-goods exported was also quite small and only on an occasional basis. Between 1660 and 1680, the largest number of pieces exported was in 1671–2 when it stood at 39,220 consisting of 37,220 pieces of fine cottons and 2,000 pieces of coarse cotton textiles.[36]

Within Asia, while small quantities of textile exports from Surat went to the Middle East (Basra, Gombroon and Mocha), the south-west coast of India (Vengurla and Malabar), Sri Lanka, Coromandel and Bengal, the bulk of the exports were directed at Batavia. From Batavia, an overwhelming proportion of these textiles was sent on to the Spice Islands and Malaya. According to an estimate prepared in 1623, the principal varieties that had a market in this region were

[33] Letter from Coen to Van den Broecke dated 6 November 1621, VOC 849, ff. 26v–27. The letter went on to say that until further orders, no funds were to be invested in any other commodity. Earlier, in his letter of 17 October 1621, Coen had told Van den Broecke to invest money in indigo only after meeting the textile orders from southeast Asia in full. The procurement of textiles for Holland was also to be postponed till such time as the availability of funds improved (letter dated 17 October 1621, VOC 849, ff. 15–16v). Also see letters from Coen to Surat dated 5 May 1622, VOC 849, ff. 85v–87v and 22 July 1622, VOC 850, ff. 1v–4.

[34] Letter from Coen to Dedel at Surat dated 22 July 1622, VOC 1076, ff. 96–96v.

[35] V.B. Gupta, 'The Dutch East India Company in Gujarat trade, 1660–1700: a study of selected aspects', unpublished PhD Thesis, Delhi University, 1991, p. 230.

[36] Gupta, 'The Dutch East India Company in Gujarat trade', p. 233.

baftas, cangans, chelas, cannikens, taffechelas and negro-cloth.[37] In the case of varieties such as *baftas* and *taffechelas*, there was a fairly large market for the medium and fine qualities. Of the Gujarat silk textiles, the most important variety procured for the southeast Asian markets was *patolas*.[38] Over the period between 1663 and 1680, for which quantitative information is available, there was an enormous fluctuation in the number of pieces exported by the Company from Surat to Batavia each year. Thus while there was a year such as 1664–5 when the number of pieces exported was as high as 396,570, at the other end of the scale there were years such as those between 1669–70 and 1672–3, when this number was under 50,000. The bulk of the textiles exported were coarse cottons, though fine cottons, silk piece-goods, as well as piece-goods made of a mixture of silk and cotton yarn, were also exported. The profitability in Indonesia was reasonable: in 1679, Surat *chintz* were reported to have yielded a gross profit of 100–128 per cent, while the following year *carricans* were sold at a profit of 70 per cent.[39]

The only other Asian region to which Gujarat textiles were exported in any quantity was the Middle East – Bandar Abbas and Basra in the Persian Gulf and Mocha in Yemen. Since the trade with these places had been organized from Surat as the base, Gujarat textiles had traditionally been included in the cargo sent there together with items such as Indonesian spices. The value of the textiles exported to Persia from the mid-1630s usually fluctuated between around ƒ.50,000 and ƒ.150,000 per annum. In the late 1630s, Surat cargo accounted for nearly half of the total value sent to Persia by the Company. The gross profit earned on the textiles was 40 per cent in 1642 but registered a steep decline thereafter to 4 per cent in 1651 and 7 to 8 per cent in 1659.The export of the textiles, therefore, was curtailed heavily. Between 1660 and 1700, the value of the exports from Surat to Persia was insignificant and often accounted for less than 1 per cent of the total Dutch exports from Gujarat. The only exceptions to this were

---

[37] An estimate prepared at Batavia by Antonio van Diemen of the textiles procured in Surat and the neighbouring areas that could be sold annually in the southern factories, 1 August 1623, VOC 1079, ff. 192v–193.

[38] In 1621, good quality *patolas* with figures of elephants and humans painted on them were reported to be selling in the Moluccas at the extremely high price of 40 to 50 rials per piece (Coen at Batavia to Van den Broecke at Surat, 6 November 1621, VOC 849, ff. 26v–27).

[39] Gupta, 'The Dutch East India Company in Gujarat trade', pp. 311, 337.

the years 1664–5, when Persia's share was a respectable 13.9 per cent, and 1668–9 when it was 8.56 per cent. The story was even more dismal in the case of Mocha. The export of Gujarat textiles to this port had begun around 1638, but was terminated in 1656 because of extremely poor profitability. It was only around the end of the seventeenth century that the Company's interest in Mocha had been revived because of coffee. The role of Gujarat textiles in the Mocha trade, however, never assumed any importance, and it was only occasionally that a gross profit of about 50 per cent was earned on these textiles.[40]

Bengal

When the Company came to Bengal in the early 1630s after having established itself in Coromandel and Gujarat, it was also mainly in quest of goods for its intra-Asian trade.[41] But the commodity this time was not textiles for southeast Asia, but raw silk for Japan. Some time later, Bihar opium also emerged as a major item of export to southeast Asia. In the closing decades of the seventeenth century, Bengal emerged as a major provider of textiles and raw silk for the European market. The average annual value of the Company's total exports from Bengal to other parts of Asia as well as to Europe registered a rapid rise from under ƒ.200,000 in the late 1640s to over a million florins a decade later (Table 5.3).

Over the following decades, the growth continued almost uninterrupted till the figure of nearly ƒ.2 million was reached in the early 1680s. Information available for 1675–6 shows that raw silk accounted for 40 per cent of the total Dutch exports from the region and textiles for another 22 per cent. The remaining 38 per cent was divided equally between saltpetre (12 per cent) and opium (7 per cent) on the one hand, and miscellaneous goods (sugar, rice, wheat, clarified butter, mustard oil, wax, borax, seashells (cauris) and gunny bags) on the other. Over the greater part of the seventeenth century, a fairly important segment of the textiles, the bulk of the raw silk and the entire lot of opium procured in the region was used by the Company for its intra-Asian trade. In the 1660s, exports to Batavia, Japan and other parts of Asia accounted for between 55 and 70 per cent of the

[40] van Santen, De Verenigde Oost-Indische Compagnie in Gujarat, p. 57; Gupta, 'The Dutch East India Company in Gujarat trade', pp. 263–6, 278.
[41] This section is based on Om Prakash, The Dutch East India Company and the Economy of Bengal, 1630–1720, Princeton, 1985, chs. 5–7.

Table 5.3 *The Dutch East India Company's exports from Bengal,*
1645–1785

	(average annual value in florins)			
Quinquenniums	Number of years for which information is available over the quinquennium	Value (f.)	Years	Value (f.)
1645–50	2	172,982	1720–1	4,615,986
1650–5	2	718,707	1722–3	4,221,093
1655–60	4	1,267,491	1725–6	4,943,337
1660–5	5	1,454,524	1731–2	2,363,138
1665–70	5	1,407,112	1735–6	4,314,042
1670–5	4	1,652,102	1741–2	3,034,504
1675–80	4	1,256,393	1751–2	4,995,786
1680–5	5	1,960,132	1761–2	2,301,796
1685–90	5	1,871,034	1771–2	1,965,350
1690–5	5	2,429,758	1780–1	2,476,844
1695–1700	4	2,777,103	1784–5	1,324,523
1700–5	3	3,294,045		
1705–10	2	3,565,194		
1710–15	5	3,258,434		
1715–20	3	3,845,882		

Source: The figures for the years 1645–50 to 1715–20, and for 1720–1, 1725–6 and 1735–6 have been calculated from the Bengal export invoices in the *Overgekomen Brieven en Papieren* series in the VOC records preserved at the *Algemeen Rijksarchief*, The Hague. (The figures until 1720–1 are also available in my *The Dutch East India Company and the Economy of Bengal, 1630–1720*, Princeton, 1985, Table 33, p. 70.) The figures for the remaining years have been calculated from the 'copie generale journalen gehouden door de boekhouder-generaal te Batavia 1700/1701–1789/90' which forms part of the series 'Copien van stukken afkomstig van de boekhouding te Batavia', available at the *Algemeen Rijksarchief*, The Hague under ARA, BGB 10751 to 10801. In order to establish the comparability across time of the values calculated from these two sources, the figures for the years 1701–2 and 1711–12 were collected from both sources. It turned out that the figures from the two sources were quite comparable, the marginal difference arising probably from various handling and other costs associated with the export of goods. For 1701–2, the figure from the invoices in the *overgekomen brieven* series was *f.*3,327,845 and that from the *Generale journalen* series *f.*3,344,910. The corresponding figures for 1711–12 were *f.*3,481,998 and *f.*3,497,270 respectively. The possibility of the figures for the years 1722–3, 1731–2 and those between 1741–2 to 1784–5 calculated from the 'copie generale journalen' differing from those that might emerge on the basis of export invoices cannot, of course, be ruled out.

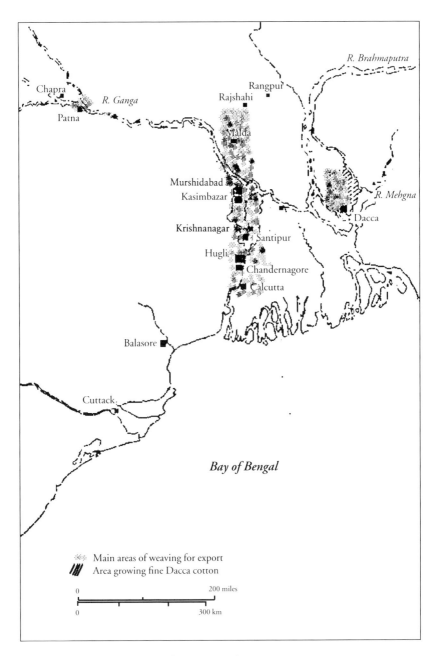

Map 7 Bengal: main textile towns c. 1720

Table 5.4 *Regional distribution of the Dutch East India Company's average annual exports from Bengal, 1660–1735 (value in florins)*

Years	Average annual exports	Europe Value (f.)	Europe % of total	Batavia Value (f.)	Batavia % of total	Japan Value (f.)	Japan % of total	Rest of Asia Value (f.)	Rest of Asia % of total
1660–1	1,325,002	NA	–	NA	–	595,000	44.90	85,155	6.42
1665–6	1,229,360	555,597	49.15	NA	–	500,704	40.72	173,059	14.07
1666–7	1,100,536	324,319	29.46	NA	–	611,349	55.55	164,868	14.98
1668–9	1,713,016	NA	–	NA	–	689,369	40.25	298,190	17.40
1673–4	1,453,107	NA	–	NA	–	796,000	54.77	206,917	14.23
1674–5	1,313,460	255,490	19.45	165,926	12.63	603,400	45.93	288,644	21.97
1675–6	1,153,769	318,039	27.56	NA	–	574,759	49.81	260,971	22.61
1681–2	1,923,665	NA	–	NA	–	530,700	27.58	249,132	12.95
1693–4	2,641,071	2,041,061	77.28	325,826	12.33	167,737	6.35	106,447	4.03
1698–1703	3,261,849	2,402,694	73.66	430,265	13.19	258,345	7.92	160,063	4.90
1708–13	3,308,529	2,300,706	69.53	526,430	15.91	348,983	10.54	131,862	3.98
1713–18	3,683,513	2,677,033	72.67	582,304	15.86	264,268	7.17	157,907	4.28
1720–1	4,615,986	3,508,911	76.01	761,890	16.50	201,756	4.37	143,429	3.10
1725–6	4,943,337	3,565,066	72.11	1,009,152	20.41	320,173	6.47	48,946	0.99
1735–6	4,314,042	3,072,662	71.22	977,512	22.65	153,878	3.56	109,990	2.54

Note: NA stands for not available.

Source: The figures for the period 1660–1721 have been calculated from Prakash, *The Dutch East India Company and the Economy of Bengal*. The figures for 1725–36 have been calculated from Bengal export invoices in the Dutch records. In the three quinquenniums included between 1698 and 1718, the annual average is based on information available for all the five years.

Company's total exports from Bengal. In 1674–75, this proportion touched an all-time peak of 80 per cent, though the following year it had again come down to 72 per cent (Table 5.4).

In Asia, by far the most important market for Bengal goods was Japan which took large quantities of raw silk in addition to silk and mixed textiles. The Japan goods sent to Bengal included, in addition to substantial quantities of silver and later gold, fairly large quantities of bar copper. Bengal raw silk was included in the Company's cargo for Japan for the first time in 1640. From 1641 onward, the profitability on the Chinese raw silk, the principal rival of the variety from Bengal, was adversely affected by the decision of the Japanese authorities to subject the entire lot of the Chinese raw silk brought in by the Company to the *pancado* arrangement.[42] The amount of Bengal raw silk sent to Nagasaki was, therefore, increased. In 1646, the Board of Directors even instructed Batavia to give priority to the orders for Bengal raw silk from Japan over those from Holland. In 1649, Bengal silk was reported to have yielded a gross profit of 200 per cent at Nagasaki. The following year, the entire lot of this silk received at Batavia was sent on to Japan. In the early 1650s, the rate of profit registered a decline, but Bengal silk still did considerably better than its rivals from Tonkin or China. In 1657, the Board of Directors went so far as to observe that 'the Bengal–Japan silk trade provides us with the largest amount of capital . . . Bengal and Japan should, therefore, be used as our milch-cows!'

In the 1660s, goods destined for Japan accounted for as much as 40 to 55 per cent of the Company's total exports from Bengal (Table 5.4). Of the total cargo sent to Japan from Batavia, the share of Bengal goods at this time was within the same range – a little under 50 per cent. Over the period 1656–72, Bengal silk accounted, on an average, for 80 per cent of the total amount of raw silk the Company sent to Nagasaki. The 1672 introduction of the appraised trade system, which effectively reintroduced the *pancado* system in relation to all goods imported into Japan, inevitably brought the profit rate down considerably. The volume of trade with Japan was, therefore, reduced. In 1679, the Batavia Council instructed the Bengal factors to supply raw silk

---

[42] Under the *pancado* arrangement, the Company was obliged to sell to the Nagasaki guild at a price unilaterally determined by the latter.

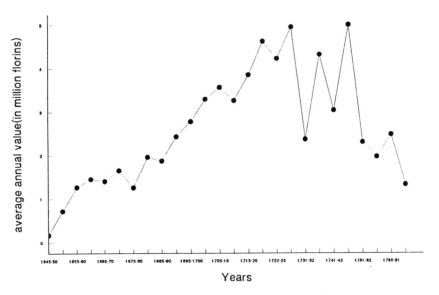

Fig. 5.3 The Dutch East India Company's exports from Bengal,
1645–1785

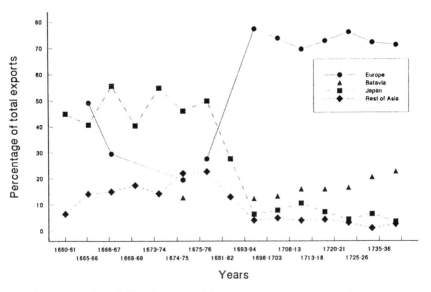

Fig. 5.4 Regional distribution of the VOC's average annual exports
from Bengal, 1660–1736 (in percentage terms)

for Japan only if a minimum gross profit of 80 per cent had been earned on it in Nagasaki the previous year.

The other major Asian region to which the Dutch Company exported Bengal goods was the Indonesian archipelago. The principal commodity that figured in this trade was Bihar opium, and by the close of the 1660s the quantity exported had reached fairly important levels. The Batavia Council sold the Bihar opium to Indonesian, Malay, Chinese and other merchants at public auctions held in the town. Opium was smoked practically all over the region. But if one were to list the various consuming markets in descending order of importance to the Company, at the top would probably be the island of Java, then Sumatra, the Malay peninsula, the island of Borneo, and the Moluccas, in that order. The greater part of the lot the merchants bought from the Company was carried to the Javanese ports of Grise, Japara and Cheribon. The other major destinations were Palembang in Sumatra and Malacca in the Malay peninsula.

The 1670s witnessed a significant rise in the amount of Bihar opium exported to the archipelago exceeding, for example, 32,000 ponds in 1674-5. In 1677, the Company succeeded in getting monopoly rights in opium in Mataram in Java. A similar privilege was obtained in 1678 in Palembang in Sumatra, and in 1681 in Cheribon in Java. The greater part of the crucial Javanese market and a considerable segment of the Sumatran market were now available to the Company on an exclusive basis. In 1679, the average auction price at Batavia was reported to be 300 rix-dollars per picul of 122 ponds, which meant a gross profit of 400 per cent. The importance the Batavia Council now attached to the opium trade was reflected in the instructions sent to Hugli to give priority to the procurement of this drug over even that of raw silk. As a provider of purchasing power to the Company in the archipelago, opium was now second only to Indian textiles. These textiles did include some varieties from Bengal, but at this time their role was quantitatively insignificant. Among the major items the Company imported from the archipelago into Bengal were spices and non-precious metals such as tin, spelter, lead, mercury and vermilion, in addition to minor items such as sandalwood from Timor.

The Coromandel coast, Sri Lanka, Malabar and Persia were the other places in Asia to which the Company sent Bengal goods. The volume and the value of trade with each of these places was, however, comparatively small. The exports to Coromandel and Sri Lanka included textiles, raw silk and provisions such as rice, sugar, long pepper, wheat and clarified butter. The items imported from Sri Lanka included cinnamon, areca-nuts and elephants. The main item of export to Malabar was opium besides small quantities of raw silk and textiles, while the principal item imported from there was pepper. Between 1663 and 1672, the Company used its newly acquired status at Cochin to wrest from the local rulers in Malabar exclusive trading rights in both pepper and opium. Even though these rights were qualified to a significant extent by the large-scale smuggling carried on by Indian merchants, the amount of opium sold in Malabar registered a substantial increase. As far as Persia was concerned, the principal exports included sugar and textiles. The profit earned on the textiles was, however, quite small and, occasionally, even a net loss was incurred. Indeed, in 1665, in order to minimize the chances of net loss, the Batavia Council ruled that a minimum of 40 per cent gross profit had to be earned on any given variety in a particular year to qualify it for export the following year.

As far as the exports to Europe were concerned, the role of Bengal was rather limited mainly because raw silk and textiles, the two principal exports from the region, had only a limited market in Europe at this time. Indeed, but for saltpetre, of which Bengal was the principal Asian supplier, the role of Bengal goods in the total Dutch exports to Europe would have been negligible. In the 1660s and the 1670s, the proportion of Bengal goods in the total exports to Europe fluctuated between 7 and 10 per cent (Table 5.5). The only exception to this was the year 1665–6 when an unusually small value of total exports to Europe coupled with a relatively high value of goods originating in Bengal led to a situation where Bengal goods accounted for as much as half of the total value sent to Holland.

As for textiles, initially it was only muslins that were ordered from Bengal, though later other varieties of cotton, cotton and silk mixed, as well as silk textiles, also figured in the orders. The performance in Holland was quite satisfactory: in 1660, the average gross profit on Bengal textiles was reported to be 200 per cent, which was considerably higher than the profit earned on the textiles from Coromandel, for example. But this happy state did not last very long with the result that, in 1665, the orders for Bengal textiles were sharply slashed and several varieties, particularly in the fine cotton group, were dropped altogether. Mainly because of the stiff competition by the English East

Table 5.5 *Share of Bengal goods in total Dutch exports to Europe,*
1665–1736

Year (1)	Total exports to Europe (f.) (2)	Bengal exports to Europe (f.) (3)	Share of Bengal exports in total exports (%) (4)
1665–6	1,124,180	555,597	49.42
1666–7	3,119,053	324,319	10.39
1674–5	3,644,173	255,490	7.01
1675–6	4,131,266	318,039	7.69
1693–4	2,794,745	2,041,061	73.03
1698–1703	5,951,011	2,402,694	40.64
1708–13	5,464,354	2,300,706	42.10
1713–18	6,735,503	2,677,033	39.74
1720–21	10,235,475	3,508,911	34.28
1725–26	10,136,882	3,565,066	34.83
1735–36	6,500,672	3,072,662	47.26

Source: The figures in column 2 have been calculated from Bruijn, Gaastra and Schöffer, *Dutch–Asiatic Shipping*, vol. III. The figures in column 3 are based on Table 5.4. The figures for the years between 1698 and 1718 are average annual figures.

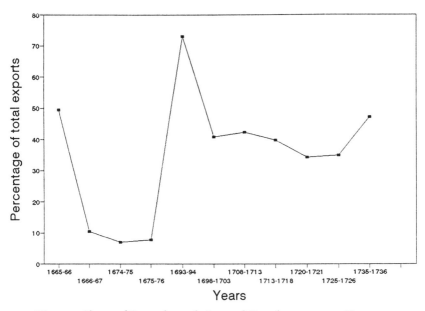

Fig. 5.5 Share of Bengal goods in total Dutch exports to Europe,
1665–1736

India Company, the cost price was almost continuously on the rise. In a moment of exasperation, the Directors went so far as to write to Batavia in 1676 that if the cost of the Bengal textiles could not be kept in check, they would seriously consider stopping further imports.

The raw silk the Company imported into Holland was procured, in addition to Bengal, in China and Persia. The principal attraction of the Bengal variety was that, while it was substantially cheaper than both the Chinese and the Persian varieties, it fetched a price only slightly lower than the former and about the same as the latter. But because of the precedence given to the orders from Japan, the quantity of Bengal silk reaching Holland remained quite small in the early years and the profit earned quite satisfactory. From the early 1660s on, however, as in the case of textiles, the competition by the English led to the twin problems of rising cost and deteriorating quality. Until the close of the 1670s, the Asian raw silk that dominated the Dutch market was still that from Persia.

The Malabar coast

As far as the Kanara and the Malabar coasts were concerned, the principal commodity the Company procured there was pepper in exchange mainly for opium. The pepper was intended primarily for the Persian market, though it was also sent elsewhere. Competition by Indian merchants was severe and, in 1639, the factors at Vengurla were obliged to pay 20 to 30 per cent more than what the Indian merchants had paid. This, Batavia pointed out, was enough to wipe the profit out or even to involve a net loss.[43] The amount of Malabar pepper imported into Batavia reached the respectable figure of around one million ponds at mid-century. But as pointed out earlier, the resumption of hostilities with the Portuguese after the end of the Ten Years' Truce in 1652 necessitated the closure of the Kayakulam factory, and it was not until 1663 that the Company resumed trade at Malabar. When that happened, however, it was on the basis of the availability to the Company of privileges that it had not been able to obtain anywhere else in the subcontinent. In return for the assistance to the raja of Cochin in throwing the Portuguese out of his territories, the Dutch were granted, among other privileges, monopsony rights in pepper in the territory between Purakkad and Cranganur, and monopoly rights

---

[43] Coolhaas (ed.), *Generale Missiven*, vol. II, pp. 33, 111.

in opium in several parts of the region. The Company estimated that it would be able to procure as much as 4 million ponds of pepper per annum at the low price of $1\frac{1}{2}$ stivers per pond.

It was, however, soon realized that getting a monopoly privilege on paper was very different from getting it in effect. Given the topography of the region, it was nearly impossible to prevent large-scale smuggling in both pepper and opium. Any attempt to police the numerous tracks used for the purpose would have involved a disproportionately high cost for the Company. The next best solution was to try and control the finances of the raja of Cochin to ensure that adequate funds were allocated for payment to guards employed by the government to check smuggling. But because of the Company's inability to penetrate the complicated structure of power at the Cochin court, this was never found feasible and smuggling continued. The result was that the pepper received by the Company was seldom delivered on time or in the promised quantity.[44]

THE ENGLISH COMPANY TRADE

We noted earlier that the English Company had already established factories in both Gujarat and Coromandel in the second decade of the seventeenth century, though it did not reach Bengal until the 1650s. Initially, the principal commodity the Company exported from Gujarat was Sarkhej and Bayana indigo for the European market. But the size of the market turned out to be relatively small and already by the 1620s the point of saturation would seem to have been reached. In the 1630s, the rise in the price of the Sarkhej variety as a result of the great Gujarat famine led to a relatively greater part of the lot being supplied in Bayana indigo. As of the late 1630s, the European demand for indigo began to shrink in view of the growing competition by the better quality lots imported from the West Indies. This trend became marked in the 1640s following which instructions were sent to Gujarat to curtail investment in this item. In 1670, the Surat factors were told by the Directors that buyers in London were complaining about the quality of the Indian indigo. The 1670s nevertheless were marked by a rapid increase in the import of Indian indigo, leading to pressure on

---

[44] H.K. s'Jacob, 'De VOC en de Malabarkust in de 17de eeuw', in M.A.P. Meilink-Roelofsz. (ed.), *De VOC in Azie*, Bussum, 1976, pp. 85–99.

the sale price in London. The other important bulk good the Company imported from India (mainly Bengal) was saltpetre, which came in handy for ballasting the return ships. It was often sold in large lots to the government and the mark-up, which was almost always in excess of 1:4, was clearly the highest amongst all East India goods.

By far the most important commodity the Company procured in India was, of course, textiles for both its intra-Asian as well as its Euro-Asian trade. Initially, as in the case of the VOC, the Company bought Indian calicoes needed for the procurement of Indonesian pepper and spices at places such as Bantam and Acheh. This was no longer the case following the establishment of the Masulipatnam factory, but given the continued uncertain position of the Company in the Indonesian archipelago, the quantity of Coromandel textiles imported into the region continued to be small. It was only after 1624 when the procurement of cloves smuggled into Makassar became important that growing quantities of Coromandel textiles were carried there via Batavia and later Bantam. But this trade declined rather sharply as of 1643 as Dutch efforts to plug the smuggling into Makassar became increasingly successful. The only other Asian market to which the Company carried Coromandel textiles was Persia, but the quantities involved were never large.

As far as the European market was concerned, the bulk of the textiles supplied over the first half of the seventeenth century origi-nated in Gujarat. Calicoes imported from Surat appeared as a regular item in the Company's sales from 1613 onward, and the 1620s witnessed a fairly rapid increase in the quantity imported. Thus the number of pieces brought in went up from 100,000 in 1620 to 221,500 five years later. But this expansion was interrupted rudely by the famine and even in 1639 the number of pieces imported was no higher than 66,000.[45]

It was during the Gujarat famine that the Company explored the possibility of importing Coromandel textiles into Europe. But success was strictly limited, and it was only after 1646 that the quantity of Coromandel textiles the Company carried to Europe became at all significant. The number of pieces ordered from Coromandel for 1658 amounted to 54,000 as against 63,500 from Surat. The 54,000 pieces

[45] K. N. Chaudhuri, *The English East India Company: The Study of an Early Joint Stock Company*, London, 1965.

included 20,000 pieces each of Guinea cloth and *salampuris*, and 14,000 pieces of other varieties. Moreland has argued that, because of their size, 20,000 pieces of Guinea cloth were in fact equivalent of 50,000 pieces of normal-sized textiles. On this basis, the orders from Coromandel would amount to 84,000 pieces and would exceed those from Surat. But in so far as the Dutch Company was still distinctly ahead (the Dutch orders were for 106,500 pieces for 1652 and possibly a larger amount for 1658) of the English in the trade in Coromandel textiles, Moreland's assertion that 'it was the English Company which opened the West European market in cotton fabrics' needs revision at least in respect of the textiles from Coromandel.[46]

The first year for which detailed quantitative information in respect of the English East India Company's imports into England is available is 1664. During that year, more than a quarter of a million pieces of textiles worth a little over £100,000, and accounting for 73 per cent of total value, were imported from India. Of these, valuewise, Coromandel textiles accounted for 48 per cent, those from Gujarat for 35 per cent, while the remaining 17 per cent worth were from Bengal. The share of the varieties from the three regions in the total sales proceeds of textiles was 58.7 per cent, 31.1 per cent and 10.2 per cent respectively. The remainder of the 1660s, the 1670s and the early 1680s were a period of considerable growth in the English Company's textile trade with the imports in 1684 standing at an all-time record of 1.76 million pieces costing nearly £670,000 and accounting for an unprecedented 83 per cent of the total value imported.[47] The period after 1670 also witnessed a sustained expansion in the Company's import of Bengal raw silk into Europe, though in absolute terms the quantities involved were still quite small.

THE DANISH COMPANY TRADE

Besides the Portuguese, the Dutch and the English, the only other European enterprise active in Asia over the first three quarters of the seventeenth century was the Danish East India Company. The first fleet on the account of this Company consisting of two men-of-war and three merchantmen had left Copenhagen in August 1618 to

[46] For Moreland's assertion, see Glamann, *Dutch–Asiatic Trade*, p. 138.
[47] K.N. Chaudhuri, *The Trading World of Asia and the English East India Company, 1660–1760*, Cambridge, 1978, Appendix 5.

explore the possibilities of trade in Sri Lanka, the Coromandel coast and the Indonesian archipelago. In November 1620, Roland Crappé obtained from the Nayak of Tanjavur the town of Tranquebar (where Fort Dansborg was built the following year) in addition to revenue-farming rights in respect of a neighbouring village. In October 1625, a factory was established at Masulipatnam as well.

The shortage of resources proved a limiting factor from the very beginning. It is remarkable that between 1623 and 1639 no more than a total of thirteen vessels left Denmark for Asia with long periods such as 1624–30 in between when not a single ship arrived in Asia. Again, between the dispatch from Copenhagen of the *Christianshavn* in November 1639 and a royal frigate, the *Færo*, in October 1668, there was a complete blank. It is not surprising, therefore, that the import of Asian goods into Denmark through this period was only occasional and extremely limited in value. Between 1622 and 1637, no more than seven ships returned to Denmark. In 1632, the *Christianshavn* was sent from Tranquebar to Denmark with a cargo worth f.90,000 consisting of 57,600 ponds of pepper, 48,000 ponds of cloves, 100 packs of cotton yarn and 36 bahars of saltpetre. Crappé himself travelled on the next shipment which left Tranquebar towards the end of 1636 and arrived in Copenhagen in January, 1638. The cargo carried aboard was 145,000 ponds of cloves and 20,000 ponds of sappanwood, besides some saltpetre and a few packs of Guinea cloth from Coromandel.[48]

By the 1640s, it had become quite clear that the East India Company venture had not been a particular success. King Frederick III, therefore, formally declared the Company liquidated in 1650. Since Tranquebar was a royal colony, Danish presence continued there and in 1668 the royal frigate *Færo* was sent there with supplies and money. The commercial side of the expedition was looked after by a group of private investors who had hired cargo space on the frigate. The factors at Tranquebar were relieved in 1669, and in September 1670 the *Færo* returned to Copenhagen with a cargo of pepper and fine spices from Bantam. This served to raise expectations about the East Indies trade once again, and on 28 November 1670 a second East India Company was chartered.

Given the grossly inadequate support in ships and capital from

---

[48] Subrahmanyam, *The Political Economy of Commerce*, pp. 185–7.

home, the first Danish venture derived its real sustenance from participation in a limited range of coastal as well as high-seas trade within Asia. The coastal trade from Tranquebar southwards extended as far as Sri Lanka. The first high-seas connection developed was that with Tenasserim, where the principal competition was provided by the Portuguese operating from Nagapattinam. The shortage of capital soon forced the conversion of this particular activity into essentially one of a freight service which too was terminated in the early 1630s. The arrival of capital and ships from Copenhagen in April 1624 had in the meantime facilitated the establishment of a more substantive link between Tranquebar and Makassar. The role of Makassar as the principal outlet for cloves smuggled out of the Moluccas has already been noted. By the late 1620s, the Danes were sending on a regular basis two ships per annum from Tranquebar to Makassar. They had emerged as reasonably important buyers of cloves in exchange mainly of coarse cotton Coromandel textiles causing a good deal of embarrassment and concern to the VOC. In 1632, the Danes were reported to have brought into Tranquebar as much as 150,000 ponds of cloves, a part of which, as already noted, was sent on to Copenhagen aboard the *Christianshavn*. In addition to Makassar, the Danish vessels also called at several other Indonesian ports open to non-VOC trade such as Acheh, Bantam and Japara. In 1638, for example, two Danish ships were reported to have brought into Bantam 39,700 rials worth of goods from Coromandel in addition to carrying textiles worth 22,000 rials for Makassar. On their return to Bantam from Makassar in June 1639, the vessels carried a cargo worth 29,709 rials including 58 bahars of cloves and 1,319 piculs of sugar (probably of Philippines origin) for Coromandel. At Bantam, they picked up cargo worth another 38,464 rials.[49] From about this time on, however, the scale of their trade with Makassar and other southeast Asian ports would seem to have registered a sharp decline. In 1653, for example, writing about the Danish resident at Makassar, the Dutch factors noted that 'he had received no funds whatever over the last two years and has no option but to live from hand to mouth'.[50]

To sum up the position around 1680 which marked the end of the first phase of the European companies' trading activities in Asia, the

[49] Subrahmanyam, *The Political Economy of Commerce*, p. 187.

[50] J.E. Heeres *et al.* (ed.), *Dagh-Register gehouden in 't Casteel Batavia*, Batavia/The Hague, 1888, 22 July 1653, p. 103.

two giants – the Dutch and the English – between themselves accounted for practically the entire Company trade. The Danish Company operations were insignificant, and the French had still to make a beginning. Between the Dutch and the English, the former were still distinctly ahead. We noted earlier that, during the triennium 1668–70, the value of Dutch imports into Europe was as much as $f.$10.78 million against the English figure of $f.$4.32 million. The 1670s, however, witnessed a remarkable growth in the English Company imports, which stood in 1680 at $f.$4.27 million against the Dutch figure of $f.$3.38 million that year.[51] But in so far as the Dutch, in addition, carried on an extensive intra-Asian trade, there can be very little doubt that in terms of the total value of trade, the Dutch were still very much ahead. In the English imports of 1680, India accounted for as much as 86 per cent of the total value, with the share of Coromandel, Gujarat and Bengal being 36.9, 27.3 and 21.9 per cent, respectively.[52] For the VOC also, the Coromandel trade was still the most important, accounting for an annual average of $f.$2 million worth of exports from the region during 1676–80 followed by Bengal ($f.$1.25 million during 1675–80) and Gujarat ($f.$1.07 million during 1676–81). Note that in the case of each of the three regions, a larger proportion of the total cargo was directed at destinations within Asia, as compared to that for Europe.[53]

[51] The English Company figure is based on Chaudhuri, *The Trading World of Asia*, Appendix 5, with the rate of conversion between the £sterling and the florin being assumed to be £1 = $f.$12. The Dutch Company figure has been calculated from Bruijn, Gaastra and Schöffer, *Dutch–Asiatic Shipping*, vol. III.

[52] Calculated from Chaudhuri, *The Trading World of Asia*, Appendix 5.

[53] In the late 1670s, the share of Asia in the total exports from Bengal ranged between 70 and 80 per cent. For Gujarat, this figure was 62 per cent in respect of the goods exported. In addition, the entire supply of silver rupees from the region was meant for other Asian factories.

CHAPTER 6

THE VOC AND THE GROWING COMPETITION BY THE ENGLISH AND THE FRENCH, 1680–1740

The last two decades of the seventeenth and the early part of the eighteenth century marked a major qualitative change in the Dutch East India Company's trade between Asia and Europe. The value of this trade continued to grow at a fairly impressive rate. Thus the triennium total of the Company's imports into Europe went up from *f.*10.79 million during 1668–70 to *f.*15 million during 1698–1700, and further to *f.*19.25 million during 1738–40. But more importantly, over the same period, the composition of the imports altered dramatically. Thus between 1668–70 and 1698–1700, the share of pepper and other spices in the total imports came down from 43 per cent to 23 per cent. By 1738–40, this figure had further come down to a mere 14 per cent (Table 4.1). Because of an almost revolutionary change in European fashions, the share of textiles and raw silk, on the other hand, increased significantly. While during 1668–70 these two items together had accounted for 36 per cent of the total imports from Asia, by 1698–1700 the figure had gone up to an impressive 55 per cent. During 1738–40, it stood at 41 per cent. An overwhelming proportion of the Asian textiles and raw silk was procured in India. Thus out of textiles worth *f.*2.35 million that reached Holland in 1697, for example, those originating in India accounted for as much as 88 per cent.[1] Again, of the Asian raw silk sold in Amsterdam between 1693 and 1720, Indian raw silk accounted, valuewise, for as much as 90 per cent. The subcontinent's share in the total Dutch imports into Europe, therefore, registered an important increase, though with the rise of tea in the 1730s, China also became an important supplier for Europe.

[1] Calculated from Kristof Glamann, *Dutch–Asiatic Trade, 1620–1740,* Copenhagen/The Hague, 1958, p. 144.

THE DUTCH COMPANY, CLANDESTINE PRIVATE TRADE AND THE INDIAN MARITIME MERCHANT

The Dutch Company trade

Bengal

Within the subcontinent, the most important region for the Company's trade now was Bengal. The entire lot of raw silk imported from India was procured in this region. In the case of textiles, Bengal accounted in 1697 for 63 per cent of the total of Indian textiles, and 55 per cent of the total of Asian textiles imported into Holland. It is no wonder, therefore, that at the turn of the century Bengal accounted for as much as 40 per cent of the total value of Dutch imports from Asia into Europe. In the process, the loss of the pre-eminence of Bengal in the Company's intra-Asian trade, largely because of the declining position of the Japan trade in the network, was fully compensated. Of the total Dutch exports from Bengal, the ratio of the cargo destined for other parts of Asia to that for Europe, which had stood in 1674–5 at 80:20, had altered dramatically by 1693–4 to 23:77.

Over the period 1680 to 1740, the average annual value of the total Dutch exports from Bengal increased significantly (Table 5.3). From *f.*1.26 million in 1675–80, this figure had gone up to *f.*3.56 million over 1705–10 and to *f.*4.94 million during 1725–6. Thereafter, there was a rather sharp decline to *f.*2.36 million during 1731–2, but by 1735–6 the figure had recovered to *f.*4.31 million. The period also witnessed a major alteration in the composition of the exports from the region (Table 6.1). Thus the share of textiles, which had stood at 22 per cent in 1675–6, had gone up to as much as 54 per cent in 1701–3, though by 1722–3 it had come down marginally to 49 per cent. The share of raw silk, on the other hand, had come down over the same period from 40 per cent to 29 per cent and further to 25 per cent. Among the less important goods, while opium had gone up from 7 to 10 per cent, saltpetre came down from 12 to 5 per cent. The decline in the share of raw silk and the phenomenal rise in that of textiles was directly related to something we have already noted, namely the region's substantially reduced role in the Company's intra-Asian trade and its new role as the principal supplier of goods for Europe.

Table 6.1 *Composition of Dutch exports from Bengal (percent),*
1675–1785

Commodity	1675–6	1701–3	1722–3	1751–2	1784–5
Textiles	21.93	54.19	49.03	58.93	53.93
Raw silk	39.57	29.44	25.46	10.11	7.84
Saltpetre	12.11	5.79	5.42	6.56	6.96
Opium	6.64	7.08	10.21	14.47	21.27
Miscellaneous	19.75	3.50	9.88	9.93	10.00
Total	100.00	100.00	100.00	100.00	100.00

Source: The figures for 1675–6 and 1701–3 are based on the Bengal export invoices in the *Overgekomen Brieven en Papieren.* The figures for 1722–3, 1751–2 and 1784–5 are based on 'Copie generale journalen, gehouden door de boekhouder-generaal te Batavia. 1700/1701–1789–90', ARA, BGB, 10751–801.

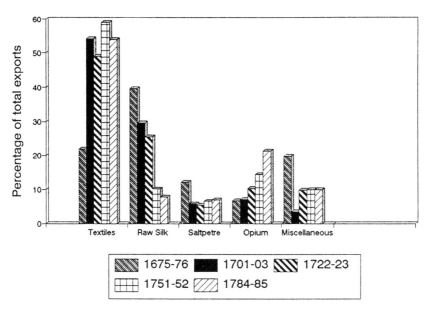

Fig. 6.1 Composition of Dutch exports from Bengal, 1675–1785

Intra-Asian trade

We noted earlier that, in the framework of the Company's intra-Asian trade, by far the most important role played by the goods produced in Bengal was in the Company's trade with Japan. Until the 1670s, the share of goods for Japan in the total cargo procured in Bengal as well as the share of Bengal goods in the total cargo sent to Japan was in both cases around 50 per cent. But this changed dramatically over the period 1680 to 1740. The share of goods for Japan in the total cargo procured in Bengal was not much more than a quarter in 1681–2, and it came down to under 10 per cent in the 1690s. In the 1720s and the 1730s, it fluctuated between 4 and 6 per cent (Table 5.4). As for the share of Bengal goods in the total exports to Japan, the figure had dipped to around a third in the 1690s, with the figure in 1699–1700, the last year for which information is available, being no more than 18 per cent.

The radically altered situation of Bengal goods in regard to the Japan trade was in a good measure the outcome of certain policies adopted by the Japanese authorities in the 1680s and 1690s. We have already noted the introduction in 1672 of the system of 'appraised trade'. But it was soon discovered that even this forced deterioration in the foreigners' terms of trade was not adequate to ensure that the annual specie loss did not assume disturbing proportions. In 1685, therefore, the system of what might be called 'limited trade' was introduced. Under the new arrangement, the Company was permitted to import annually goods whose total sales proceeds were not to exceed *f*.1.05 million. Further, the amount of raw silk the Company could sell during the course of a year was henceforth to be limited to *f*.350,000 sale value. The resultant erosion in the role of Japan in the overall trading strategy of the Company was further reinforced in 1696, when the gold content of the koban was reduced from 85.69 per cent to 56.41 per cent without a reduction in its silver price, making it a much less attractive coin to procure.

The decline of the Japan trade is apparent in the fact that the average annual value of the total Dutch exports to Nagasaki between 1686 and 1700 was reduced to *f*.630,000. Since the Company could not be certain of the precise quantity of raw silk that would fetch the ceiling amount of *f*.350,000 in Japan, and because the amount of raw silk exported to Europe was growing at a rapid rate around this time, what often happened was that the amount of raw silk sent to Japan was worth less than the maximum allowed. Throughout this period, Bengal continued to be the principal supplier of raw silk for Japan, but the absolute quantity involved had been reduced considerably.[2] The gross profit on Bengal raw silk was reported to be 63 per cent, 74 per cent, 85 per cent and 68 per cent in 1702, 1704, 1715 and 1717, respectively.

By forcing a rapid decline in the Dutch silk trade and at the same time withdrawing the appraised trade system from goods other than raw silk, the 1685 regulations actually promoted the trade in textiles. The first manifestation of this was an increase by 50 per cent in the 1686 Nagasaki orders for most varieties of Bengal textiles. Bengal *armosins* fetched a good profit of 137 per cent in 1702, and of 92 per cent two years later. In the early part of the eighteenth century, Bengal cotton textiles became a regular item of import into Japan. In 1715, whereas Bengal textiles afforded in Nagasaki an average gross profit of 151 per cent, those from the Coromandel coast fetched only 116 per cent, while the few pieces imported from Gujarat had, in fact, to be sold at a loss of 67 per cent.[3] In the 1720s and the 1730s, the quality of the Bengal textiles sent to Japan probably varied considerably from year to year. Thus while in 1728 and 1729 the quality of the *taffechelas gingams* and the *tassar alachas* was reported to be so poor as to have involved a net loss,[4] a 1731 Batavia evaluation of the lot of Bengal silk textiles received for Japan pointed out that not only had the samples on the basis of which the contracts had been put out been generally reproduced competently, but in many cases they had actually been improved upon in terms of quality.[5]

In contrast to Japan, the share of the goods destined for the Malay archipelago in the total exports from Bengal registered an important increase in the period under reference. From 12.63 per cent in 1674–5, this share had gone up to 17.81 per cent in 1698–9. The following few years were marked by sharp fluctuations, but by 1709–10 the figure of 19 per cent had been reached. In 1725–6, this figure stood at 20.4 per

---

[2] Thus the amount of Bengal raw silk exported to Japan had come down from 180,000 ponds in 1675 to 124,000 ponds in 1682, and to 44,000 ponds in 1693–4. The figure in 1700–1 was 60,700 ponds, in 1710–11, 42,845 ponds and in 1717–18, 33,806 ponds (Om Prakash, *The Dutch East India Company and the Economy of Bengal, 1630–1720*, Princeton, 1985, p. 126).

[3] Prakash, *The Dutch East India Company and the Economy of Bengal*, p. 137.

[4] *Algemeen Rijksarchief* (ARA), Hugli to Batavia, 30.11.1730, VOC 2165, ff. 20–1.

[5] Evaluation done by Hendrik Haak and Anthony Jubbels at Batavia dated 20.4.1731, ARA, VOC 2174, ff. 2427–8.

cent and in 1735–6 at 22.6 per cent. A part of this increase had been achieved by a fairly substantial expansion in the export of textiles from Bengal from about 1690 on.[6] This was related mainly to the deterioration in the situation on the Coromandel coast with regard to the availability and the price as well as the quality of the coarse cotton textiles obtained there. But the increased procurement in Bengal also involved problems of rising cost price and deteriorating quality, so much so that in 1715 Batavia reported that the quality of the *garras* – an ordinary calico – received was 'so poor that we do not recall an occasion in the past when such bad quality textiles were received from Bengal'.[7] The position did not register any particular improvement over the 1720s and the 1730s. A statement prepared at Batavia relating to the period 1 September 1728 to 30 October 1734 noted that on Indian textiles costing f.656,279 and sold at the Batavia Castle over the period, a profit of only f.194,497 amounting to 29.75 per cent had been earned. The sales at Bantam were much smaller: over the same period, a profit of only f.17,198 representing approximately a profit rate of 50 per cent was earned there.[8]

The principal Indian commodity sold in the region was now perhaps the opium from Bengal. It has been estimated that the amount annually consumed in Java and Madura, which had been around 4,000 ponds at the beginning of the seventeenth century, had gone up by 1678 to 70,000 ponds. By 1707, this figure had reportedly further gone up to 108,000 ponds.[9] Earlier in 1683, the Company had estimated the annual demand in the entire archipelago to be around 116,000 ponds.[10] It was a classic case of increased availability leading to increased consumption. To its mounting dismay, however, the Company discovered that its efforts at monopolizing this highly profitable and growing market were being severely undermined by both Asian and rival European traders engaged in the opium trade.

---

[6] Thus the number of pieces exported went up from around 7,000 in the mid-1670s to an average of 26,531 during the 1690s. There was further expansion from about 1706 on. After reaching levels such as 81,090 pieces in 1709–10 and 74,425 pieces in 1710–11, the figure stood at 46,510 pieces in 1717–18 (Prakash, *The Dutch East India Company and the Economy of Bengal*, Table 6.1, pp. 146–7).

[7] Prakash, *The Dutch East India Company and the Economy of Bengal*, p. 144.

[8] Statement signed at Batavia, VOC 2301, ff. 3416–3416v.

[9] J.C. Baud, 'Proeve van eene geschiedenis van den handel en het verbruik van opium in Nederlandsch-Indie', *Bijdragen tot de Taal-, Land-, en Volkenkunde van Nederlandsch Indie*, vol. 1, 1853, p. 115.

[10] ARA, Batavia to Hugli, 26.8.1683, VOC 909, f. 1378.

The competitors' trade not only cut deeply into the Company's potential market but, being characterized by enormous fluctuations in its total volume from year to year, had a destabilizing influence on the average auction prices at Batavia. Among the Asian traders participating in this trade were Indians, Armenians, Indonesians, Malays and Chinese, while the Europeans included the Danes, the Portuguese and, most important of all, the English, both private traders and the East India Company. Until 1682, these traders operated mainly from Bantam. But with the fall of the city to the Dutch in that year, the English East India Company moved to Benkulen in southwest Sumatra. The others moved mainly to Acheh in northern Sumatra. Besides carrying on a large amount of trade in areas where the Dutch had no special privileges, these traders appear to have succeeded in bringing limited quantities of opium into Mataram, Cheribon and Palembang as well, which were officially the exclusive 'preserves' of the Dutch. By far the most annoying of the competing groups was that of the Company's own servants engaged in a clandestine trade in the drug. Being a high-value, low bulk item, opium was ideally suited for this trade.

With a view to facing the challenge posed by the competitors (including their own servants), the Governor-General and Council at Batavia took a number of steps that included instructions to the Bengal factors to keep the cost of the drug as low as possible by confining their procurement to Patna, and to be extremely particular about the quality of the opium they sent to Batavia. In 1695, the Batavia Council decided that the only effective way to squeeze the competitors out of business was to undersell them for as long as necessary. In 1698, the Council observed that it had succeeded in bringing down the price of opium throughout Java. But the hopes of squeezing the rivals out were belied when it was discovered in 1700 that their volume of trade at both Acheh and Malacca had in fact been growing. What the Batavia Council had apparently not taken into account was the fact that its competitors usually succeeded in procuring opium at Patna at a lower price than its own factors did, and that in view of their considerably lower overhead costs (except, of course, in the case of the English East India Company) they could afford to operate at rather low rates of profit per unit of investment. In view of the intense competition, the rate of profit earned on opium by the Company continued to be relatively poor. In 1712, it was reported to be only 46 per cent, though in 1735–6, it had gone up to between 77 and 86 per cent.[11]

Euro-Asian trade

As we noted earlier, it was in the Company's imports into Europe that Bengal played a critically important role during the period 1680–1740. The region was now by far the largest Asian supplier of goods for Holland, accounting for around 40 per cent of the total imports during the 1690s (in 1693–4, this figure was as high as 73 per cent, but that probably ought to be treated as exceptional), the 1700s and the 1710s. In the 1720s, this figure was around 35 per cent, but in 1735–6 it stood at an unusually high level of 47 per cent (Table 5.5). A corollary of this was the emergence of Europe as the dominant trading partner of Bengal. While in 1675–6 Europe accounted for no more than 28 per cent of the total Dutch exports from Bengal, this figure over the last decade of the seventeenth and the first four decades of the eighteenth century was as high as between 70 and 77 per cent (Table 5.4).

The orders list sent by the Heren XVII in 1677 reflected the first major manifestation of the new pattern of demand for textiles in Europe. The orders for fine calicoes as well as those for silk and mixed piece-goods – the most important source of which was Bengal – were substantially increased whereas those for ordinary calicoes – procured mainly in Coromandel – were reduced. Initially, the greater part of the increased demand for muslins and fine calicoes for use as wearing apparel came from the well-to-do sections of the community, so that the Directors asked almost exclusively for the more expensive varieties of these textiles. With the spread of the fashion among consumers who were not so well off, however, it became profitable from the early 1690s on to import comparatively less fine qualities of these textiles as well, which in fact often afforded a higher profit. In view of the increasing shortages and rising costs of these textiles on the Coromandel coast in the 1690s, Bengal emerged as a major supplier of ordinary calicoes to Europe also.

The enormous increase in the procurement of textiles in Bengal, however, involved problems of rising cost price as well as deteriorating

[11] Prakash, *The Dutch East India Company and the Economy of Bengal*, p. 156; ARA, Statement in VOC 2361, f. 1140.

quality, particularly in the context of the growing trade carried on in the region by the English and the French East India companies. The response of the Dutch Company was limited to taking such steps as minimizing the rejection rate among the textiles received from the suppliers, and ensuring that the factors did not have to forgo supplies because of the shortage of liquid funds. In 1720, for example, the Hugli factors reported that, because of the availability of ample liquid funds, they had been able to dominate the production centres (*aurungs*). Both the English and the French, whose ships had arrived late, on the other hand, had not been able to procure more than 10 per cent of their requirements.[12] The situation could get particularly difficult in years characterized by one kind of abnormality or another. In 1730, for example, heavy floods, coupled with the loss at sea of several indigenous vessels while on their way from Surat to Hugli carrying mainly cotton, resulted in a sharp rise in the price of cotton in Bengal. Contrary to the norm whereby the merchants were obliged to supply at the price mutually agreed upon at the time of the contract irrespective of what happened in the meantime to the price of the inputs, the merchants expressed their inability to supply coarse cotton textiles at the stipulated price. Protracted negotiations obliged the Company to agree to a last-minute price rise ranging between 10 and $12\frac{1}{2}$ per cent.[13] The following year, continued uncertainty regarding the trend in the price of cotton made the merchants initially refuse to accept any textile contracts whatsoever. Eventually, as far as fine cotton textiles were concerned, the merchants were persuaded to accept contracts at the previous year's prices with the proviso that if the price of cotton continued to be high, they would be duly compensated at the time of delivery. In the case of coarse cotton textiles, however, all that the Company's broker, Hari Kishan, succeeded in doing was to persuade the merchants supplying fine cotton textiles to supply simultaneously some coarse cotton pieces. There was no formal agreement regarding the quantity or the price of these textiles. All that was agreed to was that the merchants would supply whatever number of pieces they could and would be paid a

---

[12] ARA, Hugli to Batavia, 31.10.1720, VOC 1938, ff. 86–7.
[13] ARA, Minutes of the Hugli Council meeting of 24.8.1730, enclosure to the letter from Hugli to Batavia, 30.11.1730, VOC 2165, ff. 265–74; Minutes of the Hugli Council meeting of 25.9.1730, VOC 2165, ff. 375–80; Hugli to Batavia, 30.11.1730, VOC 2165, ff. 121–6.

'fair' price at the time of delivery.[14] The average profit earned on Bengal textiles in Holland in 1735 was reported to be only 19 per cent: on Bengal and Coromandel textiles together, it was 32 per cent. This was because the intense competition by the English and the French had made the suppliers increasingly indifferent to quality, so much so that in 1735, of a particular lot of 19,390 pieces supplied to the Company, as many as 4,119 pieces had to be rejected outright. The rivals, particularly the French, were reported to have accepted such lots quite happily.[15] Later in the year, the Hugli factors reported that they had been unable to procure any *jamawars* or *armosins* whatsoever at the prices prescribed for them.[16]

The other Bengal commodity exported in large amounts to Europe was raw silk. Between 1693 and 1720, Bengal raw silk accounted, on average, for as much as 88 per cent of the total Asian raw silk sold in the Amsterdam market. In terms of value, this figure was 90 per cent. The share of Persian raw silk was 6 per cent in physical and 4 per cent in value terms, whereas Chinese raw silk accounted for 6 per cent of the total lot sold in terms of both quantity and value. Indeed, the Dutch silk textile industry had come to depend a great deal on Bengal for the supply of the necessary raw material. In July 1698, for example, the Directors wrote: 'The extremely limited amount of [Bengal raw] silk we received this year has caused very great inconvenience to the manufacturers here. Due to the shortage of raw silk, hundreds of looms are unemployed and the workmen are loitering about idle.' A similar statement was made in 1701 about the Bengal *mochta* (florette yarn) silk: 'The small amount received has inconvenienced the producers so much that a number of manufacturing units had to stop production.'[17]

The increase in the price of raw silk supplied by the merchants prompted the Hugli factors in 1714 to have as much as possible of the raw silk they exported reeled in the Company's own silk-reeling unit in the Kasimbazar factory. We have information regarding the place of reeling for 86 per cent of the total raw silk exported by the Company from Bengal to all regions between 1714 and 1718. Of this, as much as

[14] ARA, Minutes of the Hugli Council, 15.1.1731, VOC 2195, ff. 137–42; Minutes of the Hugli Council, 29.1.1731, VOC 2195, ff. 157–61; Hugli to Batavia, 10.3.1731, VOC 2195, ff. 66–70; Memorandum by Sadelyn to Berenaart dated 15.1.1732, VOC 2196, ff. 420–5.
[15] ARA, Hugli to Batavia, 18.11.1735, VOC 2348, f. 70.
[16] ARA, Hugli to Batavia, 17.1.1736, VOC 2348, ff. 560–1.
[17] Prakash, *The Dutch East India Company and the Economy of Bengal*, p. 217.

83.25 per cent was reeled in the Company's own reelery.[18] Through the 1720s and the 1730s, the growing English and French competition created problems for the Company as much in the case of raw silk as it did in that of textiles. Added to this was the growing trade in raw silk carried on by the Indian merchants between Bengal on the one hand and Gujarat and northern India on the other. In 1730–1, these merchants were reported to have made on this item a profit of 50 to 100 per cent more than they usually made.[19]

The Coromandel coast

The other principal area of the Company's trading operations in the subcontinent during 1680–1740 was the Coromandel coast, which continued to be a major supplier of textiles for both the European and the Asian markets. But the relative share of the two markets tended to change over time. While until the 1660s the value of the textiles procured in Coromandel for the rest of Asia had exceeded that of those for Europe, by the end of the century Asia accounted for only about a third of the total value of the textiles procured, the remainder being sent on to Holland. Of the total Asian textiles arriving in Holland in 1697, those procured in Coromandel accounted for 27 per cent by value. If one took into account only the textiles procured in India, this figure would go up to 30 per cent.

An analysis of the Company's textile exports from Coromandel from 1691 onwards produces interesting results (Table 6.2). With the exception of 1691 and 1697, the value of textiles exported during the 1690s and the early years of the eighteenth century generally approximated or exceeded a million florins, reaching a figure of as much as f.1.7 million in 1701. An important development characterizing this period was the growing shift in the area of procurement for both Europe and Asia from northern to southern Coromandel, where textiles were available both more cheaply and in distinctly greater abundance. Districts such as Cuddalore, Salem and Tanjavur now provided a large proportion of the total amount procured. Districts such as Madura and Tinnevelli, which lay south of Point Calimere and were under the jurisdiction not of the Dutch 'government' of Cor-

---

[18] Prakash, *The Dutch East India Company and the Economy of Bengal*, p. 219.
[19] ARA, Hugli to Batavia, 15.12.1720, VOC 1962, ff. 61–2; Hugli to Batavia, 30.11.1730, VOC 2165, ff. 58–62; Hugli to Batavia 10.3.1731, VOC 2195, ff. 33–5; Hugli to Batavia, 16.3.1736, VOC 2385, ff. 16–17.

Table 6.2 *Value of the Dutch textile exports from Coromandel,*
1691–1770 (in Dutch florins)

Year	Value	Year	Value
1691	373,762	1728	2,318,719
1692	1,296,196	1729	1,382,337
1693	1,449,993	1730	1,996,727
1694	1,080,189	1731	1,136,308
1695	1,270,911	1732	1,153,000
1696	974,164	1733–4	1,053,929
1697	691,965	1734–5	1,164,791
1698	1,050,456	1735–6	1,278,269
1699	1,171,546	1736–7	1,901,424
1700	1,395,980	1737–8	2,574,903
1701	1,699,772	1738–9	1,459,665
1702	1,647,238	1739–40	1,423,050
1703	1,560,720	1740–1	1,030,249
1704	837,780	1741–2	348,614
1705	759,321	1742–3	666,088
1706	1,073,943	1743–4	458,442
1707	1,635,813	1744–5	480,563
1708	1,991,110	1745–6	1,004,663
1709	2,138,199	1746–7	2,269,188
1710	1,905,173	1747–8	1,381,907
1711	1,760,407	1748–9	1,581,114
1712	2,037,520	1749–50	1,492,920
1713	1,834,596	1750–1	1,641,267
1714	2,215,877	1751–2	1,752,826
1715	1,840,969	1752–3	1,324,825
1716	1,175,061	1753–4	943,077
1717	723,608	1754–5	1,483,688
1718	1,038,929		
1719	1,077,475	1764–5	788,007
1720	1,433,283	1765–6	1,635,216
1721	2,134,336	1766–7	1,906,522
1722	2,133,228	1767–8	2,641,890
1723	1,865,479	1768–9	2,590,166
1724	1,852,324	1769–70	2,162,322
1725	1,977,079		
1726	1,839,472		
1727	1,654,036		

Note: The figures have been rounded to the nearest florin. From 1743–4 onward, the figures in the original document were expressed in 'heavy money' (*swaargeld*). In order to make these comparable to the preceding figures, the 'heavy money' figures have been inflated by 19.55 per cent (I am grateful to Els Jacobs and Femme S. Gaastra for providing me with this figure).

Source: The information for the period 1691–1755 is from a report on the Company's Coromandel trade prepared in November 1757 by Jacob van der Waeyen, a member of the Batavia Council, in pursuance of a secret resolution of the Council dated 11 October 1755 (ARA, HRB 341). The information for the period 1764–70 is from a memorandum prepared by Governor Pieter Haksteen of Coromandel for his successor Reijnier van Vlissingen dated 20 September 1771 (ARA, HRB 344, ff. 1–232).

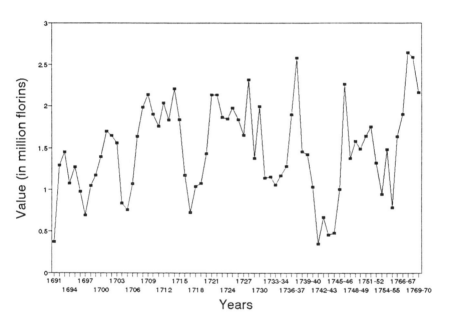

Fig 6.2 Dutch exports of textiles from Coromandel, 1691–1770

omandel but of that of Sri Lanka, were also found increasingly more attractive. Indeed, in the year 1701, the textile investment in these two districts alone was reported to have been of the order of ƒ.1.4 million against ƒ.1.7 million in the areas under the jurisdiction of the Coromandel government.[20] But the total supplies that the Company was able to get hold of were still considerably short of the orders. In the case of orders from Europe, this shortfall at times amounted to as much as 40 per cent. This evidently reflected the growing competition by the rival traders for supplies which were not rising at a fast enough rate.

Between 1708 and 1715, the average value of the textile exports from Coromandel per annum approximated two million florins. If one included the value of the textiles procured in the Tinnevelli district where the competition by fellow European traders was less severe, this figure would go up to more than ƒ.2.5 million. In southeast Asia, the Company was now concentrating more and more on the relatively captive markets of Java, southern Celebes and the Moluccas, and increasingly opting out of places such as Acheh, Johor, Kedah, Tenasserim and Pegu where the competition by Asian merchants was turning out to be crippling. These years also witnessed the revival of the export of Coromandel textiles to Persia and Mocha, which had been discontinued during the last quarter of the seventeenth century.

After a brief setback during 1716 to 1720 when the average annual exports were in the range of only a million florins because of conditions of famine in the areas of procurement, the average figure of approximately two million florins per annum was maintained again through the decade of the 1720s. While the factories in northern Coromandel did continue to supply some textiles during this period, an overwhelming bulk of the procurement was now concentrated in southern Coromandel at places such as Nagapattinam, Sadraspatnam and Porto Novo. The suppliers at these places were organized more and more into the so-called joint stock companies. As we saw earlier, the innovation in this arrangement consisted essentially in the fact that the funds needed for investment in the textiles were raised jointly by the suppliers themselves rather than being provided by the Company in the form of advances to the customary extent of 50 to 70 per cent of

---

[20] S. Arasaratnam, *Merchants, Companies and Commerce on the Coromandel Coast, 1650–1740*, Delhi, 1986, p. 177.

the value of the contract. The growing competition amongst a multiplicity of buyers, however, was leading to both a decline in quality and a continuous rise in the cost price. The latter was also related to a rise in the price of the inputs. Evidence in respect of Sadraspatnam and Porto Novo for the years 1726 to 1731 suggests a rise in the prices of cotton and yarn of the order of between 50 and 100 per cent.[21]

The years between 1731 and 1735 witnessed successive harvest failures and near famine conditions in southern Coromandel. Indeed, in the year 1732–3, there was a major famine which affected even the kingdom of Tanjavur, which traditionally was a granary of the south. The resultant rise in the price of rice and cloth was large enough to force a number of merchants out of business. The disruption in supply is reflected in the value of textile exports during this period averaging just over a million florins per annum. When the famine conditions ended, the tide was turned once again and in 1736–7 the value of the textiles exported approached $f.2$ million. The following year, the exports exceeded $f.2.5$ million, almost the highest ever figure reached over the period between 1691 and 1770. In 1738–9 and 1739–40, however, the exports were under $f.1.5$ million. Overall, the evidence on the Dutch textile exports from Coromandel over the period 1690 to 1740 would seem not to support the hypothesis put forward by scholars such as Raychaudhuri and Glamann of a substantive decline in the Dutch Company trade from the region over the first half of the eighteenth century. A decade such as that of the 1720s was evidently as vigorous as any between 1650 and 1680. The first four decades of the eighteenth century were indeed characterized more by overall stagnation in the value of Dutch trade from the region rather than by perceptible decline.

Gujarat

The hypothesis of a distinct decline in the value of the Company's trade over the period 1680–1740 would, however, go through fully in the case of Gujarat (Table 5.2). During the last two decades of the seventeenth century, the average annual value of the exports from the region went down to well under a million florins, though in the late 1690s it stood at a respectable $f.1.23$ million. The division of the

[21] S. Arasaratnam, 'The Dutch East India Company and its Coromandel trade, 1700–1740', *Bijdragen tot de Taal-, Land-, en Volkenkunde*, vol. 123 (3), 1967, pp. 325–46.

exports between silver rupees and goods had also altered dramatically over these two decades. From a peak of ƒ.700,000 worth during the late 1670s, the average annual export of silver rupees had come down in the late 1680s and the early 1690s to around ƒ.200,000, and in the late 1690s to a mere ƒ.150,000 worth. The share of goods had correspondingly increased with an all-time peak of ƒ.1.08 million worth being reached in the late 1690s. As far as the first four decades of the eighteenth century are concerned, information regarding silver rupees, if any, exported from Surat is not available and we have to rely solely on the value of goods exported to work out the trends in the exports. After a reasonably high annual average of ƒ.830,000 during 1701–5, the value of goods exported plummeted to half that level over the following decade, and to under ƒ.400,000 during 1716–40. Both Europe and Asia shared in this decline. Except for 1701–5 when the goods exported to Europe amounted to as much as ƒ.671,000 against a mere ƒ.159,000 for Asia, there was no particular pattern in the division of the goods between Europe and Asia. Sometimes more goods went to Europe: in other years more were directed at the rest of Asia (Table 5.2). Gujarat goods now constituted, on an average, no more than 4 to 5 per cent of the total Dutch imports into Holland.[22] The crisis that was engulfing the Mughal empire during this period was partly to blame for this situation. The transportation of goods from Agra to Surat, for example, was increasingly becoming more hazardous, so much so that in 1716 the Company was obliged to close its factory at Agra.

Commodity-wise, the last two decades of the seventeenth century in fact witnessed an increase in the export of both indigo and textiles from Gujarat. The export of indigo began to pick up from about 1685–6 in response to a good profit earned in Amsterdam the previous year. Between 1685 and 1700, the amount of indigo exported to Holland in a year was never under 100,000 ponds, and often was

[22] This proportion was 5.19 in 1699–1700, 3.83 in 1702–3, 3.96 in 1711–12, 3.30 in 1720–1 and 4.02 in 1735–6. Note, however, that there were some years wildly outside this range because of special circumstances. In 1693–4, for example, when the total exports to Europe were unusually low, the exports from Surat designated for Holland happened to be unusually high. This led to the highly unusual result of Gujarat goods accounting for as much as 31.05 per cent of the total Dutch Company cargo to Holland. At the other end of the spectrum was a year such as 1725–6, when this proportion was no more than 0.96 per cent. (Calculated from the Jan Schreuder memoir, ARA, HRB 838, and J.R. Bruijn, F.S. Gaastra and I. Schöffer, *Dutch–Asiatic Shipping in the 17th and 18th Centuries*, The Hague, 1987, vol. III).

considerably more. Thus the figure of 250,000 ponds was reached in 1693–4, and of 317,000 ponds three years later.[23] The principal factor behind the revival in the demand for Indian indigo was the substantive decline in the imports from the West Indies due to an unprecedented rise in the freight rates between the Caribbean and Europe.

As far as textiles were concerned, Gujarat had its share in the fast-growing European market for Indian textiles. While cotton textiles continued to dominate the textile exports from Gujarat, silk piece-goods, as well as those made from a mixture of silk and cotton yarn, also began to figure in the exports from this point on. Within cotton textiles, the role of ordinary cottons registered an important increase representing in part the growing re-export trade from Europe to the West Indies. Induced by the example set by the English and French companies, the Surat factors also increasingly introduced new varieties such as *patkas*, *berzampauts* and *savagazees* in the exports to Europe. Also, some of the traditional Coromandel varieties such as *salampuris* and *parcals* were now manufactured in Gujarat and formed part of the textile cargo from Surat. The profit earned in Holland varied considerably across different varieties, but, on the whole, the situation was quite satisfactory. In 1694–5, for example, the profit earned on most of the varieties ranged between 50 and 100 per cent. The number of pieces exported in any given year continued to fluctuate quite sharply. Glamann has shown that of the total Asian textile cargo worth *f*.2.35 million reaching Holland in 1697, that originating in Gujarat accounted for only *f*.44,078 (or 1.87 per cent). But this is not really a representative figure for the period. If we look at the average annual value of the textile exports from Surat for Holland over the three year period between 1698 and 1700, the figure turns out to be *f*.247,289, or over 10 per cent of the total textiles imports into Holland in 1697. The 1680s and the 1690s also witnessed an expansion in the export of Gujarat textiles to the Malay archipelago. The exports in 1680–1 amounted to 145,000 pieces costing *f*.250,000. The number of pieces exported was 222,000 in 1692–3 and a record 323,000 pieces in 1696–7.[24]

Unfortunately, detailed commodity-wise information is not available for the period after 1700. But the marked decline in the value of

[23] V.B. Gupta, 'The Dutch East India Company in Gujarat trade 1660–1700: a study of selected aspects', unpublished PhD thesis, Delhi University, 1991, p. 230.
[24] Gupta, 'The Dutch East India Company in Gujarat trade', pp. 233, 337.

total exports from Gujarat noted above strongly suggests that the decline would in all probability have affected all commodities.

The Malabar coast

The Malabar trade of the Company continued to be rather small in value throughout the period under discussion. For a few years in the 1690s, the Company actually stopped the procurement of pepper in the region. Pepper was then flowing into the Dutch warehouses at Palembang and Bantam in large quantities and it was decided to do without the Malabar variety. Indeed, with a view to partially disposing of the accumulated stocks, limited amounts of pepper were actually sold at Cochin. Passes were also issued to Malabar merchants for carrying their pepper to the coast of Coromandel by sea. This, however, was a very short-lived phase and things soon returned to 'normal' where the Company was trying to invoke its monopsonistic privileges and obtain a good quantity of pepper at a below-market price, but usually without much success. Irrespective of what their princes had agreed to, the suppliers did their best to escape having to supply pepper at a price below market. This was particularly so in a situation where the demand was rising and the Indian as well as the European buyers such as the English (who had established a factory at Tellicherry in northern Malabar in 1682, and at Anjengo in southern Malabar in 1688, and had gone on to be favoured with a pepper monopoly by the queen of Atingal in 1694), the French and the Danes were all perfectly happy to follow the market. Indeed, in an agreement with the king of Tekkenkur in June 1694, the VOC was obliged to agree to pay the market price in respect of the supplies delivered. Also, given the growing diversion of the supplies of Bihar opium to the more lucrative Java market, the Company was increasingly obliged to pay for the pepper in terms of precious metals.

As a part of the Directors' plans to build up large stocks of pepper in Holland, Batavia instructed Malabar in 1698 to supply as much pepper as it could. But the exports from Malabar continued to be modest. As Table 6.3 shows, the exports were no more than ƒ.216,000 worth in 1701–2 and ƒ.190,000 worth in 1711–12. By 1722–3, the figure had gone up to ƒ.424,000, but it was again down to ƒ.341,850 in 1731–2. In the meantime, the price of pepper had gone up from Rs.60–62 per kandi of 560 ponds during 1722–30 to Rs.70–78 during 1731–4 and further to Rs.88–90 per kandi during 1735–9. This

Table 6.3 *Value of the Dutch exports from Malabar, 1701–85*

Year	Exports (f.)
1701–2	215,638
1711–12	190,431
1722–3	423,717
1731–2	341,418
1741–2	231,519
1751–2	382,322
1761–2	699,760
1771–2	271,133
1784–5	593,040

Source: 'Copie generale journalen, gehouden door de boekhouder-generaal te Batavia, 1700/1701–1789/90', ARA, BGB, 10751–801.

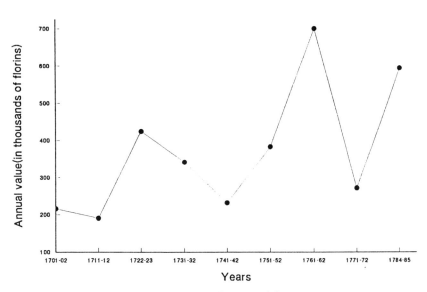

Fig. 6.3 Dutch exports from Malabar, 1701–85

remarkable phenomenon of a 50 per cent rise in the price within the space of a decade owed its origin essentially to a major shift in the pepper procurement towards Malabar. The fall of the Safavids in 1722, followed by considerable political uncertainty in Gujarat in the 1730s, had forced groups of Indian and other merchants who until then had been procuring their pepper supplies in Surat and the Persian Gulf ports to turn to Malabar. This had further intensified the problem of smuggling. To add to the Company's woes, Martanda Varma who had ascended the throne of Travancore (Venad) in 1729 annexed in 1734 two small neighbouring kingdoms whose entire pepper crop had been pledged to the Company. The Malabar Council also learnt that, with the establishment of Travancore hegemony in the region, large quantities of pepper were being diverted to the Coromandel coast. The Company sought a military solution to the problem, but in the battle between the forces of the Company and those of Martanda Varma, fought near the roadstead of Colachel in southern Malabar on 10 August 1741, the Company's forces were defeated.[25] The Dutch dream of a revived monopoly of the pepper trade had to be given up once and for all.

Clandestine private trade

In view of its own substantial stakes in intra-Asian trade, the VOC followed the policy of imposing a strict ban on its employees participating in port-to-port trade within Asia on their private account. That, however, did not prevent the latter from doing so on a fairly important scale on a clandestine basis. They used the Company's ships and often its capital resources quite blatantly. One of the most lucrative branches of trade in their network was that between Bengal and Batavia. The main item carried to Batavia was opium, a high-value low-bulk and, therefore, ideal item for contraband trade, though other Bengal goods such as raw silk and silk textiles also figured in this trade. Pieter van Dam has suggested that, at one stage, the volume of the clandestine private trade from Bengal was nearly as large as that on the Company's own account. As far as opium alone was concerned, in an unusually bountiful year such as 1676 the volume of opium smuggled into Batavia could be several times the amount imported on the account of the Company. An anonymous report submitted to the

[25] Ashin Das Gupta, *Malabar in Asian Trade 1740–1800*, Cambridge, 1967, pp. 25, 31–2.

Heren XVII in 1684 contained a detailed description of the organizational structure of this trade at the Bengal end. In the year 1679, Director Jacob Verburg founded in the name of his wife a 'small company' with the specific purpose of carrying on private trade. To facilitate its operations, two of the shareholders in the 'company' – both nephews of Verburg's wife – were appointed to the key posts of the directorate's *fiscaal* (the law-enforcement officer) and the Hugli factory's warehouse officer, respectively. In order to enable him to discharge his 'duties' properly, the *fiscaal* was provided with a staff large enough to keep an eye on all Dutch company ships entering or leaving the port of Hugli. As soon as a ship approached the port, the warehouse officer went aboard and offered to buy whatever private cargo might be on board. The prices offered were obviously considerably below the market, but usually the deals went through because everyone knew that in the event of an unsuccessful negotiation, the *fiscaal* would be promptly informed and the goods confiscated on behalf of the Company. The goods obtained by the warehouse officer in this manner were then sold on the open market at substantially higher prices on the account of the 'small company'. As far as goods procured in Bengal were concerned, the procedure was to buy them in the name of a nonexistent Bengali merchant. This was done before procurement was begun on the account of the Company, so that the 'small company' was ensured of getting the best quality goods at the lowest possible prices. These goods were then loaded aboard the Company's ships along with the regular cargo. Sometime before the ships were due into the harbour at Batavia, the contraband goods were taken out in small boats. The watch-and-ward staff at Batavia at times managed to seize part of the smuggled goods, but that made only a very minor dent in the total profit from the operation. A rough idea of the magnitude of the profit earned could probably be formed by the fact that at Verburg's death in 1681, his wife carried with her to Holland a fortune running to *f*.600,000. Even the warehouse officer had managed to save a sum of *f*.150,000 over a period of three and a half to four years.[26] In so far as the clandestine nature of this trade often obliged the servants to pay a price above the market in respect of goods procured and accept one below it for goods sold, the servants' private trade tended to spoil both the buying and the selling markets

---

[26] Anonymous report entitled ''t Oostindische Sacspiegeltje', ARA, VOC 4704.

for the Company. There was, however, very little the Company could do about this problem. One measure taken was to strengthen the cruising watch-and-ward staff deployed to detect clandestine goods carried aboard Company ships coming into Batavia. The other was periodically to issue proclamations reiterating the deterrent penalties, including dismissal from service and deportation to Holland, prescribed for those found engaging in private trade. This was done in 1677, 1678, 1680 and 1683. The last of these decrees went so far as to prescribe punishment by death. But the vested interests were far too entrenched to be dislodged easily and nothing changed.[27]

A major landmark in the Dutch Company policy towards private Dutch participation in intra-Asian trade was the partial opening up of this trade in the early 1740s. The initiative in this regard had been taken by Gustaf Willem Baron van Imhoff, the Governor-General-designate of the Dutch East Indies. In a memorandum submitted in 1741, Van Imhoff had argued that the Company's trade in the factories west of Malacca had been on the decline for some time and now compared very unfavourably with that carried on by its competitors such as the English and the French. He, therefore, suggested that it would be in the best interests of the Company to declare trade with that region, except in strategic commodities such as spices and Japanese copper, open to all. Extra customs duties charged from the private traders who, Van Imhoff believed, would mainly be the burghers from Batavia, would compensate in part for the loss of profit that the partial abandonment of its own trade in the region would entail. As for trade within the archipelago, Van Imhoff pleaded for a greater freedom of trade between Batavia and the eastern provinces of Amboyna and Celebes. Finally, in relation to Euro-Asian trade, Van Imhoff recommended that the private traders be allowed to export tea to Holland in the Company's ships. The burghers could buy the tea from the Chinese junks calling at Batavia, and the Company could charge as freight 40 per cent of the proceeds from the sale of the tea in Holland.[28]

Van Imhoff's recommendations were accepted by the Heren XVII

---

[27] Prakash, *The Dutch East India Company and the Economy of Bengal*, pp. 86–9, 154–6.
[28] J.E. Heeres, 'De consideratien van Van Imhoff', *Bijdragen tot de Taal-, Land-, en Volkenkunde van Nederlandsch Indie*, vol. 66; S. Arasaratnam, 'Monopoly and free trade in Dutch–Asian commercial policy: debate and controversy within the VOC', *Journal of Southeast Asian Studies*, vol. 4 (1), March 1973, pp. 1–15.

in 1742. The communication received by the Indian factories from Batavia in 1743 stipulated that 'the navigation and trade from and to Batavia both to the east as well as to the west of India has been declared open for everyone with the provision that the trade in spices, copper, tin, pepper as well as the import of opium will be reserved for the Company'.[29] In September 1745, Van Imhoff further outlined the geographical extent of his free-trade area. It comprised China, Batavia, Malacca, all harbours from Acheh to Bengal, and Bengal to Nagapattinam, Sri Lanka, and from Cape Comorin to Persia, then along the African coast to Madagascar and Mozambique.[30]

The private trade under the new dispensation was to be carried on under the flag and the protection of the Company. At Surat, the list of goods in which trading was to be reserved for the Company included, in addition to spices and tin, copper and opium, items such as coral, ivory and several varieties of textiles including blue *baftas*, blue *cangans*, *kannekins*, silk *patolas*, *niquanias* and so on. Not only would such goods found aboard private traders' ships be confiscated, but the owner would be subjected to further punishment. In the case of spices and opium, the punishment prescribed was death: in the case of other goods, it was left to the discretion of the judge.[31] The private traders were supposed to pay customs duty to the Company at the rate of 4 per cent at Hugli and 5 per cent at Surat. The Company would, in its turn, settle the accounts with the authorities at the locally established rates for its own goods. At Hugli, this would leave a surplus of $1\frac{1}{2}$ per cent for the Company, of which $\frac{1}{2}$ per cent would be given to the *fiscaal*. At Surat of the $2\frac{1}{2}$ per cent surplus, $\frac{1}{2}$ per cent would go to the *fiscaal*, 1 per cent to the director, and the remaining 1 per cent to the Company accounts. The additional surplus of $2\frac{1}{2}$ per cent in respect of provisions and drinks, which were exempt from government customs duties, would all accrue to the Company.[32] While it is quite clear that the 1743 provisions did indeed lead to a certain amount of additional participation in intra-Asian trade by the Dutch free burghers, the scale of this participation remains unclear. Some of the concessions granted by Van Imhoff were withdrawn by his successor, Jacob Mossel

---

[29] ARA, 'Consideratien over de opengestelde vrije Vaart en Handel-hoedanig die in Souratta sal kunnen gereguleert werden', by Director Jan Schreuder at Surat, 2 March 1746, HRB 837, para. 340.
[30] Das Gupta, *Malabar in Asian Trade, 1740–1800*, p. 86.
[31] ARA, 'Consideratien' by Jan Schreuder, HRB 837, para. 411.
[32] ARA, 'Consideratien' by Jan Schreuder, HRB 837, paras. 400, 411.

(1750–61). Later in the century, the burghers were again allowed more freedom of trade. But the overall volume of this trade does not seem to have become particularly significant at any point.[33]

The Dutch and the Indian maritime merchant

In addition to its employees, the other principal group of merchants competing with the Company in its intra-Asian trade was that of the Indian and other Asian maritime merchants. By using the device of the pass (*cartaz*) the Company tried to hinder, or at least to regulate, these merchants' trade with areas where it enjoyed monopoly privileges. We had noted earlier that by the early 1620s the VOC had acquired monopoly rights in the Moluccas where the major spices were procured. Indian and other Asian merchants were successfully excluded from the area. It was only at the port of Makassar in Celebes that trade was still possible, and this link was used by Indian merchants, particularly those from Coromandel, to break the Dutch control of the eastern archipelago. But this particular opening also came to an end in 1669 with the Dutch conquest of the port city. In the meantime, the capture of Malacca in 1641 by the VOC had occasioned a major dislocation in the Indian merchants' trade with the Malay penninsula. From the very beginning, the Company tried to divert as much of the Asian merchants' trade with the region as possible to Malacca. This would bring in a certain amount of revenue (a 10 per cent duty on imports and a 5 per cent duty on exports was to be levied at Malacca) but, more importantly, would enable the Company to control and direct the Asian merchants' trade with the region to its advantage. But already in November of 1641 the Dutch governor of Malacca pointed to the glut of Indian cloth in the area as a result of which the Company's own sales had suffered. The following year, the factors in Ayutthaya ascribed the poor sale of Indian textiles to the large imports by the merchants from Bengal and Coromandel. The situation was even worse at Perak where the Company's sale of textiles had practically been brought to a halt. Batavia's response to this situation was a twofold one. On the one hand, instructions were issued to the factors in India to require all merchants granted passes for the Malayan ports to call first at Malacca and pay the duties there. For one whole year, the Surat factors even managed to oblige the Surat

---

[33] Femme S. Gaastra, *De Geschiedenis van de VOC*, Zutphen, 1991, p. 124.

shipping granted passes for the region to pay the Malacca duties at Surat itself before sailing out. The factors at Malacca were to offer to buy the textiles brought in by the Indian ships at the market price. Sufficient stocks of goods that these merchants might want to buy at Malacca were also to be maintained in the Company's warehouses. At the same time, these merchants were to be prevented from operating in some of the more important markets in the region. This was sought to be achieved by the Company entering into exclusive contracts with the local rulers. Such contracts were made with Kedah (June 1642), Phuket (March 1643) and Bangeri (January 1645). The Kedah contract stipulated that half of the total supply of tin would be made available to the VOC at a fixed price against cash or cotton textiles. Indian merchants' ships would be allowed in only if they carried Dutch passes and produced evidence that they had first called at Malacca and paid duties there. A similar stipulation was made in the Phuket contract. The Bangeri contract was even more wide-ranging. The entire supply of tin was to be sold to the VOC and no textiles were to be bought from any foreign vessel.

The Indian merchants from Gujarat, Coromandel, Bengal and other places sought to counter this by shifting their operations to Acheh. The extensive trade carried on by the Acheh merchants with Sumatran and Malayan ports made Acheh a large market for Indian textiles, as well as a major procurement point for items such as pepper and tin. It was in this context that the Company imposed a blanket ban on the Indian merchants' trade with Acheh as well as the Malay peninsular ports. The failure of the retaliatory action taken at Surat designed to prevent the Company from implementing the decision has already been noted in Chapter 4.

Since Perak had refused to enter into an exclusive contract with the Company along the lines of its northern neighbours, the Perak river was blockaded. The immediate sufferers were the Acheh merchants whose tin trade with Perak was brought to an end. Perak was, therefore, ordered by the queen of Acheh to enter into an agreement with the VOC, which was done in August 1650. The tin trade of Perak was henceforth to be shared between the VOC and the merchants of Acheh to the exclusion of everyone else. The VOC factory at the mouth of the Perak river was attacked in 1651, but in December 1655 the 1650 treaty was reconfirmed. Soon thereafter, differences cropped up again and a fleet was dispatched against both

Perak and Acheh. It was only in June 1659 that a comprehensive treaty was finally concluded with the queen of Acheh. The Indian merchants were again to be granted passes for Acheh, though the Malay peninsular ports were to remain out of bounds for them. The tin trade of Perak was to be divided equally between the VOC and the merchants of Acheh.

From about 1660 or so, Dutch passes were issued liberally for both Acheh and Malacca. The Indian merchants made the most of the trading opportunities at Acheh, but by no means gave in to the Dutch demand of staying away from the Malay peninsular ports. Kedah, which was just outside the Dutch blockade system and, though not a producer of tin, was a major provider of it because of the existence of an efficient network of coastal trade with the neighbouring producing region, became an important port of call for shipping from Coromandel. Further north, a considerable amount of shipping went to Bangeri and Phuket in addition to the Thai port of Tenasserim and the Burmese port of Pegu. After the conclusion of the second Anglo-Dutch war in 1667, obtaining an English Company pass became yet another device to evade the Dutch control. Goods were also freighted on English ships going to the Malayan ports. At times, English Company ships flying the English flag were also hired to transport the Indian merchants' goods to the region.

The Dutch conquest of Bantam in 1682 followed by the exclusion of Indian shipping from the port did indeed involve the loss of the important Java market for Indian, particularly Coromandel, textiles. The procurement of Chinese and Japanese goods, particularly copper, which used to be obtained mainly at Bantam, also suffered in the process. But a part of this loss was made up by increased sailings to ports such as Johor, Lama and Pankor. The Dutch Company's attempts to make the sultan of Johor restrict Indian shipping to his ports were not particularly successful.[34]

The available evidence would seem to suggest that from the closing years of the seventeenth century onward, there was a distinct decline in the Indian merchants' trade with the Malay archipelago. But this decline would seem to be related in the main to political and economic

---

[34] S. Arasaratnam, 'Some notes on the Dutch in Malacca and the Indo-Malayan trade 1641–1670', *Journal of Southeast Asian History*, vol. 10 (3), 1969, pp. 480–90; S. Arasaratnam, 'The Coromandel–Southeast Asia trade 1650–1740', *Journal of Asian History*, vol. 18, 1984, pp. 113–35.

developments in the relevant Indian region and/or in the partner ports. The role of the VOC policies or trade in this regard would seem to be of no particular consequence. A case in point is the eastward trade from the Bengal ports of Hugli and Balasore. This trade consisted essentially of four sub-branches: the trade with Arakan and Pegu; the trade with Siam with Tenasserim as the principal port; the trade with the Malay peninsula and Sumatra, the principal ports of call in the area being Phuket (Ujang Salang), Kedah, Perak, Malacca and Acheh; and the trade with Manila in the Philippines. Evidence available in the Dutch shipping lists for the ports of Hugli and Balasore relating to departures for and arrivals from the eastward ports on the account of Indian and other Asian merchants suggests a pattern of marked decline in this trade between the last years of the seventeenth century and about 1720. There would seem, however, to have been no connection between this development and the policies of the VOC. If one disaggregated the nature of the decline of the Bengal-eastward trade, it turns out that it was ascribable entirely to the withdrawal from high-seas trade by Mughal state officials engaged in trade in addition to their other activities. The volume of eastward trade carried on by the ordinary merchants registered no particular decline. It would be highly unlikely that in a situation where ordinary merchants could survive the Company's trade and pass policies, state officials with a substantial resource and power base would have been obliged to withdraw from trade by the Company policies. This conclusion finds strong support in the history of the trade between Bengal and the Maldive Islands. During the closing years of the seventeenth and the early years of the eighteenth century, while this branch of trade registered an increase, the participation of state officials in it declined markedly. If these officials practically withdrew from a *growing* trade which, in addition, was characterized by the lack of Company competition and the absence of a restrictive pass policy, their withdrawal from the eastward trade must also be viewed as having had nothing to do with the policies of the VOC.[35]

If the VOC was by and large unable to disrupt the Indian merchants' eastward trade on any long-term basis, what about their trade with Sri Lanka, the other major Asian region where the Dutch

---

[35] This argument can be followed in greater detail, together with the necessary evidence, in Prakash, *The Dutch East India Company and the Economy of Bengal*, ch. 8.

enjoyed exclusive rights? Traditionally, a considerable amount of trade was carried on between the ports in Bengal, the Coromandel coast, Malabar and the Kanara coast on the one hand, and those in Sri Lanka on the other. In 1670, the VOC monopolized the Sri Lanka trade in all major commodities, the only exception being rice. Among the export goods, the commodities monopolized were cinnamon, elephants, ivory, areca-nuts and *chanks*. The major import goods declared monopoly items were cotton textiles, pepper, tin and zinc. The import of rice was not monopolized because the island depended heavily on the import of this provision from India on a continuing basis, and the shipping capacity available to the Company could simply not take care of the island's requirements. The trade restrictions inevitably led to some decline in the Indian merchants' trade with the island, but given the vast coastline which it was impossible to police effectively, a great deal of trade in the prohibited items continued on a clandestine basis.

As far as trade carried on legally was concerned, given the important role of Bengal as a supplier of provisions such as rice, sugar, clarified butter and oil, the restrictive provisions were enforced in her case only from about 1684 onward when it was considered necessary to contain the competition in the sale of cotton textiles. These textiles were consequently excluded from the list of 'permitted' goods specified in the passes issued. A similar step was taken in respect of cinnamon in 1696. That these restrictive measures turned out to be a great damper on the volume of the legally conducted Bengal–Sri Lanka trade is suggested quite unambiguously by the information available in the Dutch shipping lists for the period between the late 1690s and about 1720.[36]

The trade between south India and Sri Lanka was carried on from a number of ports stretching from Kanara round the Cape Comorin to north Coromandel. The restrictive measures of 1670 affected this trade quite adversely, but by the 1690s recovery would seem to have taken place. This process was further helped by the 1697 removal of restrictions on the trade in textiles and areca-nuts. But increased competition in the sale of cotton textiles again obliged the Company to prohibit their import. The Indian ships were henceforth also

[36] Om Prakash, 'The European trading companies and the merchants of Bengal, 1650–1725', *The Indian Economic and Social History Review*, vol. 1 (3), 1964, pp. 37–63.

required to confine their trade to the Dutch-controlled ports of Colombo, Galle and Jaffna where areca-nuts would be sold to them directly by the Company. These measures again tended to depress the trade without, of course, affecting in any way the volume of the substantial clandestine trade on this sector.[37]

To sum up, the Dutch East India Company's attempts at controlling and redirecting the Indian merchants' trade with the Malay archipelago and Sri Lanka were by and large quite ineffective. In the case of Sri Lanka, the Company was never really able to make up its mind regarding what precise course of action to follow. The policy of indecision significantly limited whatever adverse effect the restrictions imposed on the Indian merchants' trade with the island had on their trade. It was also found impossible to control the large-scale smuggling trade with the island. As for the Malay peninsula, it was only during the late 1640s and the 1650s, when the Company was willing to resort to violence, if necessary, to prevent what it perceived to be a grave threat to its long-term commercial interests in the region, that it succeeded in keeping the Indian merchants out of a number of Malay ports. For the rest, it was indeed a question of these merchants adjusting to the pressures generated by the Company by shifting their trade to another port in the area rather than by reducing the scale of their operations.

THE ENGLISH COMPANY AND THE PRIVATE TRADERS

The English Company trade

The period 1680–1740 also witnessed a tremendous expansion in the value of the Indo-European trade carried on by the English East India Company. We noted earlier that the value of the total English imports from Asia had gone up from the equivalent of a mere *f*.4.32 million during the triennium 1668–70 to *f*.13.79 million during 1698–1700, and further to *f*.23 million during 1738–40. The dominant items of import during the period were textiles and raw silk which together accounted for over 80 per cent of the total imports during both

---

[37] S. Arasaratnam, 'Dutch commercial policy in Ceylon and its effects on the Indo-Ceylon trade (1690–1750)', *The Indian Economic and Social History Review*, vol. 4 (2), 1967, pp. 109–30.

1698–1700 and 1738–40. Since both these items, together with some of the minor ones, were procured almost entirely in India, the sub-continent accounted for 95 per cent of the total English imports during 1698–1700 and 84 per cent during 1738–40. As in the case of the Dutch, within the subcontinent Bengal, which was the sole supplier of raw silk and by far the most important supplier of textiles, was now the most important region for the Company's trade. Its share in the total Asian imports of the Company, which stood at 42 per cent in 1698–1700, had further gone up to 66 per cent by 1738–40. In the latter triennium, Bengal accounted for as much as 78 per cent of the total Indian procurement, the remainder being divided between Madras and Bombay in a ratio of 2:1.[38]

The enormous increase in the Indo-European trade in textiles over the last quarter of the seventeenth century caused a commotion among the indigenous producers of linen, silk and woollen textiles. In England, the manufacturers' opposition to the import of these textiles was sufficiently vocal to lead to the passage of a Parliamentary Act in 1700 prohibiting the import of 'all wrought silks, Bengals and stuffs mixed with silk or herba, of the manufacture of Persia, China or the East Indies and all calicoes painted, dyed or printed or stained there'. But since this might simply have involved an increase in the import of white calicoes and muslins from India which were then printed in England, another Act was passed twenty years later altogether prohibiting the use or wear of printed calicoes in England. Of course, neither of the two Acts affected in any way the re-export trade in Eastern textiles, and, on the whole, their effect on the growth of the trade in textiles was not particularly marked. While the all-time 1684 peak level of textile imports into England could not be sustained in the following period, the position continued to be reasonably satisfactory. The 1690s witnessed a rise in the average sale price of these textiles. Between 1695 and 1704, the average mark-up on the English textile imports was reported to be as high as 1:3.85. The number of pieces imported in 1700 was 868,095 costing a total of £374,608 and accounting for 74.7 per cent of the total imports. All of the textiles had originated in India, with Bengal accounting for 48.5 per cent of the total value of the textiles imported. The share of Madras and Bombay

[38] Calculated from K.N. Chaudhuri, *The Trading World of Asia and the English East India Company, 1660–1760*, Cambridge, 1978, Appendix 5.

was 14.3 per cent and 37.3 per cent respectively. Forty years later, while the total number of pieces imported had come down to 648,060, the invoice value had gone up slightly to £395,570 accounting for 68.3 per cent of the total imports. Bengal now accounted for a staggering 83.4 per cent of the total value of textiles imported. The share of Madras was 13.7 per cent, while Bombay with 0.9 per cent had practically been dropped. The share of Chinese silk piece-goods in the total textile value imported was also no more than 2 per cent.[39]

The Company's procurement of raw silk in Bengal (which accounted for practically the entire amount procured in Asia) had begun to pick up from about 1680, but the conflict with the Mughals later in the decade had interrupted the process. The amount imported in 1700 stood at 96,340 lbs with an invoice value of £44,071 accounting for 8.8 per cent of the total imports. All these magnitudes had registered an increase by 1740, when the quantity imported was 129,619 lbs. costing £59,157 and accounting for 10.2 per cent of the total imports.[40]

Finally, among the bulk goods, the demand for Indian indigo had continued to be good in the 1680s, and the orders from Surat had in fact been doubled. But the supplies in the 1690s had been erratic. In the early years of the eighteenth century, there had been a significant rise in the cost price, and after 1712 it was only occasionally that the Company traded in indigo. The other bulk good, saltpetre, also remained at the margin accounting in 1720 and 1740 for no more than 1.05 and 1.7 per cent respectively of the total value imported.[41]

The English private traders

Unlike the VOC, the English East India Company usually did not own the ships it used but hired them from private parties. The 'charterparty' agreements often obliged the Company to make available to the owners a minor proportion of the shipping space, creating yet another category of private traders engaged in Euro-Asian trade. It was also customary for the Company to allow a small amount of shipping space to the ship's personnel. These groups were obliged to operate under certain rules and regulations with regard to the goods they could trade in and so on. From 1667 onward, the range of goods

---

[39] Calculated from Chaudhuri, *The Trading World of Asia*, Appendix 5.
[40] Calculated from Chaudhuri, *The Trading World of Asia*, Appendix 5.
[41] Calculated from Chaudhuri, *The Trading World of Asia*, Appendix 5.

in which trade was allowed was broadened, but it was still obligatory to operate by registration and consignment through the Company's warehouse in London.[42] Valuewise, an important item of trade figuring in the English Euro-Asian trade on private account was diamonds, which were not covered by the Company's monopoly and could be freely imported against a 4 per cent fee. The diamond trade was controlled basically by Jewish merchants, many of whom had migrated from Portugal to England around the middle of the seventeenth century. This had led to a shift in the axis of the diamond trade from Goa–Lisbon to Madras–London. The diamond merchants operated mainly by appointing 'commissioners' in India to whom funds were dispatched regularly and who looked after the procurement and the shipment of the rough stones. By and large, these commissioners were chosen from amongst the senior officials of the Company based in Madras who were simultaneously engaged in intra-Asian trade in a substantial manner on their private account. In recompense of their labours, the commissioners were entitled to a 7 per cent commission on the value of the investment.

Euro-Asian trade, however, was only on the fringes of the total English private trading activity from India. The real field of activity was the trade within Asia. The two groups of private traders engaged in this trade were the Company servants (until about the 1760s) and the so-called free merchants settled in India. In the initial stages, the Company itself was engaged in a certain amount of intra-Asian trade, and like the Dutch Company had sought to prevent its servants from participation in it. That, however, had not quite worked because the servants are known to have engaged in a fair amount of intra-Asian trade from the very beginning. As early as 1613, for example, when the *James* arrived at Bantam from Surat, it was found to be so heavily laden with 300 bales of privately owned goods that it was described as rather a 'sty for swine than a ship for men'. In 1630, the private trade to Persia was said to be worth £30,000, equivalent to nearly one third of the stock of the Company's own Persian voyage that year. Cases of Englishmen returning home with fortunes of between £30,000 and £40,000 each were recorded around this time. By the 1650s, some of

---

[42] Ian Bruce Watson, *Foundation for Empire, English Private Trade in India 1659–1760*, New Delhi, 1980, pp. 68–75.

the private traders operating from Madras were believed to have made fortunes of up to £50,000.[43]

The Company's own limited participation in intra-Asian trade, however, had in the meantime turned out to be rather disappointing, and in 1661 a decision was taken to withdraw from it. But in order to ensure that the English presence in various parts of Asia did not cease altogether, it was decided at the same time to legalize the trade carried on by the Company servants and the free merchants. By a series of 'indulgences' issued in the late 1660s and the 1670s, these two groups were formally allowed to engage in trade with all parts of Asia, the only places excluded being Tonkin and Taiwan.

The private merchants' trade embraced both the westward as well as the eastward sectors of the maritime trade from India. In addition to the ports on the west coast of India itself, the westward sector included the ports in the Red Sea and the Persian Gulf. The eastward trade embraced, in addition to the two littorals of the Bay of Bengal, the Malacca Straits, ports in the Indonesian archipelago, the Philippines and the south China coast. It was common for these traders to carry, in addition to their own goods, Indian merchants' goods on freight. There was demand for this service notwithstanding the fact that the rates charged by the English were distinctly higher than those offered by the rival Indian and other Asian shipowners. Thus in 1699 while an Asian vessel was asking for Rs.5 per maund of freight between Bengal and Persia, the rate quoted by the English was Rs.8. The corresponding figures for 1718 were Rs.6 to Rs.7 and Rs.9 per maund. The explanation was only in part in terms of the generally more efficient sailing and the greater immunity the English ships offered against piracy. Often the English shipowners were willing to assume the ownership of the freight cargo making available to the freighter the fairly substantial customs privileges enjoyed by the English in many parts of Asia.[44]

The English private traders operated from ports on both the east and the west coasts of India. Over the seventeenth and the early years of the eighteenth century, the Coromandel ports witnessed English

---

[43] P.J. Marshall, 'Private British trade in the Indian Ocean before 1800', in Ashin Das Gupta and M.N. Pearson (ed.), *India and the Indian Ocean 1500–1800*, Calcutta, 1987, pp. 278–9.
[44] Marshall, 'Private British trade', p. 283; P.J. Marshall, *East Indian Fortunes, The British in Bengal in the Eighteenth Century*, Oxford, 1976, pp. 58–60.

trading activity on a much larger scale than did ports in Bengal. Masulipatnam was the principal port used on the Coromandel coast, but around the turn of the century more and more private English shipping moved on to Madras. In Bengal, the principal port used was Hugli until it was replaced by Calcutta in the early years of the eighteenth century. In course of time, Calcutta emerged as the most important port of English private trade from India. On the west coast, English private trade began at Surat in the early years of the seventeenth century, but moved on to Bombay in the eighteenth.

Among the important private English traders operating from Coromandel during the second half of the seventeenth century were the governors of Madras. Two of these, Elihu Yale and Thomas Pitt, were particularly active and are known to have amassed huge fortunes, estimated in the case of Yale at a massive £200,000. Other governors with significant private trading interests included Edward Winter, William Langhorn, Streynsham Master, Gulston Addison, Edward Harrison and Joseph Collet. Among the chiefs of the English factory at Masulipatnam, major private traders included William Jearsey, Richard Mohun and Robert Freeman. Most, if not all, of these individuals were also diamond commissioners, an activity that contributed handsomely towards their prosperity. The accounts of a leading diamond merchant in London, John Chomley, provide for some years information on the total amount of funds remitted each year from London to Madras for investment in diamonds. While this amount fluctuated a great deal between one year and another, an exceptionally good year such as 1676 witnessed the remittance of as much as £100,000 on this account.[45] There ordinarily was a gap, sometimes as long as six months, between the receipt of the funds by the commissioner in Madras and their actual investment in the purchase of the diamonds. The resultant additional liquidity available at no extra cost often constituted a major contributory element to the commissioner's success in the country trading ventures he carried on on his private account.

William Jearsey was initially the chief of the English factory at Syriam in Burma. In 1655, when it was decided to close that factory down, Jearsey was ordered to return to Madras. An alleged delay in

---

[45] Søren Mentz, 'English private trade on the Coromandel coast, 1660–1690: diamonds and country trade', *The Indian Economic and Social History Review*, vol. 33 (2), April–June 1996, pp. 155–74.

his departure from Syriam led to a severing of Jearsey's connection with the Company, but he remained in Madras as a freeman. Later, he was reinstated in the Company's service, and in August 1662 succeeded Johnson as the chief of Masulipatnam. But jealousies and conflicts arising out of Jearsey's substantial private trading ventures led to a constant friction between him and the governor, Edward Winter. Between 1663 and 1669, Jearsey was also an important, probably the most important, diamond commissioner in the region operating in partnership with Nathaniel Chomley, the brother and the local commissioner of John Chomley. In 1669, Jearsey was discharged from his chiefship but was permitted to remain in India for a year or two if he gave the Company 'satisfaction'. Strenuous efforts in this behalf by the Company's factors notwithstanding, Jearsey managed to evade producing his accounts until, in 1686, the Company withdrew all claims of money due from him. During the forty years that Jearsey was engaged in private trade from Coromandel until his death in 1690, his trading fortunes ebbed and flowed quite considerably. In the 1660s, he is believed to have owned at least nine vessels. These ships operated between Coromandel and ports in Pegu, Phuket, Acheh, Kedah and Persia. He was evidently making a great deal of money around this time both from his diamond commissionership as well as from his private trading ventures, but also had his share of misfortunes. Around 1669, two of his ships, the *Nonsuck* and the *Adventure*, both richly laden, were taken by the Dutch. In 1672, the *Ruby* was seized by the French at São Tomé. About this time, Jearsey also lost the *York Ormuze*, which ran ashore at Balasore.[46]

Richard Mohun, also a diamond commissioner and partner of Nathaniel Chomley, had succeeded William Jearsey as the chief of Masulipatnam but was himself suspended in 1675 for misusing the Company's funds for private trade, taking commission on goods bought on the account of the Company and other such misdemeanours. But curiously enough, he was reinstated in the service of the Company in 1679 as the head of the mint. This was done without the approval of the Directors in London who ordered his dismissal when the matter came to their attention. In 1683, Mohun left Coromandel for Acheh where he died three years later. Robert Freeman was

---

[46] L.M. Anstey, 'Some Anglo-Indian worthies of the seventeenth century: William Jearsey', *The Indian Antiquary*, vol. 34, 1905, pp. 164–76.

employed at Masulipatnam in 1668, but left the service of the Company in 1675. In 1682, he reappears as the chief at Masulipatnam, joins the Council at Fort St George in 1687 and dies two years later. During his chiefship at Masulipatnam, he was probably the most substantial shipowner of all and, in addition to conducting trade on his own account, carried a large amount of freight cargo between Masulipatnam and Persia on the account of Indian merchants. He was also an important trader between Masulipatnam on the one hand and Pegu and Acheh on the other, besides carrying on a certain amount of coastal trade in rice.[47] Freeman succeeded Nathaniel Chomley in 1682 as a diamond commissioner when the former finally left for England. Chomley took the bulk of his fortune amounting to £54,000 with him, but left a small amount of £7,300 at Freeman's disposal for investment on his behalf. Streynsham Master, who left at about the same time, did the same, but eventually had reason to regret the decision. In 1703, Thomas Pitt, the governor of Madras, reported that of the 15,700 pagodas collected by Freeman from Indian merchants owing money to Master, the latter received nothing.[48]

While the bulk of the English private trade from Coromandel would seem to have been carried on on the account of individual merchants, there were several alternative patterns in use as well. Some of the governors of Madras organized 'joint stocks', that is, large syndicates of investors who would buy shares in one or more ships under the governor's management. A large segment of the English community had a stake in Madras's shipping, either as part owners or as lenders of respondentia loans. Such loans were secured on the cargo of a ship at a rate adjusted to the risk and the length of the voyage, the risk being on the lender.[49] Partnership ventures among two or more individual merchants were also quite common. Thus Richard Mohun, Matthew Mainwaring and George Chamberlain are known to have been partners in trading ventures based on a 4/9, 3/9 and 2/9 share respectively. Another noteworthy partnership was that between William Monson and Nicholas Morse, who traded on equal shares from Madras. On occasions, a vessel was owned jointly by several

---

[47] Sanjay Subrahmanyam, 'Persians, pilgrims and Portuguese: the travails of Masulipatnam shipping in the western Indian Ocean, 1590–1665', *Modern Asian Studies*, vol. 22 (3), 1988, pp. 503–30; Sanjay Subrahmanyam, 'Asian trade and European affluence? Coromandel, 1650–1740', *Modern Asian Studies*, vol. 22 (1), 1988, pp. 179–88.

[48] Søren Mentz, 'English private trade on the Coromandel coast'.

[49] Marshall, 'Private British trade', p. 287.

persons, the profit earned from its trips being shared proportionately. Thus in 1675 the *Indulgence* was reported to have been owned to the extent of one third by Richard Mohun, and the remaining two thirds jointly by William Langhorn, Harris, Matthew Mainwaring and Robert Fleetwood.[50] In the case of voyages to China, large partnerships are known to have been formed to invest in the ships, including not only Englishmen at Madras, but also those in Surat, Bombay and the Malabar ports. Many of these voyages seem to have started and finished at Surat.[51]

Joint ownership, financing and management of ships occasionally also included Indian merchants. For example, in the trade between Madras and southeast Asia, there was collaboration between Governor Harrison of Madras, Governor Joseph Collet of Benkulen (who had earlier been in Madras and after a few years returned there as governor) and Sunku Rama, the chief merchant of the English Company at Madras. In May 1713, Collet advised Sunku Rama as follows:

In such an adventure as I propose I shall constantly continue to be concern'd with you One half, not doubting but that Governour Harrison will at your request, supply my Proportion in Respondentia.[52]

The private English trade with Manila and Macao often involved Armenian, Spanish and Portuguese intermediaries. The Madras merchant, John Scattergood, had as his business partners at Malacca the Captain China Chan Yungqua and the Portuguese João de Matta. Through these two persons, Scattergood arranged second-stage investments in voyages to Trengganu, Siam, Acheh, Banjarmasin and Java. In 1720, de Matta was entrusted with the goods shipped on the *Bonita* to sell as he thought fit in the straits of Malacca and adjacent ports in return for a 5 per cent commission.[53]

The private English traders began operating from the port of Masulipatnam in the 1650s, and within two decades or so came to dominate the trade from it. Such domination during the first half of the 1680s is confirmed by the shipping lists available in the VOC records. Asian shipping based at the port appears to have declined substantially in respect of voyages to the Red Sea and the Persian

---

[50] Watson, *Foundation for Empire*, pp. 122–3, 330–1.
[51] Marshall, 'Private British trade', p. 285.
[52] D.K. Basset, 'British "country" trade and local trade networks in the Thai and Malay states, c. 1680–1770', *Modern Asian Studies*, vol. 23 (4), 1989, p. 635.
[53] Basset, 'British "country" trade', p. 635.

Gulf. The Asian merchants' cargoes to these destinations were now carried mainly as freight on English and other European shipping.[54] The English private traders also collected a good deal of freight cargo for Surat and the Persian Gulf in Bengal. Around the turn of the century when more and more of the English private shipping was moving on to Madras as its base, five or six ships were sent each year to Bengal to collect the freight cargo for Surat and Persia. But as private English trade and shipping at Calcutta came of age, the heavy dependence of the Madras shipping on freight cargo from Bengal proved to be disastrous. The political turmoil in Persia in the 1720s further cut into the profitability of the westward trade from Madras. The Coromandel famine in the early 1730s made an already difficult situation even more precarious, and the Madras merchants were reported to have made 'losses upon losses'.[55]

The decline of the Madras shipping was in part a direct consequence of the rise of the English shipping at Calcutta. The private English trade in Bengal had started out late in the seventeenth century at the Hugli and Balasore ports. Following the founding of Calcutta in 1690, the bulk of the English trade had begun shifting to that port. The principal trading links of the Calcutta shipping at this time were westward – with Surat, the Persian Gulf and the Red Sea – with the principal export goods being textiles and sugar. Carrying Indian merchants' freight cargo was an important component of the enterprise. Ships were operated on individual account as well as on partnership basis. In the eighteenth century, the Governor and the Council had also managed to set up a large joint stock enterprise involving several 'freight' ships. There is also evidence of Indians lending money to the English merchants on respondentia, and some instances of their having shares in English owned ships. We noted earlier that in its heyday the Madras shipping collected a good deal of freight cargo in Bengal for the westward sector. That business was now taken over by the Calcutta shipping and the Madras merchants repeatedly complained about the lack of access either to the freight cargo or to Bengal goods at a competitive price.

The early years of the eighteenth century witnessed a remarkable growth in the volume of English private shipping at Calcutta. The fleet

[54] Subrahmanyam, 'Persians, pilgrims and Portuguese', p. 525.
[55] Marshall, 'Private British trade', p. 288.

consisted of about twenty ships in 1715: by 1730 the number had doubled. A buoyant westward trade was largely responsible for the growing prosperity of the private English shipowning merchants of Calcutta. A Dutch shipping list pertaining to Calcutta in 1734 listed the departure of sixteen private English ships westward – nine for Surat, two for Gombroon and Basra, one for Basra alone, two for Mocha, and one each for Jeddah and Sind. A ship to Surat reportedly carried an average of Rs.70,000 worth of goods in addition to the freight cargo, a ship to the Persian Gulf Rs.150,000 to Rs.200,000 worth of goods plus freight cargo, while a ship to the Red Sea carried, in addition to the freight cargo, goods worth as much as Rs.300,000.[56] The differential advantage enjoyed by the English in the form of an exemption from transit and customs duties in Bengal subject only to the payment of a token annual sum of Rs.3,000 was evidently a factor enabling them to draw more and more trade to themselves.[57]

The short-haul trade from Calcutta in the westward direction included that with the Coromandel ports, Sri Lanka and the Maldive Islands. There was a fair amount of trade with Masulipatnam and Madras, mainly in stores and provisions such as rice. As many as 3,500 tons of rice were reported to have been shipped from Calcutta to Madras in 1737. The trade with Sri Lanka was only occasional but that with the Maldive Islands – the great provider of *cauris* and *chank* shells – was both regular and substantial.

West of Cape Comorin, the Malabar ports of call of the Calcutta shipping included Anjengo, Cochin, Calicut and Tellicherry where pepper was procured for the Red Sea and the Persian Gulf markets. While some of the ships proceeded from Malabar directly to the Red Sea or the Persian Gulf, others stayed on the coastal circuit and went on to Goa, Bombay and Surat. The last mentioned was by far the most important westward port of call for the Calcutta shipping. The goods exported there included, in addition to textiles and sugar, a large volume of raw silk, while the principal item imported was raw cotton.

---

[56] Marshall, *East Indian Fortunes*, pp. 85–6.

[57] This privilege had been secured first in 1651 by misrepresentation of facts pertaining to the *farman* granted by Emperor Shahjahan in 1650. It had been formalized in February 1691 vide a *hasb-ul-hukm* issued under the seal of wazir Asad Khan. The royal sanction was received in 1717 vide the well-known *farman* granted by Emperor Farrukhsiyar. The privilege was meant for the English Company goods alone, but was widely abused to include the private English traders' goods. The latter often abused it further by assuming, against a consideration, the ownership of the Indian merchants' goods.

That the rise in the English trade was most probably at the expense of that of the Surat merchants is strongly suggested by the Dutch shipping lists. In the early eighteenth century, these lists recorded a total of about fifty Surat ships being put to sea each year with Bengal as an important destination. By the 1730s, the number of Asian ships trading between Surat and Bengal had been reduced to a trickle. By the 1760s, a stage had been reached where the Calcutta 'freight ships' (the joint stock run by the Governor and Council) had so complete a monopoly over the main return cargo from Surat, namely Gujarat cotton, that their owners could fix its selling price in Bengal.[58]

The two principal ports in the Persian Gulf frequented by the Calcutta shipping were Gombroon in Persia and Basra in Iraq. Against the usual exports of textiles, raw silk and sugar, the principal import from the region consisted of precious metals. Commodity imports included copper, rosewater, Shiraz wine, dates and horses. As in the case of the trade with Surat, this was a major route for the Asian merchants as well and the competition the private English merchants operating on the route had to face was stiff. Many of the Asian merchants, however, used the English ships to freight their goods. By about 1710, the practice of sending to the Persian Gulf at least one Calcutta ship each year and sometimes two or more had become fairly established. In 1717, it was estimated that two ships a year carried about 500 tons of Bengal goods to Persia. Following the Afghan invasion of Persia in 1722, the focus shifted from Gombroon to Basra. In the 1720s and the 1730s, the number of ships sent to Basra normally fluctuated between two and four, though in an unusually good year such as 1738–9, it could even be five. As for the Red Sea, the principal ports of call were Mocha and Jeddah and the principal item imported again precious metals. By about 1720, the bulk of Bengal's exports to the Red Sea would seem to have been carried in private English shipping. At Mocha, English merchants' goods paid only a 3 per cent customs duty as against 9 per cent paid by the Asian merchants. At Jeddah, the corresponding rates were 8 and 10 per cent except that the Asian merchants' goods were over-valued in such a way that the real burden of the customs duties on these merchants amounted to as much as 12 to 17 per cent.

Adverse political conditions in the western Indian Ocean, combined

[58] Marshall, *East Indian Fortunes*, pp. 78–9, 86.

with the instability in Bengal in the 1740s following the Maratha incursions into the province, provided a damper on the trade between the two regions. A rise in the prices of the Bengal goods made them increasingly less competitive. Thus sugar from Java and China undersold Bengal sugar. Bengal raw silk, the price of which was said to have risen by 40 per cent between 1765 and 1780, similarly suffered from the competition by Chinese silk in the western Indian market. Even the Bengal textiles were said to be losing out in western India and the Persian Gulf. The shipping to Surat continued to maintain a good level in the 1740s (thirteen and ten ships returned from Surat in 1745 and 1746 respectively). But there was a sharp decline in the 1750s when the value of the English-owned silk and textiles was reported to be only 10 per cent of what it had been in the peak years of the 1730s. As for the Persian Gulf, the outlook was so poor in 1747 that the Bengal Council decided not to send a freight ship at all to Basra. Gombroon was captured by the French in 1759, and formally abandoned by the Company in 1763. The Red Sea proved by far the most stable of the western Indian Ocean destinations. One ship per annum continued to ply between Calcutta and Mocha, as well as between Calcutta and Jeddah right through the 1760s. It was only in the 1770s that the English trade between Calcutta and the Red Sea was finally abandoned.[59]

The private English merchants' trade from the west coast of India was carried on mainly from the port of Surat in the seventeenth century, and increasingly from that of Bombay in the eighteenth. In addition, a certain amount of trade was carried on from the Malabar ports of Anjengo and Tellicherry. As on the rest of the Indian seaboard, persons holding senior positions in the Company hierarchy dominated the trade. This group included George Oxenden, Gerald Aungier and John Child, each President at Surat between the 1660s and the 1680s. With the two ships that he owned, Oxenden carried on a vigorous freight trade to Persia. He reportedly turned a debt of Rs.50,000 into an estate worth Rs.300,000 at his death. Oxenden's ships were purchased by Aungier in association with a number of Surat merchants who included Mohammed Chellaby, belonging to a distinguished merchant family of the city. Eventually, Aungier and associates owned as many as five vessels. John Child reportedly left his

---

[59] Marshall, *East Indian Fortunes*, pp. 80–4, 92–5.

wife £100,000. Charles Boone, governor of Bombay in the second half of the 1710s, and Robert Cowan, governor during 1728–34, together with his associate Henry Lowther, chief at Surat, were other important members of this select group. Boone organized joint stocks for two China ships in 1716. Cowan was busy trying to remit £28,000 to England to increase his estate when he died at Bombay in the last months of 1737. Lowther was less fortunate materially, but he lived to return to England.[60] The trade at Anjengo and Tellicherry, consisting mainly of freight business provided by the Indian merchants, was also carried on mainly by the chiefs of the two factories: indeed, as Holden Furber notes, 'the posts were unquestionably run at a loss for the private benefit of their chiefs and factors as country traders'.[61]

The growth of the private English shipping based at the ports of western India was much more slow than it was either on the Coromandel coast or in Bengal. Until the 1770s or so, the orientation of the private English trade from the western Indian ports was almost entirely westward – ports on the Red Sea and in the Persian Gulf. But the kind of mastery and control that the Calcutta shipping was able to establish over the westward trade from the region in the early part of the eighteenth century always eluded the Surat/Bombay shipping. The westward trade from western India remained firmly in Asian hands with the share of the English shipping remaining limited. Thus in the season of 1731–2, of the twenty-four country ships that called at Mocha, the thirteen primarily Indian-financed ships totalled 4,390 tons, the remaining European-controlled ones only 2,440 tons. In the case of the Persian Gulf also, Indian shipping from the west coast around this time had about twice as much carrying capacity as the English shipping.[62]

THE FRENCH COMPANY AND
THE PRIVATE TRADERS

The French Company trade

As for the French East India Company, we have noted earlier that the enterprise founded by Colbert in 1664 had been succeeded by a new

[60] Watson, *Foundation for Empire*, pp. 82–106.
[61] Holden Furber, *Bombay Presidency in the Mid-Eighteenth Century*, London, 1965, p. 18.
[62] Furber, *Bombay Presidency in the Mid-Eighteenth Century*, pp. 32, 40.

company in 1685. This company began by procuring textiles in Surat and Pondicherry, but almost immediately was faced with protective legislation at home – the first of its kind in Europe – directed against these textiles. In January 1687, the Directors did manage to persuade the authorities to relax the new restrictions somewhat. Painted calicoes and clothes suitable for painting remained banned, but the Company was allowed to dye its stock of white clothes until the end of 1688, and sell its stock of painted calicoes until the end of 1687 to merchants who, in turn, might retail them for another year. After that, the Company would have to repossess the remainder for export abroad.[63] A large profit was made at the sales at Rouen in 1687, and at Nantes in 1689.[64] Around this time, on average, one ship was being sent to Surat each year and another to Pondicherry.

At the turn of the century, prospects for French Company trade in India appeared reasonably bright. In September 1699, on a sale of Surat and Bengal goods worth 3.5 million livres (1 livre = ƒ.0.5), a profit of 750,000 livres had been made. After the reoccupation of Pondicherry in 1699, the procurement of Coromandel textiles had also been organized on a proper basis. A sum of 100,000 pagodas was reportedly invested at Pondicherry in 1710: three years later, this figure had gone up to 180,000 pagodas.[65] But from about this time on, the financial situation of the Company became increasingly precarious. In 1716, the Company was reported to be under debt at Surat to the tune of Rs.3 million. In 1719, Pondicherry was said to be in desperate straits financially. Its governor could only carry on with the aid of loans from the leading local merchants. It was against this background that, in May 1719, the Edict of Reunion merged the Compagnie des Indes Orientales with Law's expanding enterprise. The edict attributed the Company's failure to bad administration, insufficient capitalization, premature payment of dividends and a ruinous borrowing policy. But Law's grandiose schemes for the East had hardly begun when the collapse of his 'system' forced the liquidation of the Compagnie des Indes and its restructuring in 1723 as the Compagnie Perpetuelle des Indes.

It was only after the founding of the Compagnie Perpetuelle des

---

[63] Holden Furber, *Rival Empires of Trade in the Orient, 1600–1800*, Minneapolis and Oxford, 1976, p. 113.

[64] Furber, *Rival Empires of Trade*, p. 204.

[65] Arasaratnam, *Merchants, Companies and Commerce*, p. 203.

Table 6.4 *The French East India Company's imports from Asia and India, 1725–71 (figures in livres tournois (1 LT = f.o.5))*

Years	Invoice value			Sales value			Profit (%)	
	Average annual value of total imports from Asia (LT)	Average annual value of imports from India (LT)	Proportion of imports from India to total imports (%)	Average annual value of total sales (LT)	Average annual value of sale of goods from India (LT)	Proportion of total sales accounted for by goods from India (%)	Profit on all goods from Asia (%)	Profit on goods from India (%)
1725/6 to 1734/5	5,224,506	4,348,212	83.22	10,635,214	8,800,702	82.75	103.56	102.39
1735/6 to 1744/5	8,873,867	6,647,642	74.91	16,560,826	12,307,759	74.31	86.62	85.14
1745/6 to 1754/5	6,365,383	4,354,272	68.40	12,782,027	8,518,574	66.64	100.80	95.63
1755/6 to 1764/5	3,940,648	2,650,288	67.25	6,540,701	3,969,780	60.69	65.98	49.78
1765/6 to 1770/1	8,742,583	5,197,747	59.45	15,466,131	8,839,065	57.15	76.90	70.05

Source: Calculated from Philippe Haudrère, *La Compagnie française des Indes au XVIIIe siècle 1719–1795*, Paris, 1989, vol. IV, Tables 2G and H, pp. 1199–201.

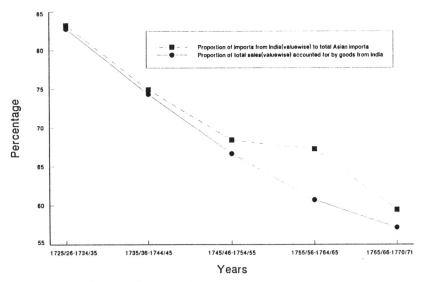

Fig. 6.4 The French East India Company's imports from Asia and
India, 1725–71

Indes that the French trade in India really picked up. In 1719, the
Compagnie des Indes had also decided to participate in intra-Asian
trade in collaboration with both its own employees as well as other
traders – both Indian and European. This trade continued on a limited
basis until 1741. But the principal business of the Company was the
trade between Asia and Europe. Quantitative information on this
trade is available on a systematic basis for the period between 1725 and
1771, and is set out in Table 6.4. Over the decade 1725/6 to 1734/5,
the average annual value of the French Company imports from Asia
into Europe was 5.22 million livres. By the following decade, this
figure had gone up to as much as 8.87 million livres. Goods procured
in India accounted for 83 and 75 per cent of the total cargo,
respectively, in the two decades, the other principal source of goods
being China. The average rate of profit on the sales in Europe during
the two decades was 104 and 87 per cent, respectively. How do these
magnitudes compare with their English and Dutch counterparts of the
time? In the triennium of 1738–40, the invoice value of the total
English imports from Asia into Europe was ƒ.23 million, and of the

Dutch *f*.19.24 million. In terms of Dutch florins, this figure in the case of the French East India Company was *f*.13.84 million.[66] While the French were still distinctly behind both the English and the Dutch, the gap was closing rather rapidly, particularly when one takes into account the fact that the catching up process had begun only some little time earlier. The French procurement had now begun to cause a fair degree of concern to the rival European companies. In November 1725, for example, the Dutch chief factor at Hugli had reported to Batavia that in view of the considerably increased competition by their European rivals, including the French, who had received a larger number of ships from home that year, it was becoming impossible to procure an adequate quantity of textiles. The new situation had made the weavers 'raise their horns not a little bit' and stop bothering about maintaining the quality, because these other Europeans 'accepted anything greedily'.[67] In 1731, four of the principal textile suppliers of the Dutch Company, Jiwan Chaudhuri, Gokul Mukund, Jagannath, and Radha Kishan Chaudhuri, after entering into contracts with the Company, chose to go over to the French at Chandernagore. The VOC could do little about it except to resolve that in the event of these suppliers offering to come back to the Company, they would not be accepted.[68] Pieces of *garras* and yarn *rumals* rejected by the Dutch in 1735 were reportedly grabbed anxiously by the French at an excessively high price.[69] When the French began procuring saltpetre at Patna in 1735, both the English and the Dutch made an application to the *nawab* to restrict the amount of saltpetre to be supplied to the French.[70]

The French private traders

Though a few Frenchmen, living mainly in Chandernagore, are known to have occasionally engaged in a certain amount of trade in the period prior to 1719, the real beginnings of French participation in intra-Asian trade ought to be traced to that year when the newly organized Compagnie des Indes decided to enter the field. It was, however, immediately obvious to the factors at Pondicherry that the

---

[66] Calculated from Philippe Haudrère, *La Compagnie française des Indes au XVIIIe siècle 1719–1795*, Paris, 1989, vol. IV, Tables 2G and H, pp. 1199–201.
[67] ARA, Hugli to Batavia, 7.11.1725, VOC 2024, ff. 91–2.
[68] ARA, Memorandum by Sadelyn for Berenaart dated 15.1.1732, VOC 2196, ff. 420–5.
[69] ARA, Hugli to Batavia, 17.1.1736, VOC 2348, ff. 559–60.
[70] Chaudhuri, *The Trading World of Asia*, p. 340.

Company's financial and other resources were simply not adequate to allow a meaningful participation in intra-Asian trade entirely on its own. A decision was, therefore, taken to invite the Company's employees as well as other traders, both Indian and European, to collaborate with the Company in the venture. The life span of this unique venture lasted for about twenty years between 1722 and 1741. During the 1720s, the Company took the lead in organizing voyages out of Pondicherry, but the sums invested on the account of the Company were strictly limited. By the end of the decade, French Company employees operating in their private capacity would seem to have become the dominant element in the enterprise. Thus while in the *Soucarama*, sent from Pondicherry to Manila in 1724, the contribution by the Company and by the employees was 51.7 per cent and 18.6 per cent, respectively (the remainder being put up by Indian and other European traders), the respective share of the two groups had altered to 9.4 per cent and 65.6 per cent in the *Pondicherry* sent to Mocha in 1729. The total capital invested in the *Soucarama* was 24,690 pagodas and in the *Pondicherry* 26,500 pagodas.[71] The Company employees and other French traders also operated independently of the Company.

It was usual for the French to form 'societies' or 'associations' which undertook one or more voyages. Each participant in the venture, which could be an independent merchant or an organization, put up a certain amount of money. The voyage of the *Pondicherry* mentioned above had been initiated in Pondicherry, but the shortage of capital there had persuaded the organizers to invite the employees and other traders at Chandernagore to participate. A sum of Rs.4,000 had also been subscribed on behalf of the Ostend Company on which a profit of 50 per cent was reported to have been made.[72]

There was a great deal of cooperation between French shipping based at Chandernagore and that based at Pondicherry in organizing voyages both westward and eastward. The bulk of the cargo as well as the freight for the westward destinations such as Basra generally originated in Bengal, and the cargo originating in Pondicherry was picked up on the way by the ship that had started out in Chanderna-

---

[71] Catherine Manning, 'French country trade on Coromandel (1720–50)', *Revista de Cultura*, Macao, nos. 13/14, January–June 1991, Table on page 168.

[72] Jan Parmentier, *De Holle Compagnie, Smokkel en Legale Handel onder Zuidernederlandse Vlag in Bengalen, ca. 1720–1744*, Hilversum, 1992, pp. 53–4.

gore. The trip to Mocha was based mainly on the Company's demand for coffee for Europe which was paid for in Pondicherry in silver. A ship usually sailed from Coromandel each year with freight and a cargo of textiles, pepper and Chinese porcelain to be sold against coffee. Another important branch of trade involving a relatively low investment and the possibility of making several trips a year was that to the Maldives.

The eastward destinations covered southeast Asia, Manila and, to a limited extent, China. In southeast Asia, the principal ports of call were Acheh, Mergui and Pegu. The principal goods carried there included Coromandel textiles, Bengal opium, saltpetre and firearms, which were exchanged against goods such as pepper, teak, eaglewood, rubies and rice. Further east, Manila was probably the most important eastward port of call for the French shipping. Between 1720 and 1750, a ship from Pondicherry is known to have called at this port each year but four. Probably because of the larger capital investment required, the trips to China were much less frequent. Thus over the same period of thirty years, no more than seven voyages were made between Pondicherry and Canton and the profit made was not particularly high.[73]

At least some of the French private traders are known to have done very well for themselves. Mahe de la Bourdonnais is believed to have left Asia with more than three million livre tournois (approximately f.1.5 million) and Duvelaer with more than five million.[74] The most well known of them, though perhaps not the one to have made most money, however, was Joseph François Dupleix, the head of the Chandernagore factory between 1731 and 1741. Immediately on arrival in Chandernagore, Dupleix had established a 'society' for trade. His associates ranged from direct participants in his ventures to providers of loans on an ordinary or respondentia basis. His French associates included Costanier, one of the directors of the French Company and two successive governors of Pondicherry, Lenoir and Dumas. English merchants of Calcutta and Madras such as Eliot, W. Price, Benet, Court and Wycht also carried on trade in association with Dupleix. His principal Dutch associate was the chief of the Dutch factory in Hugli, Jan Albert Sichterman, who is reported to

[73] Manning, 'French country trade', pp. 165–6.
[74] Philippe Haudrère, 'The French Company of the Indies in the 17th and 18th centuries: success or failure?', *The Indian Ocean Review*, vol. 1 (2), June 1988, p. 11.

have invested no less than Rs.87,000 in the *François* sent by Dupleix to Basra in 1736. In 1739, he was under debt of Rs.42,000 to Dupleix. Yet another group of European merchants deeply involved in Dupleix's ventures was that of the employees of the dissolved Ostend Company. These included Pierre Strebel, John Ray, Leendeert Meynders and, above all, François de Schonamille. Schonamille had been a free trader on the Coromandel coast between 1719 and 1723 and had associated with the French at Pondicherry. Just before the dissolution of the Ostend Company in 1731, Schonamille had been appointed the chief of the factory at Bankibazar. It was on the basis of his private trading ventures, mainly in association with Dupleix, that Schonamille formally kept the Ostend factory going until 1744. Of the four voyages organized by Dupleix in 1731, Schonamille invested Rs.7,000 in the trip to Acheh, Rs.3,000 in that to Mahe and Rs.2,000 in the trip to Surat.[75] In a subsequent venture to Manila, Schonamille put up Rs.4,000 on respondentia at 30 per cent interest. That Dupleix's own share in the capital investment in a particular voyage might not be very high is suggested by the breakdown of the total investment made in the voyage by the *Balocopal* to Manila in 1738. Of the total sum of Rs.243,000 invested, Dupleix's own share was only Rs.30,000. Of the remainder, Rs.105,000 was put up by Eliot, Rs.40,000 by one of the Carvalho brothers, Rs.30,000 by Dumas and Rs.23,500 by Costanier, the balance being subscribed probably by smaller associates. The list of persons providing loans for Dupleix's ventures was a long one and included persons such as the Jagat Seth. The respondentia loans carried a minimum of 18 per cent interest, though, as we saw above, it could be much higher. A major component of Dupleix's business was the carrying of freight cargo belonging mainly to the Armenian and Muslim merchants. The rate charged normally varied between 7 and 10 per cent of the value of the cargo carried.[76]

Between 1731 and 1741, Dupleix organized or participated in about ninety-one voyages. An overwhelming bulk of these – as many as seventy-nine – went westward, including sixteen to Surat and fourteen to Basra. The other westward destinations (apart from Pondicherry) included the Maldives and Mozambique, Malabar, Mocha and Jeddah, and Bandar Abbas. The eastward destinations included Acheh (two),

---

[75] Parmentier, *De Holle Compagnie*, p. 55.
[76] Indrani Ray, 'Dupleix's private trade in Chandernagore', *The Indian Historical Review*, vol. 1 (2), 1974, pp. 279–94.

Pegu and Malacca (one each), Manila (six) and Canton (two). Steady profits were made on most of these trips. But Dupleix would seem to have had more than his share of misfortune in the form of shipwrecks. The loss of the *Amiable* in 1735 while returning from Jeddah with Rs.500,000 worth of gold was a crippling blow. But fortunately for him, the loss he suffered in the disappearance of the *Balocopal* in the Bay of Bengal on its way back from Manila in 1739 amounted to no more than Rs.40,000. Dupleix kept on transferring his savings to France through both legitimate and unauthorized channels. In 1741, his capital in Pondicherry and Chandernagore was reported to have amounted to about Rs.550,000.[77]

The withdrawal of the French East India Company from intra-Asian trade in 1741, followed by the outbreak of hostilities between the English and the French in 1744, practically put an end to the French participation in intra-Asian trade. There was, however, a remarkable revival in the French private trade from Bengal in the 1750s. In the 1780s and the 1790s, French participation in Asian trade was based chiefly on Mauritius. While only six French vessels were recorded as having called at Cochin in 1785–6, the number had gone up to seventeen in 1791–2. Nearly all of these ships were trading between Mauritius and Mahe, Pondicherry, the Maldives and Colombo. Only one of these ships had made a China voyage and only two had gone to Bengal.[78]

THE DANISH COMPANY TRADE

The establishment of the second Danish East India Company in 1670 was noted earlier. It turned out to be a somewhat more successful venture than its predecessor. Danish neutrality in the late seventeenth-century wars among the great maritime powers helped, and considerable cargoes of pepper, saltpetre, sugar and Indian textiles were imported into Copenhagen. In addition to Tranquebar, the Company carried on trade in Bengal. A factory was maintained at Hugli until 1714. In 1717, a number of influential merchants of Hugli sent word to the Company at Tranquebar suggesting that it come back to Hugli. The message was accompanied by a *parwana* from *Subadar* Murshid Quli Khan. The Danes did in fact send some men to Hugli in 1724 to

[77] Ray, 'Dupleix's private trade', pp. 279–94.
[78] Holden Furber, *John Company at Work, A Study of European Expansion in India in the late Eighteenth Century*, Cambridge, Mass., 1948, p. 186.

whom was duly handed over possession of the erstwhile factory of the Company. But no trade was carried on and in October 1736, the Danes were still reported to be planning to resume the Bengal trade.[79]

Between 1671 and 1727, treasure and goods worth a total of 2.92 million Danish ryx-dollars (1 Danish ryx-dollar = approximately *f*.2) were dispatched to Tranquebar on the account of the Company. The return cargoes over the same period fetched a total auction value of 5.70 million Danish ryx-dollars. Goods worth 7.8 per cent of this amount were re-exported from Denmark. But ever since 1709, the Company had been facing rather severe financial problems. The outbreak of the great northern war that year had led to the State raising a forced loan from the Company. Besides, the fear of capture of its ships by Swedish privateers in the North Sea had necessitated extremely expensive stopovers in English ports. By the time peace was concluded in 1720, the Company's finances and international competitiveness had been undermined. Frederik IV refused to help out with a loan, and in 1729 the Company went into liquidation.[80] The East India trade, however, continued under the auspices of interim companies and on 12 April 1732 a new Danish Asiatic Company was chartered by King Christian VI with a forty-year monopoly of the Asia trade. The Company in fact stayed in business until 1807 – a total of seventy-five years.

THE OSTEND COMPANY TRADE

Finally, there was the Ostend Company chartered by the Habsburg Emperor Charles VI in 1722. We noted earlier that the group of merchants responsible for floating the Company had in fact been sending ships to Asia ever since the establishment of the Austrian administration in the former Spanish Netherlands in 1713. The group had established a factory at Kovilam, a few miles south of Madras, in 1719. But most of its activities were concentrated in Bengal, where in pursuance of the favourable reports received from the Scotsman Alexander Hume, the *Carolus Sextus* was sent in 1722. Pending the receipt of a formal permission to trade for which a sum of Rs.70,000 was deposited for 'expenses' with an Armenian banker in

[79] ARA, Hugli Resolution dated 19 October 1736, VOC 2385, ff. 550–4.
[80] Ole Feldbæk, 'The Danish Asia trade, 1620–1807, value and volume', *The Scandinavian Economic History Review*, vol. 39 (1), 1991, pp. 3–27.

Murshidabad, the *Carolus Sextus* sailed back in February 1724 for Ostend with a full cargo and with Hume aboard. Andreas Cobbé, who had stayed behind as the factor in charge and had found lodgings in the factory which the Danes had abandoned in 1714 after an armed conflict with the local authorities, continued with the efforts to obtain permission to trade. But he was more of a soldier than a merchant diplomat, and when permission was not forthcoming by April 1724, Cobbé had a few indigenous vessels seized. But he suffered a fatal wound in an engagement with the nawab's troops and died in June 1724. His colleagues were obliged to take refuge in the French factory at Chandernagore.[81]

When the news of the death of Cobbé reached Antwerp, Alexander Hume was named governor of the Ostend factories in India. He was offered an unusually high salary of Rs.6,000 per annum (the salary of the Dutch director of the Bengal factories at this time was Rs.2,160 per annum) besides a 6 per cent commission on all Bengal goods sold in Ostend. Soon after his arrival in Bengal in 1726, Hume reopened negotiations for a formal permission to trade and deposited another Rs.45,000 towards 'expenses'. But when nothing had happened by April 1727, Hume went on the offensive. He had a rumour spread that he and his colleagues were planning to return to Ostend with the next ship. He also ordered the seizure of indigenous shipping at Balasore. This was sufficient to alarm the local authorities who arranged a meeting with the nawab at Murshidabad, but nothing came of the meeting. In June 1727, Hume ordered the two newly arrived frigates from Ostend to seize Indian vessels in the River Hugli. On 2 July, one of the frigates, the *Aertshertoginne*, made contact with a vessel returning from the Maldives with a cargo of *cauris* worth Rs.30,000. The strategy worked and a *parwana* containing permission to set up a factory at Bankibazar was received on 5 July 1727. As in the case of the VOC, the rate of customs duty payable was fixed at $2\frac{1}{2}$ per cent. The Company was also granted the right to have its silver minted into rupees at the Murshidabad mint.[82]

The reluctance of the authorities to grant permission to trade, which ordinarily would have been done as a matter of routine, was the outcome basically of the behind-the-scenes efforts of the English and

---

[81] Parmentier, *De Holle Compagnie*, p. 21.
[82] Parmentier, *De Holle Compagnie*, pp. 27–8.

the Dutch companies to prevent the entry of the Ostenders in the lucrative Bengal trade. The English–Dutch coalition was at work both in Europe as well as in Bengal. Even before the Company had been chartered in 1722, the employees as well as the brokers and other residents of the English and the Dutch villages had been directed to have nothing whatever to do with the Ostenders.[83] The *faujdar* of Hugli, with whom Hume was in touch in connection with his efforts to obtain a *parwana*, played one party against the other. While he was assuring Hume that he would plead on the Ostenders' behalf with the nawab, he was at the same time actively considering an English–Dutch offer of Rs.200,000 to keep the Ostenders out of Bengal. In 1727, just before the Ostenders eventually received the *parwana*, the English even sought to bring them into disrepute by having a Bengali village set on fire by a party of their own soldiers carrying the Habsburg emperor's flag and shouting, 'Long live the Emperor, we are Germans.'[84]

In the meantime, the Ostend factors had been busy carrying on a limited amount of trade. In 1725–6, they were reported to have sent out 24,600 pieces of *malmals*, 13,812 pieces of *khasas* and 17,994 pieces of *garras* besides 1,600 maunds of low-grade raw silk.[85] The factors' relative lack of experience was taken full advantage of by the suppliers and brokers. It was reported by the Dutch factors at Hugli in 1726, for example, that *dungarees*, normally used as packing material, had been passed on to the Ostenders as *garras*.[86]

In the spring of 1728, news was received in Calcutta that in exchange for the English–Dutch support to his daughter Maria Theresia's succession to all his dominions, the Emperor had agreed the previous year to suspend the Ostend Company for a period of seven years. The Directors in Antwerp, however, decided to continue in business by operating under foreign flags. Two ships were dispatched to Bengal in the spring of 1729 with Polish passports and an international crew. The subterfuge, however, did not quite work because in Bengal the Ostenders claimed customs duties privileges for the two ships. In the meantime, the English and the Dutch factors in Bengal

---

[83] ARA, Hugli to Batavia, 15.12.1720, VOC 1962, ff. 80–2.
[84] Parmentier, *De Holle Compagnie*, pp. 25–7.
[85] ARA, Memorandum of goods sent by the Ostenders to Europe in February 1726 (VOC 2052, ff. 125–6).
[86] ARA, Hugli to Batavia, 21.3.1726, VOC 2052, ff. 13–18.

had equipped two armed vessels, the *Fordwich* and the *Duke of York*, to seize any Ostend vessel that might try to come in. At the request of the Ostenders, the nawab directed the English and the Dutch not to engage in enemy action. But the *Fordwich* nevertheless seized a sloop, the *l'Enfant*, on its way back from the Coromandel coast near Fulta. It was detained for a day but then released under pressure from the nawab. The English–Dutch coalition then sought to buy the nawab's support by a gift of Rs.124,000 besides 122 gold muhrs for the Mughal emperor. But the nawab asked for Rs.600,000, which sum was eventually reduced to Rs.325,000. In return, the nawab agreed to force the Ostenders to leave Bengal and allow the coalition to seize their vessels at the mouth of the river. When the *Phoenix* equipped at Cadiz and flying the Prussian flag arrived in Balasore in September 1730, the threat of capture obliged it to flee to Mergui. After a while, it returned to Balasore and then went on to Pondicherry and Tranquebar, but only to return to Mergui. It was only in December 1731 that the *Phoenix* returned to Goa and picked up a textile cargo put together for Europe under a secret arrangement with the French.[87]

Between 1726 and 1730, the Ostenders also engaged in a certain amount of intra-Asian trade. In 1726, the brigantine *Goed Success* was sent to the Coromandel coast with cotton textiles, saltpetre and rice. While the latter two commodities were sold to the Danes at Tranquebar, the cotton textiles were sold to a broker at Masulipatnam against *chintz* for Ostend. A sloop was similarly sent to Kovilam each year between 1727 and 1730 (from 1729 under a foreign flag), but the profit earned in the process was quite insignificant.[88] In 1729, Alexander Hume invested on the account of the Company a sum of Rs.8,000 in a voyage from Calcutta to Bombay, Mocha and Jeddah. The cargo in the vessel was owned in the ratio of 3:1 by Samuel Greenhill, a senior employee of the English Company, and Edward Coward, a private English merchant. The Ostend Company investment consisting of cotton and silk textiles was in the cargo ostensibly owned by Coward. A part of the cargo remained unsold at Jeddah, but a profit was nevertheless made. This profit was invested in yet another vessel operated by Coward between Calcutta and Surat. It was agreed that the Ostend Company would receive a 10 per cent

[87] Parmentier, *De Holle Compagnie*, pp. 29–35.
[88] Parmentier, *De Holle Compagnie*, pp. 23–4, 44.

interest on its investment. But it was with great difficulty that the investment was eventually recovered from Coward and then with a loss of about Rs.800.[89] Ever since 1729, the English and the Dutch had blockaded the River Hugli. They succeeded in capturing four vessels operating under cover of the Ostenders. The blockade was lifted later, but the question of the return of the four vessels was still pending in 1735.[90]

The Ostend Company was eventually dissolved in 1731 with one final voyage being authorized as part of the agreement of dissolution. The Bankibazar and the other Indian factories were formally taken over by the Emperor. Many of the merchants associated with the Ostend venture helped float the Swedish East India Company established in 1731, while others went over to the Danish Asiatic Company founded the following year. Still others continued to trade under the 'flag of convenience' of the king of Poland. François de Schonamille, an Antwerp merchant who had served the Ostend Company for many years and had been appointed governor after Hume had deserted to the English in December 1730, stayed on at Bankibazar and kept the factory going until 1744. This he was able to do by engaging in a certain amount of trade on his own account often in collaboration with other important private European traders operating in Bengal at the time. These included the chiefs of the French and the Dutch East India companies in Bengal, Joseph François Dupleix and Jan Albert Sichterman respectively.

The trade carried on by the Ostend Company during its brief existence never really amounted to anything. But in the history of the European companies' trade in India, the Ostend Company is nevertheless of interest for two reasons. In the first place, it demonstrates how deep seated the concern of the two giants – the English and the Dutch East India companies – really was when it came to keeping a potential rival out and the lengths to which they could go to prevent such a thing happening. The Ostend Company case also illustrates how the monopoly of the great chartered East India companies could be skirted, and the East India trade increasingly 'internationalized'.

If we look at the period 1680–1740 as a whole, certain important developments stand out. Probably by far the most important of these

[89] Parmentier, *De Holle Compagnie*, p. 45.
[90] ARA, Statement dated 28 February 1735, VOC 2327, f. 1141; Hugli to Batavia 18.11.1735, VOC 2348, ff. 68–9.

was the successful challenge by the French East India Company of the hitherto unqualified domination of the Euro-Asian trade by the two giants – the Dutch and the English East India companies. The growth in French trade was particularly marked after the reorganization of the French enterprise in 1723 into the Compagnie Perpetuelle des Indes. We noted above that over the three-year period 1738–40, the invoice value of the French exports from Asia to Europe stood at $f.13.84$ million as against $f.19.24$ million in the case of the Dutch, and $f.23$ million in that of the English East India Company. The French admittedly were still distinctly behind both the English and the Dutch, but they were a close third and could no longer be dismissed as inconsequential. That characterization, however, continued to be fully applicable to the Danes, the Ostenders and the Swedish East India Company.

Between the Dutch and the English East India companies, the English with an average annual import figure of $f.7.66$ million as against the Dutch figure of $f.6.41$ million were now distinctly ahead as far as the value of Euro-Asian trade was concerned. But if we add to the Dutch figure the value of the still substantial intra-Asian trade carried on by the VOC, to which there was no English counterpart, continued Dutch superiority in terms of the total value of trade carried on in Asia is unmistakable. Over the years 1738–40, India accounted for less than 50 per cent of the total Dutch imports into the Netherlands. But the average annual value of the total VOC imports from India alone – into Europe as well as to the rest of Asia – amounted around this time to $f.6.43$ million as against $f.6.41$ million which was the value of the total Dutch import of Asian goods into Europe at this time.[91] It is useful to remember that, in 1735–6, as much as 29 per cent of the Dutch imports from Bengal was still directed at the rest of Asia. In the case of Gujarat, this figure was 52 per cent during 1736–7 to 1740–1.[92]

---

[91] The figure of $f.6.43$ million includes the imports from

Bengal (1735–6)	$f.4.31$ million
Coromandel (1739–40 textiles alone)	$f.1.42$ million
Gujarat (1736–7 to 1740–41)	$f.0.36$ million
Malabar (1731–2)	$f.0.34$ million
Total	$f.6.43$ million

These figures have been taken from Tables 5.2, 5.3, 6.2 and 6.3.
[92] The Bengal figure has been taken from Table 5.4. The Gujarat figure has been calculated from Table 5.2.

During 1738–40, pepper and other spices accounted for no more than 14 per cent of the total invoice value of the Dutch imports into Europe. Textiles and raw silk accounted for another 40 per cent or so, while tea and coffee added up to nearly a third of the total imports. Since textiles and raw silk were procured overwhelmingly in India, the share of the subcontinent in the imports into Europe continued to be important. Within the subcontinent, Bengal continued to be the most important area of the Company's operations accounting in 1735–6 for total imports worth ƒ.4.3 million. Of these, the imports into Europe were worth ƒ.3.07 million, accounting for as much as 47 per cent of the total Dutch imports into Holland. Next in order of importance was the Coromandel coast accounting in 1739–40 for ƒ.1.42 million worth of textiles alone. Both Gujarat and Malabar played only a limited role, the average annual value of the imports from each being only slightly more than ƒ.300,000. In the case of the English East India Company, over the three-year period 1738–40, textiles and raw silk accounted for as much as 80 per cent of the total imports into England. The only other item of importance in the English import bill at this time was Chinese tea accounting for 10 per cent of the total value. The share of Indian goods in the total imports amounted to 84 per cent, of which Bengal alone accounted for as much as 66 per cent.

The period 1680–1740 also witnessed a fairly substantial participation in intra-Asian trade by European Company servants on their private account. In the case of the Dutch Company servants, this was done on a strictly clandestine basis until the partial opening up of the trade from the 1740s onward. The participation by the English Company servants, on the other hand, was legal and grew fairly rapidly during the period. The French tried the unique experiment of collaboration between the Company and its servants and others in engaging in a certain amount of intra-Asian trade. The scale and the duration of the experiment, however, was strictly limited.

CHAPTER 7

THE SUPREMACY OF THE ENGLISH EAST INDIA COMPANY, 1740-1800

From the standpoint of the European companies' trade in India, the second half of the eighteenth century constituted a distinct category characterized by developments of far-reaching import. We noted earlier that around 1740, in terms of its overall trading operations in Asia, the Dutch East India company was still distinctly ahead of its English rival, though in terms of Euro-Asian trade alone, the latter had already taken a lead. This situation had been altered radically by the time we reach 1780 or so. The greater part of the change took place in the years after 1760. Thus the value of the total English imports from Asia into Europe, which had stood at the equivalent of f.23 million over the triennium 1738–40 and had gone up marginally to f.25 million during 1758–60, reached the incredible figure of f.69 million over the triennium 1777–9 (Table 4.2). Bengal continued to account for over half the total imports, while the share of China came down from a third during 1758–60 to under a quarter during 1777–9 (Table 4.3). As against this, the value of the total Dutch imports into Europe had gone up only marginally from f.19 million during 1738–40 to f.21 million during 1778–80. The only major change in the composition of the Dutch imports had been a decline in the share of tea from 32 to 27 per cent, and a rise in that of textiles and raw silk from 41 to 49 per cent (Table 4.1). In absolute terms, the value of textiles and raw silk in the total imports had gone up from f.7.91 million during 1738–40 to f.10.28 million during 1778–80. The share of Indian goods in the total imports was now higher, perhaps around 55 per cent against a probable 45 per cent during 1738–40. While this would put at rest all speculation regarding the perceived decline (or even decimation) in the post-1750 period of the Dutch East India Company's Indo-European trade, there is no question that around 1780 the scale of the Dutch Company's trade was nowhere near that attained by the English Company. Whatever amount of trade the Dutch would still have been carrying on within Asia at this time (to which there was no English Company counterpart) would probably not have affected this relative ranking in any significant manner. As far as the French East India Company was concerned, the average annual value of the imports from Asia during 1765/6 to 1770/1 was no higher than it had been during 1735/6 to 1744/5 – roughly around *f*.4.4 million (giving a figure of *f*.13.2 million for a triennium). The share of India in the total French imports had in fact come down over the same period from around 75 per cent to around 60 per cent (Table 6.4).

THE POLITICAL AUTHORITY OF THE ENGLISH COMPANY IN BENGAL

A major circumstance contributing to the unprecedented growth in the English trade was the wresting of political authority by the Company in Bengal, the most important region of its trade, between 1757 and 1765. The chain of events culminating in the Company being appointed the *diwan* of the province in 1765 had started in April 1756 when, on the death of Nawab Alivardi Khan, his grandson, Siraj-ud-Daula, had taken over as the *subadar* of Bengal. For a variety of reasons, including the abuse of the transit and the customs duties exempt status of the Company goods by the Company servants for their private trade and even extending this privilege to Indian merchants for a consideration by assuming owner-ship of their goods, the relations between the new nawab and the English Company rapidly became strained to the point where the nawab's armies stormed Calcutta on 20 June 1756 and forced the English out of Fort William. Prior to the storming, both the English Company as well as the nawab had written to Adriaen Bisdom, the Dutch director, for assistance. The nawab had also written similar letters to the French, the Danes, the Portuguese and the Prussians. The Dutch, however, had chosen to maintain strict neutrality and had politely refused to provide assistance to either party. The other Europeans had also refused to get involved. On 23 June, the Dutch received word that a penalty of Rs.2 million had been imposed upon them for disregarding the request of the nawab. A similar penalty had reportedly been imposed on the French. After negotiations, however, the amount was reduced to Rs.400,000 for the Dutch, Rs.350,000 for the French, Rs.25,000 for the Danes, and Rs.5,000 each for the

Portuguese and the Prussians. Troops were deployed to attack Fort Gustavus in case the Dutch refused to comply with the demand. Bisdom did not have much of a choice, and the demand was met before he went to greet the nawab on 28 June 1756.[1]

The English, however, were not down for very long. The Company's army, which had been engaged in south India in a battle with the French for many years, was recalled to Calcutta in December 1756 and the town recaptured in January 1757. In February, the nawab agreed to the restoration of the English privileges. In June came the famous battle of Plassey which marked the inauguration of British political lien in the province. Mir Jafar, the new nawab, made available to the Company a body of commercial and other privileges. The revenues of 24 parganas were also allocated to the English to defray their military costs. In 1758, in part payment of debts, the revenues of three large districts were also allocated to the Company. In October 1760, the Company forced Mir Jafar to abdicate in favour of his son-in-law, Mir Kasim. The new nawab gave three new districts to the Company. But in 1763, trouble erupted with the new nawab as well. Following the battle of Buxar in October 1764, Mir Jafar was reinstated as the nawab. When Robert Clive arrived in 1765, he decided to introduce a new arrangement whereby the Company allocated a certain amount to the nawab and kept the rest of the provincial revenue to itself. The formal transfer of power took place on 12 August 1765 when the Mughal emperor appointed the Company the *diwan* of the province. The emperor was sanctioned an annual tribute of Rs.2.6 million. The nawabs of Bengal retained the office of *nazim* with formal responsibility for defence, law and order, and the administration of justice according to Islamic law. As a military power, however, the nawabs had already been reduced to insignificance. They were granted a fixed allowance for their court expenses and such activities as the *nazim* tried to undertake. The rest of the revenues of Bengal were at the disposal of the East India Company.

Quite apart from its long-term political implications, the English takeover of Bengal had major economic ramifications. The newly acquired political power was subject to gross misuse by the employees

[1] A.K.A. Gijsberti Hodenpijl, 'De handhavig der neutraliteyt van de Nederlandsche loge te Houghly by de overrompeling van de Engelse kolonie Calcutta, in Juni 1756', *Bijdragen tot de Taal-, Land-, en Volkenkunde van Nederlandsch Indie*, vol. 76 (III and IV), 1920, pp. 258–83.

of the English Company with a view to promoting both the Company's trade and even more their own private trade. The rival European trading companies were now reduced essentially to a position of being on sufferance and were subject to all kinds of harassment by the English. Then there were the indigenous merchant and artisan groups who were now subject to the coercive authority of the Company creating a situation where the terms on which they dealt with the Company were no longer governed by the market. At a macro-economic level, the implications of the European companies' trade for the economy of the region were altered beyond recognition.

The wresting of monopsony rights in saltpetre by the English from Nawab Mir Jafar in 1758 was the first step in the emergence of the Company as a commercial body enjoying privileges not available to its rivals.[2] When, soon after, the English also began interfering in their procurement of opium, the Dutch became convinced that their future in the region was in jeopardy. They, therefore, began looking for ways to strengthen their military presence in the subcontinent and to try and subvert the growing strength of the English Company. In the process, they embarked upon a bizarre adventure, ill-conceived and disastrously executed, which one might take note of if for no other reason than because, other than in Malabar in the 1660s, it constituted the only organized attempt by the VOC to employ naval-cum-land forces in the Indian subcontinent.

In June 1759, the Batavia Council dispatched a fleet of seven ships with 1,000 European and 1,000 Indonesian soldiers to the Coromandel coast with instructions to the chiefs of the Dutch factories in Coromandel, the Madura coast which was under the jurisdiction of the Sri Lanka government, Malabar, Gujarat and Bengal to keep in touch with each other and use the force, which was to be augmented by another 1,000 soldiers to be recruited in India, wherever necessary in the subcontinent, to the Company's best advantage. In the meantime, plans had been afoot to construct a new Dutch fort at Bankibazar to take the place of Fort Gustavus at Chinsura, which was not deemed to be strong enough. The Hugli factors were, however, worried that the English would not let the plans go through. It was at this point that they told Batavia that if they were allowed to help

---

[2] G.C. Klerk de Reus. 'De expeditie naar Bengale in 1759', *De Indische Gids*, vol. 11, 1889, pp. 2093–128, vol. 12, 1890, pp. 27–90 and 247–78.

Nawab Mir Jafar's son, Miran, against his father in the power struggle likely to erupt between the two, the growing English influence in the province could be neutralized. This was a tailor-made opportunity to use the projected force and, in February 1759, detailed instructions approving the project were communicated secretly to Adriaen Bisdom. At the right moment, the nawab's son was to be helped with men, ammunition and gunpowder against a promise of restitution of costs and restoration to the Company of its former privileges and prerogatives in matters of trade. If the conflict between the father and the son failed to erupt openly, the force was to be used simply to facilitate the construction of a fort at Bankibazar or another suitable site. In the meantime, G. Vernet, the Dutch second-in-command and the chief of the factory at Kasimbazar, had sought an audience with Nawab Mir Jafar in January 1759. In the audience, the nawab allegedly invited the Dutch to bring a force over to help him get rid of the English yoke.

It was against this confused background regarding its aims and objectives that the Dutch expedition reached India. The English had earlier come to know of the project from John Herbert, their spy at Batavia. Clive took immediate steps and, invoking a clause in the 1757 agreement with the nawab obliging the English to help him against a hostile third party, persuaded Mir Jafar to impose a ban on the entry of Dutch troops into the province in the interests of maintaining peace and order.

Of the seven ships constituting the Dutch fleet, two stayed on in Coromandel, but the remaining five had been supplemented there by another four. The first of these ships, the *Visvliet*, arrived at the mouth of the River Hugli on 21 August 1759. The Dutch claimed that the ship had been destined to go to Nagapattinam, but the winds had forced it to come to Bengal. Vernet had a secret meeting with Mir Jafar who, however, said that in view of the English position, he was unable to withdraw the ban on the entry of Dutch ships carrying troops. The remaining vessels of the Dutch fleet arrived on 1 October. For several weeks, there was complete stalemate with the English ships positioned to prevent the entry of the Dutch vessels into the river. The actual hostilities were started by the Dutch on 10 November when they captured seven English ships. Following their refusal to return the ships, the English launched an attack both on water and on land. The naval engagement, lasting no more than two and a half hours and going decisively in favour of the English, took place on 24 November between three English ships carrying 540 soldiers and four Dutch ships with 200 men aboard. Earlier, the English had taken Baranagar on 19 November and the land engagement took place on 25 November at Bedara near Chandernagore. Of a total Dutch force of 400 men consisting of 113 European soldiers, 21 artillerymen, 91 *topases* and 175 *sipahis*, against an English force of 100 Europeans and 400 *sipahis*, no more than 60 men reached Fort Gustavus alive. Thus ended the ill-fated adventure, and the Dutch were forced to sue for peace. The peace treaty obliging the Dutch to repatriate all European soldiers in excess of 125, and never to bring troops to Bengal again, was signed between the Dutch and Mir Jafar's son, Miran, at Murshidabad on 5 December 1759. It was ratified by the English on 8 December when the captured Dutch ships were returned.[3]

With the English Company (and its employees acting as merchants in their private capacity) creating all kinds of hindrance in the way of its trade, the position of the VOC continued to be rather precarious through the remaining part of the eighteenth century. In the wake of the Fourth Anglo-Dutch War, the Company's establishments were annexed by the English in 1781 and not restituted until 1784. During the Napoleonic wars, when the Company had ceased to exist, the Dutch possessions in the subcontinent were placed under British protection. Following the London Treaty of 1814, they were restored to the government of the Netherlands between 1816 and 1818. They were finally exchanged against English possessions in Sumatra in 1825 bringing the Dutch connection with the Indian subcontinent formally to a close.

DECLINING IMPORT OF BULLION INTO BENGAL

A part of the Bengal revenue resources available to the English East India Company from 1757 onward was diverted to finance the procurement of return cargoes for England not only in Bengal, but also in the presidencies of Madras and Bombay and even in China. This practice led to the beginning of the phenomenon of 'unrequited' exports and explains in part the growing divergence between the value of the total exports by the Company to India and that of its total

---

[3] Klerk de Reus 'De expeditie naar Bengale in 1759'.

imports from the subcontinent. The export of treasure to India, which traditionally had constituted by far the most important distinguishing feature of Euro-Indian trade, declined sharply and fast approached the figure of zero. In the decade of 1751–60, for example, against the average annual value of English exports to Asia amounting to nearly £1 million over the entire decade, the average for the last two years, 1759 and 1760, was only about half that figure. The contrast was even more sharp in respect of the export of treasure alone: against the annual average of £650,000 for the decade as a whole, the annual average for the last two years was under £160,000, accounting for no more than 30 per cent of the total value exported over the two years.[4] Such detailed information is not available for the post-1760 period, but an appendix to the Ninth Report from the Select Committee of the East India Company entitled 'An account of the quantity of silver exported by the East India Company to Saint Helena, India and to China' from 1758 to 1771 lists only Mocha and Benkulen under 'India'. A similar statement for the period 1771 to 1783 likewise lists only Benkulen and Balambangan under 'India'.[5] There is some evidence, however, which suggests that the import of treasure into India was resumed after 1784. The total value of treasure exported to China and India together was reported to be £369,033 in 1792–3, though during the following year this figure came down to a mere £10,290.[6] There was a substantial rise in this figure in the opening years of the nineteenth century. In the case of Bengal alone, the figure suggested for the five years between 1800–1 and 1804–5 is £3,399,093 giving us an annual average of £678,818.[7]

The other important local source used by the Company for the procurement of the return cargo was the money borrowed from private European merchants, including its own servants, against bills

[4] K.N. Chaudhuri, *The Trading World of Asia and the English East India Company, 1660–1760*, Cambridge, 1978, Table C.1, p. 507, Table C.4, p. 512.

[5] For a brief period, the Company had a settlement at Balambangan island north of Borneo. Both these statements are available in Appendix 5 to 'Ninth Report from Select Committee appointed to take into consideration the state of the administration of justice in the provinces of Bengal, Bihar and Orissa', 25 June 1783, India Office Library, L/Parl/2/15.

[6] India Office Records, L/AG/10/2/2, p. 236. Cited in Rajat Datta, 'Markets, bullion and Bengal's commercial economy: the eighteenth century perspective', in Om Prakash and D. Lombard (ed.), *Trade and Culture in the Bay of Bengal, 1500–1800* (forthcoming).

[7] India Office Records L/AG/10/2/4, p. 148; L/AG/10/2/5, pp. 92–3. Cited in Datta, 'Markets, bullion and Bengal's commercial economy'.

of exchange payable in London. In so far as it provided a safe channel to a whole host of European individuals to remit home savings made in India, the amounts available under this arrangement were usually quite large. Even the procurement of tea at Canton was organized partly on the basis of the funds made available at Calcutta by Englishmen in exchange for bills to be issued at Canton on London.[8]

The availability of rupee funds in India against bills of exchange payable in European capitals was also instrumental in significantly reducing the export of silver to the subcontinent by the other European companies as well.[9] If we look at the case of the Dutch East India Company, we find that while, at the level of Asia as a whole, the second half of the eighteenth century was indeed marked by the continued export of significant and, at times, rising quantities of precious metals from home (Table 3.1), the story was very different in the case of the most important of the Indian trading regions, namely Bengal. It will be seen from Table 3.3 that the value of precious metals the Company imported into this region came down from $f.4.72$ million in 1751–2 to $f.2.63$ million in 1761–2 and to a mere $f.390,000$ in 1770–1. No import of silver whatever was recorded in 1784–5. Admittedly, the value of the Dutch exports from Bengal had also declined over the same period, but by nothing like these values (Table 5.3).

THE DUTCH AND THE ENGLISH
PROCUREMENT OF THE RETURN CARGO
IN BENGAL

As far as the procurement of return cargo was concerned, Bengal continued to be by far the most important area of operation for both the Dutch and the English East India companies. The value of the

---

[8] For an example of this kind of a transaction, see a Company advertisement from Fort William dated 30 July 1781, Appendix 12 to Ninth Committee Report, India Office Library, L/Parl/2/15.

[9] The French, the Dutch and the Danish companies 'will be found to add their full Proportion to the Calamity brought upon Bengal by the destructive System of the ruling Power; because the greater part of the Capital of all these Companies, and perhaps the whole Capital of some of them, is furnished exactly as the British is, out of the Revenues of the Country. The Civil and Military servants of the English East India Company being restricted in drawing Bills upon Europe, and none of them ever making or proposing an Establishment in India, a very great Part of their Fortunes, well or ill-gotten, is in all Probability thrown, as fast as required, into the Cash of these Companies' (Ninth Committee Report, p. 16).

Dutch exports from the region did indeed register a decline from
ƒ.4.31 million in 1735–6 to ƒ.3.03 million in 1741–2, but the lost
ground had been more than made up by 1751–2 when an all-time peak
of ƒ.4.99 million was achieved (Table 5.3). Textiles and raw silk
between them accounted for as much as 69 per cent of the total
exports that year, with the share of saltpetre and opium being 7 and 14
per cent respectively (Table 6.1). The second half of the century was
again marked by a downward trend with the value of exports standing
at ƒ.2.3 million in 1761–2 and dropping further to as low as ƒ.1.96
million in 1771–2. In 1780–1, this figure had recovered to ƒ.2.47
million. In view of the dislocation caused by the Fourth Anglo-Dutch
War, the 1784–5 figure of ƒ.1.32 million should perhaps not be treated
as a representative one for the 1780s (Table 5.3). The share of textiles
and raw silk together that year stood at 62 per cent while that of
opium went up to 21 per cent (Table 6.1).

As for the English Company, we noted above that an incredible
increase in the value of total English imports from Asia from the
equivalent of ƒ.23 million during 1738–40 to ƒ.69 million during
1777–9 notwithstanding, Bengal accounted for over half the total
imports during the latter triennium (Tables 4.2, 4.3). Textiles and raw
silk would have accounted for an important part of the increase in the
value of the total imports from Bengal, but in the absence of detailed
information of the kind available until 1760, the precise share of these
items in the total imports, or the precise share of Bengal in the total
import of these items, cannot be indicated. In 1759, the last year for
which detailed information is available, textiles accounted for 58.8 per
cent of the total value imported from Asia. The value of the textiles
imported from Bengal that year was over £380,000 as against under
£40,000 for those from Madras and a little over £8,000 for those from
Bombay.[10]

Textiles

Even as Bengal continued to occupy a position of key importance in
the trading network of both the Dutch and the English East India
companies, the conditions under which the two companies traded
there underwent a sea change from the late 1750s onward when the
English assumed political authority in the region. The Dutch found

---

[10] Chaudhuri, *The Trading World of Asia*, Tables C.20–22, C.24, pp. 540–5, 547–8.

themselves reduced to a position of being essentially on sufferance and subject to all kinds of hindrance being placed in their way by the English, who grossly misused their newly acquired power. Before this, the 1740s had been marked by a crisis of a different kind – the Maratha incursions into the province which interfered seriously with the work of the procurement of return cargo. The depredations of the Marathas led to widespread scarcity of grain, shortage of labour and generally rising cost levels. Both the production and the procurement of textiles suffered severely, and the VOC was obliged to improvise. In January 1747, for example, when the suppliers failed to provide even the modest quantity of 40,000 pieces contracted for, the factors found it necessary to buy whatever was available in the market against cash. The situation was equally grim from the point of view of the merchants supplying to the Company. As early as 1744, the Company had suspected that the fortunes of several of the merchants doing business with it were under severe strain. These suspicions were confirmed in 1746 when it was learnt that four important merchants operating in the major textile centre of Santipur – Hinkar Chaudhuri, Jag Bhushan, Gokul Chand and Bhagwan Gopi Chand – together with their associates, Radhamohan Chaudhuri and Radhakant Chand, had been financially ruined. The Company suffered considerable losses in the form of debts owed by these merchants. The principal corrective step the factors sought to take was to require the merchants to provide sureties. But the local *sarrafs* and bankers, who would have been acceptable to the Company as guarantors, flatly refused, saying it was too risky a proposition.[11] The Company then tried the device of using the services of the *gumashtas* or individuals who bought for the Company in the *aurungs* against cash provided to them. But it was found difficult to get hold of an adequate number of reliable *gumashtas* and after being tried for three years in succession, the system was given up. At the same time that the Company was trying out the *gumashta* experiment, the *dadni* system was not abandoned. Since it was not possible to obtain sureties, what the factors did was to persuade the suppliers to form themselves into small groups (*ploegen*) and to be jointly and severally responsible for the funds advanced to each one of them. This in a way was the introduction in Bengal of the

[11] *Algemeen Rijksarchief* (ARA), Memorandum by Jan Kersseboom, the outgoing Director of the Bengal factories, addressed to his successor, Louis Taillefert, dated 16 February 1755, VOC 2862 (the volume is not foliated).

joint stock company experiment the Company had carried out in the seventeenth century on the Coromandel coast. As an additional precaution, broker Hari Krishan Ray was made a guarantor for the merchants and allowed a 3 per cent commission as compensation.[12]

The response of the English Company to this situation was somewhat different. In 1746, the Court of Directors instructed the Calcutta Council to try and persuade the merchants to accept the contracts without insisting on the usual advances being made available. The merchants, however, refused to oblige and the Company decided in 1753 to shift over to the *gumashta* system of procurement.[13] After the Company had wrested political power in the region later in the decade, the *gumashta* system became the principal vehicle through which the Dutch and the French East India companies were marginalized as rivals, and the merchants and the weavers doing business with the Company subjected to intense coercion.

For purposes of procurement, the English Company divided the province into segments each of which consisted of a group of *aurungs*. Each group contained a string of procurement stations, one of which was designated as the principal station where the chief *gumashta* of the group, responsible to the Commercial Resident, was based. The chief *gumashta* received from the Company both a salary (a modest sum of around Rs.50 per month) as well as a commission. He operated with the Company's funds and was, in principle, responsible for any bad debts that might arise from the sums advanced to him. He was provided with a staff of a *muqim* (supervisor of looms, yarn, etc.), a *muharir* (clerk), a *tagadgir*, a *dihidar* (village supervisors), cash-keepers and peons.[14] Each of the subordinate procurement stations was manned by a *gumashta* and a *dalal* who dealt with the weavers. Thus the *aurungs* of Haripal and Duniakhali had a total of eleven procurement stations with the principal station located at Duarhatta. Alternatively, the chief *gumashta* might operate directly through *paikars*, a group that would be a counterpart of the *dalals*. Thus the chief *gumashta* based at Khirpai and having under his jurisdiction the *aurungs* of Chandrakona and Hariasjoul dealt with a total of forty-one

[12] ARA, Memorandum by Kersseboom; Memorandum by Louis Taillefert for his successor, George Louis Vernet, dated 7 November 1763, *Hooge Regering Batavia* (HRB) 246, f. 104.

[13] Chaudhuri, *The Trading World of Asia*, pp. 310–12.

[14] Hameeda Hossain, *The Company Weavers of Bengal, The East India Company and the Organization of Textile Production in Bengal 1750–1813*, Delhi, 1988, p. 88.

paikars.[15] The intense coercion of the merchants and artisans that this system involved will be discussed later.

In order to counter the problem of grossly inadequate availability and the emergence of bad debts as a result of the English Company policies, the VOC adopted a series of essentially ad hoc measures. The *gumashta* system was revived in 1758 but soon given up as unworkable. New *dadni* merchants such as Murli, Birju Basu and Parbati Charan were then taken in and assigned to different groups, members of each of which undertook to be jointly and severally responsible for the funds advanced to them. But the principle of joint responsibility never really worked either and in 1761/2 bad debts to the tune of *f.*267,265 were reported to have arisen. The Company then tried to find merchants who would be willing to supply without being provided with an advance, but with an additional payment of 7 to 9 per cent in lieu thereof. This arrangement was reported to have had a fair degree of success for a few years but did not last, leaving the Company no option but to revert to the *dadni* system.[16]

Raw silk

The problems created by the English political power for the merchants and the artisans the Company dealt with, as well as for the rival European companies, were by no means confined to textiles but indeed extended to all other goods procured in the region – raw silk, saltpetre and opium. Raw silk had always been an important item of trade for the English, but its importance increased still further in the post-Plassey period. In the 1740s and the 1750s, the average annual value of the Bengal raw silk imported by the Company into England had been Rs.400,000 and Rs.300,000 respectively.[17] In 1766, however, the Company was reported to have contracted for raw silk worth as much as Rs.1.8 million to Rs.2 million. The following year, a figure of Rs.1.6 million was mentioned.[18] By 1769, the procurement of raw silk had become 'a great national object' and in 1793 the raw silk

---

[15] ARA, J.M. Ross to Director at Hugli, Appendix A, HRB 247 (the volume is not foliated).

[16] ARA, Memoir by Taillefert for his successor, George Vernet, 7 November 1763, HRB 246.

[17] Calculated from Chaudhuri, *The Trading World of Asia*, p. 534. The precise figures are Rs.416,344 and Rs.296,976 respectively.

[18] ARA, Memoir of outgoing Director Johannes Bacheracht for his successor, J.M. Ross, dated 31 July 1776, HRB 252, f. 112.

investment amounted to an unprecedented Rs.2.5 million.[19] This increase in procurement was achieved mainly by coercing the producers into supplying exclusively to the Company. In 1767, for example, a public announcement at Kasimbazar, accompanied by the beating of drums, ordered all silk reelers working for the Company not to accept work from anyone else. The wry comment made by the Dutch was 'if this is not a display of power, we do not know what is'.[20] The Dutch had good reason to be upset because although at a formal level the English took care to explain to them that such a ban did not apply to their procurement, the amount that the VOC was able to buy suffered considerably nevertheless. Hindrances were also placed regularly by the English *gumashtas* in the transportation to Hugli of whatever amounts the Dutch were able to buy.[21]

Saltpetre

Saltpetre, by virtue of being about the most profitable trading good doubling as ballast, had traditionally been an item of great interest to all the European companies. In 1728, the suppliers of saltpetre had been organized into a 'company' serving both the Dutch and the English. Eight years later, an agreement was concluded between the English, the Dutch and the French, stipulating that no Indian merchants living within their jurisdiction were to be allowed to buy saltpetre in Chapra, Purnea or any other *aurung* as far as Malda.[22] In 1745, the three companies agreed that they would share the jointly purchased lots in the ratio of 42.5:42.5:15.[23] But this arrangement was effectively sabotaged by the new *faujdar* of Chapra, Dip Chand (brother of the notorious Omi Chand) who took on farm the major saltpetre-producing areas in the district and practically monopolized the item. The VOC had no option but to buy 21,000 sacks of saltpetre from this man in 1747 at Rs.6 per maund.[24] Following the battle of

[19] N.K. Sinha, *The Economic History of Bengal from Plassey to the Permanent Settlement*, vol. I, Calcutta, 1956, pp. 17–19.

[20] ARA, Letter from Johannes Bacheracht at Kasimbazar to Director George Vernet at Hugli dated 13 March 1767, HRB 247.

[21] ARA, Letter from Johannes Bacheracht at Kasimbazar to Director George Vernet at Hugli dated 12 March 1766, HRB 247; letter from the same to same dated 14 July 1766, HRB 247.

[22] Chaudhuri, *The Trading World of Asia*, p. 340.

[23] ARA, Memoir prepared by Dutch director, George Louis Vernet, and submitted to the English on 10 May 1768, HRB 247.

[24] ARA, Memoir by Jan Kersseboom for his successor, Louis Taillefert, dated 16.2.1755, VOC 2862 (the volume is not foliated).

Plassey, however, the scenario again changed and the English obtained from Nawab Mir Jafar in 1758 exclusive rights in the commodity.[25] They offered to provide to the Dutch at cost price one third of the amount procured by them.[26] From 1763, the annual quota of the Dutch was fixed at 23,000 maunds, and that of the French at 20,000 maunds.[27] In years of shortage, the quota could be reduced as happened, for example, in 1776 when the Dutch were allotted only 18,000 maunds.[28] From the point of view of the VOC, however, the situation was not altogether too bad. On the lot supplied to them by the English, the problem of bad debts arising had been solved automatically and the additional quantity needed could always be bought in the market on the side. Also, from 1776 onward, the English began accepting payment for the saltpetre at Calcutta through bills, obviating the necessity of sending large sums of money to Patna.[29]

The Board of Trade promulgated new regulations regarding salt-petre in May 1787. Article 5 of these regulations stipulated that the rival companies 'be not permitted to work any manufactories of their own, as some of them are said to have done'.[30] The Dutch chief at Patna, Isaac Titsingh, made representation to Cornwallis to allow the inhabitants of the Dutch village of Daulatganj in Bihar to continue producing saltpetre 'which they had been doing for ages and deriving their livelihood from'.[31] The request was turned down and Titsingh was asked to 'instruct your commercial agents at Patna not to interfere in future in the manufacture of saltpetre'.[32] In 1794, the English

---

[25] ARA, Letter from Cornwallis at Calcutta to Isaac Titsingh at Hugli dated 20 July 1787, HRB 212 (the volume is not foliated); Memoir by outgoing director Bisdom for his successor, Louis Taillefert, dated 18 October 1760, HRB 245, ff. 35–6

[26] ARA, Second memoir by outgoing director Louis Taillefert for his successor, George Louis Vernet, dated 17 November 1763, HRB 246, f. 181.

[27] ARA, Memoir by outgoing director Johannes Bacheracht for his successor, J.M. Ross, dated 31 July 1776, HRB 252, ff. 9–10, 124; Memoir by outgoing director George Louis Vernet for his successor, Boudewyn Faure, dated 8 March 1770, HRB 249, f. 86.

[28] ARA, Letter from Calcutta to Hugli dated 21 September 1775, HRB 253 (the volume is not foliated).

[29] ARA, Memoir by outgoing director Johannes Bacheracht for his successor, J.M. Ross, dated 31 July 1776, HRB 252, ff. 124, 127.

[30] ARA, Letter from the English factors at Patna to the Dutch factors at Patna dated 11 June 1787, HRB 212 (the volume is not foliated).

[31] ARA, Isaac Titsingh at Hugli to Cornwallis at Calcutta dated 16 July 1787, HRB 212.

[32] ARA, letter from the English at Calcutta to the Dutch at Hugli, 20 July 1787, HRB 212.

decided to terminate the arrangement of supplying saltpetre to the rival companies altogether.[33]

Opium

The last major item procured by the VOC in Bengal was opium for the Indonesian market. The profit earned by the Company from the sale of this commodity had been growing over the years. Thus from ƒ.108,214 during 1678–87, the average annual profit made had gone up to ƒ.414,196 during 1688–97 and to ƒ.844,390 during 1738–47.[34] But the problem of the intense competition provided by its own servants engaged in a clandestine trade in the commodity had continued to defy solution. In his famous minute of 1741, 'Considerations over the Present State of the Dutch East India Company', Gustaaf Willem van Imhoff went to the extent of suggesting the withdrawal of all restrictions on private trade as the only way to get out of the rut of corruption the Company had managed to get into.[35] The Directors accepted the suggestion with the proviso that all opium handled would be subject to an export duty of Rs.50 per chest in Bengal and an import duty of 50 ryx-dollars at Batavia.[36] They evidently seem to have planned on the Company withdrawing from the opium trade altogether and leaving it completely to the private traders. But for some inexplicable reason, on becoming Governor-General in May 1743, van Imhoff himself turned against the idea. In their letter to the Directors dated 21 December 1743, the Governor-General and the Council at Batavia strongly opposed the introduction of the new arrangement and the plan seems to have been shelved.[37]

The following year, van Imhoff came up with a major alternative proposal. He recommended the setting up of an Opium Society constituted by private shareholders, who would be provided with a specified quantity of opium each year by the Company at a fixed price and who would be responsible for its sale in Indonesia. It was hoped

[33] ARA, John Shore at Calcutta to van Citters at Hugli dated 15 September 1794 and 17 October 1794, HRB 212.

[34] Calculated from J.C. Baud, 'Proeve van eene geschiedenis van den handel en het verbruik van opium in Nederlandsch Indie' (hereafter 'Opium'), *Bijdragen tot de Taal-, Land-, en Volkenkunde van Nederlandsch Indie*, vol. 1, 1853, Appendix 6.

[35] Baud, 'Opium', p. 120.

[36] The rate of exchange was approximately 1 ryx-dollar = 2 rupees.

[37] L.C.D. van Dijk, 'Byvoegsels tot de Proeve eener geschiedenis van den handel en het verbruik van opium in Nederlandsch Indie door den Heer J.C. Baud', *Bijdragen tot de Taal-, Land-, en Volkenkunde van Nederlandsch Indie*, vol. 2, 1854, p. 200.

that the problem of clandestine trade in the drug would be taken care of in so far as the unauthorized private traders would now have the option to become shareholders in the venture and to participate legitimately in the profit from the trade.[38] The Society came into being on 30 September 1745 on the basis of an exclusive charter granted for an initial term of ten years. The Company was henceforth obliged to offer its entire imports of opium to the Society who, on its part, would be obliged to accept each year a minimum of 1,200 chests at a fixed price of 450 ryx-dollars per chest. Supplies in excess of 1,200 chests and up to 1,500 chests, if accepted, would qualify for payment of 400 ryx-dollars and those in excess of 1,500 chests, of 350 ryx-dollars per chest.[39] The Society had a total share capital of 600,000 ryx-dollars divided into 300 shares of 2,000 ryx-dollars each.

Within a few years of the establishment of the Society, however, it was quite clear that the experiment had had only a limited amount of success. The plan to check contraband trade in the drug by associating private merchants engaged in it with the Society, for example, worked only up to a point. A large number of these traders never got into the orbit of the Society. Indeed, within a few years of the establishment of the Society, it was discovered that the bulk of the shares in it were held by persons who had since returned to Holland, or by their heirs. At one point, no more than 67 of the total of 300 shares were held by persons domiciled in Java.[40] Also, at times, the Company was obliged to accept payment from the Society at a rate lower than that stipulated in the charter.[41]

The big jolt both for the Company and for the Opium Society came in 1757 with the English takeover of Bengal. Private English merchants now engaged in an increasing amount of trade in opium and openly challenged the Dutch monopoly in the archipelago. Even more damaging was the fact that the unofficial English opium monopolies of the 1760s as well as the official Company monopoly established in 1773 put serious constraints on the Dutch opium procurement in Bihar. Over the nine years between 1746–7 and 1754–5, the Company

[38] Baud, 'Opium', pp. 122–3.
[39] The details of the charter are available in document No. 3 entitled 'Project associatie van geprivilegeerde kooplieden tot den amphioen geconsenteert in rade van Indie op den 24 September 1745', ARA, VOC 4832 (unfoliated).
[40] Baud, 'Opium', p. 24.
[41] Document 4 entitled 'Notitie van behaalde winsten op amphioen Bengaals in swaar geld gerekend', ARA, VOC 4832 (unfoliated).

had, on average, supplied 1,241 chests of opium per annum to the Opium Society.[42] Between 1756 and 1761, this figure averaged 1,200 chests. Over the four years, 1762 to 1765, however, when the impact of the unofficial monopolies began to be felt, the figure came down to as little as 432 chests.[43] On the other hand, between 1760 and 1764, the price the Company had to pay for the Bihar opium went up from f.222 to as much as f.402 per maund. The price charged by the Company from the Opium Society was, therefore, revised upward from 450 ryx-dollars to 550 ryx-dollars per chest. In 1776, on top of the increased price payable to the Company, the Society was obliged henceforth to give half of its net profits to the Company.[44]

Since this kind of pressure on the Company was directly related to the English monopoly, detailed negotiations followed in which the respective positions of the two companies were clearly spelt out. To begin with, the English offered to the Dutch an amount of 450 chests of opium per annum on the basis that this was the amount the latter had reportedly procured in the year preceding the one in which the English Company monopoly had been introduced. The price payable was to be the same as that paid by the English Company to its contractor. This was on the assumption that the Dutch would be willing to accept whatever quality lots the contractor chose to supply. If, on the other hand, they insisted on the right to reject poor-quality lots, they would be obliged to pay the price that they had actually paid in the last year of the pre-monopoly period.[45] The Dutch opted for the latter arrangement. The procedure was for the Dutch to apply to the contractor and make payment for the deliveries made by him to the chief of the English factory at Patna.[46]

While the Dutch really had no option but to agree to whatever the English dictated, they nevertheless kept up a steady correspondence on the issue with them. In the first place, they questioned the right of the English, who were merely the *diwan* of the sovereign, to negate the Dutch Company's privilege of a free trade in opium which had

---

[42] 'Notitie van behaalde winsten op amphioen Bengaals in swaar geld gerekend'.
[43] Calculated from table in Baud, 'Opium', p. 41.
[44] Baud, 'Opium', pp. 41, 142.
[45] ARA, Memoir by outgoing Dutch Director Bacheracht for his successor, J.M. Ross, 31 July 1776, HRB 252, ff. 121–2.
[46] ARA, Letter from Governor-General Warren Hastings and Council at Calcutta to the Dutch Council at Hugli, 29 January 1776, enclosures to the memoir of Bacheracht, HRB 253 (unfoliated).

been given to them by the sovereign.[47] In 1775, when a general proclamation by Calcutta allowing unhindered trade to the Dutch did not include opium in the list of items mentioned and was not publicised in the opium districts, the Dutch registered a strong protest with the chief factor of the English at Patna. The chief factor, Isaac Sage, wrote back saying that the omission was intentional since 'opium forms a considerable branch of the Company's revenue, and is by no means an esteemed article of public commerce'.[48] In a confidential letter dated 25 January 1776 to Gregorius Herklots, the chief of the Dutch factory at Patna, Sage referred to an unfortunate incident involving the ouster of the Dutch *paikar* from the district of Phulwari in 1775, and said that this had to be done because 'we cannot under the present restrictions suffer any person to interfere with the contractor on any account whatsoever'.[49] Later in the year, the two parties agreed to refer the matter to their respective superiors in Europe for a mutually acceptable solution.[50] In the meantime, the Dutch had been asking for an increase in their allotment to between 900 and 1,000 chests while the English steadfastly stuck to the figure of 450.[51] It is very likely that the Dutch managed to get some more on a clandestine basis, but the amount is unlikely to have been large.

The Dutch procurement of opium was also sought to be linked by the English in a rather curious manner to the China trade and the remittance question. In May 1785, Governor-General John Macpherson wrote to Gregorius Herklots, the Dutch second-in-command, making what he called a personal suggestion. He began by saying that as against the usual 400–450 chests in the 1770s, the Company had now agreed to provide 800 chests of opium to the Dutch. Since the English badly needed to finance their supra-cargo at Canton without having to send specie from Calcutta, they would appreciate it if Batavia could arrange for the payment of the opium

[47] ARA, Letter from the Dutch Director and Council at Hugli to the English Governor-General and Council at Calcutta, 2 February 1776, enclosures to the memoir of Bacheracht, HRB 253 (unfoliated).

[48] ARA, Letter from Gregorius Herklots to Isaac Sage, 30 August 1775 and Sage's reply, 31 August 1775, in enclosures to memoir of Bacheracht, HRB 253 (unfoliated).

[49] ARA, Extract from a secret resolution adopted by the Dutch Council at Hugli, 25 January 1776, enclosures to memoir of Bacheracht, HRB 253 (unfoliated)

[50] ARA, Second memorandum by the Dutch Director and Council to the English Governor-General and Council, 15 August 1785, HRB 211 (unfoliated).

[51] ARA, Minutes of the Dutch Council at Hugli, 2 February 1776, HRB 253 (unfoliated); Letter from Governor-General and Council at Calcutta to the Hugli Council, 7 February 1776, in the Minutes of the Hugli Council, 12 February 1776, HRB 253 (unfoliated).

supplied to them in Bengal at Canton. The amount of opium mentioned was between 800 and 1,000 chests on a recurring annual basis. As a further incentive, the Governor-General added that he was willing to give a guarantee that 'even in case of war, we should send the opium to Batavia under a flag of peace and leave you the full and secure preparation of it . . . It is immaterial to the English Company whether this trade is carried on by a foreign Company or by people living at Calcutta.'[52] Herklots sent a vague reply saying that he would get in touch with Batavia, but the arrangement did not appeal to the Dutch and was never put into practice.[53] From about this time, the Dutch quota was again successively reduced first to 700 and from 1787 on to 500 chests per annum.[54] Since this opium was delivered at Calcutta, the Dutch offered to sell their factories in Bihar to the English.[55] The offer was not taken up and, in July 1791, the factories were sold to a private party.[56] On 15 March 1794, the Opium Society was dissolved and the Company again took the opium trade directly into its own hands.[57] But this was a very short-lived affair in so far as the Company itself went into liquidation the following year.

THE ENGLISH PRIVATE TRADE AND THE 'COMMERCIAL REVOLUTION' IN THE INDIAN OCEAN

We have already analysed the English Company servants' private trade in the westward direction in the preceding chapter. As far as the eastward trade was concerned, it consisted essentially of three segments – southeast Asia, the Philippines and China. The first of these stretched from ports such as Pegu, Tenasserim/Mergui, Phuket, Kedah and Acheh – all on the eastern littoral of the Bay of Bengal – to Ayutthaya in the Gulf of Siam. The port frequented in the Philippines

[52] ARA, Letter from Governor-General John Macpherson to Gregorius Herklots, 19 May 1785, HRB 212 (unfoliated).

[53] ARA, Herklots and Council at Hugli to John Macpherson and Council at Calcutta, 26 May 1785, HRB 212 (unfoliated).

[54] ARA, Letter from Calcutta to Hugli, 15 April 1786; Hugli to Calcutta, 31 January 1787; Calcutta to Hugli, 7 February 1787; Hugli to Calcutta, 7 February 1787; Calcutta to Hugli, 7 January 1788; Hugli to Calcutta, 23 February 1788; Calcutta to Hugli, 25 February, 1788, HRB 212 (unfoliated).

[55] ARA, Letter from Hugli to Calcutta, 12 April 1791, HRB 212 (unfoliated).

[56] ARA, Letter from Calcutta to Hugli, 4 May 1791, HRB 212 (unfoliated); Hugli to Calcutta, 9 August 1792, HRB 212 (unfoliated).

[57] Baud, 'Opium', pp. 142–3.

was Manila and that in China Canton. In an analysis of the English private trade with the region, it is useful to distinguish between the period before about 1760 and that after. This is because the second half of the eighteenth century witnessed a substantive growth in the relative weight of the eastward trade in the overall trading operations of the private English merchants from India. Holden Furber has described this turning from the west to the east as an important element in the 'commercial revolution' in the Indian Ocean. The great expansion in the eastward trade in the post-1760 period, carried on by the private English merchants, was the outcome basically of a substantial growth in the trade with Canton which, in turn, was related in a large measure to the growth of English power in the Indian subcontinent. The English had become the actual rulers of Bengal, they were the dominant power on most of the Coromandel coast, and they had strengthened their position in western India. The special position of the English Company, and by association of that of the private English merchants, vis-à-vis the suppliers and producers of goods in regions such as Bengal, significantly increased the margin of profit from private trade. This was reflected in a sharp increase in the volume of trade in high-value commodities such as Bengal opium which together with Bombay cotton provided the basis of the enormous increase in the trade with China. This trade, incidentally, also served as an important vehicle for the transmission home of the large private English fortunes made in India. The newly found power and the expanded resource base had now enabled private English shipping to go beyond the Asian networks within which it had until then operated, and create new ones of its own.

The changing destination pattern of the eastward trade had its counterpart in the changing relative weight of the various Indian ports where English shipping directed at the region originated. Over the seventeenth and the first half of the eighteenth century, the bulk of the English trade with southeast Asia, which accounted for an overwhelming proportion of the total trade with the eastward region, was carried on from the Coromandel coast. This picture underwent a complete overhaul in the second half of the eighteenth century when the Madras shipping essentially took a back seat and the bulk of the eastward trade was carried on by the English shipping based at Calcutta and Bombay.

A rough idea of the growth as well as the changing destination pattern of the private English merchants' eastward trade from India can be formed by reference to the fact that while in the first half of the eighteenth century the Dutch at Malacca recorded a maximum of ten English private ships heading east through the straits in any one year, the number had gone up to twenty-four in 1764, and to as many as fifty in 1774. Simultaneously, more ships were going through the Sunda straits.[58] While a large part of this would be ascribable to the growth of the China trade, it also reflects a more thorough penetration of the southeast Asian markets by the English private traders. The Dutch control of Malacca as of 1641 and their special position in the archipelago notwithstanding, it had always been possible to do a certain amount of trading in the region in items such as opium, tin and pepper which the Dutch by and large had sought to reserve for themselves. The Dutch control over the Malay sultans' trade had always been tenuous and English country captains, by paying higher prices and with the aid of some discreet bribery, had found it possible to trade even at Malacca itself. But in the post-1760 period, it was no longer necessary to be discreet and the Dutch claims of monopoly could be countered quite openly.

Until the middle of the eighteenth century, by far the most important destination for private English shipping from India was southeast Asia, and the principal Indian port from which shipping was directed at the region was Madras. The principal ports called at were Pegu, Tenasserim/Mergui and Ayutthaya, Kedah, Acheh and Malacca besides Bantam and Batavia. At Batavia, the English ships were obliged to operate under stringent restrictions as to the commodities in which they traded, while the trade to Bantam was lost as of 1682 when the port was taken over by the Dutch and declared closed to others. Pegu remained an important destination, but trade with the port was subject to vigorous competition by the Indian merchants. During the 1720s and the 1730s, between six and twelve ships left Madras for Pegu each year. In 1720, 1722 and 1737, the number of incoming ships from Pegu rose to thirteen or fourteen, and in 1739, as many as twenty-one arrivals were recorded. The number of Indian ships in these lists often exceeded that of the private English

---

[58] P.J. Marshall, 'Private British trade in the Indian Ocean before 1800', in Ashin Das Gupta and M.N. Pearson (ed.), *India and the Indian Ocean 1500–1800*, Calcutta, 1987, p. 297.

merchants.[59] The principal items procured in Pegu were gold, timber and rice.

At the Siamese ports of Mergui and Tenasserim in the Bay of Bengal, and of Ayutthaya in the Gulf of Siam, the private English traders encountered the dynamic trading organization of the king of Siam. The trade between Madras and Mergui/Tenasserim was dominated throughout by the Asian merchants. A large number of Chinese junks regularly called at Ayutthaya making it an important meeting point between the east and the west. Between October 1683 and November 1684, as many as forty-two ships including eleven belonging to the English are recorded as having called at the port. At the beginning of 1685, more than a dozen English, French and Portuguese ships are recorded as having left Ayutthaya westward with Japanese bar copper bought from the foreign trade minister of Siam, the Greek Constantine Phaulkon.[60] But the Mergui massacre of July 1687 followed by the Anglo-Thai War of 1687–8 put a temporary stop to the English trade at the Siamese ports, and it was not until 1705–6 that Governor Thomas Pitt and associates resumed this trade. Initially, they used ships with Asian or Portuguese title or captaincy, but by 1708–9 English ships were being used again. In 1718, a private agreement was signed at Ayutthaya promising favourable treatment for Madras ships. The English Madras–Ayutthaya connection would seem to have continued on a regular basis in the 1720s and on a less regular basis in the 1730s. Occasionally, a Madras ship also called at Tonkin.[61]

Other important southeast Asian ports frequented by English shipping included Kedah and, above all, Acheh. Chinese junks regularly called at Acheh, making it an important source for Far Eastern goods. The exports to Acheh included Coromandel textiles, rice and slaves besides fair quantities of Bengal opium. The imports into Madras included camphor, benzoin, wax and pepper besides goods of Far Eastern origin. A 1660 agreement between Acheh and the English Company had exempted ships flying English colours from the payment of customs duties at the port subject to the requirement that the English shippers would trade exclusively through the *shahbandar*

[59] D.K. Bassett, 'British "country" trade and local trade networks in the Thai and Malay states, c. 1680–1770', *Modern Asian Studies*, vol. 23 (4), 1989, p. 636.
[60] Bassett, 'British "country" trade', pp. 628–9.
[61] Marshall, 'Private British trade', p. 286.

and other royal officials. While that would almost certainly have cut into the profit margin, the turnover would have been rendered quicker. Indian ships visiting Acheh were not bound by this requirement, but paid a 12 per cent import duty. The attraction of Acheh for the English traders increased further in 1687 following their temporary exclusion from Siam. The years around the turn of the century witnessed a certain amount of dislocation in this trade even involving a private British naval blockade of the port organized by Alexander Hamilton in 1702 to enforce English exemption from customs duties. There was another blockade for a few weeks in 1706 organized this time by Delton and Griffith. Repeated invitations from the sultan to resume trade with the port did lead to a resumption of voyages to Acheh from both Madras and Bengal around 1715. But soon thereafter, some gold was seized from the Madras ship *Messiah* by the Acheh government. In retaliation, the sultan's ship was seized at Madras by Governor Joseph Collet in October 1717. Trade to Acheh under British colours did not resume apparently until the 1730s.[62]

From the 1760s onward, the British country traders operating from Madras began to organize themselves into powerful syndicates. This, combined with the greater political and economic leverage available to the British all over India from about this time onward, generally increased their competitive strength in Acheh and the southeast Asian markets. The Gowan–Harrop syndicate significantly expanded its operations in Acheh from about 1766. The syndicate, taken over by Jourdan, Sulivan and De Souza in 1770, included several members of the Fort St George Council. It loaned mercenaries to the sultan and eventually dominated the port of Acheh. Kedah was also emerging as a major trading port for the English around this time. Indeed, in 1772, the Madras Presidency ranked Kedah above Acheh as an outlet for opium and piece-goods. Acheh was assumed to have a market for 150 chests of opium as against 250 chests in Kedah. The anticipated profit on the Acheh investment was 30,000 pagodas compared to 45,000 pagodas in Kedah.[63]

In addition to southeast Asia, private English shipping from Madras also went to Manila and China, the former from about the 1670s and the latter from about the 1690s onward. Trade with both these

[62] Bassett, 'British "country" trade', pp. 629–32.
[63] Bassett, 'British "country" trade', pp. 639–40.

destinations seems to have been carried on on a fairly regular, but relatively small, scale. Until 1789, the only European ships permitted into Manila were Portuguese ones. From 1674, English-owned ships based at Madras began making regular trips to Manila under Portuguese colours. For most of the eighteenth century, an average of three ships a year went from Madras to Manila. The 1789 repeal of the restrictive Spaniard regulations enabled the private English vessels to go to Manila under their own colours.[64] As far as the Madras–Canton trade was concerned, it was based on the export of silver to Canton to be exchanged against gold and commodities such as tutenag, quicksilver, alum and sugar. The bulk of these goods was re-exported from Madras to western India. From about 1760 onward, the India–China trade assumed important proportions. But the share of Madras shipping in the revitalized China trade was negligible: that was a trade carried on mainly by the private English shipping based at Bombay and Calcutta.

Until the 1760s, the private English merchants' eastward trade was practically nonexistent from Bombay and relatively quite small from Calcutta. We noted earlier that Governor Charles Boone of Bombay had organized joint stocks for two China ships in 1716. But that kind of venture would seem to have been a relatively isolated one. The trade from Calcutta was on a more regular, but relatively small, scale. The relative smallness of this trade is highlighted when it is compared to Calcutta's trade westward. Thus in 1734 against sixteen departures from Calcutta westward, only four were recorded to the ports eastward. The situation had not been very different in the early years of the century. Thus the number of vessels going eastward was reported to be four each in 1704–5 and 1705–6 and three in 1706–7. A large proportion of these vessels, if not all of them, were directed at southeast Asia, mainly ports in Malaya and Sumatra. The principal ports the ships called at in the region were Kedah and Acheh, though other ports such as Pegu and Tenasserim were also visited. The principal exports to the region were textiles and opium and the principal imports sandalwood, sappanwood, tin and pepper.[65]

Over the first half of the eighteenth century, Bengal shipping also went further east to Manila and Canton. Between these two destina-

<hr />

[64] Marshall, 'Private British trade', pp. 285, 299.
[65] P.J. Marshall, *East Indian Fortunes, The British in Bengal in the Eighteenth Century*, Oxford, 1976, pp. 85–8.

tions, the Manila connection was more regular. Bengal textiles were sold there mainly against Mexican silver. In the early part of the century, there was also a certain amount of cooperation with the Madras shipping in the trips to Manila, though by 1727 Madras was beginning to complain of Bengal's competition at the port. In the 1720s, a total of ten Calcutta ships are believed to have gone to Manila: in the 1730s, this number had come down to six or seven. Between 1740 and 1748, another seven Bengal ships are reported to have called at Manila. After a gap until 1759, the arrival of Bengal ships was again recorded at Manila in 1760, 1764 and 1767. Thereafter, there is no evidence of shipping on this route until the late 1780s, when it was no longer necessary to operate under Portuguese or Asian colours. Contacts were now officially made between Calcutta merchants and the new Spanish Royal Philippine Company for Bengal goods to be delivered openly at Manila in English ships. The Canton connection was much more irregular until about 1760. Bengal ships are known to have called at Canton only in 1725 and 1736, though another ship, the *Shah Alam*, the largest of the Calcutta fleet, was also reportedly being fitted for a voyage to Canton in 1730.[66]

The situation had, however, changed completely by the 1760s when what Furber has termed the 'commercial revolution' in the Indian Ocean was well under way. This revolution, completed by the 1780s, consisted in the first place of a clear domination of trade in the Indian Ocean and the South China Sea by private English shipping based at Calcutta and Bombay, and in the second, of an increasingly central and indeed dominant position of the trade with China and Malaya in the private English merchants' trade from India. This was the consequence of a variety of factors at work, both economic and political. These ranged from the growing popularity of Chinese tea in the European market and the growing prosperity of the private English traders engaged in country trade, to the wresting of formal political control by the English East India Company in Bengal and of considerable political leverage in western India.

An approximate idea of the orders of magnitude involved in the growth of the China trade could perhaps be formed by reference to the fact that, between 1774–82 and 1785–6, the imports by the English country ships at Canton had doubled. By 1797–8, these had nearly

---

[66] Marshall, *East Indian Fortunes*, pp. 89, 104.

trebled again.[67] The two principal items carried to Canton were Gujarat cotton and Bengal opium. In 1760, David Cuming had remarked that the only big Bombay ships he had noted at Canton were those belonging to the English East India Company. But in 1787, Cuming counted forty sails of large, privately owned ships from Bombay which had imported 60,000 bales of cotton. On average, over the last quarter of the eighteenth century, cotton accounted for approximately half of the total English exports to China. In the early years of the nineteenth century, the cotton exports were marked by large annual fluctuations. Against the peak of Rs.9 million worth in 1807–8, for example, the exports in 1812–13 were worth only Rs.2.3 million. The bulk of the cotton exports from Bombay were on the account of the private traders. Thus in 1810–11, these merchants accounted for as much as 91.4 per cent of the total cotton exports from Bombay, the remainder being on the account of the English East India Company. A certain amount of Bengal cotton was also carried to China by the Calcutta shipping. Thus in 1810–11, the private Calcutta shipping carried nearly one third (31.3 per cent) of the amount of cotton carried by the Bombay shipping on the account of both the Company as well as the private traders.[68] The principal Bengal commodity carried to China was, of course, opium. As opposed to an average of one per season in the 1760s, the number of Bengal-based ships going to Canton had gone up by 1778 to as many as ten. Valuewise, Bengal opium did not overtake Indian cotton until 1823,[69] but from the perspective of the private traders, opium had already superseded cotton as the most lucrative item by the early years of the nineteenth century.[70]

The starting point of the China trade was the growing involvement of the English East India Company in the import of Chinese tea into England. By 1758–60, tea was already accounting for a quarter of the total English Company imports from Asia into Europe. Since the British government levied duties of as much as 115 per cent on all imports of tea, smuggling by rival bodies operating from the European continent was a highly profitable enterprise. This, however, ceased to

[67] Marshall, 'Private British trade', p. 297.
[68] Pamela Nightingale, *Trade and Empire in Western India 1784–1806*, Cambridge, 1970, pp. 23, 233.
[69] Michael Greenberg, *British Trade and the Opening of China 1800–42*, Cambridge, 1951, p. 81.
[70] Nightingale, *Trade and Empire*, p. 233.

be the case following the Commutation Bill of 1784 which reduced the duties to a mere 12 per cent. The result was that the English Company was able to price the competitors out of the market and further increase its imports from China. As with most Asian commodities, however, Chinese tea had to be paid for mainly in specie. Once Bengal revenues became available to the Company following the acquisition of *diwani* rights in 1765, the Directors asked the Bengal Council to ship Rs.4 million annually to Canton. But this was not found feasible, and indeed after 1768 no specie could be spared from Bengal. As far as Indian goods were concerned, Gujarat cotton and Bengal opium were the only items with a large market in China. Opium was a contraband item and the Company obviously could not handle it on its own, but a certain amount of cotton was indeed carried by the Company ships to Canton on a regular basis. The close collaboration between the Company servants and the private traders, however, ensured that the bulk of the cotton trade was left to the latter. This, together with a large and growing clandestine trade in opium, made the China trade by far the most lucrative branch of trade for the private English merchants operating from India.

By a curious intermingling of the private traders' interests with those of the Company, the China trade became not only an important vehicle for the generation of private European fortunes in India, but also the leading medium of the remittance home of these fortunes. The proceeds from the goods the private merchants sold in China invariably exceeded the value of the goods such as silk, sugar-candy, tea, mercury and camphor that they procured there by a considerable margin. It was in the mutual interest of these merchants as well as the Company for this surplus purchasing power to be put at the disposal of the supercargoes at Canton for investment in tea on the account of the Company. The Company would then be spared the necessity of carrying specie to China, or at least could reduce the amount, and the bills of exchange issued at Canton on the directors in London for the money received would ensure for the merchants a safe avenue for the transfer home of their fortunes on a regular basis. In the event that they needed the money in India, the bills of exchange were made payable in Calcutta. The private traders were often able to expand the size of their outward cargoes by raising fairly large sums of money in respondentia from individuals who were looking for avenues to transmit their savings home. Between 1770 and 1783, approximately

£3 million worth of bills of exchange were issued at Canton: this figure would have gone up substantially with the striking growth of the China trade after 1784.

The fact that there was a great degree of collaboration between the private English traders and the governments of Bombay and Bengal is fully borne out in the case of both the cotton and the opium exports to China. In the case of cotton, this collaboration was at times even at the expense of the Company itself. Following the Commutation Act of 1784, the average annual sales of cotton in Canton had leaped from around 300,000 taels worth to as much as 2.16 million taels worth within a period of three years. The private trading interests in collaboration with the Company officials, however, ensured that the Company itself was allowed to partake of this bounty only up to a point. In April 1789, for example, the Directors deplored the fact that against a capacity of 1,500 to 2,000 bales, the Company ships carried at the most 800 bales for the Company and made the remaining space available to the private traders. The factors were, therefore, instructed to send as much cotton as possible to Canton on the Company's own account. In April 1790, the Directors even sent 600 chests of dollars to Bombay specifically for the purchase of cotton. Six years later, Bombay was ordered to send as many as 15,000 bales of cotton to China to repair the finances of the Company at Canton. But the factors by and large managed to disregard these instructions, and the Company's share in the total cotton exports to China never reached important proportions. Instead, the Company's power and authority at Surat and elsewhere was made available in ample measure to the private traders in their efforts to control the cotton dealers. Such control was deemed necessary to check the rise in price as well as the problem of adulteration of the cotton supplied. In December 1801, an agreement was concluded between the government on the one hand, and three agency houses of Bombay trading in cotton together with three Parsi merchants, on the other. The private traders and the government agreed to buy the cotton jointly, and to divide it between them. The Company's share was no larger than that assigned to each firm. It was also realized that the problem of adulteration could be tackled effectively and on a long-term basis only if the Company extended its power in Gujarat. As Pamela Nightingale has emphasized, it was this consideration rather than the menace of French imperialism that determined the British policy of territorial expansion in the region around this time. But from about 1805 onward, the Directors succeeded in obliging the Bombay government to increase the Company's share in the cotton trade substantially. The domination of the government by the private traders evidently was over, though they continued to be important participants in the cotton trade with Canton.[71]

The principal item carried to China by the private English shipping based at Calcutta was, of course, opium. Being contraband, it was completely outside the Canton commercial system. It was not channelled through the Hong merchants but was smuggled to outside brokers against cash payment. In addition to opium, the Calcutta ships also carried to Canton commodities such as Malayan tin and Sumatran pepper purchased en route in Batavia and other Malay ports against items such as Bengal opium and textiles. On the return trip, some of the China goods were sold in southeast Asia. The trade from Calcutta to Canton and southeast Asia thus became part of an integrated mechanism in which the export of opium played the central role. Ever since the middle of the seventeenth century, the opium trade between Bengal and southeast Asia had been handled predominantly by the Dutch East India Company. But the British conquest of Bengal had changed all that and the private English trader had emerged as the principal dealer in Bengal opium. In the 1760s, the procurement of opium in Bihar had been monopolized by a succession of English Company servants operating in their private capacity. In 1773, the Company itself had taken over the opium monopoly and made the drug available to the private traders through public auctions held at Calcutta. To the great advantage of these traders, the amount made available to the Dutch Company under a newly introduced quota system was kept at the relatively low level of 450 chests per annum.[72] The English private traders operated with impunity in the former Dutch preserves in the archipelago and sold large quantities of Bengal opium in the region. The shipping records at Batavia showed that British private tonnage calling at that port increased from 3,000 to 5,000 tons between 1784 and 1786.

Already in 1764 private British traders were believed to have

[71] Nightingale, *Trade and Empire*, chs. 5–7.
[72] Om Prakash, 'Opium monopoly in India and Indonesia in the eighteenth century', *The Indian Economic and Social History Review*, vol. 24 (1), 1987, pp. 63–80.

brought 500 chests of opium into the straits of Malacca. In 1777, the value of Calcutta's trade with Malaya and Indonesia was estimated as being equal to the value of its trade with China. Up to between 1,500 and 2,000 chests of opium could be sold in the port of Riau alone, which the sultan of Johor had opened to the English around 1768, and a considerable amount of pepper and tin obtained there. The American War and a Dutch counter-offensive in the Malacca straits, which closed Riau in 1784, temporarily checked the Calcutta shipping's commercial expansion into Malaya, but in 1786 it took a more concrete form with the annexation of Penang, the first British settlement in Malaya. This was the culmination of the British private traders' attempt at finding a foothold in southeast Asia which could serve as a base for their shipping and trade. Several places such as Acheh, Balambangan and Phuket had earlier been explored for the purpose but without success. In March 1789, the English traders were reported to be smuggling at least 2,000 chests of opium annually into China. Calcutta's eastward trade as a whole was estimated in 1793 at around Rs.5 million of which about Rs.3 million worth consisted of opium. This sum would have bought about 4,500 chests of which around 2,000–2,500 seem to have reached China and a roughly similar amount to have been sold on the way in the Malay archipelago.[73]

THE COROMANDEL COAST

Next to Bengal, the Coromandel coast continued to be the principal theatre of the VOC's trading operations in India over the period 1740–1800. The value of the textiles exported by the Company from the region, after slumping to $f.1$ million during 1740–1 and to only around half that figure during 1741–5, recovered remarkably from the mid-1740s onward. In 1746–7, the figure stood at as much as $f.2.26$ million. Between 1747 and 1755, this value was generally around $f.1.5$ million. Over the last block of years for which information is available, namely 1764–70, the value of the textiles exported again fluctuated considerably with a trough of $f.780,000$ being recorded in 1764–5 and

[73] Holden Furber, *John Company at Work, A Study of European Expansion in India in the Late Eighteenth Century*, Cambridge, Mass., 1948, pp. 174–5, 183.

a peak of ƒ.2.64 million in 1767–8 (Table 6.2). Overall, the wide annual fluctuations make it impossible not only to identify any particular trend in the value of the Company's textile exports from the region over the three decades between 1740 and 1770, but also to distinguish this phase from the preceding one in any meaningful way. There is, for example, very little to distinguish the decade of the 1760s from that of the 1730s. The kind of upheaval in its trading position that the Company witnessed in Bengal in the 1760s clearly did not have a counterpart on the Coromandel coast. The English Company no doubt had acquired a special position in the region, but on nowhere near the scale it had been able to do in Bengal. The French presence on the coast had at best a nuisance value.

The available data do not permit a precise division of the value of the textiles exported by the Company from Coromandel between the European and the Asian markets. There is, however, evidence which suggests that around the middle of the eighteenth century, the share of the two markets was broadly the same with Europe having a slight edge over the East Indies. Thus of the total of ƒ.13.87 million worth of textiles exported between 1744–5 and 1753–4, ƒ.6.79 million worth (or 49 per cent) was destined for the East Indies, the share for Holland being ƒ.7.08 million. The rate of profit earned on these textiles in the East Indies was reported to be around 35 per cent.[74] The fact that the Indian merchants operating from Coromandel were still a major force is also suggested by the same report. It is pointed out that from Porto Novo alone, the textiles exported by these merchants to ports such as Manila, Malacca, Acheh, Arakan, Pegu, Mocha and those in Persia and other places amounted each year to 200,000 pagodas (or approximately ƒ.1 million).[75]

The southern part of the Coromandel coast continued to be the principal supplier of textiles to the Company. The factory at Pulicat in central Coromandel provided expensive varieties such as extra fine

---

[74] These calculations are based on the report by Jacob van der Waeyen dated 25 November 1757, ARA, HRB 341 (unfoliated). According to van der Waeyen, a total profit of ƒ.2,126,041 was earned on Coromandel textiles in Holland over the ten-year period, assuming a rate of profit of 30 per cent. On this basis, the value of the textiles sold in Holland works out at ƒ.7.08 million. That leaves ƒ.6.79 million worth for the East Indies, on which a profit of ƒ.2,367,212 (actual and not assumed) was reported to have been earned, suggesting a figure of 34.8 per cent.

[75] ARA, Report by Jacob van der Waeyen, HRB 341 (unfoliated).

rumals, bethilles, gingams, taftas, chelas and fine *muris* etc. The *chintz* procured at Sadraspatnam were said to be the best available anywhere on the coast in terms both of the quality of the material as well as of the workmanship in the 'painting' on it. The most important centre of procurement in southern Coromandel continued to be Nagapattinam where Guinea-cloth and *muris* were woven in the Company's own villages.[76] But as everywhere else, the problem of rising cost and deteriorating quality was getting increasingly more acute at Nagapattinam also. In 1754–5, for example, it was noted that a piece of an ordinary *guinea*, a *salampuri* and a *parcal*, which cost *f*.5.90, *f*.2.60 and *f*.1.40, respectively, in 1690–1, now cost respectively as much as *f*.9.15, *f*.4.00 and *f*.2.10 (both reckoned in heavy money) representing an increase of between 50 and 55 per cent. But the fact that the profit on these and other varieties both in Holland as well as in the East Indies continued to be satisfactory is borne out by Batavia's exhortations to the factors in 1756 to ensure that the orders for varieties such as fine bleached *guineas* were met in full even if the price paid had to be pushed up somewhat. Half of these *guineas* had to be sent on to Holland while the other half was intended for the markets of the East Indies. The other item for the East Indies to whose procurement priority was to be attached was *salampuris*. The blue textiles for Malacca were to be procured at Porto Novo.[77]

As for northern Coromandel, the procurement at Masulipatnam had to be suspended as of 1750 following the town's takeover by the French. It is not clear whether an attempt to bribe the French governor, De Morain (who had been born in The Hague) with the offer of a 3 per cent commission on all textiles bought in the town clandestinely on behalf of the Company was successful.[78] The varieties hitherto procured at Masulipatnam were now bought at Narsapur, Bimilipatnam, Palakollu and, above all, Jagannathpuram. The last-mentioned town had been taken in farm from the Mughal governor Rustam Khan Bahadur in 1734. In the second half of the eighteenth century, it became an important centre of procurement. The washing, bleaching and starching of the Company's textiles procured in the region had been organized for over a century at its own village of

---

[76] ARA, Memoir of the outgoing Governor of Coromandel, Pieter Haksteen, for his successor, Reynier van Vlissingen, dated 20 September 1771, HRB 344, ff. 119, 207.
[77] ARA, Report by Jacob van der Waeyen, HRB 341 (unfoliated).
[78] ARA, Report by Jacob van der Waeyen, HRB 341 (unfoliated.).

Gondawaran located at the edge of a large tank noted for its alkaline water. Another of the Company's villages, Golepallem, also in the Eastern Godavari delta, similarly specialized in painting and dyeing. These processes were helped by the existence in the village of ground water with specific chemical properties.[79]

We noted earlier that, in the wake of the Fourth Anglo-Dutch War, the Indian factories of the VOC were annexed by the English in 1781. When the factories on the Coromandel coast were restored to the Dutch in 1784 along with those elsewhere on the subcontinent, the one at Nagapattinam was kept back by the British. This forced the VOC to move its Coromandel headquarters back to Pulicat. In 1791–2, the value of the Company's exports from the region, the bulk of which would have been in the form of textiles, was put by the Coromandel factors at ƒ.600,000. It was believed that a profit of approximately 75 per cent would be made on the lot sent to Holland. But given the establishment and other costs, this was not considered attractive enough. In a secret communication to Batavia in 1791, the Heren XVII had already suggested the folding up of the Coromandel factories. This decision was formally incorporated in a resolution of the Batavia Council dated 19 June 1792, and communicated to Pulicat with instructions to move the Company's effects at the six factories at Pulicat, Sadraspatnam, Porto Novo, Jagannathpuram, Palakollu and Bimilipatnam to the Dutch establishment in Sri Lanka.[80] The Company's interpreter at Pulicat, Mandalam Venkatasalam Naikar, whose family had served the Company for over a century and who himself had been an employee since 1777, offered to keep all the factories going at his own expense provided he was allowed to keep the income from the Company's villages. The profits on the sale of the Company's spices and other goods, which he would continue to organize on the Company's behalf, would be remitted by him in cash or in the form of textiles.[81] No serious attention was, however, paid to this offer and it was decided to go ahead with the closure of the factories.

[79] ARA, Haksteen memoir, HRB 344, ff. 53–4; Sanjay Subrahmanyam, 'Rural industry and commercial agriculture in late seventeenth century south eastern India', *Past and Present*, Number 126, 1990, p. 92.

[80] ARA, Secret letter from Jacob Eilbracht at Pulicat to Batavia dated 28 December 1792, HRB 362, ff. 5, 13–14.

[81] ARA, Letter from Mandalam Venkatasalam Naikar at Pulicat to Jacob Eilbracht dated 19 December 1792 (Telegu original available), HRB 362, ff. 113–20.

GUJARAT

On the west coast, when Jan Schreuder took up in October 1740 his new responsibilities as the Director of the Company's factories in Gujarat, he found things 'in a very poor shape'. Over the first half of the 1740s, the average annual exports to both Europe and the rest of Asia continued to be low, and were only marginally higher than over the preceding several quinquenniums (Table 5.2). In a review exercise carried out by him in March 1746, Schreuder put the Company's performance in a comparative perspective. He pointed out that while, during 1694/5 to 1698/9, the average annual value of the Company's exports from Surat, and of the goods sold by it in the region, had been Rs.601,373 and Rs.823,618 respectively, making a total of Rs.1,424,991, the corresponding figures during 1740/1 to 1744/5 were no higher than Rs.283,467, Rs.257,928 and Rs.541,395 respectively.[82] A comparison with the trade carried on by its rivals further highlighted the relative smallness of the Company's trade in the early 1740s. The Asian merchants' trade from Surat at this time was estimated at Rs.2 million, that of the Portuguese at Rs.500,000, of the French at Rs.160,000, and of the English at as much as Rs.2.43 million.[83] Considering that the English Company trade at Surat at this time was quite small (between 1741 and 1745, the average annual value of the Gujarat textiles the Company imported into England was no more than Rs.322,280),[84] an overwhelming proportion of the English figure was evidently accounted for by the private traders. If these figures are at all reliable, the share of the VOC in the total trade at Surat would work out at under 10 per cent.[85]

An important factor held responsible for the poor performance by the Company was the situation arising out of the Maratha incursions into the province. The additional heavy tolls charged by them were reported to be cutting deeply into the sale of goods.[86] It was also largely because of the Maratha menace that the Company was forced

---

[82] ARA, 'Considerations over the opening up of free navigation and trade – how this could be guaranteed at Surat', by Jan Schreuder, 2 March 1746, HRB 837 (unfoliated), paras. 260–3. The slight difference between these figures when converted into florins at the usual rate of *f*.1.5 to a rupee, and those in Table 4.5 arises because of the different years covered by the quinquenniums in the Table.

[83] ARA, 'Considerations', HRB 837, para. 262.

[84] Calculated from Chaudhuri, *The Trading World of Asia*, p. 541.

[85] The exact share works out at 9.61 per cent.

[86] ARA, 'Considerations', HRB 837, para. 116.

in 1744 to abandon its factory at Ahmedabad, the principal procurement centre for silk textiles, as also for some varieties of cotton textiles.[87] Silk textiles procured at places such as Surat were not of the same quality as those earlier procured at Ahmedabad. This was notwithstanding the fact that the raw materials used were the same, and in many cases even the weavers were the ones who had moved out of Ahmedabad in the wake of the Maratha troubles. The explanation given was in terms of the specific chemical properties of the water in a particular pond in Ahmedabad used for washing the silk textiles, which gave them that specific brightness and lustre.[88]

With a view to improving this state of affairs, Schreuder suggested a more vigorous and better-coordinated participation by the Company in Surat's trade. As against the average of one or two ships over the preceding several years, he made out a case for the employment of five ships each year in the trade to and from Surat. Two of these ships could come from Batavia with European and Asian goods. On their return voyage, they could carry cargo not only for Batavia and Europe, but also for Malabar and Sri Lanka to be offloaded on the way. Another two ships could come from Bengal with raw silk, sugar, textiles and freight goods. They could make stopovers on the way in Sri Lanka and Malabar and pick up goods such as sandalwood, coir and areca-nuts. On the return voyage, these ships could carry cotton to Bengal. If, however, it was felt that Bengal, Sri Lanka and Malabar together could not send two shiploads each year, then all four ships could originate at Batavia. On their return voyage, two of these ships could travel via Bengal. Finally, the fifth ship could come from China with sugar, spelter, quicksilver and alum and carry back items such as cotton. On its way back, it could also pick up goods such as pepper and sandalwood at Malabar.[89]

The plan was duly implemented for a while but then modified. The Bengal shipments stopped after two years as did the one from China soon after. In the memoir that Schreuder prepared in September 1750 for his successor, Johannes Pecock, he endorsed the discontinuation of

---

[87] ARA, 'Considerations', HRB 837, para. 136; Memoir by outgoing Director Jan Schreuder for his successor, Johannes Pecock, dated 30 September 1750, HRB 838, f. 17.

[88] ARA, 'Considerations', HRB 837, para. 137; Report to Governor-General Mossel and Council at Batavia on the state of affairs at Surat by D. van Rheede, extraordinary member of the Council, dated 15 May 1758, HRB 843, f. 90.

[89] ARA, 'Considerations', HRB 837, paras. 322–5.

the China voyage. It would be more profitable, he now felt, to invest funds in China in goods for Holland rather than for Gujarat. Also, the principal item imported from China, namely sugar, could more profitably be imported from Batavia. In any case, a profit of just 50 to 60 per cent earned on the China goods was not good enough. He therefore proposed that all the five ships originate at Batavia and carry goods such as sugar, Japanese bar copper, spices, tin, lead, iron, spelter, ivory and Siamese sappanwood to Surat. For the return voyage, while two of the ships could return to Batavia, another two could be sent to Bengal, while the fifth could go on to China. Alternatively, one ship could travel back to Batavia, another to China, and a third to Sri Lanka via Malabar. From Sri Lanka, it could go on either to Batavia or to Holland. The fourth and the fifth ships could carry freight cargo to Basra and Mocha respectively and then return to Bengal via Surat where they could pick up cotton.[90]

Whether it was the efficacy of the Schreuder plan or the result of other factors at work, the fact remains that the position of the Company's trade at Surat improved remarkably from the mid-1740s on. The value of the exports to Europe increased considerably, but the increase in the value of the goods destined for the rest of Asia to an average annual level of between $f.600,000$ and $f.700,000$ was little short of spectacular. The total value of the goods exported now approached a million florins. In addition, there was the cash sent to the various Asian factories taking the figure up to $f.1.25$ million (Table 5.2). At the same time, the profit earned on goods sold in Surat jumped from an average annual level of $f.200,000$ in the 1740s to a remarkable $f.670,000$ in the 1750s, and further to $f.720,000$ in the 1760s. While spices continued to be the single largest profit earner, the share of other goods such as Japanese bar copper consistently went up. In the eighteenth century, the period between 1745 and 1760 clearly constituted the high point of the Dutch Company's trade in Gujarat.

The 1760s, however, again witnessed a downturn in the value of the Company's trade from Gujarat. The increase in the average annual value of the exports for Holland was more than neutralized by the steep decline in the value of the goods for the rest of Asia, which now averaged only $f.250,000$ per annum against more than $f.600,000$ during the 1750s. The total value of the goods exported came down on

[90] ARA, Memoir of Jan Schreuder, HRB 838, ff. 204–17.

average to half a million florins, and that of total exports, including cash, to under a million florins (Table 5.2). Details available for the year 1764–5 show that of the total of f.743,000 worth of goods exported, 37 per cent by value, consisting entirely of textiles, were destined for Holland, and the remainder for the East Indies. The cash exports of f.450,000 were destined for the East Indies and Sri Lanka in the ratio of 1:2.[91]

A part of the Company's problems at this time emanated from the growing influence of the English East India Company at Surat. An important landmark in that development was the English takeover of the Surat castle in 1759. Meah Achan was allowed to continue as the nawab but was made subordinate to the authority of the new English *qiladar*. The English also appropriated for themselves the right to mediate in all disputes between the local merchants and the rival European companies. While the Dutch Company was formally assured both before and after the takeover that its right to trade in the province unhindered would in no way stand compromised, the facts were slightly different.[92] The English took full advantage of their special authority and created all kinds of irritants for the Dutch. In May 1765, for example, the English chief, Hodges, issued orders that in view of the possibility of fraud being perpetrated in the matter of the payment of customs duties, the Dutch would henceforth be obliged to pay these duties on the imported spices in the city rather than at the harbour. Senff, the Dutch director, while publicly threatening in protest to send the ships back without having them unloaded, privately asked the brokers to approach Hodges with the offer of a bribe if he would withdraw the order. The strategy worked and the Dutch were allowed to pay duties on all goods imported at the harbour itself. The following year, the English decided that as proof of having paid the duties, the Dutch Company goods must carry the stamp of the English in addition to that of the governor. Initially, they took the position that the measure was designed simply to prevent fraud being perpetrated by the officials of the governor. When the Dutch insisted that this violated their rights, they were simply

---

[91] ARA, 'Reflections of Director C.L. Senff on the Surat sugar trade', dated 1 March 1766, HRB 846, Appendix A, unfoliated.

[92] ARA, Memoir by outgoing director C.L. Senff for his successor, M.J. Bosman, dated 31 December 1768, HRB 848, para. 37.

informed that 'our superiors at Bombay have issued orders that the goods of the Dutch should carry our stamp'.[93]

The only other factory the Dutch had in Gujarat at this time, in addition to that at Surat, was the one at Broach. In 1772, the English asked that this factory be closed down. It was only after a deputation was sent to Bombay that the order was withdrawn. But after the peace treaty of 1783 ending the Fourth Anglo-Dutch War, the Broach factory was not returned to the Dutch, but was instead handed over to Madhav Rao Scindia. A protest to the English and a plea to Scindia went unheeded. The Dutch factors, however, noted that since they in any case carried on only a very small amount of trade at Broach, this would be no great hardship.[94] What did matter more was the use by the English of their authority to do at Surat, though on a much smaller scale, what they had been doing in Bengal, namely to insist that the weavers work for no one else till such time as they had completed their engagement with the English Company.[95] This would obviously have hurt the VOC's textile procurement at Surat, though going by the value of the Company's average annual exports in the 1780s, the adverse effect was probably only of a limited order (Table 5.2).

THE MALABAR COAST

The years between 1740 and 1800 also witnessed fluctuations in the VOC's fortunes on the Malabar coast. By far the most important development of the period was the establishment of a pepper monopoly by Martanda Varma of Travancore, whose territorial jurisdiction now stretched as far up the coast as Cranganur. It was in 1743–4 that Martanda Varma first declared his intention 'to take upon himself the Direction of the pepper trade'. Initially the English Company was allowed a certain measure of relaxation from the new arrangement. The merchants it chose to deal with were allowed to buy pepper freely in a specified area within the kingdom of Travancore. But in November 1746, the Anjengo factors were directed to enter into contracts only with designated merchants at predetermined prices. The

---

[93] ARA, Memoir of Senff, HRB 848, paras. 46–9, 56.

[94] ARA, Memorandum on Surat submitted to the Governor-General and Council at Batavia by Surat director, A.J. Sluisken dated 1 October 1786, HRB 851, paras. 149–52.

[95] ARA, Memoir of outgoing Director A.J. Sluisken for his successor, Pieter Sluisken, dated 31 December 1792, HRB 854, paras. 60–1.

result was that the English were unable to obtain any pepper during 1747–8 and 1748–9. In 1750, it was the government's contract that supplied pepper to the English at Anjengo.[96] The average annual value of the Malabar pepper the Company imported into England was £33,306 (f.399,672) in the 1740s, and £29,971 (f.359,652) in the 1750s.[97]

The position of the Dutch Company was equally precarious. In 1741–2, the value of its exports from Malabar was no more than f.232,000 (Table 6.3). The pepper it procured at this time was supplied principally by merchants engaged in business in south Malabar. The procurement in the north was negligible because of the pull of Calicut. In May 1743, the Company entered into an agreement with Martanda Varma under which the raja agreed to supply 1,200 kandis of pepper per annum at Rs.54 per kandi. This amount was often not supplied in full, but it was now the mainstay of the Company's total procurement in Malabar. At the close of 1751, the price was increased to Rs.75 per kandi. The necessity of enhancing the supply obliged the Company to enter into yet another treaty with Martanda Varma in 1753. Under the treaty of Mavalikara, the Dutch agreed to supply the raja with Rs.12,000 worth of military supplies annually, to aid him against external attack, and to denounce their treaties with all other Malabar princes, most of whom had long since come under the raja's control. In return, Martanda Varma undertook to enhance the amount of pepper supplied to the Company each year to 3,000 kandis at Rs.65 per kandi. He also undertook to supply another 2,000 kandis at Rs.55 per kandi from principalities he might later conquer. One might note that this price was no more than about half the market price and the raja was able to offer it only because of his complete control over both the production and the trade in pepper.[98] The target of 3,000 kandis per annum was not always met, but there is no question that the export capability of the Company now improved enormously. This is reflected in the rise in the value of the annual exports to as much as f.700,000 in 1761–2, and nearly f.600,000 in 1784–5, though the figure was much smaller during 1771–2 (Table 6.3).

Partly because of the expenses the maintenance of fortresses and garrisons involved, the annual expenditure of the Company incurred

---

[96] A. Das Gupta, *Malabar in Asian Trade, 1740–1800*, Cambridge, 1967, pp. 34–9.
[97] Calculated from Chaudhuri, *Trading World of Asia*, p. 525.
[98] Das Gupta, *Malabar in Asian Trade*, pp. 42–4.

in Malabar was always considerably in excess of the income earned locally through profit on the sale of goods and so on. Thus over the forty-year period ending in 1754–5, it was estimated that against the total income of ƒ.8.56 million, the total expenditure had been as much as ƒ.18.93 million, producing a staggering deficit of ƒ.10.37 million.[99] It was with a view to cutting into this deficit to the extent possible that the Cochin factors decided in the 1740s to participate in the textile trade of Malabar. The plan was to buy textiles in Tengapatnam in the south and sell them at Cochin. The beginning was quite good and, in 1752, the factors managed to sell as many as 14,000 pieces. But this phase did not last very long. In October 1758, the factors complained of a significant rise in the cost price and found that they could not quite compete with the merchants from the north. In February 1759, therefore, it was decided to get out of this trade.[100]

The Dutch connection with Malabar came to an end in the 1790s. From 1792, the factors at Cochin were trying to sell the Company's establishments to the raja of Travancore. But since it was generally believed that the English wanted the Cochin factory for themselves, the raja refrained from finalizing the deal. Trading operations were terminated in November 1793, and Dutch rule finally ended in Cochin in October 1795.[101]

THE FRENCH COMPANY TRADE

Apart from the English and the Dutch East India companies, the only European company of any consequence operating in India in the mid-eighteenth century was the French Compagnie Perpetuelle des Indes. We noted earlier that ever since its establishment in 1723, this Company had done quite well and that by the mid-1730s it had become a major competitor of the English and the Dutch. The subsequent history of the Company until its liquidation in 1769 was characterized by marked fluctuations in the value of the trade it carried on between Asia and Europe. From a peak of LT 8.87 million

---

[99] ARA, A short account, dated 31 December 1756, prepared by van Hooreman, ordinary member of the Batavia Council, for Governor-General Mossel, about Malabar in pursuance of the XVII's directive dated March 1754, and Batavia's secret decision dated 4 October 1755, VOC 4903 (unfoliated).
[100] Das Gupta, *Malabar in Asian Trade*, pp. 79–82.
[101] Das Gupta, *Malabar in Asian Trade*, pp. 124–5.

during 1735–6 to 1744–5, the average annual value of the Company's total imports from Asia came down to LT 6.36 million during 1745–6 to 1754–5, and further to a trough of LT 3.94 million during 1755–6 to 1764–5. But the last few years of the Company's existence (the last sales on the account of the Company took place in 1770–1) witnessed a remarkable revival in its fortunes. Thus, between 1765–6 and 1770–1, the average annual value of its imports into Europe was as much as LT 8.74 million, being nearly the same as during the peak years of 1735–6 to 1744–5. How did this performance compare with that of the Dutch and the English around this time? The average annual value of the Dutch imports from Asia during 1778–80 was *f.*6.93 million (Table 4.1). In the case of the English, this figure was *f.*8.36 million during 1758–60 and as much as *f.*23.11 million during 1777–9 (Table 4.2). The French figure of *f.*4.37 million (LT 8.74 million) during 1765–6 to 1770–1 was still the lowest of the three, but nevertheless one not to be dismissed lightly. The share of the India goods in the total Asian cargoes was around 75 per cent during 1735–6 to 1744–5, but came down steadily over the following decades till it reached 60 per cent during 1765–6 to 1770–1 (Table 6.4). The average mark-up on the Asia goods fluctuated between around 65 and 100 per cent. The mark-up on India goods alone was somewhat lower – roughly between 50 and 95 per cent (Table 6.4). At the time of the liquidation of the Company in 1769, the government paid the shareholders a sum of 30 million livres and threw the trade open to private merchants.

Following the peace treaties of 1783, a number of private French merchants engaged in the India trade formed in 1785 the so-called new French East India Company of Calonne. During its brief five-year existence, the Company sent out to India a total cargo worth 36.17 million livres consisting mainly of silver. A certain amount of purchasing power was also generated in India by issuing bills of exchange on Paris against rupees received. Such transactions were carried on both with individual European merchants looking for a safe avenue to transmit their savings home, as well as with agency houses at Calcutta and Madras. The total value of the return cargo received was 34.98 million livres working out to an average annual figure of approximately 7 million livres.[102] The return cargo consisted overwhelmingly of textiles procured at Chandernagore in Bengal, and Pondicherry,

---

[102] Furber, *John Company at Work*, p. 57, note 62.

Yanaon and Karikal on the Coromandel coast. At Mahe on the Malabar coast, where the Company sought to buy pepper, an embargo imposed by Tipu Sultan effectively blocked all progress. Little progress was similarly made at Surat, though in a move clearly ahead of its time, the Company had planned to import Surat cotton into Europe for manufacture by the new machines in the English cotton mills.

A treaty concluded in 1787 recognized the right of the French to sell to the English factors each year 200,000 maunds of salt and to buy from them 18,000 maunds of saltpetre and 300 chests of opium. As far as textiles were concerned, the procurement in Bengal was subject to the usual hindrances that the Dutch also had to face at the hands of the English Company *gumashtas*. The situation on the Coromandel coast, on the other hand, was reasonably satisfactory. At Pondicherry, for example, the long-established links with the weaving communities ensured regular supplies.

In April 1790, the French National Assembly issued a decree declaring the trade with India again open to all Frenchmen. Since an immediate liquidation of the Calonne Company would have left it in the red, it was allowed to reorganize itself with a new board of directors and to continue in business on a small scale for some time more. The last deliberations of its agents in Bengal are recorded as having taken place in September 1795.[103]

THE DANISH COMPANY TRADE

As for the Danes, we had noted earlier that King Christian VI had chartered the Danish Asiatic Company in April 1732 with a forty-year monopoly of the trade with Asia. Table 7.1 sets out the value of the trade carried on by this Company with India. Until 1772, when its first charter expired, the India trade of the Company was both irregular and limited in value. The cargo from India consisted mainly of cotton textiles procured at Tranquebar and in Serampore in Bengal, where a factory was re-established in 1755 after a gap of over forty years. Over the period 1734–71, the auction value of the total cargo imported from Asia was 41.69 million Danish ryx-dollars. At 10.46 million ryx-dollars, the value of the goods imported from India accounted for only a quarter of the total, the remaining three quarters

---

[103] Furber, *John Company at Work*, pp. 53, 65.

Table 7.1 *Average annual value of the Danish Asiatic Company's imports from India, 1734–1807*

Years	Invoice value of the cargo (in Danish ryx-dollars; 1 Danish ryx-dollar = approx. $f.2$)	Sales proceeds of the cargo (in Danish ryx-dollars)	Gross profit (percentage)
1734–43	NA	257,035	
1744–53	NA	256,953	
1754–63	NA	335,826	
1764–71	NA	171,189	
1772–9	290,941	363,130	24.81
1780–9	746,766	951,831	27.46
1790–9	982,784	1,361,162	38.50
1800–7	941,739	1,154,656	22.60

Note: NA stands for not available.
Source: Calculated from:
Rows 1–4 Ole Feldbæk, 'The Danish Asia trade 1620–1807, value and volume', *The Scandinavian Economic History Review*, vol. 39 (1), 1991, Table 1, p. 6.
Rows 5–8 Ole Feldbæk, *India Trade Under the Danish Flag, 1772–1808*, Copenhagen, 1969, Appendix III, pp. 246–7.

being accounted for by the goods from China.[104] The average annual value of the goods imported from India was also marked by considerable fluctuations. From an average of 250,000 ryx-dollars between 1734 and 1753, the figure went up to 335,000 ryx-dollars during 1754–63, but came down sharply to a mere 171,000 ryx-dollars during 1764–71.

The cargo exported by the Company to India during this period consisted mainly of silver, though a certain amount of value was also carried in the form of ballast goods such as lead, copper and iron. This silver constituted the principal component of the purchasing power at the disposal of the factors in India. A smaller component was the resources generated locally by issuing bills of exchange to English and other European private traders on London and Amsterdam etc. The relative smallness of this source is borne out by the fact that over the period 1732 to 1758, the bills issued amounted to no more than

---

[104] Ole Feldbæk, 'The Danish Asia trade 1620–1807, value and volume', *Scandinavian Economic History Review*, vol. 39 (1), 1991, p. 6.

£44,000 worth repayable in London and ƒ.409,000 worth repayable in Amsterdam.[105]

When the date for the expiry of the charter of 1732 approached, the Company applied in 1769 for a fresh forty-year charter. The new charter was granted in July 1772 but for a period of only twenty years. Also, while the Company was allowed to retain its monopoly of the China trade, the India trade was thrown open to all Danish subjects. The Company was allowed to continue to administer the Indian establishments, but in 1777 this function was taken over by the Crown. In 1792, the charter was renewed for yet another period of twenty years.[106]

For the period 1772–1807, both invoice and auction values of the cargoes received from India are available. An examination of these values shows that it is not without reason that this phase has been called the 'golden age' of the Danish Asiatic trade. The total auction value of the Asian cargo imported during this period both on the account of the Company as well as on that of the private traders was 132 million Danish ryx-dollars. The share of India goods in this total was as much as 75 million ryx-dollars (57 per cent), that of China goods 40 million ryx-dollars (30 per cent), and of the goods procured in the rest of Asia at places such as Java and Mauritius, the remaining 17 million ryx-dollars (13 per cent). The share of the Danish Asiatic Company in the total auction value of the imports from India and China worth 115 million ryx-dollars was 75 million ryx-dollars (65 per cent), the remaining 40 million ryx-dollars worth (35 per cent) having been imported on private account, all from India. Of the cargo imported on the account of the Company, 40 million ryx-dollars worth (53 per cent) consisted of China goods and the remaining 35 million ryx-dollars worth (47 per cent) of goods from India representing a distinct improvement in the share of the India goods compared to the preceding period.[107] The substantive increase in the cargoes from India started in the 1780s (Table 7.1). In the closing decade of the eighteenth and the early years of the nineteenth century, the average annual invoice value of this cargo approached a million Danish ryx-dollars (equivalent to approximately two million Dutch florins). The

---

[105] Holden Furber, *The Rival Empires of Trade in the Orient 1600–1800*, Minneapolis and Oxford, 1976, p. 215.
[106] Feldbæk, 'The Danish Asia trade', pp. 7–8.
[107] Calculated from Feldbæk, 'The Danish Asia trade', Table 3 (p. 14) and Table 6 (p. 24).

value imported on the account of the private traders was in addition to this. While in relation to the English Company trade from India at this time this figure does not sound particularly impressive, it nevertheless represented a great advance over whatever the Danish Company had been able to achieve earlier. The gross profit on the India goods reportedly fluctuated between about 22 and 38 per cent (Table 7.1).

Another significant feature that distinguishes the post-1772 period from the one preceding it is the considerably enhanced use now made by the Company of bills of exchange to finance its procurement of the return cargo. Between 1772 and 1775, silver formed on average no more than 32.3 per cent of the outward cargo. And for a whole decade between 1775 and 1785, no silver whatsoever was sent to India. This clearly was the highpoint of the business in bills of exchange as far as the Danish Company was concerned. But as the bill market in India became tighter and the rate of interest increased, the Company reverted to silver. Silver exports were resumed in 1786 and between 1788 and 1807 silver, on average, accounted for 75.6 per cent of the outward cargoes to India.

Between 1778 and 1808, textiles accounted for over 80 per cent of the return cargo imported on the account of the Company. The remainder consisted of ballast goods such as saltpetre and pepper. More and more of the textiles were now being procured in Bengal. While during 1772–5 the share of Bengal goods in the Indian cargo was between 18 and 30 per cent, the proportion went up to 48 per cent in 1777, and was 43 per cent in 1778. The wars in southern India in the 1780s leading to the closure of the factory at Tranquebar in 1796 further strengthened this trend.[108] As Feldbæk has shown, there was an interesting pattern of complementarity between the India trade of the Company and that of the private Danish merchants engaged in this trade. When the latter had a downward trend, the former boomed, and vice versa. In a general situation of faltering demand, the Company did not want to glut the market, though it did not always succeed. In the early years of the nineteenth century, stocks of Indian textiles piled up in the Company's warehouses and instructions were sent in 1807 to Serampore to reduce drastically the textile component in the return cargo.[109] But the war with England intervened and the Danish

[108] Ole Feldbæk, *India Trade Under the Danish Flag 1772–1808*, Copenhagen, 1969, pp. 15–22.
[109] Feldbæk, 'The Danish Asia trade', pp. 16–17.

trade with India came to an end. Tranquebar and the other Indian establishments were under the occupation of the British between 1808 and 1815, and were eventually sold to them in 1845.[110]

To summarize, the second half of the eighteenth century, and particularly the period from about 1760 onward, was characterized by an unquestioned domination of Euro-Asian trade by the English East India Company and of trade in the Indian Ocean–South China Sea complex by private English traders. Even during its 'golden age' over the last decade of the eighteenth and the early years of the nineteenth century, the average annual value of the Danish Company imports from Asia was under ƒ.2 million. The French Company imports over the period had been marked by violent fluctuations as well as interruption, and the highest average annual value achieved was ƒ.4.37 million during 1765/6 to 1770/1. In the case of the VOC, the average annual value figure had gone up only slightly from ƒ.6.4 million during 1738–40 to ƒ.6.93 million during 1778–80. In comparison, the growth in the average annual value of the English Company imports from ƒ.7.66 million during 1738–40 to ƒ.8.36 million during 1758–60, and to as much as ƒ.23.11 million during 1777–9, was nothing short of spectacular. At the latter date, India accounted for 78 per cent of the total imports. This figure was 60 per cent in the case of the French and 47 per cent in that of the Danish Company. In the case of the VOC, this figure was around 50 per cent.

Within India, the Dutch trade at Coromandel was characterized by large annual fluctuations with the peak years registering fairly important levels of trade. Gujarat contributed only marginally to the Company's Euro-Asian trade, though it continued to be of significance in its intra-Asian trade. The trade at Malabar, however, was quite small throughout the period. That left Bengal, which was by far the most important region of trade for all the European companies. In the case of the English Company, Bengal accounted for as much as 59 per cent of the total Asian imports in 1759, and 54 per cent of a very much higher figure during 1777–9. The Bengal trade was clearly the key to the English domination of the Euro-Asian trade.

The unprecedented success of the English in Bengal owed a great deal to the gross misuse of the political authority wielded by the Company in the province since about 1760. The rival European

---

[110] Feldbæk, *India Trade Under the Danish Flag*, p. 9.

companies were now essentially on sufference and subject to all kinds of hindrances put in their way. The political leverage of the Company also had significant implications for the economy of the region. For one thing, the Company diverted a part of the revenue income from the province to investment in the purchase of the return cargo for England. Another major source used to augment the rupee funds available to the Company was the sums borrowed from private European merchants, including its own servants, against bills of exchange payable in London and other European capitals. Indeed, this particular source was used extensively by the rival European companies as well. The result was that the companies no longer found it necessary to import significant amounts of silver from home or from elsewhere in Asia, leading to a fundamental alteration in the structure of Euro-Asian trade. Perhaps even more important was a basic alteration in the nature of the relationship the English Company had with merchants and artisans with whom it did business in the region. This relationship was no longer governed by the forces of demand and supply in the market, but had degenerated into one of intense coercion by the Company of the trading and the artisanal groups.

CHAPTER 8

EUROPEAN TRADE AND THE INDIAN ECONOMY

TRADE AS AN INSTRUMENT OF GROWTH

The principal distinguishing feature of Euro-Asian trade in the early modern period was its bullion-based character. In view of the inability of Europe to supply western products with a potential market in Asia at prices that would generate a large enough demand for them to provide the necessary revenue for the purchase of the Asian goods, the Europeans were obliged to import the bulk of the purchasing power they brought to India (and other parts of Asia) in precious metals, mainly silver. It is indeed quite immaterial whether the imported precious metals are treated as a traded commodity or as a balancing item settling trade surpluses. Traditionally, trade between the Indian subcontinent and neighbouring regions such as southeast Asia had essentially been one involving the exchange of commodities such as Indian textiles against items such as Indonesian spices and Malayan tin. But at the same time, trade with other regions such as west Asia had involved the exchange of Indian textiles overwhelmingly against precious metals. It is not without reason that the port of Mocha in the Red Sea was described as the treasure chest of the Mughal empire. The Euro-Asian trade was thus essentially a continuation of the earlier pattern of trade with regions such as west Asia.

In so far as a country is relatively more efficient in the production of export goods than in that of import goods, an increase in trade between nations is ordinarily to the advantage of both the trading partners, involving an increase in the value of the total output in each of the two economies. The 'gains from trade' tend to become much more substantial in special situations such as in the case of the Euro-Asian trade in the early modern period. This is because the decline in the domestic production of import-competing goods, which would usually accompany an increase in the output of export goods in an ordinary trade situation involving the exchange of goods against goods, would be avoided when the imports consisted not of goods but of precious metals (which in any case were not produced domestically in countries such as India). An increase in the output of export goods attendant upon an increase in trade would then involve a net increase in total output and income in the economy. This would be so irrespective of whether the imported precious metals are treated as a commodity import or as a mechanism for settling trade balances.

The increase in the output of export goods in the subcontinent in response to the secularly rising demand for these goods by the Europeans would seem to have been achieved through a reallocation of resources, a fuller utilization of existing productive capacity and an increase over time in the capacity itself. A reallocation of resources in favour of the production of export goods such as raw silk and particular varieties of textiles would have been signalled, among other things, by a continuous rise in the prices of these goods in the markets where they were procured. Evidence regarding such a rise is available in plenty in the European company documentation. The available evidence also suggests both a fuller utilization of existing capacity as well as expansion thereof over time. In the case of textile manufacturing, for example, artisans engaged in the activity on a part-time basis seem to have increasingly found it worth their while to become full-time producers and to relocate themselves in the so-called *aurungs* – localized centres of manufacturing production, where the Europeans were increasingly concentrating their procurement through the intermediary merchants. Among the other factors of production required, land was clearly in abundant supply practically all over the subcontinent at this time. As far as the necessary capital resources needed for the production of new spindles, wheels and looms etc. was concerned, given the extremely small amounts involved, and the fact that the European companies were ever willing to advance the necessary sums, the availability of funds also is highly unlikely to have been a constraining factor. It need hardly be stressed that across a country of the size of the Indian subcontinent, there are likely to have been regional variations with regard to the degree of dynamism, flexibility and potential for continuing expansion in the scale of production that this scenario envisages. However, evidence available at least in respect of regions such as Bengal, which was by far the most important theatre of company activity on the subcontinent, would generally seem to confirm the presence of such attributes in ample measure.

In this scenario, the Europeans' trade would have become a vehicle for an expansion in income, output and employment in the subconti-

nent. As far as additional employment generated in the textile manufacturing sector as a result of European procurement is concerned, an
exercise carried out in respect of the average annual procurement of
textiles and raw silk in Bengal by the Dutch East India Company over
the period 1678–1718 suggested that a total of 33,770 to 44,364
additional full-time jobs would have been created by the Company's
procurement of these two items. If one extended the exercise to cover
the English East India Company, but considered only the early years
of the eighteenth century between 1709 and 1718, the number of
additional full-time jobs created was estimated at 86,967 to 111,151.
The probable total size of the workforce in the textile manufacturing
sector in the province of Bengal was estimated at one million. The full-
time jobs associated with the Dutch Company's trade thus accounted
for between 3.37 per cent and 4.43 per cent of the total workforce in
the sector: the proportion went up to between 8.69 and 11.11 per cent
when the trade of the Dutch and the English East India Companies
was considered together.[1]

The fact that the rate of growth of the Europeans' demand for
goods such as textiles and raw silk was almost always greater than the
rate at which their output increased turned the market increasingly
into a sellers' market. This was reflected in the growing bargaining
strength of the merchants vis-à-vis the companies. For example, in
1709 a number of textile suppliers dealing with the Dutch Company in
Bengal refused to accept fresh contracts unless the Company gave
them an assurance that henceforth in the event of only a limited
variation between the quality of the sample given out and that of the
pieces actually supplied by them, there would be no deduction made
from the price mutually agreed upon at the time of the contract. The
suppliers even insisted upon a refund of the price deductions made on
this count on textiles supplied during the preceding season. A similar

---

[1] This is based on a more detailed analysis carried out in Om Prakash, *The Dutch East
India Company and the Economy of Bengal, 1630–1720*, Princeton, 1985, ch. 8. The
subsequent detection by Sushil Chaudhury of an error in the rate of conversion between the
covid and the yard suggested that the figure of 33,770 jobs ought to be revised to 38,195, and
that of 86,967 to 94,517. In that case, the proportion that these additional full-time jobs
would have formed of the probable total size of the workforce in the sector would go up
from between 3.37 and 4.43 to between 3.81 and 4.43 per cent, and from between 8.69 and
11.11 to between 9.45 and 11.11 per cent, respectively. (See Sushil Chaudhury, 'European
companies and the Bengal textile industry in the eighteenth century: the pitfalls of applying
quantitative techniques', *Modern Asian Studies*, vol. 27 (2), 1993, pp. 321–40. My response,
'On estimating the employment implications of European trade for the eighteenth century
Bengal textile industry – A reply', appeared in the same number of the journal, pp. 341–56.)

distinct improvement would also seem to have taken place in the bargaining strength of the weavers vis-à-vis the textile suppliers ensuring that the 'gains from trade' indeed percolated all the way down. Writing in 1700, for example, the Dutch factors at Hugli made the following observation:

The merchants inform us (and on investigation we find that they are speaking the truth) that because of the large number of buyers in the weaving centres and the large sale of textiles, the weavers can no longer be coerced. They weave what is most profitable for them. If one does not accommodate oneself to this situation, then one is not able to procure very much and the supplies go to one's competitors.[2]

THE MONETARY ASPECTS OF
THE EUROPEAN TRADE

Quite apart from the implications of European trade for real variables such as income, output and employment, there was an important range of issues in the monetary domain which were affected by this trade. The import of large quantities of precious metals by the European companies into India on a continuing basis would have had certain consequences for the economy of the subcontinent. There is a considerable body of literature that assigns an important role to the imported American silver in shaping the growth of a number of European economies in the early modern period. According to Immanuel Wallerstein, for example, without the American silver

Europe would have lacked the collective confidence to develop a capitalist system, wherein profit is based on various deferrals of realized value. This is *a fortiori* true given the system of a nonimperial world-economy which, for other reasons, was essential. Given this phenomenon of collective psychology, an integral element of the social structure of the time, bullion must be seen as an essential crop for a prospering world-economy.[3]

This is what made South America so valuable. In Wallerstein's words,

the production of gold and silver as a commodity made the Americas a peripheral area of the European world-economy in so far as this commodity was essential to the operation of this world-economy, and it was essential to the extent that it was used as *money* . . . In short, they [the Europeans] incorporated the Americas into

---

[2] *Algemeen Rijksarchief* (ARA), Explanation by the Dutch factors of why the orders were not supplied in full, 1700, VOC 1638, ff. 17–19, II Section.

[3] Immanuel Wallerstein, *The Modern World-System, Capitalist Agriculture and the Origins of the European World-Economy in the Sixteenth Century*, New York, 1974, p. 46.

their world-economy, primarily because they needed a solid currency base for an expanding capitalist system and secondarily to use the surplus in trade with Asia.[4]

But according to the proponents of this position, Asia was different. To quote Wallerstein once again,

At this epoch, the relationship of Europe and Asia might be summed up as the exchange of preciosities. The bullion flowed east to decorate the temples, palaces, and clothing of Asian aristocratic classes and the jewels and spices flowed west. The accidents of cultural history (perhaps nothing more than physical scarcity) determined these complementary preferences.[5]

Another western scholar, Rudolph Blitz, makes essentially a similar point, 'In the Orient, much of the specie went promptly into hoards or was demonetized and became a commodity satisfying the oriental penchant for ornaments.'[6] The otherness of Asia in this view thus derives essentially from the fact that while, in the case of Europe, the imported silver involved an accretion to the supply of money in the system, in Asia this valuable asset was frittered away by being used 'for hoarding or jewelry'.[7]

There is reason to believe that such a clear-cut dichotomy between Europe and Asia is indeed quite untenable and does not conform to a wide body of evidence available to us. By far the most concrete of the effects associated with the import of American silver into Europe was the so-called 'price revolution' of the sixteenth century. A similar response is ruled out in the case of Asia for the simple reason that the first link in the chain, namely an increase in the supply of money, would not have come about in the Asian economies. But such a position is demonstrably false. In the case of Mughal India, for example, the treasure brought in by the European companies was intended for investment in Indian silk, textiles and other goods. In so far as foreign coins were not allowed to circulate locally, the very first step that would need to be taken by these companies in the matter of raising the necessary purchasing power would be the conversion of imported bullion and coins into Mughal Indian rupees. This could be

---

[4] Immanuel Wallerstein, *The Modern World-System II, Mercantilism and the Consolidation of the European World-Economy, 1600–1750*, New York, 1980, p. 109.

[5] Wallerstein, *The Modern World-System, Capitalist Agriculture*, p. 41.

[6] Rudolph C. Blitz, 'Mercantilist policies and the pattern of world trade, 1500–1750', *Journal of Economic History*, vol. 27 (1), March 1967, p. 40.

[7] J. Sperling, 'The international payments mechanisms in the seventeenth and eighteenth centuries', *Economic History Review*, 2nd series, vol. 14 (3), 1962, p. 450. Quoted in Wallerstein, *The Modern World System II*, p. 109.

done either through professional dealers in money known as *sarrafs* or by recourse to one of the imperial mints in the empire. In either event, there would be an automatic and corresponding increase in the supply of money in the economy. It is, of course, perfectly possible that a part of the increased money supply might eventually have been hoarded or withdrawn from active circulation. But in the present state of our knowledge, it would probably be futile to surmise how significant or marginal this phenomenon might have been. Some observations could nevertheless be made on this behalf. In any society, hoarding of precious metals in the form of bullion or coins would be a function of the structure of asset preferences. Given the virtual absence of deposit banking facilities in India, hoarding on a reasonable scale can very well be interpreted as a perfectly legitimate and rational form of holding liquidity. The point is that the implied irrationality in the 'Oriental penchant for hoarding' kind of story might in fact never have been there except perhaps at the margin.

A growing supply of money in response to a continuing import of precious metals would presumably have had implications for the functioning of an Asian economy along lines not necessarily very different from those in Europe. In relation to late Ming China, this is what William Atwell has to say,

Japanese and Spanish-American silver may well have been the most significant factor in the vigorous economic expansion which occurred in China during the period in question. This is true not only because of its direct impact on the silk and porcelain industries, although this clearly was of great importance; but also because an increase in the country's stock of precious metals upon which economic growth and business confidence seem to have depended would have been determined almost entirely by how much silver entered the country through foreign trade.[8]

The situation is unlikely to have been different in Mughal India, where it would seem that the rising supply of money was leading to a significant acceleration in the process of monetization in the economy. The well-known growing monetization of the land-revenue demand during the period was clearly a part of this larger process. Another significant feature of the Mughal Indian economy was the rise of banking firms all over the empire dealing in extremely sophisticated instruments of credit. Many of these firms had enormous resources at

---

[8] William S. Atwell, 'Notes on silver, foreign trade, and the late Ming economy', *Ching-Shih Wen-t'i*, vol. 3 (8), 1977, p. 5.

their command. Probably the best known of these was the house of the Jagat Seths operating from its headquarters at Murshidabad in Bengal. Along with its other activities, the firm organized the transfer of Delhi's share in the land revenues collected in the province. It need hardly be stressed that there was an important organic link between the rise in the money supply and the growth of the banking firms in the Mughal Indian economy.

What about the relationship between a rise in the money supply and the notional general price level in the economy? In other words, was there a counterpart in India to the European price revolution of the sixteenth century? A considerable body of work done over the past quarter of a century or so on the history of prices in different regions of India during the seventeenth and the first half of the eighteenth century has consistently negated the possibility of a general price rise (as opposed to a rise in the prices of goods procured by the Europeans). This includes my own earlier work on the price history of Bengal based mainly on the evidence available in the records of the Dutch East India Company. The evidence regarding movements in the prices of wage-goods such as rice, wheat, sugar and clarified butter, which I had argued could indeed be treated as proxies for movements in the notional general price level in the economy, suggested considerable fluctuations in the prices of these goods but no statistically significant upward or downward trend.[9]

How does one reconcile the phenomenon of a rise in the supply of money with the absence of a rise in the notional general price level? While no definitive answer is possible, we might consider the following. Together with looking at the supply of money, we ought also to look at the demand for it. We have already noted that the 'bullion for goods' character of the Euro-Asian trade in the early modern period turned the foreign trade sector into an instrument of growth with the savings, investment and production in the economy registering an increase. The rising supply of money in the system would then have been absorbed by rising output, essentially obviating the need for the general price level necessarily to go up. This process would be further reinforced by

---

[9] Om Prakash, 'Precious metal flows, coinage and prices in India in the 17th and the early 18th century', in Eddy H.G. van Cauwenberghe (ed.), *Money, Coins, and Commerce: Essays in the Monetary History of Asia and Europe (from Antiquity to Modern Times)*, Leuven University Press, 1991, pp. 55–74. Reprinted in Om Prakash, *Precious Metals and Commerce, The Dutch East India Company in the Indian Ocean Trade*, Variorum, 1994.

the increasing monetization in the economy whereby monetized transactions as a proportion of total transactions in the economy would have gone up. Finally, over the fairly long period with which we are concerned, natural increases in population would also have necessitated a secular rise in output and transactions if the per-capita output and availability were not to go down. All these factors would tend to check a general rise in prices consequent upon an increase in the supply of money caused by an increased inflow of precious metals.

Certain deviations from the above scenario across both space and time must be noted. Across space, the above analysis will not be fully applicable to the Malabar coast, for example. The Portuguese had enjoyed special rights in pepper procurement in parts of the region until 1663 when they were thrown out of Cochin by the raja with the active assistance of the VOC. But then the VOC got its pound of flesh consisting, among other privileges, in a monopsony in the procurement of pepper in the area between Purakkad and Cranganur, and a monopoly in the sale of opium. Given the terrain, it was impossible to prevent large-scale smuggling by Indian merchants, which substantially limited the scope of the Dutch monopoly privileges. But even so, in respect of that part of the total marketed output of pepper that the Dutch East India Company procured, the price paid to the intermediary merchants, which eventually also determined the return reaching the producer, was lower, possibly substantially lower, than what the free market forces of demand and supply would have dictated. The macro-economic implications of the European procurement would thus have been grossly vitiated.

THE EARLY COLONIAL PERIOD

Across time, the situation during the second half of the eighteenth century was very different from that in the preceding period. The political control now exercised by the English East India Company in several major areas of the subcontinent placed it in a position of substantial differential advantage vis-à-vis both the rival European companies as well as the intermediary merchants and artisans. The terms and conditions the Company imposed on those doing business with it were no longer determined by the market: indeed, these people were no longer always free even to determine whether to do business with the Company at all. In Gujarat, this situation developed after the

English takeover of the Surat castle in 1759. On the Coromandel coast, the 1750s and the 1760s witnessed the acquisition by the Company of extensive land revenue collection rights in key textile-producing districts in the northern Circars and central Coromandel, giving it an unprecedented degree of control over the textile merchants and weavers in the area. S. Arasaratnam has described in some detail the coercive measures adopted by the Company in its textile procurement in the region, including the demarcation of looms on which textiles would henceforth be produced exclusively for the Company.[10]

It was, however, in Bengal where the Company first obtained formal *diwani* rights in 1765 that the full impact of the new status of the Company was in evidence. The availability against bills of exchange of large amounts of rupee funds that individual European merchants of different nationalities were interested in remitting home enabled the English and other companies operating in Bengal to cut down substantially on the import of silver from Europe. Indeed, in the case of the English Company, this source, combined with the funds raised by the diversion of a part of the Bengal revenues to the procurement of goods for Europe, led to a total suspension of the import of precious metals from home. It was only in 1784 that the import of these metals was resumed.

Textiles

This phase also witnessed a fundamental alteration for the worse in the nature of the relationship between the English Company on the one hand and the intermediary merchant and artisanal groups on the other. A gross abuse of the newly found political power available to the English factors turned this relationship into one of widespread coercion and oppression. In the matter of the procurement of textiles in Bengal, the Company's operations at Khirpai provide a good example of the manner in which the system was run. Soon after the assumption of *diwani* rights in 1765, the Commercial Resident of the area arranged for information to be collected regarding the number of weavers, looms, pieces of textiles of different kinds manufactured in each *aurung* in his area in a year, the number ordinarily procured by rival European trading companies as well as private merchants each

[10] S. Arasaratnam, 'Weavers, merchants and Company: the handloom industry in southeastern India 1750–1790', *The Indian Economic and Social History Review*, vol. 17 (3), 1980, pp. 257–81.

year, and so on.[11] Since the Company's textile requirements took precedence over everyone else's, individual *paikars* of the Company were allotted weavers who were banned from working for anyone else till such time as they had met their contractual obligations towards the Company. The terms offered by the Company to the *paikars*, and, in turn, by the latter to the weavers, were extraordinarily poor. The perennial complaint of the weavers was that the price allowed them by the Company hardly enabled them to cover the cost of the raw materials. In 1767, the weavers went so far as to send a delegation to Calcutta with a petition (*arzi*) requesting that the prices offered to them be increased by at least so much as to afford them a subsistence wage. They did manage to obtain an order directing the Commercial Resident, identified in a Dutch report as one Bathoe, to do the needful. But this evidently was no more than eyewash because Bathoe not only openly disregarded the order but indeed threatened to have the weavers arrested in the event that they continued with their efforts.[12]

The pieces of textile received from the *paikars* were classified by the Company's evaluators from quality one to five. Pieces not found good enough to make even quality five were rejected as 'firty' (ferreted). A rough idea of what the Company subjected the weavers to can be formed by the fact that pieces classified as third quality would gladly have been accepted by the Dutch Company as first quality at a considerably higher price.[13] It is remarkable that even the pieces rejected by the Company as 'firty' had a profitable market. The margin between the price that these pieces fetched in the open market, and the rate at which they had been evaluated by the Company before being rejected, would convey some idea of the extent of the exploitation of the weavers. This margin was shared clandestinely between the Commercial Resident, the chief *gumashta* and the *paikars*. To take an example from 1767, Resident Bathoe rejected 896 pieces of textiles as 'firty' that year. Many of these pieces were eventually sold by the *paikars* in the open market at between Rs.$6\frac{1}{2}$ and Rs.7 per piece higher than the price at which they had been evaluated by the Company's

---

[11] ARA, J.M. Ross at Khirpai to Director at Hugli, 18 July 1767, Appendix D, *Hooge Regering Batavia* (hereafter HRB), 247.

[12] ARA, J.M. Ross at Khirpai to Director at Hugli, 16 May 1767, Appendix C2, HRB 247.

[13] ARA, J.M. Ross at Khirpai to Director of Hugli, Appendix A, HRB 247.

factors before being rejected. Bathoe had returned the pieces to the *paikars* after keeping a margin of Rs.3 per piece for himself and Rs.$\frac{1}{2}$ per piece for the chief *gumashta* Radhamohan Basak. But even after paying Rs. $3\frac{1}{2}$ extra, the *paikars* managed to earn a net profit of Rs.3 to Rs.$3\frac{1}{2}$ per piece in the market for themselves.[14] Besides, the Company also exploited the weaver by manipulating the raw material market to its advantage. It was reported in 1767, for example, that Resident Bathoe had bought silk yarn from the producers at 16 tolas to a rupee and had supplied it to the weavers of silk textiles at 7 to 9 tolas per rupee. The profits were shown in the Bardwan accounts of the Company.[15]

In 1771, the Board of Trade reverted to the contract system and formally invited local merchants to undertake to supply to the Company. But in its actual working, the new arrangement represented no more than a change in form and left the content by and large unchanged. Often, the Commercial Residents themselves undertook the responsibility of supplying to the Company on a contractual basis. After 1774, their names were listed as direct suppliers to the Company and an official agency commission payable to them was agreed upon.[16]

A by-product of the political ascendancy of the English Company in Bengal was the growing range of problems created for its European rivals, the Dutch and the French East India companies. The growing English stranglehold on the weavers, obliging an increasing number of them to work exclusively for the English Company, made it difficult for the Dutch and the French to procure an adequate quantity of textiles. Within a few months of Plassey, the English factors were reported to be forcibly taking away pieces woven for the Dutch.[17] In October 1758, when the Dutch protested against the English high-handedness in having pieces under production for their Company torn away from the looms, the English officials promised redress but nothing was actually done.[18] In the early 1760s, the Commercial

---

[14] ARA, J.M. Ross at Khirpai to Director at Hugli, 18 July 1767, Appendix D, HRB 247.

[15] ARA, J.M. Ross to Director at Hugli, Appendix A, HRB 247; also Appendix D, HRB 247.

[16] Hameeda Hossain, *The Company Weavers of Bengal, the East India Company and the Organization of Textile Production in Bengal, 1750–1813*, Delhi, 1988, pp. 90–1.

[17] G.C. Klerk de Reus, 'De expeditie naar Bengale in 1759', *De Indische Gids*, vol. 11, 1889, p. 2099.

[18] ARA, Memoir prepared by Dutch director, George Louis Vernet, and submitted to the English on 10 May 1768, HRB 247.

Residents at Malda and Midnapur were instructed to ensure that the best weavers of Jagannathpur, Olmara and the neighbouring *aurungs* worked exclusively for the English.[19]

With a view to finding a more lasting solution to the problem, the Dutch proposed to the English in 1767 that they should be assigned weavers in the various *aurungs* who would then be allowed to work for them without hindrance. Since formally the English took the position that the Dutch, as indeed all other Europeans, were perfectly free to carry on their trade in the region, this was agreed to in principle, but eventually nothing came of the proposal.[20] A Fort William public notification dated 28 April 1775 even asserted

that the weavers of the province of Bengal and Bihar should enjoy a perfect and entire liberty to deal with any persons whom they pleased and that no person should use force of any kind to oblige the weavers or other manufacturers to receive advances of money or to engage in contracts for the provision of clothes against their will, and that all persons offending against this order should suffer severe punishment.[21]

The charade was continued in the English response dated 8 September 1785 to a Dutch memorandum:

Under your agents, they [the weavers] may work more freely perhaps than under our own, and you may rest assured that we shall not countenance the servants or gomastahs of our own Board of Trade in any attempts that they may make to oppress the natives who work for you and not us, or prevent your employment of their industry. The weaver who works for your Company contributes equally to pay the revenue, with the weaver who works for our own Board of Trade, and perhaps more so. And an extension to the sale of Bengal manufacture is more profitable to Great Britain than a monopoly in the purchase of such goods as would restrain the manufacture.[22]

The truth, however, was otherwise and the Dutch procurement continued to suffer heavily. The situation was exploited fully by the merchants. On average, the Dutch factors were obliged to pay a price about 25 per cent higher than the price the English company paid for

---

[19] ARA, Memoir by Taillefert for his successor, George Vernet, 7 November 1763, HRB 246 (the volume is not foliated).

[20] ARA, Memoir prepared by Dutch director, George Louis Vernet, and submitted to the English on 10 May 1768, HRB 247; J.M. Ross at Khirpai to Director at Hugli, 8 July 1767, Appendix D, HRB 247.

[21] ARA, The notification was signed by J.P. Auriol, Assistant Secretary, HRB 253.

[22] ARA, The English Company reply dated 8 September 1785 to the second Dutch memorandum, Macpherson and Council to Eilbracht and van Citters, HRB 211.

comparable varieties.[23] Also, the VOC often found it difficult to get an adequate number of merchants unless a continuous increase in the price was agreed to.[24]

Opium

The agrarian sector counterpart of the aggrieved Bengal textile weaver was the opium peasant who was similarly subjected to significant non-market pressures by the English East India Company as well as by its employees operating in their private capacity. Soon after the takeover of the province, Company servants tried to establish private monopolies in the drug. The first such case available to use is that of William McGwire, the chief of the English factory at Patna. In 1761, he 'persuaded' *Naib-Subadar* Ram Narain to issue a *parwana* stipulating that McGwire would have the exclusive right to engage with the suppliers of opium for the procurement of the drug. McGwire tried to have this arrangement legitimized by Calcutta and in the process even offered a share in the profit from the venture to Governor Vansittart. But the latter refused to succumb to the temptation and ordered the withdrawal of the *parwana*.[25] That, however, did not deter McGwire's successor, William Ellis, from grossly misusing his official position to coerce the suppliers into providing him with the drug at prices considerably below the market.[26] From 1765 on, the English Company factors at Patna agreed to carry on this business on a somewhat more organized basis. They decided to act jointly and divide the profits from the venture on the basis of each person's status

[23] To take a specific example, in 1767, against Rs.10 per piece paid by the English for a particular variety, the Dutch had to pay Rs.12.44, ARA, J.M. Ross to Director at Hugli, Appendix A, HRB 247; J.M. Ross to Director at Hugli dated 12 May 1767, Appendix C, HRB 247.

[24] ARA, Memoir by George Vernet for his successor, Faure, 8 March 1770, HRB 249; Memoir by outgoing Director Johannes Bacheracht for his successor, J.M. Ross, dated 31 July 1776, HRB 252.

[25] 'Secret memoir concerning the Directorate of Bengal left by outgoing Dutch Director Louis Taillefert for his successor, George Louis Vernet', dated 17 November 1763, ARA, HRB 246, f. 205; Memoir of Dutch Director in Bengal at Hugli, Johannes Bacheracht, for his successor, J.M. Ross, dated 31 July 1776, ARA, HRB 252, ff. 114–15; 'Extract of the Proceedings of the President and Council at Fort William in Bengal in their Revenue Department, the 15th October, 1773', 'Appendix 57 to the Ninth Report from the Select Committee appointed to take into consideration the State of the administration of justice in the provinces of Bengal, Bihar and Orissa', 25 June 1783, India Office Library (hereafter IOL), L/Parl/2/15; P.J. Marshall, *East Indian Fortunes, The British in Bengal in the Eighteenth Century*, Oxford, 1976, pp. 118–19.

[26] Memoir of Bacheracht for Ross dated 31 July 1776, ARA, HRB 252, ff. 115–16; Enclosures to the memoir of Bacheracht for Ross dated 31 July 1776, ARA, HRB 253, f. 6.

in the hierarchy. These individuals generally did not engage in internal or international trade in the item on their own and sold it on a monopoly basis to the prospective traders in the drug who would include Indian merchants, other private English traders, the Dutch Company, etc. The gross profit earned by the Patna factors has been estimated to have ranged between 175 per cent and as much as 300 per cent.[27] But considering that the arrangement did not have Calcutta's approval and the machinery of enforcement available to the Patna factors was of necessity limited, it would seem that the proportion of total marketed output that passed through the hands of these factors was perhaps not very large.

This situation was altered radically in 1773 when the English Company decided to assume monopoly rights in the drug for itself. The arrangement was for the Company to organize the procurement of the drug on an exclusive basis and then arrange for its sale to prospective traders through public auctions held at Calcutta. It was maintained that given the 'dispositions and the habits of the natives', a monopoly was essential.[28] Earlier, Vansittart's minute which had formed the basis of the 1773 decision had elaborated on these 'dispositions and habits' by noting that 'had every merchant free liberty to make them [the suppliers and the producers] Advances, they would receive Money in Abundance, they would dissipate a part of it, they would be unable to manufacture opium sufficient to complete their Engagements'.[29] In order to justify the measure further, the Company even helped create a myth that a state monopoly of opium had always been the norm for India. In a memorandum sent to the Dutch factors at Hugli, Governor-General John Macpherson and the Calcutta Council observed:

The opium of this country was always managed by the native government as a monopoly and we have the evidence before us of a person who held a considerable office at the Buxbandar for above sixty years, and who is now alive that opium and saltpetre were purchased by the foreign companies as they could from the

---

[27] Memoir of outgoing Dutch Director of Bengal, George Louis Vernet for his successor Boudewyn Verselewel Faure, dated 8 March 1770, ARA, HRB 249, ff. 85–6; Extract, Bengal Revenue Consultations, 23 November 1773, Appendix 57, Ninth Report, IOL, L/Parl/2/15; Marshall, *East Indian Fortunes*, p. 146.

[28] Governor-General John Macpherson and Council at Calcutta to Eilbracht and van Citters, members of the Dutch Council at Hugli, 8 September 1785, ARA, HRB 211 (unfoliated).

[29] Extract, Bengal Revenue Consultations, 23 November 1773, Appendix 57, Ninth Report, IOL, L/Parl/2/15.

persons enjoying the exclusive privilege of this monopoly in like manner as by private merchants.[30]

An examination of the extensive reports filed by the factors of the Dutch Company, the single largest buyer of opium in the market on the eve of the British takeover, however, does not point towards any such arrangement.[31] The 1773 English Company monopoly, therefore, must be viewed as an 'innovation' with rather important consequences.

Initially, the monopoly pertained to the Bihar opium and excluded the marginal amount produced in the province of Bengal. In principle, the monopoly implied that the entire output of the drug in Bihar would have to be handed over to the Company at a price determined unilaterally for the year. The amount so collected was then sold off to traders in the drug at public auctions held in Calcutta. The mechanics of the system of collection was as follows. Initially, this was done through a contractor awarded the contract for a year at a time. Although applications were invited from interested persons through public notices in English, Persian and Bengali,[32] the selection was made by the Governor-General-in-Council essentially on a patronage basis rather than on the basis of any objective criteria prescribed for the purpose. From 1781, the contract was given for a period of four years at a time. When the first four-year contract expired in 1785, the patronage system of awarding it was replaced by one where it was given to the highest bidder at a public auction organized for the purpose.

The Company paid the contractor at a specific price communicated to him in advance for each chest of opium delivered.[33] Half the value

---

[30] Governor-General John Macpherson and Council at Calcutta to Eilbracht and van Citters, members of the Dutch Council at Hugli, 8 September 1785, in 'Correspondence exchanged between the English authorities in Bengal and the servants of the Dutch Company there, 1785', ARA, HRB, 211 (unfoliated).

[31] Indeed, a Dutch memoir from 1776 explicitly says that while some attempts had been made during the pre-1757 period to monopsonize opium, these had never been successful (Memoir of Director Bacheracht for his successor, Ross, dated 31 July 1776, ARA, HRB 252, f. 117).

[32] For a sample of the public notice, see Extract, Bengal Revenue Consultations, 23 May 1775, Appendix 62, Ninth Report, IOL, L/Parl/2/15.

[33] The price paid to the first opium contractor, Mir Manir, was Sicca Rs.320 per chest. In respect of the lots procured in Ghazipur and some other districts outside Bihar and held in *jagir* by Nawab Shuja-ud-Daula, a price of Sicca Rs.350 per chest was stipulated (Extract, Bengal Revenue Consultations, 23 May 1775, Appendix 62, Ninth Report, IOL, L/Parl/2/15).

of the entire lot was given to him in advance out of which he was expected to give cash advances to the peasants producing opium. The contractor was subject to a penalty of Rs.100,000 in the event of being found supplying opium to anyone other than the Company.[34] All opium was to be collected at Calcutta in a crude state where it was to be 'manufactured' under the superintendence of a nominee of the Company.[35] From 1775 on, the revenues from opium were treated as excise or tax funds rather than as profit from trade. The management of the opium business continued to be with the Board of Revenue till 1793 when it was transferred to the Board of Trade.[36]

In 1797, the contract system was abolished in favour of an agency system involving direct control by the Company of the cultivation of opium. The production was henceforth to be restricted to Bihar and Banaras and discontinued in Bengal. Two Company officers were appointed Opium Agents with headquarters at Patna and Banaras respectively. The formal legislation defining the basic principles of the new system was set out under Regulation VI of 1799. This edict, although supplemented by further Acts in 1816, 1857 and 1870, continued to regulate the opium production and marketing enterprise until the early twentieth century.[37] All private cultivation of poppy was banned. The peasant was forced to cultivate a specified plot of land and to deliver its entire production at the fixed government price to the Agent. If a peasant failed to cultivate the full amount of land that he was required to and on which he had been given an advance, he was obliged to pay back pro-rata three times the value of the advance for the shortfall in the total area cultivated. If it were established that the shortfall in output had been due to negligence on the part of the peasant, he was to repay the proportional amount of advance with 12 per cent interest. If an illicit sale was established, the rules provided for the confiscation of the lot besides a fine at the rate of Rs.4 per seer. If confiscation of the lot was not feasible, the fine was to go up to Rs.10 per seer. In 1816, the rates of the fine were increased to Rs.8 and Rs.16 per seer, respectively. The rate of interest to be

---

[34] Extract, Bengal Revenue Consultations, 23 November 1773, Appendix 57, Ninth Report, IOL, L/Parl/2/15.

[35] Extract, Bengal Revenue Consultations, 23 November 1773, Appendix 57, Ninth Report.

[36] Second Report of the Select Committee, 1805, Collection 55, f. 21, IOL, L/Parl/2/15.

[37] J.F. Richards, 'The Indian empire and the peasant production of opium in the nineteenth century', *Modern Asian Studies*, vol. 15 (1), 1981, p. 64.

charged on the advances returned because of shortfall in supply was at the same time doubled to 24 per cent.[38]

If a peasant decided to be in the business of producing opium, he had no option but to deal with the Company. But in principle, he had the right not to be in the business of producing opium and to reject the offer of a cash advance in return for pledging his crop to the English Company Agent. The 1773 document which had specified the clauses of the opium monopoly had clearly laid down that 'no cultivator will be forced to cultivate poppy against his inclination'.[39] Regulation VI of 1799 had repeated '. . . but it is left entirely at the option of the Ryot or Cultivator, to enter into engagements on account of Government at a settled price, or to decline it altogether'.[40] But the possibility that the rights of the peasants were not fully protected and that an element of compulsion was introduced into the picture is strongly suggested by the need for Governor-General Cornwallis to make the following stipulation in 1789. He decreed that henceforth a contractor could not 'compel the ryots to engage for the cultivation of a greater number of *beeghas* than they cultivated the preceding year'.[41] Also, if for some reason a particular peasant was simply not able to continue engaging in opium cultivation, then he was required to give up his land as well since it had been earmarked for opium. The land was then assigned to another peasant undertaking to produce opium.[42]

The terms of the contract given to the peasants were enforced quite rigorously. The true beginnings of the Company's monopoly system could perhaps be placed around September 1775, when the opium contract was awarded to one Griffith. This man arranged for *parwanas* to be issued to officials in the opium districts obliging them to ensure that nobody other than his agents had access to the drug.[43] In 1776, when some Bengali merchants managed to give out opium advances clandestinely, a strongly worded letter was dispatched to the *pargana*

[38] Benoy Chowdhury, *Growth of Commercial Agriculture in Bengal (1757–1900)*, vol. I, Calcutta, 1964, p. 42.

[39] Extract, Bengal Revenue Consultations, 23 November 1773, Appendix 57, Ninth Report, IOL.

[40] Second Report of the Select Committee, 1805, collection 55, IOL, L/Parl/2/55.

[41] Chowdhury, *Growth of Commercial Agriculture in Bengal*, p. 51.

[42] Chowdhury, *Growth of Commercial Agriculture in Bengal*, p. 51.

[43] Minutes of the Dutch Council at Hugli, 13 October 1775, in Enclosures to the memoir of outgoing Director Bacheracht, ARA, HRB 253 (unfoliated); Letter from Gregorius Herklots to the Council at Hugli, 20 October 1775, ARA, HRB 253 (unfoliated).

officials holding them directly responsible for such unauthorized deals. They were directed to have a public announcement made that if an opium supplier or cultivator had accepted a cash advance as part of a clandestine deal, he was not to feel obliged either to honour the contract or to return the advance. Any complaint that might be preferred against him in this connection would not be entertained by the administration.[44]

The opium enterprise was clearly of great advantage to the English East India Company, the contractors and other intermediaries participating in the enterprise, as well as to the private English traders engaged in the opium trade. Many of the intermediaries and the traders were servants of the Company. From the point of view of the Company, an obvious advantage was in terms of an accretion to the revenues of Bengal. Some evidence available in the documentation of the Company suggests that between 1773–4 and 1784–5, though there were significant annual fluctuations, there was generally an upward trend in the revenue from opium. From a low of £14,256 in 1774–5, the revenue went up to £49,572 in 1778–9 and to £78,300 in 1783–4, though in 1784–5 it came down to £53,348.[45] As a proportion of total Bengal revenues, the revenue from opium is estimated to have accounted for 5.2 per cent in 1792, 7 per cent in 1812, 10 per cent in 1822 and as much as 20 per cent in 1842.[46]

The opium contractors were also known to have made handsome profits from the enterprise. It has been suggested that in the early years of the monopoly system, a contractor could stipulate for £10,000 from a subcontractor, who could himself stipulate for £17,000 from yet another subcontractor, who was still able to make a handsome profit.[47] While it is not at all certain how representative these figures are over time, they nevertheless suggest the existence of a very positive situation from the point of view of these people. Finally, as far as the private English traders engaged in the trade were concerned, the advantages from the opium enterprise consisted not only in facilitating

---

[44] *Parwana* dated 8 March 1776, available in Minutes of the Hugli Council meeting, 28 May 1776, Enclosures to the memoir of Bacheracht, ARA, HRB 253 (unfoliated).

[45] 'An account of the annual profits arising to the Company from Opium in Bengal from the acquisition of Diwani to the date of the latest advices from Bengal', Collection 20, f. 1, IOL, Parl/L/2/20.

[46] Tan Chung, 'The British–China–India trade triangle (1771–1840)', *The Indian Economic and Social History Review*, vol. 11 (4), 1974, pp. 422–3.

[47] Marshall, *East Indian Fortunes*, p. 203.

the earning of a high rate of profit, but also in the use of the trade in the item with China as the principal vehicle for the transmission home of the profits earned in India. This was done by placing the proceeds from the China sales of opium at the disposal of the Company factors in Canton in exchange for bills on London.

As for the peasants participating in the opium enterprise, the position was more complex. There can be no question that the opium monopoly involved a certain amount of coercion over the peasants and it is likely that the degree of this coercion exceeded the officially stipulated limits. For example, the provision regarding the peasant not being forced to increase the acreage under opium may well have been grossly violated. Despite the best efforts of the English Company, a certain amount of opium continued to be sold clandestinely to Indian and other merchants by the peasants. To take up only one such case in the Dutch Company records relating to 1775, when the *paikar* of the Dutch Company reached the opium tract of Phulwari, he was enthusiastically received by the cultivators who offered to enter into contracts with him for the supply of the drug. The arrangement made was for the cultivators to call quietly the following day at the place where the *paikar* was staying. But before the deal could go through, the *gumashtas* of the English Company's contractor, Griffith, came to know of it and the *paikar* was apprehended and taken to the contractor. Since this was the man's first offence, he was let off with the warning that if he were ever seen anywhere in the area again, he would be subjected to severe punishment.[48] While it is obvious that the price that the peasants would have obtained on these clandestine deals would have been higher than the Company price, there really is no reliable information available on the extent of this difference which, incidentally, could have served as a broad indicator of the extent of the coercion on the peasants.

The cause of the opium peasant did find occasional support even at the highest levels of the English Company hierarchy. Thus in a communication to their Calcutta factors in December 1776, the Court of Directors observed:

If you shall be of Opinion that abolishing the monopoly of opium will contribute in any great Degree to the Relief of the Natives, we authorize you to give up that

[48] Letter from Gregorius Herklots at Patna to the Dutch Council at Hugli, 20 October 1775, in Enclosures to the memoir of outgoing Director Bacheracht, ARA, HRB 253 (unfoliated).

Commodity as an Article of Commerce, only fixing and reserving a reasonable Duty thereon to the Company, which we think should not exceed 30 Rupees per maund.[49]

But the advice was perhaps not meant to be taken seriously and no note was taken of it. The peasants' resentment of the system occasionally did find expression in their refusal to accept opium advances but this problem did not assume serious proportions at any stage.[50]

What can we say about the overall implications of the English Company's opium monopoly? Was the expansion in output over time solely a function of the coercion that the peasant was subjected to? Or is it possible that the peasant found even the monopoly price, particularly after it was periodically increased between 1823 and 1838, preferable to the option of growing alternative crops? While no definitive answers are as yet possible to these questions, certain tentative suggestions might be made. The cultivation of opium did involve a four- to five-month commitment to demanding, arduous work. C.A. Bayly has argued that 'when labour costs were taken into account, opium production was relatively unprofitable for the farmer'.[51] The reason the acreage still went on increasing was because of the liberal policy the government followed in the matter of giving advances to the actual and prospective opium growers. These advances came in handy for meeting the peasants' land rent obligations and were extremely welcome. The fact that the government monopoly provided an assured market for the peasants' output at a predetermined price not subject to alteration by the size of the crop also worked as a positive factor.[52] The cash advances involved the injection of fairly large sums of money into the commercial agricultural sector of the region directly through the peasants. The crop that this helped the expansion of was both of high value as well as being intended entirely for the market.

The opium obtained by the Company from the peasants was sold through public auctions held at Calcutta overwhelmingly to the private English traders engaged in the China trade. This arrangement was mutually beneficial to the Company as well as the private traders.

[49] English Company Directors to factors in Calcutta, 24 December 1776, Appendix 33, Ninth Report, IOL.

[50] Chowdhury, *Growth of Commercial Agriculture in Bengal*, p. 27.

[51] C.A. Bayly, *Rulers, Townsmen and Bazaars, North Indian Society in the Age of British Expansion, 1770–1870*, Cambridge, 1983, p. 289.

[52] Richards, 'The Indian empire and the peasant production of opium', p. 79.

The bulk of the proceeds from the sale of the drug in China was placed at the disposal of the Company's supercargo at Canton for investment in Chinese silk and tea. In exchange, the Company made available to the private traders for value received bills of exchange on London providing for these traders a convenient channel for remitting their savings home. Holden Furber has termed the rise of the China trade a 'commercial revolution' involving a clear domination of trade in the Indian Ocean and the South China Sea by the private English traders.

Such a domination would almost certainly have had a certain amount of adverse impact on the trading operations of the Indian merchants engaged in trade in the Eastern Indian Ocean. It is, however, important to keep the matter in perspective. In earlier chapters, we noted that the Portuguese and the Dutch attempts to squeeze the Indian maritime merchants out of business were not particularly successful at any point. With a certain amount of readjustment in the matter of ports operated from and specific routes along which trade was carried on, Indian merchants were by and large able to withstand quite successfully the efforts directed at squeezing them out of participation in intra-Asian trade. In so far as the English private traders were indirect beneficiaries of the new political status of the English East India Company, the situation had admittedly become somewhat more complicated in the second half of the eighteenth century. But the overall adverse impact on the fortunes of the Indian merchants engaged in intra-Asian trade would still not seem to have been anything like catastrophic. The direct involvement of the Indian merchants in the China trade had never been of any significance, and to that extent, a growth in the English private trade in the sector had no specific and immediate implication for these merchants except that English ships also did a fair amount of business in southeast Asia on the way to and from China. It would seem that initially the increased competition by the English was injurious to the Indian merchants engaged in trade with this region. But over time the volume and value of trade on the India–southeast Asia sector would in fact seem to have registered a significant increase with the Indian merchants getting their due share in the rising volume of trade.

To summarize, given its 'bullion for goods' character, Euro-Asian trade in the early modern period would seem to have acted as a vehicle for an expansion in income, output and employment in the subcontinent. The fact that the rate of growth of the Europeans' demand for goods such as textiles and raw silk almost always exceeded the rate at which their output increased turned the market increasingly into a sellers' market with significant positive implications for the share of the producers and the intermediary merchant groups in the value of the total marketed output. The import of large quantities of precious metals by the European companies also had important consequences for variables such as the supply of money and the degree of monetization in the subcontinent.

This particular configuration of circumstances, however, underwent a certain amount of modification during the early colonial period, particularly in relation to Bengal, the first of the subcontinental regions to come under the sway of the English East India Company. It is true that a colonial pattern of trade with agricultural and other raw materials together with food constituting the bulk of the exports from the colony to the metropolitan world in exchange for finished manufactured goods produced on the machine did not emerge in the case of India until after our period. But already in the second half of the eighteenth century, important distortions had been introduced into the system. For one thing, the relationship between the English Company on the one hand and the intermediary merchant and artisanal groups on the other had turned into one of widespread coercion and oppression of the latter depriving them of a good part of their legitimate share in the total value of the output produced. This happened on a fairly widespread scale in relation to the procurement of goods such as textiles and raw silk in the manufacturing sector and opium in the commercial crop sector.

CHAPTER 9

CONCLUSION

One of the principal outcomes of the great discoveries of the closing years of the fifteenth century was the rise of a pre-modern world economy. It was the almost simultaneous discovery of the Americas and of the all-water route to the East Indies via the Cape of Good Hope that had brought the three potential constituent segments of this economy, namely Europe, the New World and Asia, together for the first time. By providing a wide range of goods for both Europe and the New World, and by absorbing in return an important segment of the New World output of silver, Asia played a key role in the creation and the subsequent successful functioning of this global network of exchange. The nature of the relationship between Europe and Asia during this early period was essentially one of mutual advantage with each side perfectly capable of a market-determined response structure and rational process of decision making.

The principal agencies instrumental in the running of the Euro-Asian commercial network in the early modern period were the European corporate enterprises – the Portuguese Estado da India in the sixteenth, and the Dutch, the English and the French East India companies in the seventeenth and the eighteenth centuries. A certain amount of Euro-Asian trade was also carried on by private European traders, though it would seem to have been quantitatively significant only in the case of the Portuguese private traders. Traditionally, pepper and other spices such as cloves, nutmeg and mace had accounted for an overwhelming proportion of the total Asian imports into Europe. This continued to be the case through the sixteenth and the greater part of the seventeenth century. The last quarter of the latter century, however, witnessed an almost revolutionary increase in the European demand for Asian textiles and raw silk, leading to a remarkable shift in the composition of the Asian imports into Europe. In the case of the Dutch East India Company, for example, the second half of the century was marked by an increase in the share of these two items in the total imports from a mere 14 per cent to as much as 55 per cent. In so far as India at this time was without any

337

doubt the largest, and the most cost-competitive, producer of textiles in Asia – and perhaps in the entire world – and a major producer of raw silk, an important implication of the shift in the European pattern of demand was a significant enhancement in the relative role of India in Euro-Asian trade. Indeed, the principal Indian region supplying these goods, namely Bengal, by itself now accounted for as much as 40 per cent of the total Asian imports by the Dutch and the English East India companies into Europe. This created a situation of near panic among the European producers of various kinds of textiles. In England, the manufacturers' opposition to the import of Asian textiles was sufficiently vocal to lead to the passage of a Parliamentary Act in 1700 prohibiting the import of 'all wrought silks, Bengals and stuffs mixed with silk or herba, of the manufacture of Persia, China or the East Indies and all calicoes painted, dyed or printed or stained there'. But since this simply involved an increase in the import of white calicoes and muslins from India, which were then printed in England, another Act was passed twenty years later altogether prohibiting the use or wear of printed calicoes in England. Of course, neither of the two Acts affected in any way the re-export trade in Eastern textiles. Holland also had a fairly well-developed linen and silk-textile industry. As early as 1643, several manufacturers of silk textiles in Amsterdam had complained to the States of Holland that, as a result of the import of silk textiles from the East Indies, a number of their apprentices had been thrown out of work. They, therefore, petitioned the States for a total prohibition on the import of silk textiles by the Dutch East India Company. While nothing came of these efforts, the matter came up again at the time of the renewal of the Company's charter in 1694–5. At the behest of the silk-textiles manufacturers and merchants of their province, the representatives of Haarlem in the States-General declared their intention of not voting for the renewal unless a ban was imposed on the Company's imports of cotton textiles, silk textiles and twisted silk. But all that the representatives eventually achieved was the extraction of a promise from the Company that in future it would 'consult' the Haarlem silk industry each year before placing orders with the factors in the East. The industry's 'advice' was not to be binding, and in 1740 a number of 'leading manufacturers of gold-, silk-, wool-, and cotton stuffs' informed the States of Holland that the Company had in any case not bothered to carry out the promised consultations.[1] The difference in this regard between the English and the Dutch East India companies was obviously due to the latter's much stronger position in national politics. Such perceived threats of a 'deindustrializing' Europe in response to the invasion by Indian textiles, however, makes one wonder as to which, between north-western Europe and south Asia in the early modern period, was the 'core' and which the 'periphery'.

THE SIXTEENTH CENTURY

In keeping with the traditional composition of the Asian imports into Europe, the principal item sought by the Portuguese Crown in Asia was spices – overwhelmingly pepper. The procurement of pepper in India was organized by the Estado da India, while the sales in Europe were through contract sales based until the middle of the century at Antwerp and thereafter at Lisbon. The manner in which the Crown dealt with the matter of the procurement, the transportation, and particularly the disposal of the Asian pepper in the European market, has led Niels Steensgaard to characterize the Portuguese Euro-Asian pepper trade as a redistributive enterprise. As he so succinctly puts it 'the Portuguese pepper monopoly was not a business but a custom house'. It is, however, imperative that one keeps the matter in perspective and does not overstate the redistributive dimensions of the Portuguese Euro-Asian trade in its entirety. Pepper was indeed the *raison d'être* of the Portuguese Euro-Asian trade in the beginning, accounting in the first two decades of the sixteenth century for as much as 95 per cent of the total Asian cargo in physical and 85 per cent in value terms. The recent work of James Boyajian suggests that this picture, however, changed drastically from the 1580s onward. The key factor at work was the extremely important role now played by the private Portuguese traders – mainly New Christians – in the Euro-Asian *carreira* trade. According to Boyajian, private cargoes accounted for an almost unbelievable 93 per cent of the total value imported over the period 1580–1640 from Asia. By far the most important consti-tuent of this cargo was textiles accounting for as much as 62 per cent of the total imports valuewise, followed by items such as precious

[1] Om Prakash, *The Dutch East India Company and the Economy of Bengal, 1630–1720*, Princeton, 1985, pp. 203–7.

stones and indigo. Pepper, which continued to be imported under official auspices, now accounted for no more than 10 per cent of the total imports. It is indeed true that there are serious problems of both methodology and evidence with the Boyajian estimates of the private merchants' trade, but there would seem to be little doubt that his revision of current orthodoxy is in the right direction. Since the redistributive-trade characterization of the Portuguese enterprise at the European end is overwhelmingly dependent on the role of pepper in the Euro-Asian trade, such a revision involves a serious erosion of the appropriateness and validity of this characterization.

What about the Asian end of the Portuguese trading operations as an element in the redistributive potential of these operations? It is indeed true that the Estado da India's attempt at monopolizing the spice trade was quite unambiguous and called for a total exclusion of Asian shipping from the Persian Gulf and the Red Sea. But the financial priorities and compulsions of the Estado soon made it relent and subject Asian shipping only to the requirement of obtaining a *cartaz* involving a small additional cost. The procurement of pepper and the attendant *cartaz* system was, however, only a part – and an increasingly smaller one at that – of the total Portuguese trading activity in the Indian Ocean. In respect of the bulk of the remainder of the trading activity carried on by the Portuguese either on an official or on a private basis, there was no component of a redistributive enterprise whatsoever. The brief phase of the Crown involvement in intra-Asian trade was followed from the second half of the sixteenth century onward by a fairly intensive participation in this trade by private Portuguese traders, many of whom were at the same time employees of the Estado. Besides investing in the Carreira da India, the New Christian merchants of Goa also participated in intra-Asian trade. Indeed, the profits from intra-Asian trade financed a good part of the cargo that these merchants put on the *carreira* ships at Goa for Lisbon on their private account. There was nothing redistributive about this trade.

THE SEVENTEENTH CENTURY

The seventeenth century was marked by a fundamental change in the character of the Euro-Asian commercial encounter. The 'Asian trade revolution' of the early seventeenth century, however, consisted only to a certain extent in the Portuguese 'redistributive enterprise' giving way to the pursuit by the Dutch and the English companies of rational and productivity-maximizing commercial policies. From the vantage point of India, the 'revolution' consisted even more in the extension of the Europeans' trading links to all major segments of coastal India, an enormous increase in the volume and value of their trade in the subcontinent in the course of the century, its diversification to include a whole range of new trade goods for the European and various Asian markets and, perhaps most important of all, the manner in which the procurement of goods for trade was organized.

While the Portuguese official presence in India was confined basically to the southwest coast of the subcontinent, the Dutch and the English soon extended their respective trading networks to include the Coromandel coast, Bengal and Gujarat. Their presence in these areas was essentially coastal, but trading stations were also established at places in the interior, including places such as Ahmedabad in Gujarat and Agra in the heartland of the Mughal empire. In the case of the Dutch East India Company, over the greater part of the century the importance of the Indian trade was derived chiefly from its role in the Company's intra-Asian trade. Textiles from Coromandel and Gujarat were indispensable for the procurement of pepper and other spices in the Indonesian archipelago, while raw silk from Bengal was the principal item exported to Japan. Bengal opium also figured prominently in the exports to the archipelago. The century was also characterized by a substantial expansion in the value of the Company's Asian imports into Europe. Thus from a modest figure of under f.3 million over the three-year period 1619–21, the imports had gone up to f.15 million during 1698–1700. The composition of these imports had also changed dramatically over this period with pepper and other spices, which had accounted for as much as 74 per cent of the total at the beginning of the period, accounting for no more than 23 per cent at its end. The share of textiles and raw silk, on the other hand, had gone up over the same period from 16 per cent to as much as 55 per cent. Since Bengal was by far the largest Asian supplier of these two items, it should come as no surprise that goods procured in this region accounted for as much as 40 per cent of the total Asian cargo imported by the Dutch and the English East India companies into Europe at the turn of the eighteenth century. The English East India Company did not participate in intra-Asian trade, but the value of its imports into Europe had risen at a rate even faster than that in the case of the

Dutch, so that at the end of the century, with its three-year total of $f.13.79$ million, it had nearly caught up with the VOC. Goods procured in India accounted for as much as 95 per cent of its total imports into Europe at this time. The Company allowed its employees a small amount of trade on their private account on the return voyages from India. In addition, trade in certain items, including diamonds, was outside the Company's monopoly leading to a fair amount of trade in these precious stones on private account. Indeed, many of the Company's senior employees actively engaged in intra-Asian or 'country' trade on their private account with the Company's permission, used their intermediary role in the diamond trade as commissioners to raise the necessary capital resources for investment in this trade.

Considerably more important in its implications than the significant expansion in the value and the volume of trade from India carried on by the northern European trading companies and the private European traders was the manner in which the procurement of goods for this trade was organized in contrast to the pepper trade of the Portuguese Estado in the sixteenth and the early part of the seventeenth centuries. The pepper monopsony, involving the payment of a price substantially lower than would otherwise have obtained in the market, that the Estado was able to extract from the rulers in Malabar, represented a new and sinister form of coercion that the indigenous producers of and merchants dealing in this spice were up against. The rapid deterioration in the relationship between the Estado and the local merchants first at Calicut and then at other places on the Malabar coast was, therefore, not surprising. The only saving grace in the situation was the near impossibility, given the terrain of the region, of enforcing the pepper monopsony in any effective sense. The procurement by the New Christian and other private Portuguese merchants of textiles and other goods in Malabar and elsewhere in India for both intra-Asian and Euro-Asian trade, which became quantitatively significant from the last quarter of the sixteenth century onward, was, of course, outside the monopsony framework.

The Dutch East India Company helped the raja of Cochin get rid of the Portuguese in 1663. In return, the raja was obliged to make monopoly privileges with regard to the purchase of pepper and the sale of opium available to the VOC, which left the situation on the ground largely unchanged from the Portuguese period. But Malabar was an exception and must be regarded as such. In the rest of the

Indian subcontinent, none of the European corporate enterprises at work had access to any kind of coercive authority over the producers and merchants with whom they did business. They were allowed complete freedom of trade and had full access to the use of various elements of a rather efficient economic infrastructure characterizing the commercial and the monetary sectors of the Indian economy of the period. But when it came to dealing with the producers and the merchants supplying the export goods, the corporate enterprises (and the private European traders) were just another group operating in the market. The completely market-determined relationship between the Europeans and the Indian artisanal and intermediary merchant groups is one of the principal distinguishing characteristic features of the seventeenth and the first half of the eighteenth century. The period around the turn of the eighteenth century witnessed a sharply widening gap between the rate of growth of the Europeans' demand for Indian goods such as textiles and raw silk and the rate of growth of their supply, increasingly turning the market into a sellers' market.

The political counterpart of the absence of coercion in the market-place was the nature of the relationship between the European corporate enterprises and the Indian ruling authorities. The relationship of domination between the Dutch and the raja of Cochin was an exception: the norm was for this relationship to be generally positive, free of coercion and businesslike, based on a perception of mutual advantage. In the event of the emergence of areas of disagreement, both sides generally took steps to ensure that the conflict did not escalate beyond a certain point. At work was indeed a rather finely tuned balance between the Europeans' unquestioned armed superiority on the sea as against their almost total vulnerability on land for a long time. The latter situation was sought to be partially remedied by the construction of fortified settlements which often became the core around which European-dominated coastal cities grew up. The Indian ruling authorities permitted the construction of such fortified settlements little realizing the inherent danger such a policy entailed for their own survival till it was too late to do anything about it.

THE EIGHTEENTH CENTURY

The death of the Mughal emperor Aurangzeb in 1707 was the symbolic beginning of the process of the collapse of the centralized

Mughal empire, the rise of the so-called successor states in provinces such as Awadh, Hyderabad and Bengal, and eventually the takeover of large parts of the country by the English East India Company, beginning with Bengal, where it was officially recognized by the Mughal emperor as the *diwan* of the province in 1765. Aurangzeb was followed in quick succession by Bahadur Shah (1707–12), Jahandar Shah (1712–13), Farrukhsiyar (1713–19) and Muhammad Shah (1719–48). The imperial fabric was subjected to serious strain during the early part of the century marked by disaffection of the Rajputs, growing militancy among the Sikhs and Jats in the north, and continuing Maratha insurgency in the south. Weakened central authority encouraged governors in several provinces to establish near-autonomous regional states only paying lip-service to the emperor's authority. The financial bankruptcy of the central government – dramatized by episodes such as Jahandar Shah's own troops remaining unpaid from the time of his accession – was further accentuated by the increasing irregularity and default in the receipt of the imperial government's share in the land revenues due from the newly emerging successor states.

The rapid deterioration in the state of law and order seriously affected the flows of long distance overland trade within the empire. An important route that suffered particular damage was the one that connected the heartland of the empire to Gujarat. Caravans organized by private merchants, even though protected by hired guards, could no longer travel safely from Agra to Surat. In view of the problems faced in the procurement and the transportation of textiles and Bayana indigo from Agra to Surat, the VOC was obliged to close its factory at Agra in 1716. The cost of the bills of exchange between these two cities, which ordinarily used to be no more than 1 to 2 per cent, now shot up to as much as 12 per cent. In Surat, the imperial mint was shut down for several years and numerous dealers in money were reported to have gone bankrupt.[2]

The nature and the extent of the dislocation described above should, however, be kept in perspective and care taken that its negative implications for the overall standard of economic performance are not overstated. Research done over the past two decades or so suggests the

[2] Ashin Das Gupta, *Indian Merchants and the Decline of Surat, 1700–1750*, Wiesbaden, 1979, p. 142; John F. Richards, *The Mughal Empire*, vol. 1.5 in the *New Cambridge History of India* series, Cambridge, 1993, pp. 278–9.

strong possibility of various sectors in the Indian economy continuing to perform well during the course of the century. In the words of Burton Stein, scholars maintaining this position

agree that the rural economy over most of the 18th century India enjoyed substantial, if uneven, growth notwithstanding both the destructive wars culminating in those which won the subcontinent for the British, and the supposed political disorder in many areas. It is claimed that new, smaller states with efficient tax-gathering procedures replaced the Mughal military imperial order, that market networks proliferated and became to a degree interlinked, that a more prosperous agriculture came into being with increased commodity production as a result of rural investments by the revenue farmers of the time, that all of this was buoyed up by an ever-increasing level of international trade in which Indian artisans, merchants and especially bankers played key and lucrative roles, and that this phase of political economy obtained until the first quarter of the 19th century.[3]

From the perspective of the European trading companies, the most crucial developments were those taking place in Bengal, by far the most important of the Asian trading regions, supplying at the turn of the eighteenth century as much as 40 per cent of the total Asian cargo that the Dutch and the English East India companies imported into Europe each year. It is vitally important to note that as far as this province was concerned, the situation over the greater part of the eighteenth century was not materially different from that in the heyday of the Mughal empire in the seventeenth. The man mainly responsible for this in the early part of the century was Murshid Quli Khan, who dominated the history of the province between 1701, when he was sent there as the imperial *diwan* with a specific brief to try and increase the flow of revenues due to the imperial government from the province, and his death in 1727. By scrupulously ensuring that the annual flow of the *khalisa* revenues to Delhi not only continued uninterrupted but in fact registered an increase over time, Murshid Quli succeeded in creating a mutually beneficial working partnership with the imperial government. In the domain of political stability and the state of law and order, the first four decades of the eighteenth century were certainly no worse than had been the case during the seventeenth. It is true that a certain amount of dislocation was caused in the early 1740s as a result of the Maratha incursions into the province. But that was essentially a temporary phase and things were

---

[3] Burton Stein, 'A decade of historical efflorescence', *South Asia Research*, vol. 10 (2), November 1990, pp. 132–3.

by and large back to normal by the end of the decade. In brief, the picture of political confusion and unrest usually associated with the declining power of the Mughals in the first half of the eighteenth century is certainly not applicable to Bengal. In fact, the growing weakness of the centre, particularly in the wake of Nadir Shah's invasion during 1739–43, further strengthened regional polities, and successor states such as Bengal, Hyderabad and Awadh stopped paying their customary tribute to Delhi on a regular basis making larger resources available for internal deployment. The Europeans' trade from Bengal also registered a significant increase during the period. Thus of the rising total Dutch exports from Asia to Europe amounting to ƒ.19.24 million over the triennium 1738–40 as against ƒ.15 million during 1698–1700, the share of goods procured in the province had gone up to 47 per cent as against 41 per cent at the turn of the century. The corresponding figures in the case of the English East India Company were ƒ.23 million as against ƒ.13.79 million with the share of Bengal goods being at the all-time peak of 66 per cent during 1738–40 as against 42 per cent during 1698–1700.

The second half of the eighteenth century witnessed a fundamental alteration in the nature of the Indo-European encounter. The takeover of Bengal by the English East India Company following the battle of Plassey in 1757 marked the inauguration of the colonial phase in this encounter. The nawab's army, though ten times the size of Clive's 2,000 sepoys and 900 Europeans, was routed providing the English Company its first foothold in the subcontinent. The formal acquisition of *diwani* rights in 1765 provided it with access to the province's revenues. These were used in part to strengthen further the Company's military strength. By 1782, the Company was able to maintain 115,000 men in India (90 per cent of them sepoys) enabling it to intervene effectively in other parts of the subcontinent such as the Deccan.

A part of the surplus from the Bengal revenues was also used to finance the procurement of goods for export to Europe. To that extent, these exports now became 'unrequited' involving a drain of resources from the country – a theme that has legitimately attracted a great deal of attention in the Indian nationalist historical writings of the nineteenth century. The bulk of the English Company exports during this period, however, were financed by rupee receipts obtained by the Company locally against bills of exchange issued to English and other European private traders payable in London and other European capitals enabling these traders to transmit their Indian earnings home. Between the Bengal surplus revenues and the rupee receipts obtained against the bills of exchange, the Company found itself in a position to suspend altogether the import of treasure from home for nearly a quarter of a century. It was only in 1784 that these imports were resumed partly for investment in the procurement of export goods and partly to strengthen further the Company's military presence – a necessary prelude to the conquest of other parts of the subcontinent.

The altered situation held important consequences for the economy of the province. For one thing, the substantial reduction in the silver imports would seem to have been an important element behind the shortage of money that several contemporaries noted and commented upon. More importantly, there was a marked deterioration in the relative share in the total value of the output produced as far as the Bengali artisanal and the mercantile groups engaged in business with the English East India Company were concerned. This was a necessary corollary of the replacement of a market-determined relationship between the Company and these groups until about 1760 by a relationship marked by a clear-cut domination by the Company in the decades that followed. On the basis of its political muscle power, the Company now enforced unilaterally determined below-market terms on the producers of and the dealers in commodities such as textiles and opium. The blatant manner in which this was done, robbing in the process the producers and the merchants of a good part of what was legitimately due to them, would, in turn, have introduced distortions in the incentive structure in the domain of manufacturing and other production in the province. This, combined with the official Company and the unofficial private English traders' monopolies in commodities such as salt and opium, is likely to have brought about a certain amount of decline in the value of the total output produced in the province, though in the present state of our knowledge it is not possible to indicate even broadly the extent of this decline.

There is a distinct possibility, however, that this decline was not altogether massive or irreversible and that the structure of both agricultural and non-agricultural production in the province continued to be marked by a reasonable degree of vitality and capacity to deliver. An important, though by no means conclusive, index suggesting this scenario is the continuing growth of both the Euro-Asian and the intra-Asian trade from the province. It is true that, under the pressure of the increasingly monopsonistic policies adopted by the English Company, the trade of the rival companies operating in the region was on the decline. Thus in the case of the VOC, although the overall value of its Asian exports to Europe between the trienniums of 1738–40 and 1778–80 went up from f.19 million to f.21 million, the average annual value of the Company's exports from Bengal came down from the all-time peak of f.5 million in 1751–2 to a measly f.1.32 million in 1784–5. But such a decline was much more than made up for by the English Company's own total exports to Europe going up from f.23 million in 1738–40 to f.25 million in 1758–60 and to an almost incredible figure of f.69 million in 1777–9 giving us an annual average figure of f.23 million. Bengal accounted for as much as half of this value. In intra-Asian trade, the decline in the Dutch Company exports as well as in those by the Indian merchants engaged in this trade was similarly much more than made up for by the spectacular rise in the English private merchants' trade with China.

The Indo-European encounter over the three-hundred-year period between 1500 and 1800 was a historical process with extremely significant and wide-ranging implications for both sides. Within the overall rubric of the desire to procure Indian goods, the precise motivation and mechanism behind the arrival of each of the European trading groups into the subcontinent was different. The Portuguese came basically for pepper, and throughout the sixteenth and the early part of the seventeenth century India provided an overwhelming bulk of the total pepper supplies reaching Lisbon. The Bay of Bengal figured prominently in the intra-Asian trading network of the Estado da India, and later also in the trading operations of the private Portuguese merchants both within Asia as well as between Asia and Europe. The Dutch East India Company, on the other hand, procured its pepper and other spices in the Indonesian archipelago and came to India looking mainly for the relatively inexpensive mass-consumption cotton textiles produced on the Coromandel coast, and to a smaller extent in Gujarat, with a view to using them as a medium of exchange to procure the Indonesian spices. This became the first link in a chain that eventually developed into a massive involvement in intra-Asian trade with other Indian commodities such as Bengal raw silk and opium also playing a critical role in the successful functioning of the complex network. In the last quarter of the seventeenth century, the fashion revolution in Europe put Indian textiles and raw silk at the head of the imports from Asia catapulting India into the position of being by far the most important supplier of goods for Europe. The key role of India in the Dutch East India Company's overall framework of trade continued well into the early years of the second half of the eighteenth century when the English East India Company, on the strength of its newly acquired special status in Bengal, overwhelmed the Dutch and forced them into reducing the scale of their operations in the subcontinent substantially. The French were latecomers on the scene having set up an East India Company only in 1664. In fact, it was only from the beginning of the second quarter of the eighteenth century onward that the French trade in the subcontinent became quantitatively significant. They were engaged in an almost continuous conflict with the English in south India, but like the Dutch were eventually unable to withstand the English hostility.

The English involvement in the trade of the subcontinent became significant only from the second quarter of the seventeenth century, after they had found it impossible to carry on profitable trade in the Indonesian archipelago due in part to the opposition by the Dutch. From this point on, India figured even more prominently in the total English exports to Europe than was the case with the Dutch. With the English Company's takeover of Bengal in the second half of the eighteenth century, India assumed an altogether new role for Britain. Bengal revenues provided an indirect subsidy to the British exchequer and the enormous opportunities – legal and clandestine – for private gain now available to the Company servants in their personal capacity created a whole new class of the new-rich 'nabobs' returning to England with fortunes unheard of before. It is, however, highly unlikely that these private fortunes constituted an element of any importance in the financing of the Industrial Revolution in Britain which was then getting under way.

As far as India was concerned, the substantial amount of trade carried on from her ports by the Europeans, both with Europe as well as with other parts of Asia, particularly from the early part of the seventeenth century onward, served to strengthen her status considerably as a premier trading and manufacturing nation in Asia. At the turn of the eighteenth century, India was probably the largest and the most cost-competitive textile-manufacturing country in the world. An increase in trade being beneficial for a country is an axiom: in India's case the 'bullion for goods' character of the European trade considerably enhanced its positive implications and indeed turned it into an important instrument of growth in the Indian economy. The gold and silver the Europeans imported from Europe and other Asian countries such as Japan led to a substantial increase in the supply of money in the country. The growing level of monetization in the economy, in turn, facilitated reform measures such as the growing conversion of the land revenue demand from kind into cash, which led to a further increase in market exchange and trade. The growing availability of precious metals in the system also helped the rise of banking firms, and generally became an important factor in facilitating the expansion of the Mughal empire.

By not involving a decline in the domestic output of import-competing goods, the 'bullion for goods' character of the European trade also implied that the positive implications of the growth in trade for the level of income, output and employment in the economy were considerably more substantial than would have been the case if this trade had been of the ordinary 'goods for goods' variety. In the agricultural sector, there was an increase in the acreage under cultivation, particularly in the case of high-value commercial crops such as cotton and opium. The increase in output and employment in the manufacturing sector was clearly on a scale that was not entirely insignificant. Job opportunities in several segments of the services sector such as that providing brokerage services would also have gone up. Besides, the fact that, on average, the rate of growth of the European demand for Indian goods such as textiles and raw silk was greater than the rate of growth of their supply, increasingly turned the market into a sellers' market. The fact that this involved not only an increase in the bargaining strength of the intermediary merchants vis-à-vis the Europeans but also a continuous improvement in the bargaining strength of the weavers vis-à-vis the intermediary merchants, implied that the benefits of the continuing rise in the level of output, income and employment were not confined to the intermediary groups but percolated all the way down to the weavers and the other constituents of the producing groups.

During the early colonial phase in the post-1760 period, this situation continued unaltered in many respects but underwent major modification in others. The composition of the trade with Europe remained unchanged, and except for the 'unrequited' part of the exports financed through the investment of the Bengal surplus revenues, the 'bullion for goods' character of the trade continued to be valid, though in a more restrictive and limited way. From the point of view of the English Company, the suspension of silver imports for a while and the financing of the exports mainly through the bills of exchange only meant that the payment in silver was now made in Europe rather than in India. But of course, this silver never reached India. Also, in so far as the relationship between the English East India Company on the one hand and the Indian intermediary merchants and producers on the other was no longer governed by the market but was dictated by the Company, a good part of the legitimate share of the producers and the merchants in the total output was now appropriated by the Company. As the Industrial Revolution began to mature in Britain, more fundamental changes followed. From the second quarter of the nineteenth century onward, India began to lose the European market for its textiles. Later in the century, the so-called colonial pattern of trade came into operation in a full-fledged manner and India was converted into an important market for textiles manufactured in Manchester and Lancashire.

BIBLIOGRAPHIC ESSAY

General studies

A useful starting point for the necessary background material would be the *Cambridge Economic History of India*, vol. I (Cambridge, 1982) edited by T. Raychaudhuri and Irfan Habib. Part I of vol. II (Cambridge, 1983) edited by Dharma Kumar would also be found useful. A concise history of Mughal India is now available in John Richards' *The Mughal Empire* (Cambridge, 1993) in the *New Cambridge History of India* series. Richards' earlier *Mughal Administration in Golconda* (Oxford, 1975) is the standard work on the subject. Irfan Habib's *The Agrarian System of Mughal India* (Bombay, 1963), with its detailed discussion of the fiscal structure of the empire, continues to be indispensable. Also see Shireen Moosvi, *The Economy of the Mughal Empire c. 1595* (Delhi, 1987). For south India, Burton Stein's *Vijayanagara* (Cambridge, 1989) in the *New Cambridge History of India* series may be used profitably. Frank Perlin's 'Proto-industrialization and pre-colonial South Asia', *Past and Present*, No. 98 (1983), is valuable in as much as it raises a number of important issues.

The nature of economic change in the subcontinent during the eighteenth century consequent upon the collapse of the Mughal empire has been the subject of a lively debate over the past two decades or so. Many of the issues raised in that debate are of direct interest for our field of enquiry. Among the more important contributions which make a case for a positive interpretation of the developments in the eighteenth century are C.A. Bayly's *Rulers, Townsmen and Bazaars, North Indian Society in the Age of British Expansion 1770–1870* (Cambridge, 1983) and *Indian Society and the Making of the British Empire* (Cambridge, 1988) in the *New Cambridge History of India* series. Muzaffar Alam's *The Crisis of Empire in Mughal North India, Awadh and the Punjab, 1707–48* (Delhi, 1986) and Chetan Singh, 'Centre and periphery in the Mughal state: the case of seventeenth century Panjab', *Modern Asian Studies*, vol. 22 (1988) are in the same broad genre. D.A. Washbrook's 'Progress and problems: South Asian economic and social history c. 1720–1860', *Modern Asian Studies*, vol. 22 (1988) and Burton Stein's 'A decade of historical efflorescence', *South Asia Research*, vol. 10 (1990) and 'Eighteenth century India: another view', *Studies in History*, vol. 5 (1989) are among the other important contributions subscribing to a non-negative view of the eighteenth century. This view has been contested by scholars such as M. Athar Ali in several papers including 'Recent theories of eighteenth century India', *Indian Historical Review*, vol. 13 (1986–7) and

'The Mughal polity – a critique of revisionist approaches', *Modern Asian Studies*, vol. 27 (1993).

Important studies relating to eighteenth-century Bengal include N.K. Sinha, *The Economic History of Bengal From Plassey to the Permanent Settlement* (Calcutta, 1956) and P.J. Marshall, *Bengal, The British Bridgehead: Eastern India 1740–1828* (Cambridge, 1987) in the *New Cambridge History of India* series. Abdul Karim's *Murshid Quli Khan and His Times* (Dhaka, 1963) and K.K. Datta's *Alivardi and His Times* (Calcutta, 1963) continue to be important. Two papers by Philip B. Calkins, 'The formation of a regionally oriented ruling group in Bengal 1700–40', *Journal of Asian Studies*, vol. 22 (1970) and 'The role of Murshidabad as a regional and sub-regional center in Bengal', in R.L. Park (ed.), *Urban Bengal* (East Lansing, Michigan, 1969) may also be used profitably. Zahiruddin Malik's *Reign of Muhammad Shah 1719–48* (Delhi, 1977) contains a useful discussion of Bengal's relations with the Mughal centre. Benoy Chowdhury's *Growth of Commercial Agriculture in Bengal (1757–1900)*, vol. 1 (Calcutta, 1964) continues to be indispensable.

Studies relating to the field

Over the past two decades or so, there has been a fair amount of work in our field. This is partly in the form of collections of essays published as proceedings of international seminars, as *festschrift* volumes, and as volumes on selected themes to which groups of scholars were invited to contribute. L. Blussé and F.S. Gaastra (ed.), *Companies and Trade, Essays on Overseas Trading Companies during the Ancien Regime* (The Hague, 1981) and J.R. Bruijn and F.S. Gaastra (ed.), *Ships, Sailors and Spices, East India Companies and their Shipping in the 16th, 17th and 18th Centuries* (Amsterdam, 1993) are mainly concerned with the European end of the Companies' operations, though the former volume also contains some essays dealing with Asia. The two volumes edited by James D. Tracy, *The Rise of Merchant Empires, Long-distance Trade in the Early Modern World 1350–1750* (Cambridge, 1990) and *The Political Economy of Merchant Empires, State Power and World Trade 1350–1750* (Cambridge, 1991) contain several major pieces in our area. Among the collections of essays specifically dealing with trade in the Indian Ocean and the South China Sea, one might note first of all, Ashin Das Gupta and M.N. Pearson (ed.), *India and the Indian Ocean, 1500–1800* (Calcutta, 1987) which might almost be regarded as a textbook on the subject. Other major collections in the field include Blair B. Kling and M.N. Pearson (ed.), *The Age of Partnership, Europeans in Asia before Dominion* (Honolulu, 1979), Roderich Ptak and Dietmar Rothermund (ed.), *Emporia, Commodities and Entrepreneurs in Asian Maritime Trade (1400–1750)* (Stuttgart, 1991) and Jorge Manuel Flores (ed.), *The Asian Seas 1500–1800, Local Societies, European Expansion and the Portuguese, Revista de Cultura*, vols. 13/14 (1991), which contains papers on trading entities other than the Portuguese as well. Finally, one might note the two volumes edited by K.S. Mathew, *Studies in Maritime History (Pondicherry, 1990) and Mariners, Merchants and Oceans, Studies in Maritime History* (Delhi, 1995).

The Variorum Collected Studies Series published by Ashgate Publishing Ltd, Aldershot, Hampshire, UK, where papers published by an individual scholar around a particular theme are reprinted in a volume, is well known to researchers in our field mainly through the four volumes of essays by C.R. Boxer, *From Lisbon to Goa, 1500–1750, Studies in Portuguese Maritime Enterprise* (1984), *Portuguese Conquest and Commerce in Southern Asia, 1500–1750* (1985), *Portuguese Merchants and Missionaries in Feudal Japan, 1543–1640* (1986) and *Dutch Merchants and Mariners in Asia, 1602–1795* (1988). Another early volume was Geneviève Bouchon, *L'Asie du sud à l'époque des grandes découvertes* (1987). The coverage of the series has now been substantially expanded and the volumes published over the past few years include P.J. Marshall, *Trade and Conquest, Studies on the Rise of British Dominance in India* (1993), John F. Richards, *Power, Administration and Finance in Mughal India* (1993), Om Prakash, *Precious Metals and Commerce, The Dutch East India Company in the Indian Ocean Trade* (1994), Ashin Das Gupta, *Merchants of Maritime India, 1500–1800* (1994), S. Arasaratnam, *Maritime Trade, Society and European Influence in Southern Asia, 1600–1800* (1995), G.V. Scammell, *Ships, Oceans and Empires, Studies in European Maritime and Colonial History 1400–1750* (1995), S. Arasaratnam, *Ceylon and the Dutch, 1600–1800, External Influences and Internal Change in Early Modern Sri Lanka* (1996) and Dennis O. Flynn, *World Silver and Monetary History in the 16th and 17th Centuries* (1996). The publishers of the Variorum series have recently also launched a thirty-volume reprint series, *An Expanding World, The European Impact on World History 1450–1800* under the general editorship of A.J.R. Russell-Wood. Volumes in our area already published include Anthony Disney (ed.), *Historiography of Europeans in Africa and Asia* (No. 4), Sanjay Subrahmanyam (ed.), *Merchant Networks in the Early Modern World (1450–1800)* (No. 8), Om Prakash (ed.), *European Commercial Expansion in Early Modern Asia* (No. 10), M.N. Pearson (ed.), *Spices in the Indian Ocean World* (No. 11) and Pieter Emmer and Femme Gaastra (ed.), *The Organization of Interoceanic Trade in European Expansion, 1450–1800* (No. 13).

Among the major general works concerned with our field, one might begin with Fernand Braudel's *The Mediterranean and the Mediterranean World in the Age of Philip II* (2 vols., second edition, London, 1981). K.N. Chaudhuri's *Trade and Civilization in the Indian Ocean, An Ecnomic History from the Rise of Islam to 1750* (Cambridge, 1985) and *Asia Before Europe: Economy and Civilization of the Indian Ocean from the Rise of Islam to 1750* (Cambridge, 1990) are very much in the Braudilian tradition. Parts of Donald F. Lach's *Asia in the Making of Europe* (3 vols. in 9 books, vol. III with Edwin J. van Kley, Chicago, 1965–93) also contain useful material. More immediately relevant is Holden Furber's masterly *Rival Empires of Trade in the Orient, 1600–1800* (Minneapolis and Oxford, 1976). A slim volume by Dietmar Rothermund, *Asian Trade and European Expansion in the Age of*

Mercantilism (Delhi, 1981) may also be used with profit. Jacob van Leur's classic *Indonesian Trade and Society: Essays in Asian Social and Economic History* (The Hague, 1955) and M.A.P. Meilink–Roelofsz. *Asian Trade and European Influence in the Indonesian Archipelago between 1500 and about 1630* (The Hague, 1962) are valuable for their theoretical ideas, and in the case of the latter also for its detailed empirical content.

The Portuguese

There is a great deal of primary source material pertaining to the Portuguese which is available in printed form. This material has been described in some detail in a bibliographical essay in the recent George D. Winius (ed.), *Portugal, the Pathfinder: Journeys from the Medieval towards the Modern World 1300–ca.1600* (Madison, 1995). The twenty essays in this volume deal with the geographical explorations of the Portuguese as well as with their commercial and diplomatic activities. Many of the essays deal with Asia. Another useful collection of essays dealing exclusively with Asia is Roderich Ptak (ed.), *Portuguese Asia: Aspects in History and Economic History (Sixteenth and Seventeenth Centuries)* (Stuttgart, 1987). The Proceedings of the International Seminar on Indo-Portuguese History usually held every two years alternately in India and Portugal also contain important contributions in this area. Eight seminars have been organized in the series so far and the published Proceedings include John Correia-Afonso (ed.), *Indo-Portuguese History: Sources and Problems* (Bombay, 1981), Teotonio R. de Souza (ed.) *Indo-Portuguese History: Old Issues, New Questions* (Delhi, 1985), Artur Teodoro de Matos and Luís Filipe F. R. Thomaz (ed.), *As Relações entre a Índia Portugesa a Ásia Do Sueste eo Extremo Oriente* (Macau/Lisbon, 1993) and *Portuguese India and its Northern Province, Mare Liberum* (No. 9, July 1995).

Charles Boxer's *The Portuguese Seaborne Empire, 1415–1825* (London, 1969) continues to be valuable as an entry point into the field. Bailey W. Diffie and George D. Winius, *Foundations of the Portuguese Empire 1415–1580* (Minneapolis, 1977) is strong in the domain of political, military and administrative history of the Portuguese expansion. Another major work in the field, especially useful for economic history, is V. Magalhães-Godinho, *Os Descobrimentos e a Economia Mundial* (3 vols., Lisbon, 1981–4). Niels Steensgaard's *The Asian Trade Revolution of the Seventeenth Century, The East India Companies and the Decline of Caravan Trade* (Chicago, 1974) is also an important work. Valuable studies pertaining to the operations of the Portuguese in Asia include Sanjay Subrahmanyam, *The Portuguese Empire in Asia 1500–1700, A Political and Economic History* (London, 1993) and *Improvising Empire: Portuguese Trade and Settlement in the Bay of Bengal 1500–1700* (Delhi, 1990), M.N. Pearson, *The Portuguese in India* in the *New Cambridge History of India* series (Cambridge, 1987), *Coastal Western India, Studies from the Portuguese Records* (Delhi, 1981) and *Merchants and Rulers in Gujarat: the Response to the Portuguese in the Sixteenth Century* (Berkeley, 1976), Geneviève Bouchon, *Regent of the Sea, Cannanore's Response to*

Portuguese Expansion, 1507–1528 (Delhi, 1988) and George B. Souza, *The Survival of Empire: Portuguese Trade and Society in China and South China Sea, 1630–1754* (Cambridge, 1986).

The literature on the Portuguese Euro-Asian pepper trade includes Magalhães-Godinho's, *Os Descobrimentos e a Economia Mundial*, Geneviève Bouchon's 'L'Inventaire de la Cargaison rapportée de l'Inde en 1505', *Mare Luso Indicum*, vol. 3 (1976) and *Navires et cargaisons retour de l'Inde en 1518* (Paris, 1977), and Hermann Kellenbenz, 'Autour de 1600: le commerce du poivre de Fugger et le marché international du poivre', *Annales, ESC*, vol. 11 (1956). An excellent study dealing with the pepper trade in the early part of the seventeenth century is A.R. Disney, *Twilight of the Pepper Empire, Portuguese Trade in Southwest India in the Early Seventeenth Century* (Cambridge, Mass. and London, 1978). The question of the relative amount of pepper shipments via the Cape as against those via the water-cum-land route is covered in two papers by Frederic C. Lane, 'Venetian shipping during the commercial revolution', and 'The Mediterranean spice trade, further evidence on its revival in the sixteenth century', published in the *American Historical Review*, vol. 38 (1933) and vol. 45 (1940) respectively, in a paper by C.H.H. Wake, 'The changing pattern of Europe's pepper and spice imports, ca 1400–1700', *Journal of European Economic History*, vol. 8 (1979), and in C.R. Boxer's 'A note on Portuguese reactions to the revival of the Red Sea spice trade and the rise of Atjeh, 1540–1600', *Journal of Southeast Asian History*, vol. 10 (1969). In his 'Navigation between Portugal and Asia in the sixteenth and seventeenth centuries' in E.J. van Kley and C.K. Pullapilly (ed.), *Asia and the West: Encounters and Exchanges from the Age of Explorations* (Notre Dame, 1986), T. Bentley Duncan provides a new series of shipping movements between Portugal and Asia. In the recent *Portuguese Trade in Asia under the Habsburgs, 1580–1640* (Baltimore and London, 1993), James C. Boyajian provides an almost revolutionary revision of current orthodoxy in the matter of the relative role of the private Portuguese traders in the Euro-Asian carreira trade. Boyajian's book also deals extensively with the Asian end of the Portuguese enterprise. Regional studies in that domain include Sanjay Subrahmanyam, *The Political Economy of Commerce, Southern India 1500–1650* (Cambridge, 1990), Jan Kieniewicz, 'The Portuguese factory and the trade in pepper in Malabar during the sixteenth century', *Indian Economic and Social History Review*, vol. 6 (1969), and K.S. Mathew, *Portuguese Trade in India in the Sixteenth Century* (Delhi, 1983). An important paper dealing with the private Portuguese merchants' intra-Asian trading operations is Luís Filipe F.R. Thomaz, 'Les Portugais dans les mers de l'Archipel au XVIe siècle', *Archipel*, vol. 18 (1979).

The Dutch

The manuscript and printed sources in respect of the Dutch East India Company are described in an appendix and the bibliography of Om Prakash, *The Dutch East India Company and the Economy of Bengal, 1630–1720*

(Princeton, 1985). His 'Dutch source material on Indian maritime history in the early modern period: an evaluation', *Indian Historical Review*, vol. 8 (1981–2) can be consulted usefully as an entry point into the Dutch archives. A small volume of the manuscript sources is available in English translation and annotation in Om Prakash, *The Dutch Factories in India, 1617–1623, A Collection of Dutch East India Company Documents Pertaining to India* (Delhi, 1984).

As in the case of the Portuguese, C.R. Boxer's general survey of the Dutch expansion, *The Dutch Seaborne Empire* (London, 1965) is a useful introductory volume. The organizational structure of the Dutch East India Company at the European end is discussed in F.S. Gaastra, *Bewind en Beleid by the VOC 1672–1702* (Zutphen, 1989). The best general account of the Company is also by Gaastra, *De Geschiedenis van de VOC* (Zutphen, 1991). The financial accounting of the Company is described in detail in J.P. de Korte, *De Jaarlykse Financiele Verantwoording in de Verenigde Oost-Indische Compagnie* (Leiden, 1984). Jonathan I. Israel's *Dutch Primacy in World Trade, 1585–1740* (Oxford, 1989) is a comprehensive survey of the rise of the Dutch as a commercial power from the closing decades of the sixteenth century onward. Niels Steensgaard in his 'The Dutch East India Company as an institutional innovation', in Maurice Aymard (ed.), *Dutch Capitalism and World Capitalism* (Cambridge, 1982) argues the case for a qualitative difference between the Portuguese enterprise and the Dutch East India Company. The Dutch Company's expansion into the Indonesian archipelago during the early decades of the seventeenth century is best analysed in the much-neglected *The Cradle of Colonialism* (New Haven, 1963) by George Masselman. Kristof Glamann's masterly *Dutch–Asiatic Trade 1620–1740* (Copenhagen/The Hague, 1958, reprint 1981) continues to be indispensable. Also extremely useful is the three-volume *Dutch–Asiatic Shipping in the 17th and 18th Centuries* (The Hague, 1979–87) by J.R. Bruijn, F.S. Gaastra and I. Schöffer. While the second and the third volumes contain a full listing respectively of the outward- and the homeward-bound ships operating on the account of the Company, the first volume contains useful details regarding the organizational structure and the shipping of the Company. A general survey of the Company's expansion into India is provided by George D. Winius and M.P.M. Vink, *The Merchant-Warrior Pacified, The VOC and its Changing Political Economy in India* (Delhi, 1991).

On the Dutch East India Company's trading operations in Asia, several useful studies are available in M.A.P. Meilink- Roelofsz. (ed.), *De VOC in Azie* (Bussum, 1976). Other studies on the Dutch in Asia include Om Prakash, 'Restrictive trade regimes: VOC and the Asian spice trade in the seventeenth century', in R. Ptak and Dietmar Rothermund (ed.), *Emporia, Commodities and Entrepreneurs in Asian Maritime Trade, c.1400–1750* (Stuttgart, 1991), and 'Trade in a culturally hostile environment: Europeans in the Japan trade, 1550–1700', in Jens Christian V. Johansen, Erling Ladewig Petersen and Henrik Stevnsborg (ed.), *Clashes of Culture, Essays in Honour of Niels Steensgaard* (Odense, 1992), and S. Arasaratnam 'Some notes on the

Dutch in Malacca and the Indo-Malayan trade', *Journal of Southeast Asian History*, vol. 10 (1969) and 'Dutch commercial policy in Ceylon and its effect on Indo-Ceylon trade, 1690–1750', *Indian Economic and Social History Review*, vol. 4 (1967).

For the Indian subcontinent, regional studies include, for Coromandel, T. Raychaudhuri, *Jan Company in Coromandel 1605–1690* (The Hague, 1962), S. Arasaratnam, *Merchants, Companies and Commerce on the Coromandel Coast, 1650–1740* (Delhi, 1986) and Sanjay Subrahmanyam, *The Political Economy of Commerce, Southern India, 1500–1650* (Cambridge, 1990). Unpublished PhD theses dealing with this region include Joseph J. Brennig, 'The textile trade of seventeenth century northern Coromandel: a study of a pre-modern Asian export industry' (University of Wisconsin, Madison, 1975) and Bhaswati Bhattacharya, 'The Dutch East India Company on the Coromandel coast' (Visva Bharati University, Santiniketan, 1993). Studies on Bengal include Om Prakash, *The Dutch East India Company and the Economy of Bengal, 1630–1720* (Princeton, 1985) and Frank Lequin, *Het Personnel van de Verenigde Oost-Indische Compagnie in Azie in de Achttiende Eeuw, meer in het byzonder in de Vestiging Bengalen* (2 vols., Leiden, 1982). As far as Gujarat and its north Indian hinterland is concerned, an important study is that by H.W. van Santen, *De Verenigde Oost-Indische Compagnie in Gujarat en Hindustan, 1620–1660* (Leiden, 1982). Ann Bos Radwan's *The Dutch in Western India, 1601–1632* (Calcutta, 1978) is rather thin. An unpublished doctoral dissertation is that by V.B. Gupta, 'The Dutch East India Company in Gujarat trade 1660–1700: a study of selected aspects' (Delhi School of Economics, University of Delhi, 1991). Finally, as far as the Malabar coast is concerned, the first work done on the region was *De Vestiging der Nederlanders ter Kuste Malabar* (The Hague, 1943) by M.A.P. Roelofsz. More recent is H.K. s' Jacob, *De Nederlanders in Kerala 1663–1701* (The Hague, 1976) which is a collection of the memoirs and the instructions left behind by the outgoing Dutch 'commandeurs' of the region. Ashin Das Gupta's *Malabar in Asian Trade, 1740–1800* (Cambridge, 1967) while dealing with the Dutch Company trade also goes into other issues such as the Indian merchants' trade from the region.

The English

The English Factories in India 1618–1669 (ed. W. Foster, 13 volumes, Oxford, 1906–27) and *The English Factories in India (New Series 1670–1684* ed. C. Fawcett, 4 volumes, Oxford, 1936–55) have been used extensively over the years by researchers working on the English East India Company. For a description of the manuscript and other printed sources in respect of the English Company, see the bibliography in K.N. Chaudhuri, *The Trading World of Asia and the English East India Company 1660–1760* (Cambridge, 1978) which is a definitive account of the trading operations of the Company in India. The earlier phase of the Company's trade in Asia is covered by Chaudhuri in his *The English East India Company: the Study of an Early*

Joint-Stock Company, 1600–1640 (London, 1965). The Company's trading operations in the Far East are described in D.K. Bassett, 'The trade of the English East India Company in the Far East, 1623–1684', *Journal of the Royal Asiatic Society of Great Britain and Ireland* (1960). Two useful papers dealing with Persia are by R.W. Ferrier, 'The trade between India and the Persian Gulf and the East India Company in the 17th century', *Bengal Past and Present*, No. 89 (1970) and 'The Armenians and the East India Company in Persia in the seventeenth and early eighteenth centuries', *Economic History Review*, vol. 26 (1973).

Specifically for the Indian subcontinent, in addition to K.N. Chaudhuri's *Trading World of Asia*, we have for the Coromandel coast the little-noticed *Economic Progress of the East India Company on the Coromandel Coast 1702–1746* (Nagpur, 1974) by R.N. Banerji, and the recent *Maritime Commerce and English Power, Southeast India 1750–1800* (Delhi, 1996) by S. Arasaratnam. Arasaratnam's earlier *Merchants, Companies and Commerce on the Coromandel Coast 1650–1740* (Delhi, 1986) also contains material on the English Company's activities on the coast. The two volumes by Sushil Chaudhury, *Trade and Commercial Organization in Bengal, 1650–1720* (Calcutta, 1975) and *From Prosperity to Decline, Eighteenth Century Bengal* (Delhi, 1995) deal, among other things, with the Company's trade in the region. Ashin Das Gupta's *Malabar in Asian Trade, 1740–1800* (Cambridge, 1967) and Sanjay Subrahmanyam's *The Political Economy of Commerce, Southern India, 1500–1650* (Cambridge, 1990) also contain material on the English Company on the Malabar coast.

There is also an extensive literature on the commercial activities of the private English traders engaged in the Indian Ocean trade. Holden Furber's pioneering *John Company at Work, A Study of European Expansion in India in the Late Eighteenth Century* (Cambridge, Mass., 1948) continues to be valuable. Ian Bruce Watson's *Foundation for Empire, English Private Trade in India 1659–1760* (Delhi, 1980) is a detailed account of the subject. P.J. Marshall's 'British private trade in the Indian Ocean before 1800', in Ashin Das Gupta and M.N. Pearson (ed.), *India and the Indian Ocean 1500–1800* (Calcutta, 1987) is of fundamental importance. The English private merchants' trade with southeast Asia is covered in S.D. Quaison, *English 'Country Trade' with the Philippines* (Quezon City, 1966) and D.K. Bassett, *British Trade and Policy in Indonesia and Malaysia in the late Eighteenth Century* (Zug, 1971). For an analysis of the China trade, see Michael Greenberg, *British Trade and the Opening of China 1800–1841* (Cambridge, 1951) and Tan Chung, 'The British–China–India trade triangle (1771–1840)', *Indian Economic and Social History Review*, vol. 11 (1974).

The private English trade between the Coromandel coast and southeast Asia is discussed by D.K. Bassett in an important paper 'British "country" trade and local trade networks in the Thai and the Malay states, c.1680–1770', *Modern Asian Studies*, vol. 23 (1989). 'English private trade on the Coromandel Coast, 1660–1690: diamonds and country-trade', *Indian Economic and Social History Review*, vol. 33 (1996) by Søren Mentz breaks new ground by emphasizing the contribution made to the total resource base of several of the leading English private traders by the remuneration earned by them in their capacity as commissioners for diamond merchants based in England. The private English traders' commercial activities in and from Bengal are discussed in great detail in P.J. Marshall, *East Indian Fortunes: The British in Bengal in the Eighteenth Century* (Oxford, 1976), 'Masters and banians in eighteenth century Calcutta', in Blair B. Kling and M.N. Pearson (ed.), *The Age of Partnership, Europeans in Asia before Dominion* (Honolulu, 1979), and 'Private British investment in eighteenth century Bengal', *Bengal Past and Present*, No. 86 (1967). Amales Tripathi's *Trade and Finance in the Bengal Presidency* (Calcutta, 1979) continues to be useful. For the English private merchants' involvement in the opium trade, see Om Prakash, 'Opium monopoly in India and Indonesia in the eighteenth century', *Indian Economic and Social History Review*, vol. 24 (1987). Elizabeth Saxe's unpublished 1979 Yale PhD thesis, 'Fortune's tangled web: trading networks of English enterprises in eastern India 1657–1717' is also useful. Finally, as far as the private English trade from the West Coast is concerned, Holden Furber's *Bombay Presidency in the Mid-eighteenth Century* (Bombay and New York, 1965) contains useful material. Pamela Nightingale's *Trade and Empire in Western India, 1784–1806* (Cambridge, 1970) has not received as much attention as it deserves. Lakshmi Subramanian's *Indigenous Capital and Imperial Expansion, Bombay, Surat and the West Coast* (Delhi, 1996) is an important recent addition.

The French and the minor companies

For a description of the manuscript and printed sources on the French, reference might be made to the bibliographies in two recent volumes, Glenn J. Ames, *Colbert, Mercantilism and the French Quest for Asian Trade* (Dekalb, Illinois, 1996) and Catherine Manning, *Fortunes à faire, The French in Asian Trade, 1719–48* (Aldershot, 1996). The Ames volume deals in some detail with the first decade of the French attempts at finding a niche for themselves in the Indian Ocean trade. Philippe Haudrère's authoritative four-volume, *La Compagnie française des Indes au XVIIIe siècle 1719–1795* (Paris, 1989) is on a much wider canvas and deals with both commercial as well as naval issues. Pierre H. Boulle's 'French mercantilism, commercial companies and colonial profitability', in L. Blussé and F.S. Gaastra (ed.), *Companies and Trade: Essays on Overseas Trading Companies during the Ancien Regime* (The Hague, 1981) may also be used profitably.

The early history of the French in India is covered in S.P. Sen, *The French in India: First Establishment and Struggle* (Calcutta, 1947). An excellent work on French participation in intra-Asian trade is Catherine Manning's *Fortunes à faire, The French in Asian Trade, 1719–48*. Her article 'French country trade in Coromandel 1720–50', *Revista de Cultura*, vols. 13/14 (1991) is also useful. Indrani Ray's 'Dupleix's private trade in Chandernagore', *Indian Historical Review*, vol. 1 (1974) is a substantial paper. Another study dealing with the private trade of Dupleix and other French private traders, particularly that in association with the merchants from Ostend, is Jan Parmentier, *De Holle Compagnie, Smokkel en Legale Handel onder Zuidernederlandse Vlag in Bengalen, ca.1720–1744* (Hilversum, 1992). Parmentier's slim volume is also the only account dealing with the short-lived Ostend Company. The authoritative study on another minor company, the Swedish East India Company, is that by C. Koninckx, *The First and Second Charters of the Swedish East India Company* (Kortrijk, 1988). Finally, the work on the Danish East India Company comes almost exclusively from Ole Feldbæk. In addition to *India Trade Under the Danish Flag, 1772–1808* (Copenhagen, 1969), reference might be made to some of his papers, such as 'The organization and structure of Danish East India, West India and Guinea Companies in the 17th and 18th centuries' in Blussé and Gaastra (ed.), *Companies and Trade*, and the comprehensive 'The Danish Asia trade, 1620–1807, value and volume', *Scandinavian Economic History Review*, vol. 39 (1991).

Indian merchants in the Indian Ocean trade

A good part of the work on the Indian merchants appears in collections of essays and the volumes in the Variorum Collected Studies series already discussed in the section on 'Studies relating to the field'. Other important studies may be noted as follows. For trade in the western Indian Ocean, see Edward Alpers, 'Gujarat and the trade of East Africa, c.1500–1800', *International Journal of African Historical Studies*, vol. 9 (1976). H.W. van Santen's 'Trade between Mughal India and the Middle East and Mughal monetary policy', in K.R. Haellquist (ed.), *Asian Trade Routes, Continental and Maritime* (London, 1991) is useful for an analysis of the relative strengths and weaknesses of the Asian merchants vis-à-vis the Europeans. For the eighteenth century, an important study is Ashin Das Gupta's *Indian Merchants and the Decline of Surat, c.1700–1750* (Wiesbaden, 1979). Also see M. Torri, 'In the deep blue sea; Surat and its merchant class during the dyarchic era 1759–1800', *Indian Economic and Social History Review*, vol. 19 (1982).

In the Bay of Bengal, the port of Masulipatnam is discussed in Shah Manzoor Alam, 'Masulipatnam, a metropolitan port in the XVIIth century', *Islamic Culture*, vol. 33 (1959), Sanjay Subrahmanyam, 'The port city of Masulipatnam, 1550–1750: a bird's-eye view', in Narayani Gupta (ed.), *Craftsmen and Merchants: Essays in South Indian Urbanism* (Chandigarh, 1993), and S. Arasaratnam and A. Ray, *Masulipatnam and Cambay, a History of Two Port Towns, 1500–1850* (Delhi, 1994). For trade from Bengal, see Sanjay Subrahmanyam, 'Notes on the sixteenth century Bengal trade', *Indian Economic and Social History Review*, vol. 24 (1987), Om Prakash, 'The European trading companies and the merchants of Bengal, 1650–1725', *Indian Economic and Social History Review*, vol. 1 (1964), and Indrani Ray, 'The French Company and the merchants of Bengal, 1680–1730', *Indian Economic and Social History Review*, vol. 8 (1971).

The technological and other dimensions of Indian shipping are analysed in

A.J. Qaisar, *The Indian Response to European Technology and Culture* (Delhi, 1982), 'Shipbuilding in India during the seventeenth century', *Indian Economic and Social History Review*, vol. 5 (1968), and 'Merchant shipping in India during the seventeenth century', *Medieval India: A Miscellany* (Delhi, 1970). Also see Lotika Varadarajan, 'Traditions of indigenous navigation in Gujarat', *South Asia*, vol. 3 (1980).

The structure of production and procurement

The structure of production in the textile industry is discussed in K.N. Chaudhuri, 'The structure of Indian textile industry in the seventeenth and eighteenth centuries', *Indian Economic and Social History Review*, vol. 11 (1974). For the Coromandel coast, a detailed discussion is available in Joseph J. Brennig, 'The textile trade of seventeenth-century northern Coromandel: a study of a pre-modern Asian export industry' (University of Wisconsin PhD Thesis, 1975), and 'Textile producers and production in late seventeenth-century Coromandel', *Indian Economic and Social History Review*, vol. 23 (1986). Sanjay Subrahmanyam deals with the same theme in 'Rural industry and commercial agriculture in late seventeenth century southeastern India', *Past and Present*, No. 126 (1990). S. Arasaratnam's 'Weavers, merchants and the Company: the handloom industry in southeastern India, 1750–1790', *Indian Economic and Social History Review*, vol. 17 (1980) is also useful. The period between the tenth and the seventeenth centuries is covered in Vijaya Ramaswamy, *Textiles and Weavers in Medieval South India* (Delhi, 1985). The structure of textile procurement by the European companies is discussed in Joseph J. Brennig, 'Chief merchants and the European enclaves of seventeenth century Coromandel', *Modern Asian Studies*, vol. 2 (1977).

The structure of textile production and procurement in Bengal is analysed in Om Prakash, *The Dutch East India Company and the Economy of Bengal 1630–1720* (Princeton, 1985), and for the later period in Hameeda Hossain, *The Company Weavers of Bengal, The East India Company and the Organization of Textile Production in Bengal 1750–1813* (Delhi, 1988) and D.B. Mitra, *The Cotton Weavers of Bengal 1757–1833* (Calcutta, 1978).

In the agricultural sector, an important segment for which a fair amount of work is available is that of opium production and procurement in Bengal. This work includes S. Sanyal, 'Ram Chand Pandit's Report on opium cultivation in 18th century Bihar', *Bengal Past and Present*, No. 78 (1968), John F. Richards, 'The Indian empire and the peasant production of opium in the nineteenth century', *Modern Asian Studies*, vol. 15 (1981), and Om Prakash, 'Opium monopoly in India and Indonesia in the eighteenth century', *Indian Economic and Social History Review*, vol. 24 (1987).

International bullion flows and monetary history

Important collections of essays in this area include Hermann Kellenbenz (ed.), *Precious Metals in the Age of Expansion: Papers of the XIVth Interna-*

tional Congress of Historical Sciences (Stuttgart, 1981), John F. Richards (ed.), *Precious Metals in the Late Medieval and Early Modern Worlds* (Durham, 1983) and *The Imperial Monetary System of Mughal India* (Delhi, 1987), Wolfram Fischer, R. Marvin McInnis and Jürgen Schneider (ed.), *The Emergence of a World Economy, 1500–1914*, Part I, *1500–1850* (Wiesbaden, 1986), H.G. van Cauwenberghe (ed.), *Precious Metals, Coinage, and the Changes of Monetary Structures in Latin America, Europe and Asia (Late Middle Ages–Early Modern Times* (Leuven 1989), and *Money, Coins and Commerce: Essays in the Monetary History of Asia and Europe (from Antiquity to Modern Times)* (Leuven, 1991), and Sanjay Subrahmanyam (ed.), *Money and the Market in India 1100–1700* (Delhi, 1994). In addition, we have several of Frank Perlin's pieces in his *The Invisible City: Monetary, Administrative and Popular Infrastructures in Asia and Europe, 1500–1900* (Variorum collected studies series, 1993). A recent addition is Dennis O. Flynn and Arturo Giráldez (ed.), *Metals and Monies in an Emerging Global Economy* (No. 14 in the Variorum *Expanding World* series).

On the specific theme of international precious metal flows, see Artur Attman, *The Bullion Flow between Europe and the East, 1000–1750* (Goteborg, 1983), and the more recent Ward Barrett, 'World bullion flows, 1450–1800', in James D. Tracy (ed.), *The Rise of Merchant Empires: Long-distance Trade in the Early Modern World, 1350–1750* (Cambridge, 1990). The rise of Amsterdam as a centre for international trade in precious metals is analysed in J.G. van Dillen, 'Amsterdam als wereldmarkt der edele metalen in de 17de en 18de eeuw', *De Economist*, vol. 72 (1923). The rise of Japan as a major Asian producer of precious metals, and of its role as a source of these metals for use elsewhere in Asia, is discussed respectively in A. Kobata, 'The production and uses of gold and silver in 16th and 17th century Japan', *Economic History Review*, vol. 18 (1965), and Om Prakash, 'Precious metal flows in Asia and world economic integration in the seventeenth century' in W. Fischer, R. Marvin McInnis and Jürgen Schneider (ed.), *The Emergence of a World Economy, 1500–1914*, Part I, 1500–1850 (Wiesbaden, 1986). The presumed difference between Europe and Asia in the matter of the relationship between the import of precious metals and the general price level, among other things, is discussed in Earl J. Hamilton, 'American treasure and the rise of capitalism, 1500–1700', *Economica*, vol. 27 (1929), Rudolph C. Blitz, 'Mercantilist policies and the pattern of world trade, 1500–1750', *Journal of Economic History*, vol. 27 (1967), J. Sperling, 'The international payments mechanism in the seventeenth and eighteenth centuries', *Economic History Review*, vol. 14 (1962), and Immanuel Wallerstein, *The Modern World System, Capitalist Agriculture and the Origins of the European World-Economy in the Sixteenth Century* (New York, 1974), and *The Modern World-System II, Mercantilism and the Consolidation of the European World-Economy 1600–1750* (New York, 1980). This view is contested for China in W.S. Atwell, 'International bullion flows and the Chinese economy, circa 1530–1650', *Past and Present* No. 95 (1982) and 'Notes on silver, foreign trade, and the late Ming economy', *Ching-Shih wen-t'i*, vol. 3 (1977), and for

India in Om Prakash, *Asia and the Pre-Modern World Economy* (IIAS, Leiden, 1995). The price history of the subcontinent is discussed in Irfan Habib, *The Agrarian System of Mughal India* (Bombay, 1963), Appendix C, Om Prakash, 'Precious metal flows, coinage and prices in India in the 17th and the early 18th century', and Sanjay Subrahmanyam, 'Precious metal flows and prices in western and southern Asia 1500–1750: some comparative and conjunctural aspects', both in H.G. van Cauwenberghe (ed.), *Money, Coins and Commerce: Essays in the Monetary History of Asia and Europe (From Antiquity to Modern Times)* (Leuven, 1991).

On Indian coinage, recent work includes Om Prakash, 'On coinage in Mughal India', *Indian Economic and Social History Review*, vol. 25 (1988) and 'Foreign merchants and Indian mints in the 17th and the early 18th century', in J.F. Richards (ed.), *The Imperial Monetary System of Mughal India* (Delhi, 1987). Aziza Hasan's was the first attempt to estimate the amount of money stock and the money in circulation in Mughal India in 'The silver currency output of the Mughal empire and prices in India during the 16th and 17th centuries', *Indian Economic and Social History Review*, vol. 6 (1969). This piece generated two critiques, one by Om Prakash and J. Krishnamurty, 'Mughal silver currency – A critique', *Indian Economic and Social History Review*, vol. 7 (1970) (Hasan's response, 'Mughal silver currency – A reply', appeared in the same number), and the other by John Deyell, 'Numismatic methodology in the estimation of Mughal currency output', *Indian Economic and Social History Review*, vol. 13 (1976). Subsequent attempts made in this direction include Shireen Moosvi, 'The silver influx, prices and revenue extraction in Mughal India', *Journal of the Economic and Social History of the Orient*, vol. 30 (1987) and Najaf Haidar, 'Precious metal flows and currency circulation in the Mughal empire', *Journal of the Economic and Social History of the Orient*, vol. 39 (1996).

On the structure of credit in Mughal India, an important study is that by the Dutch historian H.W. van Santen, *The Verenigde Oost-Indische Compagnie in Gujarat en Hindustan, 1620–1660* (Leiden, 1982), which unfortunately is not available in English translation. Some of the same ground is covered in Om Prakash, 'Sarrafs, financial intermediation and credit network in Mughal India', in H.G. van Cauwenberghe (ed.), *Money, Coins and Commerce*. The role of bankers in the functioning of the Mughal Indian economy is discussed in Karen Leonard, 'The Great Firm theory of the decline of the Mughal empire', *Comparative Studies in Society and History*, vol. 21 (1979) and in John F. Richards, 'Mughal state finance and the premodern world economy', *Comparative Studies in Society and History*, vol. 23 (1981). The biggest of the great firms is the subject matter of J.H. Little, *The House of Jagatseth* (Calcutta, 1967). Two other important studies in this area include Lakshmi Subramanian, 'The banias and the British: the role of indigenous credit in the process of imperial expansion in western India in the second half of the eighteenth century', *Modern Asian Studies*, vol. 21 (1987) and Kumkum Chatterjee, *Merchants, Politics and Society in Early Modern India, Bihar: 1733–1820* (Leiden, 1996).

The rise of coastal cities

Important among the collections of essays on this theme are Kenneth Ballhatchet and John Harrison (ed.), *The City in South Asia: Pre-Modern and Modern* (London, 1980), Dilip K. Basu (ed.), *The Rise and Growth of the Colonial Port Cities in Asia* (New York, 1985), Frank Broeze (ed.), *Brides of the Sea, Port Cities of Asia from the 16th–20th Centuries* (Kensington, 1989) and Indu Banga (ed.), *Ports and their Hinterlands in India, 1700–1950* (Delhi, 1991). The European companies' policies in the matter of the fortification of their settlements are discussed in Om Prakash, 'The Sobha Singh Revolt: Dutch policy and response', *Bengal Past and Present*, No. 94 (1975) and I.B. Watson, 'Fortifications and the "idea" of force in early English East India Company relations with India', *Past and Present*, No. 88 (1980).

Studies on southern India include H.D. Love, *Vestiges of Old Madras 1640–1800*, (4 vols., London, 1913), John F. Richards, 'European city states on the Coromandel coast', in P.M. Joshi and M.A. Nayeem (ed.) *Studies in the Foreign Relationships of India* (1975), Susan M. Nield, 'Colonial urbanism: the development of Madras city in the eighteenth and nineteenth centuries', *Modern Asian Studies*, vol. 13 (1979) and Susan J. Lewandowski, 'Changing form and function in the ceremonial and the colonial port city in India: an historical analysis of Madurai and Madras', *Modern Asian Studies*, vol. 11 (1977). Important among the studies on western and eastern India are K.N. Chaudhuri and Jonathan I. Israel, 'The English and Dutch East India Companies and the Glorious Revolution of 1688–9', in Jonathan I. Israel (ed.), *The Anglo-Dutch Moment, Essays on the Glorious Revolution and its World Impact* (Cambridge, 1991), P.J. Marshall, 'Eighteenth century Calcutta', in Robert Ross and G.J. Telkamp (ed.), *Colonial Cities, Essays on Urbanism in a Colonial Context* (Leiden, 1985) and Farhat Hasan, 'Indigenous cooperation and the birth of a colonial city: Calcutta c.1698–1750', *Modern Asian Studies*, vol. 26 (1992).

INDEX

Abdul Ghafur, 145–6
Acapulco, 93
Acheh, 8, 16, 20, 46, 62, 65–6, 69, 91, 106,
    141–3, 206, 209, 217, 224, 233, 235–7,
    245–7, 258–9, 286, 288–91, 297–8
Addison, Gulston, 244
Aden, 8, 9, 16–17, 45–6
Agra, 91, 94, 108, 131, 142, 155–7, 162–4,
    166, 169–70, 187–9, 192, 226, 341, 344
Ahmadnagar, 189
Ahmedabad, 108, 131, 136, 164, 192, 302,
    341
Akbar, Mughal emperor, 69, 154
Albuquerque, Afonso de, 46, 49
Aleppo, 45
Alexandria, 16–17, 45, 47–8
Alivardi Khan, 269
alum, 30, 291, 302
Amboyna, 91, 107, 130, 232
Amsterdam, 29, 73–4, 76, 84–6, 92, 188, 190,
    220, 226, 310–11, 338
Amsterdam Exchange Bank, 86
Anjengo, 62, 228, 249, 251–2, 305–6
Ankleshwar, 164
Annam, 93
Antwerp, 28, 72–3, 262–3, 265, 339
Arabia, 17–18, 66, 92, 140
Arabian Sea, 8, 9, 14
Arakan, 69, 144, 151, 237, 298
Arasaratnam, S., 323
areca-nuts, 20–1, 68, 124, 202, 238–9, 302
Armagon, 160
aromatics, 15, 18
Asad Khan, 134, 151
Asian trade, 5, 6, 8, 9, 12–13, 15, 45, 58, 92,
    95–6, 140
Asian trade revolution, 81–3, 340–1
Astrakhan, 156
Atheunis, Lucas, 106
Atlantic Ocean, 23
Atwell, William, 320
Aungier, Gerald, 251
Aurangzeb, Mughal emperor, 133, 147–8,
    150–1, 157, 343–4
Austria, 80, 261
Awadh, 344, 346
Ayutthaya, 107, 234, 286, 288–9

Bab-el-Mandeb, 45–6
badams (bitter almonds), 161
Baghdad, 45
Bahadur Shah, Mughal emperor, 133, 344
Balambangan, 274, 297
Balasore, 18–19, 62, 110, 132, 134, 140, 165,
    237, 245, 248, 264
Banaras, 330
Banda, 50–1, 55, 91, 107, 130, 175
Bandar Abbas, 156, 194, 259
Bangeri, 235–6
Banjarmasin, 247
Bankibazar, 259, 262, 265, 271–2
Bantam, 92, 105–6, 108, 137, 143, 206,
    208–9, 216–17, 228, 236, 242, 288
Baranagar, 132, 273
Barbosa, Duarte, 21
Bardoli, 164
Bardwan, 325
Barhanpur, 108, 131
Barkur, 17
Baroda, 131, 164
Basra, 45, 136, 193–4, 249–51, 257, 259, 303
Basrur, 64, 66
Bassein, 64, 70
Bassett, D.K., 107
Batavia, 88–9, 92, 94–7, 101, 107, 127, 129,
    132, 135, 136–9, 141–2, 144, 146, 178,
    180–2, 184, 189, 191–5, 199, 201–2, 204,
    206, 215–17, 230–4, 256, 271–2, 282,
    285–6, 288, 296, 299, 300, 302–3
Bayana, 157, 169, 171, 192, 205, 344
Bayly, C.A., 334
Bazar Mirzapur, 132–3
Bedara, 273
beer, 85
Beirut, 16–17, 45
Bengal, 4–6, 8, 14, 16–21, 53, 58, 60, 62, 64,
    68–9, 83, 94, 97, 100, 108, 110–11, 133–9,
    141, 144, 150, 155–7, 160–3, 165, 168, 174,
    182, 184, 192–3, 195–205, 207, 212–21,
    233–4, 237–8, 240–1, 243–4, 248–53, 257,
    260, 263, 268–73, 275–87, 290–2, 294–7,
    302, 305, 308–9, 316–17, 321, 323–36, 338,
    341, 344–7, 349
Bengal, Bay of, 8, 9, 14, 18, 20, 22, 46, 50, 52,
    57–8, 60, 69–71, 141, 243, 260, 286, 289, 348

Benkulen, 217, 247, 274
benzoin, 289
Berar, 156
Bernier, François, 62
Best, Thomas, 108
Bhagwan Gopi Chand, 277
Bhatkal, 17, 66, 71
Bhusna, 144
Bihar, 20, 133, 165, 195, 201, 228, 281, 284, 286, 296, 326, 329, 330
Bijapur, 95, 135
bills of exchange: between Agra and Surat, 344; financing of European procurement through, 274–5; issued by Danish East India Company, 310–12; issued by Dutch East India Company, 88–9; issued by English East India Company and others, 105, 294–5, 314, 323, 333, 335, 346–7, 351; issued by French East India Company, 308
Bima, 51
Bimilipatnam, 299, 300
Birbhum, 165
Birju Basu, 279
Bisdom, Adriaen, 269–70, 272
Blitz, Rudolph, 319
Bocarro, António, 49, 56, 68
Bokhara, 156
Bombay, 108, 119, 136, 140, 146, 150–1, 240–1, 244, 249, 251–2, 264, 273, 276, 295, 305; ceded by the Portuguese to the English, 150; naval engagement with the Mughal authorities at, 150–1; pattern of settlement of, 151; population of, 150
Boone, Charles, 252, 291
borax, 195
Borneo, 50, 58, 79, 201
Both, Pieter, 137
Bouchon, Geneviève, 34–5, 40–1
Bourdonnais, Mahe de la, 258
Boxer, C.R., 46, 59, 65
Boyajian, James C., 37–9, 339–40
Brazil, 55
Broach, 91, 131, 136, 164, 305
Broer, Hans, 75
Brouwer, Hendrik, 92
Bruijn, J.R., 114
Brunei, 51
Burma, 8, 12–13, 19, 21, 50, 52, 70–1, 123, 175, 236, 244
butter, clarified, 16, 20, 195, 202, 238
Buxar, 270
Buzurg Ummed Khan, 144

Cabral, Pedro Alvarez, 27, 44
Cadiz, 264

Cairo, 18, 45
Calcutta, 81, 110, 134, 136, 138–9, 146, 151–3, 258, 263–4, 275, 281, 285–6, 308, 324, 327–30, 333; black town of, 152–3; English procurement of zamindari rights in, 152; English takeover of, 269–70; European companies' fortifications in, 151–2; hostilities with the Mughals in, 151; population of, 152–3; seat of government for British India, 153; white town of, 152–3
Calicut, 8, 9, 15–16, 18, 23, 43–5, 63, 67–8, 71, 94–5, 124, 249, 306, 342
Cambay, 8, 9, 15–17, 21, 44, 64–5, 67, 91, 131
Cambodia, 93
Campbell, Colin, 80
Campbell, Hugh, 80
camphor, 21, 50, 289, 294
Cannanore, 15, 18, 43, 64, 67–8, 71
Conton, 8, 258, 260, 275, 286–7, 291–4, 296, 333, 335
Cape Comorin, 64, 69, 233, 238, 249
Cape of Good Hope, 2, 23, 28, 44, 46–8, 50, 65, 72–3, 93, 337
cardamom, 18
Caribbean, 227
carpets, 51
carreira da Índia, 33, 37, 340
carreira de Bengala, 53, 69
cartaz (pass system), Portuguese: 44, 46, 61, 64, 66, 70–1, 140–1, 340; Dutch: 82, 141, 234–5; English: 236
Casa da Índia, 26, 29, 30, 37
casados, 55–6, 66, 68–9
Catherine of Braganza, 150
cauris, 3, 21, 161, 195, 249, 262
Ceaser, Martinus, 127
Celebes, 175, 224, 232, 234
Central Asia, 155–6
Ceuta, 23
Chamberlain, George, 246
Chandernagore, 110, 256–8, 260, 262, 273, 308
chank shells, 238, 249
Chapra, 280
Charles I, king of England, 76
Charles II, king of England, 150
Charles VI, Habsburg emperor, 80, 261, 263
Charnock, Job, 110
chatins, 55, 60, 66–7, 144
Chatwa-Barda, 151
Chaul, 15–17, 22, 64, 68
Cheng-Ho, Admiral, 9, 58
Cheribon, 201, 217
Child, John, 150, 251

Child, Josia, 150
China (Chinese), 1, 9, 14–15, 26–7, 50, 53,
 60, 68, 79, 80, 84, 93, 109, 119, 233, 236,
 240–1, 247, 251, 255, 258, 260, 268, 273–4,
 285–8, 290–7, 302–3, 310–11, 320, 333,
 335, 338, 348
China Chan Yungqua, Captain, 247
Chinese junks, 9, 232, 289
Chinsura, 132, 152, 271
Chittagong, 18, 21, 53, 58, 60, 69, 144, 151
Chomley, John, 244–5
Chomley, Nathaniel, 245–6
Christian IV, king of Denmark, 78
Christian VI, king of Denmark, 261, 309
cinnamon, 20–1, 27, 34, 37, 67, 124, 202, 238
Clive, Robert, 270, 272, 346
cloves, 13, 15, 27, 34, 49, 50–2, 208; trade by
 the Asian merchants, 189; trade by
 Danish East India Company, 189, 208–9;
 trade by Dutch East India Company:
 75–6, 143, 182, 337; monopoly in, 91, 124,
 minimum sale price for Asia, 190–1, sale
 at Coromandel, 189–90, sale at Surat,
 187–92; trade by English East India
 Company, 91, 107, 189, 206
Cobbé, Andreas, 262
Cochin, 18, 30, 34, 42, 43, 62–4, 68–9, 71,
 95, 100, 124, 135, 202, 204–5, 228, 249,
 260, 307, 322, 342–3
coconut, 18
Coen, Jan Pietersz., 92–3, 130–8, 178, 188,
 193
coffee, 114, 118, 195, 258, 267
coir, 302
Colachel, 230
Colbert, Jean Baptiste, 252
Collet, Joseph, 244, 247, 290
Colombo, 67, 239, 260
concession system, 55–60, 69, 70, 90
conserves, 21
Copenhagen, 207–9, 260
copper, 17, 19, 21, 30, 50–1, 59, 70, 143, 155,
 157, 159, 236, 250, 310; Japanese bar
 copper, 95, 100–1, 186, 199, 232–3, 289,
 303: sale at Surat, 186, 303
coral, 30, 233
Cornwallis, Charles, 281, 331
Coromandel coast, 8, 13, 18–20, 53–4, 57–8,
 60–2, 64, 68–71, 91–4, 100, 106, 108,
 110–11, 125, 127–30, 132, 135–6, 141–3,
 146–7, 156, 160, 163, 175–8, 180–2, 184,
 188–9, 192–3, 195, 201–2, 205–9, 221–5,
 228, 230, 234, 236, 238, 243–5, 249, 252,
 258–9, 264, 271–2, 278, 287, 289, 297–300,
 309, 323, 341, 348
Cosmin, 19, 21

cotton, 12, 20, 68, 156–7, 165, 219, 249–50,
 287, 293–4, 302–3, 309, 350
Courteen's Association, 76
Cowan, Robert, 252
Coward, Edward, 264–5
Coxinga (Cheng Cheng-kung), 94
Cranganur, 204, 305, 322
Crappé, Roland, 208
credit system, 4, 154, 161–3; borrowing at
 Surat, 186; commenda loans, 53; hundi
 system, 4, 161–3, 344; interest rates, 4,
 161; rise of banking firms, 320–1, 350;
 respondentia loans, 4, 246–8, 258–9, 294;
 sarrafs, 4, 158–9, 162–3, 277, 320
Croock, Paulus, 131
Cuddalore, 131, 221
Cuming, David, 293

Dabhol, 16–17, 22, 95
Dagon, 21
Daman, 64
Danish East India Company: 83, 207–10,
 217, 260–1, 309–13; Bengal trade, 260–1,
 309, 312; establishment of, 78; Euro-
 Asian trade, 261, 309–13; intra-Asian
 trade, 209; successor companies, 79–81,
 260–1, 265
dates, 250
Daud Khan Panni, 147–8
de Houtman, Cornelis, 73
de Korte, J.P., 103
de Matta, João, 247
de Witt, Pieter, 191
Deccan, 189
Delft, 74
Delhi, 155, 157, 162, 164, 345–6
Denmark, 79, 208, 261
Deshima, 94, 100, 126
Dhaka, 12, 134, 140, 144, 156–7, 165, 168
Dholka, 164
diamonds, 175, 242
Dias, Bartolomeu, 23
Dihi-Kalkatta, 152
Dinis, António, 19, 21
Dip Chand, 280
Diu, 45, 64–5, 68
Draksharama, 164
Duncan, T. Bentley, 31–3
Dupleix, Joseph François, 258–60, 265
Dutch East India Company: 2, 6, 27, 29,
 48–9, 61, 65, 71, 78, 80–3, 150, 155, 161,
 163, 167, 170, 175, 210, 256, 266, 268, 275,
 280, 317, 322, 324–5, 328–9, 335, 337–9,
 341–3, 345, 348–9; administrative
 functioning of factories, 135–9;
 clandestine private trade by employees,

Dutch East India Company (*cont.*)
88, 129, 133, 139, 217, 230–4, 267;
establishment of, 72–3; Euro-Asian trade,
81, 96–7, 111, 211–21: value and
composition of Asian imports into
Europe, 114, 211, 266–8, 308, 313, 337,
341, 346, 348: value of imports from
India, 266; impact of Company policies
on Indian maritime merchants' trade,
234–9; intra-Asian trade, 3, 5, 7, 82, 89,
90–6, 100–5, 111, 118–19, 132, 137, 141,
181, 195, 210, 212–18, 266, 269, 341, 348:
profit from intra-Asian trade, 96, 102–3;
naval assistance in Mughal campaigns,
143–4; organization of sales, 75;
organizational structure, 73–5; role of
India in total trade, 111, 118, 266, 341; use
of violence by, 82
  Bengal trade: 94, 97, 132–3, 192, 195–204,
212–21, 297–8; armed engagement with
the English, 271–3; composition,
destination and value of trade from, 195,
199, 212, 218, 267, 276, 348; relative share
of Europe and Asia in total exports from,
212: value of total exports for and share in
total imports into Europe, 202, 210, 212,
218, 341, 345–6; establishment of factories
in, 132–3; intra-Asian trade from, 212,
214–18: trade with Coromandel, Malabar,
Persia and Sri Lanka, 201 2: trade with
Japan, 214: trade with Malay-Indonesian
archipelago, 215; personnel in, 133–4
  Coromandel trade: 91–3, 97, 123, 127–9,
175, 178, 180–2, 184, 192, 297, 313;
establishment of factories in, 127–8;
personnel and social life, 128–9; value of
trade from, 178, 180–2, 184, 267; share in
total imports into Europe, 210
  Gujarat trade: 91–2, 97, 100, 184, 186–7,
192, 225–8, 301–5, 313; establishment of
factories, 131; personnel and social life,
131, 133; intra-Asian trade from, 303:
Mughal silver rupees exported from, 100,
192, 303–4; value of trade from, 192,
225–6, 266–7, 301, 303–4; share in total
imports into Europe, 210, 226; value of
goods sold in, 301: profit on goods sold,
303
  Japan trade: 60, 93–5, 97, 100–2, 111,
126–7, 132, 212, 214–15
  Malabar trade: 6, 94–5, 100, 134–5, 192,
228–30, 305–7, 313, 342; personnel, 135;
value of trade from, 228, 230, 267, 306
Dutch pre-companies, 73, 90

eaglewood, 258

East Africa, 8, 9, 12, 17, 26
East Asia, 12
East Indies, 2, 73, 76, 78, 85, 90–2, 240,
298–9, 304, 337–8
Edo (Tokyo), 100, 126
Egypt, 16, 17, 45
elephants, 20, 70, 202, 238
Ellis, William, 327
Emden, 81
England (Great Britain), 240, 242, 252, 273,
293, 301, 306, 326, 338, 349, 351
English East India Company: 2, 6, 27, 29,
48–9, 62, 65, 80–1, 83, 85, 105–8, 145, 148,
150, 160, 210, 217, 232, 256, 266, 268, 273,
275, 293–4, 301, 304–5, 308, 313, 317,
322–39, 341, 344–7, 349; administrative
functioning of factories, 136, 138–9;
coercion over intermediary merchants
and artisans, 322–3, 336, 341, 351;
establishment of, 76; establishment of
factories in Asia, 105–8, 129–31, 134–5;
Euro-Asian trade, 76, 108, 111, 118:
exports to Asia, 105, 274: value and
composition of Asian imports into
England, 118–19, 239, 266–8, 276, 308,
313, 341–2, 346, 348: Indo-European
trade, 119, 210, 239–40, 267, 341–2;
founding of fortified cities by, 146;
hostilities with the Dutch, 106–7, 129;
organization of sales, 77–8; organizational
structure, 77–8
  Bengal trade, 119, 134, 138–9, 275–86, 341;
acquisition of political power, 6, 111, 139,
269–73, 322, 346, 349; diwani rights in,
77, 269–70, 294, 323, 344, 346; share of
Bengal in total imports from Asia, 210,
240, 268, 313, 341, 345–6, 348;
  Coromandel trade, 119, 130, 206, 210;
  Gujarat trade, 108, 119, 205, 210, 301, 304;
takeover of Surat castle, 304, 323; Malabar
trade, 135, 228, 305–6
English East India Company (New), 77
English private traders: Euro-Asian trade,
241–2: trade in diamonds, 242, 244–5,
342; fortunes earned, 242–4, 246, 251–2,
349; intra-Asian trade, 3, 6, 63, 242, 267:
Indian merchants' freight carried, 243,
246, 248–50, 252: eastward trade, 286–97,
313: destination pattern, 288: distribution
by port of origin, 287: from Bombay, 252,
287, 291–6; from Calcutta, 283, 287,
291–7; from Madras, 247: westward trade,
242–8, 251–2: from Bombay, 244, 247,
251–2: from Calcutta, 244, 248–51, 291:
from Madras, 244–8: from Malabar, 251:
from Surat, 251–2

Enkhuizen, 74
Estado da Índia, 26–8, 37, 43, 45–6, 55–7, 60–1, 64, 68, 70–1, 337, 339–40, 342, 348
European trade, generation of additional income, output and employment, 111–12, 315–18, 321–2, 335–6, 350; monetary aspects of, 318–322: monetization, 320, 322, 336, 350: money supply in the economy, 320–2, 336, 350; price level, 321–2

Falcáo, Luís de Figueiredo, 31, 37
Far East, 70, 175, 289
Farrukhsiyar, Mughal emperor, 134, 344
Feldbæk, Ole, 312
Fishery coast, 18, 61
Fleetwood, Robert, 247
Floris, Pieter, 106
Fort Dansburg, 208
Fort Geldria, 127–8, 143, 147, 160
Fort Gustavus, 152, 270–1, 273
Fort St George, 131, 147, 149, 246, 290
Fort William, 136, 152–3, 269, 326
Frederik III, king of Denmark, 208
Frederik IV, king of Denmark, 261
Freeman, Robert, 244–6
French East India Company, 6, 72, 81, 109–10, 145, 148, 210, 232, 252–6, 264, 266, 269, 280, 295, 298, 307–9, 325, 337, 349; Bengal trade, 110; establishment of, 2, 79, Euro-Asian trade: exports to Asia, 109, 308: profit on India goods, 253, 255: share of India in total imports into France, 255, 269, 308: value of imports into France, 255–6, 266, 269, 307–8, 313; intra-Asian trade, 255–7, 260; Pondicherry trade, 253, 299; successor companies, 79, 80, 252–3, 308–9; Surat trade, 253, 301
French private traders, 256–60, 267, 289
Fulta, 264
Furber, Holden, 252, 287, 292, 335

Gaastra, F.S., 114
Galego, Afonso, 53
Galle, 239
Gama, Vasco da, 23, 27
Gandevi, 164
Gaur, 19
Genoa, 17, 45
Genoese Company, 79, 83
Germany, 78
Gilani, Khwaja Shams-ud-din, 46
Gingelly coast, 18, 20
ginger, 17–18, 37, 66–8, 94
Glamann, Kristof, 114, 225, 227

glassware, 15
Goa, 22, 26, 28–9, 41–2, 45, 49, 50, 53–6, 58–9, 61–2, 64, 66–8, 90, 95, 242, 249, 264, 340
Godavari (river and delta), 163–4, 300
Gokul Chand, 277
Gokul Mukund, 256
Greenhill, Samuel, 264
Golconda, 4, 70, 128, 143, 147, 159–60
gold, 4, 17–19, 23, 30, 50, 59, 70, 93, 155–7, 159–60, 165, 199, 260, 264, 289–91, 350; Dutch procurement in Japan, 94, 100–1, 126, 195, 214: in Persia, 96: in Sumatra, 92: in Taiwan, 94; role in Euro-Asian trade, 86
Golepallem, 164, 300
Gombroon, 95, 136, 193, 249–51
Gondawaran, 164, 300
Govindpur, 152
grain, 68
gram, 20
Grise, 201
Gresik, 51
Gujarat, 12, 14–18, 20–1, 65, 67–9, 91–3, 97, 100, 111, 131, 136, 155, 157, 163–4, 182, 184, 192–3, 195, 205–7, 221, 225–8, 271, 295, 301, 303, 305, 322, 341, 344, 348
gunny-bags, 195

Haarlem, 338
Hague, the, 75, 299
Hamburg, 29, 85
Hamilton, Alexander, 290
Haqiqat Khan, 142
Hari Kishan Ray, 219, 278
Hariharpur, 94, 132
Harrison, Edward, 244, 247
Hasan Hamadani, 145
Hawkins, William, 108
Haye, Commander de la, 110
Henrique, dom, 28
Henry the Navigator, Prince, 23
Herbert, John, 272
Herklots, Gregorius, 285–6
Hinkar Chaudhuri, 277
Hirado, 59, 93
hoarding, 84, 157, 319–20
Holland (the Netherlands), 49, 72–3, 75, 78, 80, 88–9, 92, 95, 97–8, 101, 103, 129, 134, 137, 180, 191–2, 199, 202, 212, 218, 221, 226–8, 231–2, 273, 283, 298–9, 303–4, 338
Holland, States of, 73, 338
Honawar, 17, 64
Hoorn, 74
horses, 13, 17–18, 66–7, 70, 156, 250
Hugli, 19, 58, 62, 68–9, 94, 108, 133–5, 139,

151–2, 161, 169, 201, 219–20, 231, 233, 237, 244, 248, 256, 260, 263, 271, 280, 318, 328
Hume, Alexander, 261–5
Hyderabad, 160, 344, 346

Ibrahim Khan, 152
Imperial East India Company of Trieste, 81
Indian merchant shipping, attacks by European pirates on, 143, 145–6, 148
Indian Ocean, 1, 6, 8, 13–15, 21–2, 52, 56, 58, 62–3, 65–6, 71, 90, 140, 154, 287, 292, 335, 340
indigo, 12, 15, 34, 37, 108, 118–19, 157, 167, 169–71, 175, 182, 192–3, 340, 344; Dutch procurement at Bayana, 169–71, 192: at Sarkhej, 192; Dutch exports to Holland, 226–7; English procurement at Bayana and Sarkhej, 205, 241
Indonesia, 3, 8, 12–14, 16, 50, 84, 91, 175, 193–4, 282, 297, 315, 348
Indonesian archipelago, 1, 19, 27, 50, 57, 84, 91, 93, 106, 108, 123, 127, 129, 131–2, 145, 175, 201, 206, 208, 215, 232, 234, 253, 283, 288, 296, 341, 348–9
Industrial Revolution, 84, 349, 351
internal trade, 156–7
Iraq, 16, 18, 250
iron, 17, 20, 51, 66, 85, 303, 310
Irrawaddy delta, 19
Isfahan, 136, 155–6
ivory, 19, 233, 238, 303

Jacatra, 92
Jaffna, 20, 143, 239
Jag Bhushan, 277
Jagannath, 256
Jagannathpuram, 172, 299, 300
Jagat Seth, 162, 259, 321
Jahandar Shah, Mughal emperor, 133, 344
Janjira, 140
Japan (Japanese), 1, 6, 8, 14, 27, 50, 56–7, 59, 60, 93–5, 97, 100–2, 107, 126–7, 155, 159, 175, 195, 199, 201, 204, 212, 214–15, 236, 341, 350
Japara, 201, 209
Java, 15, 51, 105, 146, 175, 178, 182, 201, 216–17, 224, 236, 247, 251, 283, 311
jazia, 133
Jearsey, William, 244–5
Jeddah, 8, 16, 46, 66, 249–51, 259–60, 264
jewellery (Chinese), 50
Jinji, 147
Jiwan Chaudhuri, 256
Johor, 141, 224, 236, 297

Kabul, 156

Kalahasti, 147
Kampferbeck, Hans, 47
Kanara coast, 4, 15–16, 20–1, 27, 43–4, 46, 64, 66, 71, 94–5, 134–5, 204, 238
Kandi, 143
Karikal, 309
karkhanas, 174
Karnatak, 148
Karwal, 136
Karwar, 15
Kasimbazar, 110, 132, 134, 136, 165, 174, 220, 272, 280
Kaveri delta, 20
Kayakulam, 95, 135, 204
Kayal, 136
Kedah, 16, 58, 70, 141–3, 224, 235–7, 245, 286, 288–91
Khem Chand Shah, 168
Khurram, Prince, 131
Khyber Pass, 156
Kilwa, 8, 17
Kollam, 9, 18, 43, 67
Koenig, Henry, 80
Koninckx, C., 80
Konkan coast, 15–17, 20, 67
Kovilam, 261, 264
Krishna (river and delta), 19, 163–4
Kumbla, 17
Kunjimedu, 18
Kyoto, 100, 126

lac, 34
lacquer (Chinese), 50
Lahore, 155–6
Lake Balkh, 156
Lama, 236
Lancashire, 351
Lane, Frederic C., 34, 47, 139
Langhorn, William, 244, 247
Law, John, 80, 253
lead, 21, 30, 51, 85, 93, 105, 161, 201, 303, 310
leather, 51
Leghorn, 29, 81
Leiden, 85
Levant, 44, 47–8, 76, 93
Lisbon, 23, 26–30, 32–3, 36–9, 42–4, 46–50, 68, 84, 242, 339–40, 348
London, 76, 78, 84, 105, 107–8, 136, 139, 201, 206, 242, 244, 275, 294, 310–11, 333, 335, 347
long pepper, 20–1, 202
Lowther, Henry, 252
Lubeck, 29

Macao, 26, 50, 58–60, 62–3, 68, 93, 247

mace, 13, 15, 27, 34, 50–1; trade by Dutch East India Company: 73, 75, 337, minimum sale price for Asia, 190, monopoly in, 91, 124, sale in Surat, 187, 192
Macpherson, John, 285, 328
Madagascar, 145, 233
Madhav Rao Scindia, 305
Madras, 62–3, 108, 119, 131, 136, 146–8, 152, 160, 240–4, 249, 258, 261, 273, 276, 308; black town of, 148–9; English mint at, 160; fortification of, 147; military personnel at, 148–9; population of, 148–9; racial separateness in, 149; revenues of, 148; size of the settlement of, 148; white town of, 149
Madrid, 57
Madura, 216
Magalhães-Godinho, V., 30, 31–4, 40–2, 47–8, 54
Magellan, Strait of, 73
Magh pirates, 144
Mahe, 259–60, 309
Mainwaring, Matthew, 246–7
Makassar, 91, 107, 143, 189, 206, 209, 234
Malabar coast, 4, 6, 9, 14–16, 18–21, 27, 43–4, 46, 62–4, 66–8, 71, 94–5, 100, 124, 134–5, 184, 192–3, 201–2, 204, 228–30, 238, 247, 249, 259, 271, 302–3, 305–7, 309, 322
Malacca, 5, 9, 12, 14–21, 27, 43, 45, 50–4, 57–9, 61–2, 64, 68–71, 123, 141, 143, 182, 201, 217, 232–7, 260, 288, 297–9
Malacca, Straits of, 8, 14, 243, 247, 297
Malaya (Malay peninsula, archipelego), 8, 12–13, 50, 58, 61, 70–1, 82, 93, 108, 141, 145, 175, 193, 201, 234–7, 239, 288, 291–2, 296–7, 315
Malda, 133–4, 165–7, 280, 326
Maldive Islands, 20–1, 67, 140, 156, 237, 249, 258–60, 262
Male, 67
Malindi, 9, 17
Manar (island), 18
Manchester, 351
Mandalam Venkatasalam Naikar, 300
Mangalore, 17, 64
Manila, 62, 68, 79, 93, 237, 257–60, 287, 290–2, 298
Margarita, Queen Doña, 57
Maria Theresia, 80, 263
Martaban, 19, 21, 52, 58, 70
Martanda Varma, 230, 305–6
Martin, François, 110, 147
Master, Streynsham, 244, 246
Masulipatnam, 18, 20, 70–1, 127–30, 136, 143, 172, 178, 181, 188, 206, 208, 244–9, 264, 299

Mataram, 217
Mauritius, 260, 311
Mavalikara, 306
McGwire, William, 327
Meah Achan, 304
Mecca, 71
Mediterranean, 1, 14–17, 65
Meghna river, 144
Meilink-Roelofsz., M.A.P., 20
merchants: Abyssinian, 22; Arab, 9, 13, 15–16, 19, 22, 152; Armenian, 19, 131, 153, 217, 247, 259; Bengal, 4, 5, 13, 18, 21, 67, 234–5; Cannanore, 67; Chetti, 13, 19; Chinese, 9, 12–13, 60, 94, 123, 182, 201, 217; Chulia, 13, 19; Coromandel, 234–5; Gujarati, 12–13, 15–17, 46, 51, 65, 67, 123, 142, 152, 157, 235; Greek, 153; Hong, 296; Indian, 12, 65–6, 69–71, 82, 90–1, 94, 123, 125, 140–1, 204, 217, 221, 234–9, 246–7, 288, 298, 322, 328, 333, 335, 348; Indonesian, 14, 201, 217; Jain, 18; Japanese, 12, 123; Jewish, 242; Keling, 5, 19, 21, 50–2; Khatri, 153, 157; Malay, 14, 182, 201, 217; Mappila, 6, 18, 43, 67; Marakkayar, 19; Marwari, 153; Navayat Muslim, 18; New Christian, 37, 55, 339–40, 342; Okinawa, 12; Oriya, 13; pardesi, 6, 18, 43, 67; Parsi, 152, 295; Persian, 8, 15–16, 21; Red Sea, 43; Rumi, 22; Saraswat, 18, 66; Southeast Asian, 12, 123; Syrian Christian, 43; Spanish, 247; Turkish, 15, 22; Venetian, 48; West Asian, 16–17
mercury, 21, 30, 51, 85, 201, 294
Mergui, 16, 19, 58, 258, 264, 286, 288–9
Meulman, Hendrik, 79
Meulman, Willem, 79
Mexico, 292
Meynders, Leendert, 259
Middleburg, 29, 74
Middle East, 2, 23, 50–1, 93, 97, 155, 157, 193
Middleton, Henry, 108
Midnapore, 151, 166, 326
Minangkabau, 70
Mir Jafar, 270–3, 281
Mir Jumla, 142–3
Mir Kasim, 270
Miran, 272–3
Mirjan, 17
Mirza Hasan Ali, 152
Mocha, 13, 21, 95, 136, 142, 193–5, 224, 249–52, 257–9, 264, 274, 298, 303, 315
Mogadishu, 8, 9, 17
Mohammed Chellaby, 251
Mohun, Richard, 244–7

Moluccas, 21, 27, 37, 50–1, 58, 92, 107, 130, 175, 182, 201, 209, 224, 234
monetary system and coinage: 4, 154, 157–63; Mughal Indian coinage system, 4, 86, 155, 157–61, 320, 344; south Indian coinage system, 86, 159–61
Moreland, W.H., 207
Morse, Nicholas, 246
Mossel, Jacob, 233
Mount Eli, 15
Mouson, William, 246
Mozambique, 233, 259
Mughal empire, 13, 226, 315, 319–21, 341, 344–5, 350
Muhammad Shah, Mughal emperor, 344
Murli, 279
Murshid Quli Khan, 260, 345
Murshidabad, 157, 162, 165, 262, 273, 321
Muscat, 66
musk, 93
Mysore, 148

Nabakrishna, 153
Nadia, 165
Nadir Shah, 346
Nagapattinam, 18, 20, 58, 60–2, 70, 128, 147, 160, 163, 172–3, 209, 224, 233, 272, 299, 300
Nagasaki, 58–60, 90, 94, 100–1, 126–7, 199, 201, 214–15
Naguru, 18
Najabat Khan, 146
nakhuda, 53
Nantes, 253
Narsapur, 299
Nausari, 164
Near East, 50
Nediad, 164
Nightingale, Pamela, 295
Nina Chatu, 19, 52
Nina Suryadev, 19
Northern Circars, 323
nutmeg, 13, 15, 27, 34, 50–2: trade by Dutch East India Company, 73, 75, 337, minimum sale price for Asia, 190, monopoly in, 91, 124, sale in Surat, 187–8, 192

oil, 12, 16, 156, 195, 238
olive oil, 30
Omi Chand, 280
opium, 15, 20, 68, 167, 169, 195, 201, 233, 271, 279, 282–6, 336; Dutch East India Company: clandestine private trade by employees, 230–2, 282–3; exports to Malabar, 202–4: to Malay-Indonesian archipelago, 195, 201, 216–18, 282–4, 296, 341, 346; monopoly rights in Malabar, 204–5, 322, 343: in Malay-Indonesian archipelago, 201; Opium Society, 282–4, 286; procurement in Bengal, 3, 118, 212, 276; English East India Company: Bengal monopoly, 283, 296, 328–35, 347: cultivation of, 330–4, 347, 350: impact on Dutch Company procurement, 283–6, 296: impact on Indian merchants' trade, 335; profit made by opium contractors, 332; public auctions held at Calcutta, 296, 328–9, 334; private monopolies, 283–4, 296, 327–8, 347; private trade in, 283, 287–91, 293–7, 332–4; revenues, 330–2; French private trade, 258, 309
Orissa, 18–19, 57, 94, 132–3, 165
Ormuz, 8, 9, 45, 64, 66, 68–9
Osaka, 100, 126
Ostend, 81, 262, 264
Ostend Company, 2, 72, 80, 83, 257, 259, 261–6
Ottoman empire, 45
overland trade, 155–6
Oxenden, George, 251

Palakollu, 299, 300
Palembang, 9, 201, 217, 228
Panarukan, 51
pancado system, 100, 126
Pankor, 236
Pappillon, Thomas, 150
Parbati Charan, 279
Paris, 308
Paris, Giraldo, 29
Pasai, 19–21, 67
Patani, 93, 167
Patna, 110, 132, 134, 165, 217, 256, 281, 285, 327–8
Pecock, Johannes, 302
Pegu, 16, 19, 53, 57–8, 62, 70, 141, 166, 224, 236–7, 245–6, 258, 260, 286, 288–9, 291, 298
Pelsaert, Francisco, 188
Penang, 297
Penukonda, 18
Perak, 70, 141–2, 234–7
Persia, 17–18, 45, 50, 95–7, 108, 136, 155, 166, 175, 194–5, 201, 204, 206, 224, 233, 240, 242, 245–6, 248, 250–1, 298, 338
Persian Gulf, 1, 6, 8, 9, 12, 14, 16–18, 20–1, 44–5, 48, 63, 66, 68, 93, 95, 136, 145, 194, 230, 247–52, 340
Pescadores, 93
Peshawar, 156
Petapuli, 127–8

Phaulkon, Constantine, 289
Philippines, 12, 123, 209, 237, 243, 286
Phuket, 58, 142, 235–7, 245, 286, 297
Pidie, 19–21
Pinto, Manuel Teixeira, 62
Pipli, 18–19, 57–8, 142, 165, 168
Pires, Tomé, 15, 21, 51
Pitt, Thomas, 148, 244, 246, 289
Plancius, Petrus, 73
Plassey, 153, 270, 279, 281, 325, 346
Point Calimere, 221
Point Godavari, 18
Poland (Polish), 263, 265
Pondicherry, 110, 147–8, 253, 256–60, 264, 308
Porto Novo, 61–2, 172, 224–5, 298–300
Portugal, 27, 30–3, 49, 56, 150, 242
Portuguese, 2, 19, 22–3, 26–7, 63–71, 73, 81–4, 93, 95, 108, 124, 126, 131, 135, 140–1, 143, 150, 154, 204, 207, 209, 217, 269–70, 289, 291–2, 335, 339–41; Euro-Asian trade, 37, 48–9, 72: by the Crown, 3, 5, 23, 26–9, 34–5, 37, 39, 41, 48, 72, 90–1, 339–40, 342, 348; by private traders, 37, 39, 337, 339–40, 342, 348; intra-Asian trade: by the Crown, 3, 5, 27, 49, 50–5, 66, 68–70, 90, 340, 348: by private traders, 26–7, 49–50, 55, 61–2, 70, 90, 247, 340, 342, 348
Portuguese India Company, 29, 42, 49
Portuguese nau, 33, 50, 54
Priaman, 106
Price, W., 258
Prussian 'Bengal' Company, 81
Publicat, 18–21, 52–4, 60–1, 69–71, 127–30, 132, 147, 160–1, 163, 298, 300
Purakkad, 204, 322
Purnea, 280

qafila system, 64
Qandahar, 155
quicksilver, 19, 30, 93, 291, 302
Qutb Shah, Ibrahim, 70
Qutb Shah, Muhammad Quli, 71

Radha Kishan Chaudhuri, 256
Radhakant Chand, 277
Radhamohan Basak, 325
Radhamohan Chaudhuri, 277
Radhanagar, 166
Raedt, Gert Dircksz., 75
Rajapur, 136
Ram Narain, 327
Rambu, 144
Ray, John, 259
Raychaudhuri, Tapan, 225

Red Sea, 1, 8, 12, 14, 16–18, 20–1, 44–6, 48, 63, 65–9, 71, 93, 95, 145, 243, 247–9, 251–2, 315, 340
red yarn, 19
redistributive enterprise, 45, 81–2, 339–40
Riau, 297
rice, 12, 16–17, 20–1, 51, 64, 66–8, 70–1, 91, 156, 195, 202, 225, 238, 246, 249, 258, 264, 289
rosewater, 13, 15, 250
Rott, Konrad, 28–9, 47
Rotterdam, 73–4
Rouen, 253
Rovalesca, Giovanni Batista, 28–9
rubies, 13, 19, 258
Rustam Khan Bahadur, 299

Saadutullah Khan, 148
Sadraspatnam, 224–5, 299, 300
Sage, Isaac, 285
Saint Helena, 274
Sakai, 100, 126
Salem, 221
salt, 309, 347
saltpetre, 20, 94, 118–19, 175, 182, 195, 202, 206, 208, 212, 241, 256, 258, 260, 264, 271, 276, 279–82, 312, 328; English Company monopoly in, 281, 309; quota fixed by the English for the Dutch and the French, 281
Samudri raja, 43, 46, 94, 124
sandalwood, 21, 50, 63, 92, 201, 291, 302
Santipur, 165, 277
São Tomé, 20, 57, 60, 69, 110, 245
sappanwood, 208, 291, 303
Sarkhej, 192, 205
Satgaon, 19, 53, 58, 60
Scattergood, John, 247
Scheldt river, 72
Schöffer, I., 114
Schonamille, François de, 259, 265
Schreuder, Jan, 301–3
Senff, C.L., 304
Serampore, 309, 312
Shah Alam, Mughal emperor, 77
Shah Shuja, Prince, 134
shahbandar, 123
Shahjahan, Mughal emperor, 133–4, 142, 189
Shaista Khan, 144
Shogun, 60
Siam (Thailand), 8, 12, 64, 93, 175, 236–7, 247, 286, 289–90
Sichterman, Jan Albert, 258, 265
Siddi Yakut Khan, 151
silk, raw:
    Dutch East India Company: Bengal raw

silk: dependence of Dutch silk textile industry on, 220; procurement of, 34, 94, 111, 132, 195, 202, 204, 302; reeling unit at Kasimbazar, 174, 220; trade in: Euro-Asian: 3, 84, 114, 118, 204, 212, 220, 276: share in Asian raw silk sold in Holland, 211, 268; intra-Asian: 3, 195, 212, 348: for Japan, 195, 199, 214–15, 341: for Malabar, 202; Chinese raw silk: 15, 19, 21, 50, 59, 93, 100, 126, 195, 204, 251, 294, 335, share in Asian silk sold in Holland, 220; Persian raw silk: 95–6, 204, share in Asian silk sold in Holland, 220; English East India Company: Bengal raw silk: coercion over intermediary merchants and producers after Plassey, 279–80, 314; import into England, 119, 207, 239–41, 276, 279–80; procurement of, 204, 221, 279–80; French East India Company: 221

Silveira, D. João da, 53

silver, 4, 13, 15, 18, 21, 30–1, 56, 93, 155–9, 165, 258, 262, 273–5, 291–2, 308, 310, 312, 315, 318–20, 323, 337, 347, 350–1; Dutch export of silver rupees from Gujarat, 184, 226; Dutch procurement of silver in Japan, 95, 92–4, 97, 100–1, 199, 214: in Persia, 95–7; production in Spanish America, 2, 85, 93; role in Euro-Asian trade, 86; silver rials, 30, 86, 92

Sind, 136, 249

Siraj-ud-Daula, 269

Sironj, 164

slaves, 23, 289

Sobha Singh, 151–2

Sonargaon, 165

Soto, João Gomes de, 62

South America, 318

South China Sea, 1, 8, 9, 14, 22, 56–8, 62–3, 90, 243, 292, 335

Southeast Asia, 12, 50, 53, 65, 67–8, 70, 119, 154, 175, 180–2, 184, 193, 195, 209, 224, 258, 286–91, 296–7, 315, 335

Spain, (Spanish, Spaniard), 57, 80, 85, 93, 291

Spanish Royal Philippine Company, 81, 292

Specx, Jacques, 59

spelter, 201, 302–3

Spice Islands, 82, 91, 107, 146, 175, 182, 193

spices, 13, 15–19, 21, 27–8, 34–5, 37–8, 44–6, 50–2, 59, 63, 65, 67–8, 70, 90, 156, 315; trade by Dutch East India Company: 3, 27, 90–3, 95, 114, 175, 194, 201, 211, 232–3, 303, 341, 348, spice monopoly, 82, 91, 100, 114, 119, 124, 234, European

monopoly, 188, 190–1, sale in Asia: prescription of minimum prices, 190–1, in Agra, 187–9, in Bengal, 192, in Coromandel, 188–9, 192, 300, in Malabar, 192, in Persia, 192, in Surat, 100, 186–9, 191–2, 303–4; trade by English East India Company, 3, 27, 91, 105, 107–8, 206 (see also individual spices)

Sri Lanka, 8, 9, 18–21, 27, 37, 67, 71, 100, 124, 127, 137, 143, 156, 175, 184, 193, 201, 208–9, 224, 233, 237–9, 249, 271, 300, 302–4

States-General, 72, 86, 338

steel, crucible, 20

Steensgaard, Niels, 31, 34–5, 38, 45, 47–8, 81–3, 139, 339

Stein, Burton, 345

Sterthemius, Pieter, 101

Steur, Dirck, 143

Strebel, Pierre, 259

Subrahmanyam, Sanjay, 54

sugar, 12, 16–17, 21, 66, 93–4, 156, 195, 202, 209, 238, 248, 250–1, 260, 291, 302–3

sugar-candy (Chinese), 62, 294

Sumatra, 8, 9, 15, 19, 27, 50, 92, 106, 108, 141, 175, 201, 217, 235, 237, 273, 291, 296

Sunda (Straits), 50, 58, 66, 83, 288

Sunku Rama, 247

Surat, 62–5, 68, 91, 95, 100, 108, 110, 131, 133, 135–7, 141–2, 145–6, 150–1, 156–7, 159, 161–4, 166, 184, 186–94, 205–7, 219, 226–7, 230, 233–5, 241–2, 244, 247–53, 259, 264, 295, 301–5, 309, 323, 344

Sutanati, 134, 151–2

Swedish East India Company, 80–1, 265–6

Syria, 16

Syriam, 244–5

Tack, Johan, 142

Taiwan, 93–4, 175, 243

Tanjavur, 208, 221

Tatta, 136

Tavernier, Jean Baptiste, 164

Tavoy, 70

tea (Chinese), 3, 84, 111, 114, 118–19, 232, 267–8, 275, 292–4, 335

teak, 258

Tekkenkur, 228

Tellicherry, 62–3, 228, 249, 251–2

Tenasserim, 16, 209, 224, 236–7, 286, 288–9, 291

Tengapatnam, 307

Ternate, 52, 91

textiles, procurement structure: 4, 5, 167–74, 277–9; bad debts and joint stock companies, 5, 171–3, 277–9; English

textiles, procurement structure (*cont.*)
procurement in Bengal after Plassey and
misuse of authority vis-à-vis rival
companies, intermediary merchants and
the weavers, 276–9, 323–7, 347
textiles, production structure: 3–5, 163–8;
weavers' costs and merchants' mark-up,
166–7
textiles, trade by Danish East India
Company: Indian textiles as a proportion
of total imports, 312; procurement in
Bengal, 312; procurement in Coromandel,
209, 266, 269, 309
textiles, trade by Dutch East India
Company: Asian textiles: demand by
Dutch manufacturers for ban on import
of Asian silk textiles, 338–9; share of
Asian textiles and raw silk in total imports
into Europe, 211, 267–8; Indian textiles: 3,
12, 91, 93, 211, 216, 234–6
Bengal textiles: impediments created by
English Company in procurement, 276–9;
for Holland-procurement, 138, 139, 195,
202, 204, 218–19: profit in Holland, 220:
share in total imported into Holland, 212;
for Japan, 199, 215; for Malabar, 202; for
Malay-Indonesian archipelago, 201; for
Persia, 20
Coromandel textiles: 91–3, 111, 143, 175,
178, 180–2, 184, 216, 218: total value of
exports, 221, 224–5, 297–8, 300: share of
Euro-Asian and intra-Asian trade, 221,
298; for Holland, 220–1, 299–300; for
Japan, 215; for Malay-Indonesian
archipelago, 224, 231; for Mocha, 224; for
Persia, 224
Gujarat textiles: 91–2, 111, 184, 186, 302,
305; for Bengal, 193; for Coromandel,
193; for Holland, 193, 227, 304; for Japan,
215; for Malabar, 193; for Malay-
Indonesian archipelago, 193–4, 227, 341;
for Middle-East, 193–5; for Sri Lanka, 193
Malabar textiles, 307
textiles, trade by English East India
Company:
Indian textiles: 119, 239–40, 276;
commotion among English producers,
240, 338; share in total imported into
England, 240; value of total imports,
239–41
Bengal textiles: Euro-Asian trade, 138–9,
202, 204, 207, 219–20, 240–1, 276
Coromandel textiles: 106, 298; agreement
with Dutch regarding joint procurement,
129–30; Euro-Asian trade, 206–7, 240–1,
276; intra-Asian trade, 206

Gujarat textiles: Euro-Asian trade, 206–7,
227, 240–1, 276, 301
textiles, trade by French East India
Company, protective legislation at home,
253; Bengal textiles, 219–20, 309;
Coromandel textiles, 309; Gujarat textiles,
227
Thomaz, Luís Filipe F.R., 49, 50, 53, 57, 61
Tiku, 106
timber, 19–20, 68, 289
Timor, 50, 201
tin, 13, 15, 19, 21, 30, 50, 141–3, 161, 201,
233, 235–6, 238, 288, 291, 296–7, 303,
315
Tinnevelli, 221, 224
Tipu Sultan, 309
Tirupapaliyur, 127–8
Tirupati, 18
Titsingh, Isaac, 281
tobacco, 20
Tonkin, 93, 199, 243, 289
Tranquebar, 208–9, 260–1, 264, 309, 312–13
Travancore (Venad), 230, 305, 307
Trengganu, 247
Trieste, 81
Tripoli, 16
Turkey, 18
tutenag, 291

Ujang Salang, 58, 237

van Adrichem, 133
van Campen, Cornelis, 75
van Dam, Pieter, 48, 191, 230
van den Broecke, Pieter, 186, 193
van den Heuvel, Jakob, 79
van Helsdingen, Pieter, 191
van Imhoff, Gustaf Willem Baron, 232–3,
282
van Leenen, Commander, 144
van Linschoten, Jan Huyghen, 73
van Oldenbarnevelt, Johan, 73
van Rheede, Hendrik Adriaan, 4, 133
van Zwaardecroon, 191
Vansittart, 327–8
Vasconcelos, Diogo Mendes de, 28
Venetian galleys, 45
Vengurla, 95, 135, 193, 204
Venice, 17, 45, 47–8
Venkata II, king of Vijayanagar, 128
Verburg, Jacob, 231
vermilion, 19, 85, 201
Vernet, G., 272
Vienna, 80
Vijayanagar, 18, 66, 70, 128
Virji Vohra, 162

Vizagapatnam, 131

Wake, C.H.H., 34, 42, 48
Wallerstein, Immanuel, 318–19
wax, 195, 289
West Asia, 9, 12–13, 15–18, 45, 48, 66, 154, 315
West Indies, 175, 193, 205, 227
wheat, 20, 195
wines, 30, 85, 250
Winter, Edward, 244–5

woods, 15, 19

Yale, Elihu, 244
Yanaon, 309
Yemen, 136, 194

Zaiton, 8
Zambezi valley, 26
Zeeland, 73–4
zinc, 238
Zulfiqar Khan, 147

THE NEW CAMBRIDGE HISTORY OF INDIA

I The Mughals and their contemporaries

*M.N. Pearson, *The Portuguese in India*
*Burton Stein, *Vijayanagara*
*Milo Cleveland Beach, *Mughal and Rajput painting*
*Catherine Asher, *Architecture of Mughal India*
+*John F. Richards, *The Mughal Empire*
*George Michell, *Architecture and art of Southern India*
Richard M. Eaton, *Social history of the Deccan*
Bruce R. Lawrence, *Indian Sufism and the Islamic world*
George Michell and Mark Zebrowski, *Architecture and art of the Deccan Sultanates*

II Indian states and the transition to colonialism

+*C.A. Bayly, *Indian society and the making of the British Empire*
*P.J. Marshall, *Bengal: the British bridgehead: eastern India 1740–1828*
+*J.S. Grewal, *The Sikhs of the Punjab*
*Stewart Gordon, *The Marathas 1600–1818*
*Om Prakash, *European commercial enterprise in pre-colonial India*
Richard B. Barnett, *Muslim successor states*
David Washbrook, *South India*

III The Indian Empire and the beginnings of modern society

*Kenneth W. Jones, *Social and religious reform movements in British India*
*Sugata Bose, *Peasant labour and colonial capital: rural Bengal since 1770*
+*B.R. Tomlinson, *The economy of modern India, 1860–1970*
+*Thomas R. Metcalf, *Ideologies of the Raj*
David Arnold, *Science, technology and medicine, c. 1750–1947*
Susan Bayly, *Caste in India*
Gordon Johnson, *Government and politics in India*
David Ludden, *Agriculture in Indian history*
B.N. Ramusack, *The Indian princes and their states*

IV The evolution of contemporary South Asia

+*Paul R. Brass, *The politics of India since Independence: second edition*
*Geraldine Forbes, *Women in modern India*
Rajnarayan Chandavarkar, *The urban working classes*
Nita Kumar, *Education and the rise of a new intelligentsia*
Francis Robinson, *Islam in South Asia*
Anil Seal, *The transfer of power and the partition of India*

Already published
+ *Available in paperback*